D0165291

TAIWAN IN THE MODERN WORLD

At Cross Purposes

U.S.-Taiwan Relations Since 1942

Richard C. Bush

AN EAST GATE BOOK

M.E.Sharpe
Armonk, New York
London, England

An East Gate Book

Copyright © 2004 by M.E. Sharpe, Inc.

All rights reserved. No part of this book may be reproduced in any form
without written permission from the publisher, M.E. Sharpe, Inc.,
80 Business Park Drive, Armonk, New York 10504.

Library of Congress Cataloging-in-Publication Data

Bush, Richard C., 1947–
    At cross purposes : U.S.-Taiwan relations since 1942 / Richard C. Bush
      p. cm. — (Taiwan in the modern world)
    "An East gate book."
    Includes bibliographical references and index.
    ISBN 0-7656-1372-7 (alk. paper) — ISBN 0-7656-1373-5 (pbk. : alk. paper)
  1. United States—Foreign relations—Taiwan. 2. Taiwan—Foreign relations—United
States. 3. United States—Foreign relations—1945–1989. United States—Foreign
relations—1989– I. Title. II. Series.
E183.8.T3 B87 2004
327.7305124′9—dc22

                                        2003018882

Printed in the United States of America

The paper used in this publication meets the minimum requirements of
American National Standard for Information Sciences
Permanence of Paper for Printed Library Materials,
ANSI Z 39.48-1984.

BM (c) 10 9 8 7 6 5 4 3 2 1
BM (p) 10 9 8 7 6 5 4 3 2 1

At Cross Purposes

TAIWAN IN THE MODERN WORLD
Series Editor
Murray A. Rubinstein

ASSESSING THE LEE TENG-HUI LEGACY IN TAIWAN'S POLITICS
Democratic Consolidation and
External Relations
*Edited by Bruce J. Dickson
and Chien-min Chao*

AT CROSS PURPOSES
U.S.–Taiwan Relations Since 1942
Richard Bush

**CONSTITUTIONAL REFORM
AND THE FUTURE
OF THE REPUBLIC OF CHINA**
Edited by Harvey J. Feldman

**CONTENDING APPROACHES
TO THE POLITICAL ECONOMY
OF TAIWAN**
*Edited by Edwin A. Winckler and Susan
Greenhalgh*

THE GREAT TRANSFORMATION
Social Change in Taipei, Taiwan Since
the 1960s
Robert M. Marsh

HEIJIN
Organized Crime, Business, and
Politics in Taiwan
Ko-lin Chin

**THE INDIGENOUS DYNAMIC IN
TAIWAN'S POSTWAR
DEVELOPMENT**
The Religious and Historical Roots
of Entrepreneurship
Ian A. Skoggard

MEMORIES OF THE FUTURE
National Identity Issues and
the Search for a New Taiwan
Edited by Stéphane Corcuff

**THE OTHER TAIWAN: 1945
TO THE PRESENT**
Edited by Murray A. Rubinstein

**POLLUTION, POLITICS, AND
FOREIGN INVESTMENT
IN TAIWAN**
The Lukang Rebellion
James Reardon-Anderson

**THE PROTESTANT COMMUNITY ON
MODERN TAIWAN**
Mission, Seminary, and Church
Murray A. Rubinstein

**THE ROLE OF THE STATE
IN TAIWAN'S DEVELOPMENT**
*Edited by Joel D. Aberbach,
David Dollar, and Kenneth L. Sokoloff*

THE SOLDIER AND THE CITIZEN
The Role of the Military in Taiwan's
Development
Monte Bullard

**STATE AND SOCIETY IN THE
TAIWAN MIRACLE**
Thomas B. Gold

TAIWAN
A New History
Murray A. Rubinstein

TAIWAN
Beyond the Economic Miracle
*Edited by Denis Fred Simon and
Michael Ying-mao Kau*

TAIWAN
National Identity and Democratization
Alan M. Wachman

**TAIWAN ENTERPRISES
IN GLOBAL PERSPECTIVE**
Edited by N.T. Wang

**TAIWAN'S ELECTORAL POLITICS
AND DEMOCRATIC TRANSITION**
Riding the Third Wave
Edited by Hung-mao Tien

**TAIWAN'S EXPANDING ROLE IN
THE INTERNATIONAL ARENA**
Edited by Maysing H. Yang

**TAIWAN'S
PRESIDENTIAL POLITICS**
Democratization and Cross-Strait
Relations in the Twenty-first Century
Edited by Muthiah Alagappa

WOMEN IN THE NEW TAIWAN
Gender Roles and Gender
Consciousness in a Changing Society
*Edited by Catherine Farris, Anru Lee, and
Murray Rubinstein*

For Sharmon and Andrew

Contents

List of Boxes   ix
Acknowledgments   xi

1. Introduction   3

2. The Wartime Decision to Return Taiwan to China   9

3. Difficult Dilemmas: The United States and Kuomintang
   Repression, 1947–1979   40

4. The Status of the ROC and Taiwan, 1950–1972: Explorations
   in United States Policy   85

5. The "Sacred Texts" of United States–China–Taiwan Relations   124

6. Congress Gets into the Taiwan Human Rights Act   179

7. Taiwan Policy Making Since Tiananmen: Navigating
   Through Shifting Waters   219

8. Epilogue   239

Notes   245
Index   279
About the Author   287

List of Boxes

2.1 Wartime Options for Taiwan's Future   18

5.1 The Shanghai Communiqué   128

5.2 The Normalization Communiqué and Associated Documents   138

5.3 The Taiwan Relations Act and Taiwan's Security   155

5.4 The August 1982 Communiqué and Associated Documents   169

Acknowledgments

Although my name is on the cover of this volume, many people contributed to its seeing the light of day.

Murray Rubinstein, general editor of M.E. Sharpe's Taiwan in the Modern World series, offered immediate and warm support for the book. Patricia Loo managed the whole project and Amy Albert, Angela Piliouras, and Therese Malhame guided me through the editorial process.

Rowman & Littlefield Publishers kindly gave its permission to reprint "Taiwan Policy Making Since Tiananmen: Navigating Through Shifting Waters," which originally appeared in *Making China Policy: Lessons from the Bush and Clinton Administrations*, edited by Ramon H. Myers, Michel C. Oksenberg, and David Shambaugh and published in 2001. It is reprinted here with minimal changes.

I got valuable and cheerful assistance from the staffs at the Library of Congress, particularly the Manuscript Collection, the National Archives facility in College Park, Maryland (where Elizabeth Lipford removed unexpected obstacles), the State Department Library, and the Harvard-Yenching Library of Harvard University.

A number of friends, old and new, were willing to answer questions or read chapters in draft, or both. They include Fulton Armstrong, Chen Lung-chu, Mark Tan Sun Chen, Hung-dah Chiu, Ralph Clough, Roberta Cohen, Winston Dang, David Dean, Cynthia Sprunger Fogelman, Edward Friedman, John Garver, Bob Hathaway, Keelung Hong, Michel Oksenberg, Mark Pratt, Alan Romberg, Stanley Roth, John Salzberg, Steve Solarz, David Tsai, Nancy Tucker, and Gerrit vander Wees. Shen Lyu-shun acquired for me a collection of ROC wartime documents. He, Stephen S.F. Chen, C.J. Chen, and many other ROC diplomats indulged my interest in the history of Taiwan's relationship with the United States.

I owe a lot to the good friends and colleagues with whom I served while chairman and managing director of the American Institute in Taiwan. Among them were Barbara Schrage, Ray Sander, Gary Weis, Rick Ruzica, Greg Man, and Renee Bemish at the Washington office; Darryl Johnson, Ray Burghardt, Lauren Moriarty, Steve Young, and Pam Slutz in the Taipei office; and Susan Shirk, Sylvia Stanfield, John Norris, and David Keegan at the State Department.

The late Mike Oksenberg was my first adviser at Columbia University. He provided critical support at the beginning and remains a powerful inspiration and example. Stephen J. Solarz was the reason my professional career came to focus on Taiwan. The intelligence, energy, and desire to do good that Steve directed toward Taiwan and many other issues during his eighteen years in Congress are all too missing in American public life today.

Finally, my family—my parents, my wife, Marty, and my children, Sharmon and Andrew—have given me continuous and unqualified support throughout my career. None of this would have been possible without them.

Note: Chinese proper names are rendered in the pinyin system except for a few individuals (Chiang Kai-shek, Chiang Ching-kuo, etc.) and when other systems are used in quoted material.

At Cross Purposes

1

Introduction

I wrote most of these essays during the period that I was chairman and managing director of the American Institute in Taiwan (AIT), from September 1997 to June 2002. During my time at AIT several questions of a historical nature piqued my curiosity. How was it that Franklin Roosevelt decided that Taiwan should be returned to China? What stance did the United States take toward the Kuomintang (KMT) regime's repression from the 1940s to the 1970s? What was the substance of the so-called two-China policy that the United States pursued between the beginning of the Korean War and the Nixon opening to China? What do the three U.S.–PRC communiqués and the Taiwan Relations Act really say?

This volume offers answers to those questions, answers that I hope will have value beyond the satisfaction of my personal curiosity. These are relatively unstudied issues. On some, there exists a conventional wisdom but little supporting documentation. Filling out the historical record on an important chapter in the history of American foreign relations is important for its own sake.

The outlines of that history are well known.[1] After Pearl Harbor, the United States and the Republic of China (ROC) were allies in the World War II fight against Japan. The relationship was a rocky one, however, upset by disputes over military strategy, allocation of resources, and the role of the Chinese Communist Party. Still, President Roosevelt was prepared to give Chiang Kai-shek the benefit of the doubt and take steps to keep him in the war. Moreover, he concurred in Chiang's territorial war aims, including the return of Taiwan to China after almost fifty years of Japanese colonial rule. That intention was proclaimed in the Cairo Conference of December 1943. After Tokyo's surrender, it was ROC forces, authorized by Douglas MacArthur, Supreme Commander of the Far East, that accepted the surrender on the island. The residents of the island, Chinese in their social and cultural background, welcomed reversion to China.[2]

The American focus, however, was not on Taiwan but on the looming civil war on the Chinese mainland. President Truman sent George Marshall to try to broker peace between the Nationalists and the Communists, but he failed in the face of mutual Chinese mistrust and the efforts of each side to gain a tactical advantage over the other. Fighting broke out in earnest, just around the time that KMT misrule on Taiwan sparked a revolt by the Taiwanese. In spite of efforts by local leaders to resolve the latter conflict through negotiation, the ROC government sent troops to the island who brutally ended any resistance.[3]

The United States provided some support to Chiang's forces during the civil war, but increasingly concluded that Nationalist incompetence would lead to military defeat. Washington then distanced itself from Chiang, in the hope of ultimately driving a wedge between the Chinese Communists and the Soviet Union. The ROC government was able to slow the process of disassociation by mobilizing its supporters in the U.S. Congress but could not stop it.

Once the Nationalist cause seemed lost, Washington then worried about the vulnerability of Taiwan, to which the KMT was retreating. There was a consensus that a Communist takeover was both likely—again because of Nationalist political and military ineptitude—and detrimental to American security interests. On the other hand, the United States lacked the military assets to defend it. Various schemes were considered and abandoned, and President Truman signaled in January 1950 that Washington would not intervene.[4]

Taiwan and the ROC were saved by North Korea's invasion of South Korea in June 1950. Washington decided to deploy ships of the Seventh Fleet to the Taiwan Strait, in order to prevent either the PRC or the ROC from attacking each other. In order to justify this policy reversal, the Truman administration asserted that Taiwan's legal status (whether it was indeed part of China) had not yet been determined, and so was an international issue, not a purely domestic one.

Over time, Taiwan became part of the American structure of anti-Communist containment. The United States established a significant military assistance and training relationship with the ROC armed forces, and the two governments concluded a mutual defense treaty in late 1954. Still, it was a case of same bed, different dreams. Chiang wanted to fight his way back to the mainland with American help but American presidents sought to avoid being drawn into an unwanted war. The United States recognized that limited contact with China would help in managing conflict. Chiang simply saw that contact as a degradation of his legitimacy.[5]

In the meantime, the KMT regime imposed harsh repression on Taiwan. This was a minority government, made up of mainlanders from China who ruled over the 85 percent of the population whose ancestors had migrated from southeastern China to the island from the sixteenth century on. As a minority regime, the KMT rationalized its denial of majority rule on the grounds that it was the government of all of China. Thus the memberships in the Legislative Yuan and the National Assembly were frozen because it was not possible to hold elections in districts throughout China. Taiwan representation had to be limited, more or less, to its share of the Chinese population. Political freedoms were severely restricted, it was asserted, because of a national emergency to suppress the Communist rebellion. Under martial law, challenges to KMT rule were tried in military courts. Countless Taiwanese dissidents lost their lives or their freedom, and those who chose caution still regarded their rulers with silent, sullen hostility. The U.S. government concluded that this was a reality it should not change (for geopolitical reasons) or could not change (because of Chiang Kai-shek's rigid opposition). To be sure, the ROC did embark on a program of export-led growth with substantial American assistance and persuasion. That produced impressive prosperity and removed poverty as a source of instability, but did not translate into an early, parallel program of political liberalization.[6]

This configuration—containment of China, ambiguous alliance with the ROC, and KMT repression—began to change in the early 1970s. The starting point was Richard Nixon's and Henry Kissinger's strategic calculation that China could make a significant contribution to the struggle against the Soviet Union, sufficient to justify a reduction of ties with Taiwan. Jimmy Carter continued this process by "normalizing" relations with the PRC and acceding to Beijing's demands that it break diplomatic relations with Taipei, end the mutual defense treaty, and withdraw the remaining military personnel and facilities. Washington now inclined more toward the view that Taiwan was a part of China, but continued to state a strong interest in a peaceful resolution to the Taiwan Strait issue and an intention to sell defensive weapons to Taiwan. Ronald Reagan reaffirmed the fundamentals of the new arrangement in August 1982, while agreeing to exercise restraint on arms sales. Simultaneously, the ROC lost its presence in most international organizations and the number of countries that had diplomatic relations with it shrank to around thirty. Over the course of a decade, Taiwan's international standing had seriously deteriorated. Beijing, now in a position of relative strength, mounted a new offensive for reunification, and there was some expectation that the three-decade state of division was about to end.[7]

International isolation for Taiwan triggered internal political ferment. Each new blow to the ROC's legitimacy as the government of China diminished its right to maintain a political monopoly on the island, at least in the eyes of its political opponents. Under the emerging leadership of Chiang Ching-kuo (Chiang Kai-shek's son), the regime began moving toward a soft authoritarianism, in which limited political expression and elections would serve as a barometer of KMT performance. Yet the critics wanted reform to go further and faster, and they called for a democratic system. They were coalescing into an opposition party, which was a violation of KMT limits.

Simultaneously, Taiwanese exiles in the United States, in order to exert some pressure on the Taiwan government, were beginning to cultivate members of the U.S. Congress (which was an irony, since the ROC government had used Congress for decades to constrain the U.S. Executive Branch).

The regime cracked down on the growing opposition movement, most notably at the Kaohsiung Incident of December 1979, but the pressure for change continued. Reformers around Chiang Ching-kuo argued that a democratic Taiwan could make a stronger appeal for American support, and Chiang himself came to the counterintuitive conclusion that the KMT could better maintain its hold on power by opening up the political system than by continuing repression. Once the process of liberalization began, KMT conservatives complained that it was too fast and leaders of the newly formed Democratic Progressive Party (DPP) thought it was too slow, but the direction was clear. Lee Teng-hui, a Taiwanese, succeeded Chiang as president after the latter's death in January 1988, and he soon accelerated the process. By the mid-1990s, Taiwan had a vibrant and fractious democratic system.

The United States was a bit ambivalent about this outcome. In terms of American values, this could only be a welcome development, and it did indeed solidify U.S. support for Taiwan. On the other hand, the open discussion of independence, the emergence of a strong Taiwanese identity, and the possibility that the DPP might come to power could not be ignored because of their potential implications for peace and stability.[8]

The late 1980s and early 1990s brought three other developments. The first was the growing economic and human interaction between Taiwan and the mainland. A no-man's-land for four decades, the Taiwan Strait became a highway for trade, investment, and family reunification. Taiwan companies needed a new production platform for labor-intensive goods like shoes as wages rose on the island itself and the New Taiwan dollar appreciated under American pressure. Aging mainlanders leapt at the chance to see their relatives and native places again. There was even hope that economic intercourse might lead to political reconciliation. Semiofficial channels were established to manage problems like document certification and illegal immigration that stemmed from greater contact.

The second development was the Tiananmen Incident of 1989 and its profound impact on U.S.–China relations. This shattered the consensus that had existed in the United States in favor of ties with Beijing, and led to intense conflict within the American political system over China. The contrast between a repressive China and a democratizing Taiwan was stark, and the impact on American political opinion was profound.[9]

The third development was the fall of the Soviet Union. Containing Moscow had long since lost its value as a geopolitical basis for U.S.–China relations, and the sudden decline in the prospects for international conflict had a very practical consequence: a radical shift in the international arms market. The new Russia was desperate to find new markets for its producers of military equipment. Western defense contractors were in the same predicament as their traditional customers cut back on orders in light of a more benign security environment. China was able to purchase relatively advanced systems from Russia, thus increasing the threat to Taiwan. American companies pressured the Bush administration to ease the policy of restraint on arms sales to Taiwan that in 1982 it had pledged Beijing it would follow. In the end, the Bush administration agreed.

Cross-strait reconciliation stalled over the fundamental issue of the legal status of Taiwan in a unified China. Beijing asserted that it would be an autonomous yet subordinate unit. Taipei claimed that its government was a sovereign entity, essentially equal to the PRC government. In part to improve his negotiating position with China, President Lee Teng-hui sought to take advantage of Taiwan's new approval in the United States by making a trip to his alma mater, Cornell University. He mobilized Taiwan's supporters in the Congress, who in turn were successful in pressuring the Clinton administration into approving the visit, which occurred in June 1995. That sparked a crisis in both cross-strait and U.S.–China relations. Beijing concluded that there was a dangerous trend toward the permanent separation of Taiwan from China, a trend that could be stopped only by cutting back both relationships and displays of military force. The United States shifted to an approach of dual deterrence: deterring the PRC from using its growing military assets and restraining Taiwan from taking actions that might provoke a Chinese attack.

That is basically where the situation is today. In some respects, we see parallels with the past. Dual deterrence was essentially what Washington pursued in the 1950s and 1960s, making it harder for China to "liberate" Taiwan and for Chiang Kai-shek to "retake the mainland." The legal status of Taiwan and its government is the key sticking point now as it was then. What has changed is the emergence of a democratic system on the island, which not only complicates the task of managing a delicate triangular relationship but also reduces the possibility that Washington will make decisions on Taiwan's fate without regard to the views of its citizens, as was the case in 1943, 1950, 1972, and 1978.

The chapters that follow fill in some of the gaps in our understanding of this history. Chapter 2 details the background of Roosevelt's decision to return Taiwan to China after Japan's defeat in World War II. Chapter 3 documents U.S. actions—or inaction—in the major cases of KMT repression from the 1940s to the 1970s. Chapter 4 reveals how in a conceptual sense five administrations addressed Taiwan's legal status from 1950 to 1971, the period in which it took the explicit position that the status was undetermined. Chapter 5 explores how the United States treated Taiwan—both its legal status and its security—in the key documents of U.S.–PRC normalization. Chapter 6 presents the story of how a few members of the U.S. Congress mounted an effort to pressure the Taiwan government to end its repressive regime and move toward a democratic system. Chapter 7 describes American policy making regarding Taiwan in the administrations of George H.W. Bush and Bill Clinton.

There is, I think, a reason for going over old ground that is far more significant than satisfying personal curiosity or filling historical lacunae. For the people of Taiwan, this is not ancient history or the stuff of musty archives. They are in the process of recovering their past, and these issues are relevant as they assess how the island crafts its relationships with both China and the United States.

It thus matters for them that Franklin Roosevelt chose to ignore for Taiwan the option of a trusteeship and plebiscite even as he favored it for Japan's other colony, Korea. It matters that American diplomats sometimes gently pushed Chiang Kai-shek to create a system that could attract Taiwanese support but most of the time accommodated to his harsh repression. It matters that for more than a decade the United States explored the idea that there were equivalent, sovereign entities on each side of the Taiwan Strait in order to ensure that the ROC could keep its seat in international organizations, but that this creativity was spurned for too long by an ideologically rigid Chiang Kai-shek. It matters that U.S. officials, in negotiating normalization with the PRC, tended to make their concessions up front and then had to struggle to assert America's—and Taiwan's—interests. And it matters to the people of Taiwan that in the 1980s the KMT regime faced for the first time a good-cop, bad-cop approach from the United States on human rights and democracy, with the administration as the good cop and congressional activists as the bad cop. This book represents a small effort to give them back their history.

2

The Wartime Decision
to Return Taiwan to China

How did it happen that Taiwan was transferred to China after World War II? It is well known that the first public signal of the island's postwar fate came in the Cairo Declaration of December 1943, in which Prime Minister Churchill and Presidents Roosevelt and Chiang Kai-shek announced that it was "their purpose that . . . all the territories Japan has stolen from the Chinese, such as Manchuria, Formosa, and the Pescadores, shall be restored to the Republic of China." Joseph Stalin concurred in that intention at the Teheran Conference.[1] Yet the process of decision making that led up to that announcement has never been explored.

I became intrigued with these questions because of periodic conversations with Taiwan friends who tend to support a Republic of Taiwan. They point to the Cairo Declaration as the primary reason that the island was subjected to Kuomintang (KMT) rule and all that came with it. Why, they ask, did the native residents of the island not have a choice as to who their new rulers would be, whether Chiang Kai-shek (Jiang Jieshi), Taiwanese themselves, or someone else? Instead, they assert, the decision at Cairo denied the people of Taiwan a say in their fate and therefore their right of national self-determination. Some have not given up the hope that the claim of the people of Taiwan to ownership of "their land" might, with external help, still be realized.[2]

It is certainly true that the People's Republic of China, which most countries recognize as the government of the state called China, asserts vigorously that Taiwan is part of China. The government of the Republic of China (ROC), which has jurisdiction over Taiwan and the Pescadores, was in full agreement up until the late 1990s (at which point its position became more ambiguous). Moreover, the intention of the World War II great powers to transfer ownership of Taiwan from Japan to China follows a long tradition whereby the victors in war dispose of territories previously held by the enemies they have vanquished and, more generally, existing states decide on the formation of new states.[3] It might be argued, moreover, that existing states *should* make such decisions because they have a strong interest in assuring future stability and avoiding the territorial causes of new wars.

Yet the peoples subject to territorial and state changes have sometimes been given a say in the disposition of the land in which they live. That has happened not only for areas whose status may change as the result of a war but also as a mechanism employed with non–self-governing territories that have been under colonial rule or international trusteeship. Thus the peoples of the trust territories of Micronesia, the Marshall Islands, and Palau voted in plebiscites to approve compacts of free association with the United States upon gaining their independence.

This essay seeks to bring together the available information on when and how it was decided to return Taiwan to China in the first place. Four factors appear to have been at play: U.S. government planning; Washington's desire to keep China in the war; Roosevelt's vision for postwar security; and the impact of personal diplomacy. And the decision was actually made as much as a year before the Cairo Conference.

China Takes a Position

First we must establish how it was that the ROC government placed the future of Taiwan on the postwar agenda in the first place.

Before 1942, neither the Nationalist government under the Kuomintang nor the Chinese Communist Party placed much emphasis on Taiwan as a territorial issue, and the CCP would not change its position until after the Cairo Declaration. Frank Hsiao and Lawrence Sullivan have demonstrated that neither actor initially regarded the island as an integral part of China that had to be taken back from Japan. To the extent that either mentioned Taiwan at all, each equated it with Korea and regarded the Taiwanese as a distinct nation or nationality that deserved some measure of independence, even de jure independence. (Hsiao and Sullivan speculate that this diffidence was born of the sense that decades of Japanese rule had leached the Taiwanese of their Chinese soul.)[4]

With the Japanese attack on Pearl Harbor, China declared war on Japan and declared that "all treaties, conventions, agreements and contracts concerning the relations between China and Japan are and remain null and void." Thus China renounced the Treaty of Shimonoseki of 1895 by which Taiwan was ceded to China, but it did not make a claim to the island. Some people in KMT areas of China were not so reticent. In the ROC-controlled territory there were around a thousand Taiwan natives engaged in political causes. These people had formed at least nine organizations dedicated to opposing Japan's rule of their homeland and favoring its return to China. Beginning in late 1938, these organizations had gradually come together to form the Taiwan Revolutionary League (Taiwan geming tongmenghui), which was formally established on February 10, 1941, and brought under the KMT's aegis. The League's constitution stated its fundamental objective: "This association, under the leadership of the Chinese Nationalist Party, will concentrate all Taiwanese revolutionary strength in order to overthrow Japanese imperialism, recover Taiwan, and help the Fatherland establish a new China constructed on the basis of the Three People's Principles." The League's main activity was propaganda and education to anyone who would listen. To foreigners, the League sought to make the case that Taiwan should be returned to China. To the ROC government, it asserted the idea that after the war the island should be a full province of China rather than a special district of the ROC or a part of occupied Japan.[5]

The League held a meeting in Chongqing in March 1942, a few months after Pearl Harbor. Among the subjects under discussion were formation of a Taiwanese army, establishment of a Taiwan provincial government under ROC auspices, and assurance of China's repossession of the island. It was probably at this meeting that Sun Fo, president of the Judicial Yuan and son of Sun Yat-sen, said in a public speech that after the war "Formosa will come back to China." On April 2, the *Yishibao*, a Catholic paper in Chongqing, devoted its editorial to Taiwan and hoped-for recovery of the island, and noted that April 5 was to be celebrated in Chongqing as "Formosa Day." The editorial further urged that "the Chinese government should make a fresh declaration of its claim of sovereignty over the island and thus remove from the minds of other nations the conception of Formosa as a colony, and encourage the Formosans themselves to redouble their efforts against the enemy." (American diplomats surmised that the League had begun agitating for Taiwan's return because of public discussion of independence for Korea, which was also a Japanese colony and which the ROC government had previously viewed on a par with Taiwan.)[6]

The first conversation on Taiwan between American and ROC officials that is a matter of record came in June 1942, when John Stewart Service approached Yang Yunzhu, the director of the East Asiatic Affairs Department of the ROC's Ministry of Foreign Affairs, about press articles on the return of Taiwan to China. Yang replied that the island's "return seemed fitting to the Chinese because the greater part of the population was Chinese and had continued to maintain close ties with China." Yet Yang's remark should not be taken necessarily as an official position of his government, since he made

it in response to Service's question, and, as reported, did so somewhat diffi-
dently.[7] Later in the summer, Owen Lattimore, who served as Roosevelt's
political adviser to Chiang Kai-shek, indicated that ROC intentions remained
ambiguous. He told a State Department committee that "If any western power
wants Formosa, the Chinese will claim it, but otherwise they may not insist
on possessing it, since they lack the sea power to hold it."[8]

It was not until the fall of 1942 that the ROC can be said to have conveyed
its official intentions. This came first privately in Chiang Kai-shek's meeting
on October 7 with Wendell Willkie, who was visiting China as Roosevelt's
representative. According to Chinese diplomatic archives, Chiang told Wilkie
that "after the war China's coastal fortresses like Lushun, Dalian, and Taiwan must be returned to China." The public announcement of the official
ROC position came a month later, on November 3, when T.V. Soong (Song
Ziwen), in his first press conference after appointment as minister of foreign affairs, said that China "will recover Manchuria, and Formosa and the
Ryukyu Islands."[9]

It was around this time that Chiang began drafting *Zhongguo zhi mingyun*
(China's Destiny). In it, he identified "Formosa, the Pescadores, the Four
Northeastern Provinces, Inner and Outer Mongolia, Sinkiang, and Tibet"
each as "a fortress essential for the nation's defense and security" since
China proper had no natural frontiers. Taiwan and the Pescadores, he said,
were opened by Han Chinese, occupied by the Dutch, and recovered by
Zheng Chenggong (Koxinga). The loss of Taiwan to the Japanese was part
of China's humiliation, "and not until all lost territories have been recovered can we relax our efforts to wipe out this humiliation and save our-
selves from destruction."[10]

Chinese officials had another opportunity to state their views on Taiwan
to both American and British officials at the conference of the Institute of
Pacific Relations (IPR) held at Mont Tremblant, Quebec, in early December
1942. Heading the ROC delegation was Shi Zhaoji (Sao-ke Alfred Sze), a
former ambassador to London and Washington and head delegate to the
League of Nations in 1931. Among the American officials were Laughlin
Currie, administrative assistant to Roosevelt, who had visited China during
the summer; Stanley Hornbeck, adviser on political relations in the State
Department and a long-time China hand; Maxwell Hamilton, chief of the Far
Eastern Affairs division in the State Department; and Owen Lattimore,
Roosevelt's political adviser to Chiang.[11] (The IPR was, in today's parlance,
a venue for Track II dialogue, in which government officials meet in their
personal capacity.)

The Chinese delegation took several opportunities to assert the ROC's claim to Taiwan. Shi Zhaoji asserted that: "During the years of military weakness, China has lost control of various portions of her territory, and it is but reasonable and just that, when the present war is victoriously ended, she should expect the return of such of her possessions as have been taken from her by force or by threat of force." Another member of the Chinese delegation said that the island of Taiwan was "Chinese from every point of view and should go back to China—without strings." A focus of the conference discussion was a scheme associated with Winston Churchill for the postwar supervision of dependent territories. The plan contemplated an international organization supported by regional councils and an array of international bases. At one point, British and Dutch delegates, supported by one American, argued that Taiwan should be treated the same way as Malaya or the Netherlands Indies. The Chinese delegates categorically rejected any effort to lump the three territories together. They also noted that Taiwan and the Penghu (Pescadore) islands might be a good site for such an Allied base, "provided that they were previously restored unconditionally to Chinese sovereignty."[12]

Clearly then, some key American officials knew of the ROC's territorial demands as of late 1942. We can also be virtually certain that Roosevelt knew as well. On November 16 and 17, Lattimore had met with Chiang Kai-shek before leaving to return to the United States to take up an assignment with the Office of War Information. In his handwritten notes of Chiang's statements, in a section titled "For President," is the sentence: "In Western Pacific: China must recover full sovereignty in Taiwan & Northeast" (i.e., Manchuria). On December 7, Lattimore briefed Roosevelt. As Lattimore wrote to Chiang in a follow-up letter drafted in mid-December, "Several days ago I had an interview with the President in which I mentioned to him your views on certain matters as you discussed them with me just before I left China."[13]

American Agencies Plan

The working levels of the American government had not been idle during 1941 and 1942 in thinking about Taiwan's future. Officials in the War, Navy, and State Departments were engaged in what one later called "the battle of the memoranda." Yet the Taiwan decision was of minor importance compared to other issues facing the Allied leaders and compared to its post-1949 salience. "Formosa" appears rarely in the histories of the time and in the papers of the key actors. The time and paper devoted to the island by U.S. government agencies was minuscule relative to that consumed on European issues and on fighting Japan. For Washington, Taiwan was at most a tertiary issue on the third front of the war. Arguably, the war in Europe and the naval conflict in the Pacific were far more significant than the struggle on the mainland of Asia. Even within the China arena, the Taiwan question was far outweighed by such issues as the strategy to be pursued (air power versus ground power), who would command (Chiang versus Stilwell), and the degree of Allied support at any given time.[14]

In February 1942, officers in the State Department's Far Eastern Affairs Division prepared a background memorandum on Taiwan's history, economy, and society. One of the authors drew this conclusion concerning Taiwan's future:

> Formosa's people were predominantly Chinese, its trade was chiefly with China, and the nearby provinces of China depended largely on its crops for their food supply. Despite the lapse of years, there is every reason, economic, ethnical and moral, that Formosa should once more belong to China. The national interest of the United States in Formosa is commercial and strategic. . . . Thus it is in our national interest that the island should be in the hands of a nation traditionally liberal in trade regulation such as China. But far more important than the commercial aspects of the question are the strategic aspects. Formosa in the hands of an unfriendly power, especially a naval power, is a standing threat to the peaceful development and security of the peoples of southeastern Asia and Oceania and to our free intercourse with those peoples so vital to our national well-being.

This memo should not, however, be read on its own as the policy position or proposal of the Department of State. Written less than three months after Pearl Harbor, it was a historical overview, probably prepared for planning purposes.[15]

For their part, the armed services had two priorities from the beginning of the war. The first was to deny the island to the Japanese military (if not to use it as a base to attack the home islands). The second was to ensure that it would not be used again as a platform to threaten U.S. interests in the Pacific. George Kerr, who had lived on Taiwan before the beginning of the Pacific War and who was working for the Military Intelligence Service after Pearl Harbor, prepared a memorandum in early 1942 that discussed the possible alternatives for postwar settlements. He advocated "some form of international control, the creation of a policing base on the island at the south, and the use of Formosa's abundant resources in postwar reconstruction programs. I ventured to suggest that China would not be able to assume exclusive control of Formosa." Kerr therefore agreed with those at the State

Department who felt that Taiwan should be denied to a hostile power, but disagreed with it on the island's future legal status.[16]

In July 1942, the Military Intelligence Service tasked the Far Eastern Division to prepare views on an occupation of Formosa and Kerr responded with a memorandum on July 31. He urged that the United States tailor its bombing and propaganda efforts toward the island with a view to encouraging local opposition to Japanese rule. He arrayed the reasons why the United States and the United Nations should, as a matter of self-interest, regard the island as an ideal location for "policing" of the East Asian region in the latter part of the war and during the reconstruction period thereafter. In any event, Taiwan should be denied to any power hostile to the United States. At the same time, "China must be assured that Formosa will not be exploited by Western powers to her disadvantage, or with apparent threat, to her coastal security."

Regarding who would run Taiwan during the occupation period, Kerr placed greater priority on U.S. security interests and the wishes of the Taiwanese than he did on ROC claims. He recommended that "Formosa must be occupied by a United Nations force which includes the Chinese. The alternatives are occupation by an exclusively Chinese force (scarcely possible) or internal chaos." He suggested that the United States establish a "military reservation" in the southwestern part of the island, centered on Kaohsiung, from which air forces would police the wider region. The reservation would be governed by a United Nations command in which China would have representation. As for the rest of the island, it "could be governed by a Formosan administration chosen by the Formosans themselves (an electoral machinery already exists) but subject of the approval of the United Nations Formosan council. In other words, Formosans could be given freedom of self determination so long as it remains consonant with United Nations' whole Asiatic interest." It should be emphasized that Kerr's July 1942 memorandum addressed only the occupation and administration of Taiwan, and not the island's postwar legal status.[17]

For its part, the State Department created an Advisory Committee on Post-War Foreign Policy and a set of subcommittees to formalize the discussion of postwar issues. Some subcommittees were inter-agency and most drew on experts outside the government. These were not decision-making bodies, and the discussion was exploratory, sometimes rambling and unfocused. They may have been formed for the partial and ulterior motive of building support for a postwar internationalist foreign policy. Yet their deliberations on Taiwan's future were probably the most extensive in terms of time and paper consumed in the U.S. government, and so constitute one stream of decision making.

The advisory committee did not turn its attention to Taiwan until the latter part of 1942, and even then its discussions were inconclusive and not inconsistent with the military's point of view. On August 1, the Subcommittee on Political Problems agreed that Japan should be stripped of Manchuria, Korea, and Taiwan. It also proposed that China would regain Manchuria but it was only after some prompting from Under Secretary of State Sumner Welles that "there seemed to be general agreement" that Taiwan should be returned as well. Even so, Maxwell Hamilton of the State Department's Far Eastern Division suggested that "this might be subject to some security considerations which the Army and Navy would have in mind." The Security Subcommittee was more explicit on September 22, when it came to the "tentative conclusion" that Japan should be deprived of Formosa and other territories, but "the United States should not commit itself as to the ultimate disposition of any territory suitable for air or naval bases until the relevant strategic considerations have been carefully examined by the Army and Navy."[18]

Coterminous with these passing references to Taiwan, there was extensive discussion that went beyond the disposition of territories to a systematic consideration of decolonization, international trusteeship, and international security mechanisms. On August 8, for example, the Subcommittee on Political Problems had a wide-ranging discussion that tended to support the ultimate objective of independence for peoples around the world. Those peoples who were judged not ready for self-government would be subject to international trusteeship, as opposed to the old mandate system under the League of Nations. In some cases there would be direct international administration; in others, a country would be given the authority to administer the territory, subject to the supervision of regional councils made up of other countries. The subcommittee approved recommendations to this effect on November 14, 1942. With specific reference to East Asia, the discussion appears to have focused on the evils of imperialism in Indochina, Korea, and Timor. Although arguably Taiwan might be included in the category of dependent territories and subject to one of these approaches, it was not discussed.[19]

The Subcommittee on International Organizations was simultaneously addressing the details of a trusteeship system. Liberation of colonial peoples was still the ultimate goal, in the sense of freedom from foreign subjugation, but continued association with the colonial power with the right of self-government was acknowledged as an alternative to independence. In the interim, an international executive would retain final authority, and regional councils would play a role as well. With respect to East Asia, there was a recommendation that Korea should be administered directly as a trust territory, rather than have the task delegated to a specific country (again, no reference to Taiwan). Hull approved the proposal around the end of the year, but confined its application to the former mandates and colonies of the Axis powers, rather than all colonies. Roosevelt later gave his nominal approval.[20]

Meanwhile, the navy formed its own views. In February 1943, its general board began work on an independent study on which Pacific territories the United States should seek in negotiations with other countries. Generally, the navy suspected the intentions of other U.S. government agencies and was skeptical of the capacity of any international organization to preserve international peace and security, even with a network of bases from which to take action. In its view, the best way to protect U.S. interests was to secure American bases. So on March 20, the board sent its report to the Secretary of the Navy. In an annex, it projected bases in various places in the Pacific Rim, including Taiwan "and even Shanghai."[21]

The State Department's planning subcommittees did not return to the disposition of Taiwan until March 1943. On March 12, the Political Problems Subcommittee came to the "tentative view" that "China should regain Manchuria and Formosa, and that the question of Mongolia and Tibet may be settled by agreement." The Security Subcommittee, however, reaffirmed on the same day its view of the previous September that disposition of Taiwan and other territories should be subject to the review of the army and navy on strategic grounds. Then on April 17, the same subcommittee reviewed a document on trusteeships that proposed that Taiwan and the Pescadore islands would be under the jurisdiction of the regional council of the north Pacific region, made up of the United States, Russia, and China. Taiwan would be administered by China and the Pescadores by the Council, "conditional upon security arrangements." Stanley Hornbeck intervened to counter an apparent trend of emphasizing U.S. strategic interests over China's claims. "He wondered whether, if Formosa should be restored to China without conditions, it really belonged in here at all [in a discussion of trusteeships]. Mr. Welles suggested that for Formosa this arrangement might be made transitional to cover the period of transfer of populations. Mr. Hornbeck agreed that such a provision would be desirable but that he understood the Chinese were insisting upon an outright transfer of Formosa." In a later summary of its views, the subcommittee tended to split the difference: not oppose the return of Taiwan to China but suggest that some parts of the island be under the jurisdiction of the United States or an international organization for purposes of preserving security.[22]

Box 2.1
Wartime Options for Taiwan's Future

Extract on "Alternative Political Solutions," from "Formosa," Document 325 of the Territorial Subcommittee of the State Department's Advisory Committee on Post-War Foreign Policy, May 25, 1943, pp. 8–12, Box 63, Notter Files, Record Group 59, U.S. National Archives and Records Administration, College Park, MD; drafted by Cabot Colville of the Department's Division of Political Studies.

1. *Continuance of Japanese Sovereignty*

To allow Japan to retain Formosa would be to endorse a seizure effected by war as recently as 1894, a seizure which has never had even such sanction as derives from heavy colonizing by the conquering nation. In 1894 the number of Japanese residents in Formosa was insignificant, and to the present time the number has never exceeded 6 percent of the population of Formosa. Furthermore, the record in economic terms is clearly one of exploitation.

The United Nations through the Atlantic Charter have stated that they "respect the right of all peoples to choose the form of government under which they will live." There is, however, no evidence that the people of Formosa will after the war choose a form of government which would keep them a part of the Japanese empire. Unless such a choice is made by them, there appears to be no commitment which requires the continuation of Japanese sovereignty. The common principle of the United Nations that they seek no aggrandizement, territorial or other, might in itself be held to be a commitment that an area which was part of the territory of an enemy state at the commencement of the war will not be detached from her; in the instance of Formosa the area has been Japanese only by recent aggrandizement based on force, and other principles declared by the United Nations would be violated by Japanese retention.

Continued Japanese sovereignty over Formosa would presumably have the same unsatisfactory consequences as heretofore.

2. *Independence of Formosa*

Under the principle of the United Nations regarding respect for the right of all people to choose the form of government under which they will live, it is conceivable both that the Formosans might claim to be a people and that they should choose to live under an independent government of their own. There is, however, little likelihood of such a movement developing. The populace has not been articulate, and the dominantly Chinese make-up of the population has resulted in a general tendency to favor the cause of China rather than to organize a movement for self-government.

The severe wrench to the existing economic interdependence between Formosa and Japan proper which would be produced by the setting up of an independent Formosa would give rise to mutual need for the continuation of trade. Present heavy reliance on Japanese skill and capital in Formosa would, in event of independence, give rise to further problems which would call for solution by special action.

Box 2.1 *(continued)*

3. *Internationalization*

The placing of the sovereignty of Formosa directly and solely under an international body set up by the United Nations or under some other international administration would be to assume responsibility for administration of the civil affairs of a predominantly Chinese population, affairs in which there is no direct international interest other than that of security. For such a function there does not exist at present, deriving from previous international machinery, a corps of specialists experienced and ready to perform the duties necessary; however, the building up of an international corps of qualified personnel does not appear outside the realm of practicability.

Chinese suspicion of the basic motive underlying any program of complete internationalization of Formosa should be anticipated. The strategically dominating position of Formosa in relation to the coast of China would give rise to a natural Chinese query as to why, with the population of Formosa Chinese in race and under Chinese sovereignty before 1895, internationalization rather than restoration of Chinese sovereignty would be required by the purposes of the victorious United Nations.

4. *Restoration of Chinese Sovereignty*

A. *Unconditional*. China having been forcibly deprived in 1894–1895 of sovereign rights over Formosa, the restoration of Formosa to China is one logical alternative.

Formosan Chinese, comprising 91.5 percent of the population, have retained, even under Japanese rule, an outlook which is more Chinese than Formosan. The toughness of China in holding out against Japanese attack since 1937 has added to the Chinese nationalistic sense among the people of the island. It seems probable that Chinese sovereignty would generally be welcomed in Formosa.

The administration of government in Formosa would require the assignment there of a number of experienced Chinese from China, inasmuch as the form of rule by the Japanese has left no room for the development of political talent among the Formosans.

Economic adjustment would be a more serious problem. However, the rice-deficient provinces of Fukien and Kwangtung could easily absorb export surpluses of Formosan rice. China does not naturally offer a market for sugar, but the recent tendency for Manchuria to import Formosan sugar might be encouraged. Continuation of similar trade with Japan, but on a two-way balanced basis, would probably be wise economics for Formosa even under a change of sovereignty.

If China should require mandatory repatriation to Japan of the Japanese residents of Formosa, industry in Formosa would suffer badly as a consequence of present dependence on Japanese skilled personnel. It appears that China could not soon supply such personnel.

Restoration of sovereignty to China would not alter the fact that Formosa, by reason of strategic location, is a key to international security. It does not appear that China in her present stage of development is capable of making use of Formosa in execution of the international interest in security.

Box 2.1 *(continued)*

B. *With Special Arrangements in the Interests of International Security.*
If Chinese sovereignty is restored over Formosa, the international interest
in the use of points in Formosa for purposes of security might be met by
special arrangement. Some opposition has already been expressed in China
to the restoring of Formosa to China under restrictions over the exercise of
its sovereign rights. It is possible that this opposition could be overcome by
China's granting to an international organization stipulated rights in Formosa
to be exercised for the purposes of international security, this grant by China
to be subsequent to (or coincident with) full legal restoration to China of
sovereignty over Formosa. Participation by China as a member of the international organization to which this grant of rights would be made would
facilitate this procedure, particularly if in other parts of the world other sovereign states granted to the international organization similar rights over
crucial areas. The use of Formosa for security purposes on a restricted
basis would of course leave the way open for many conflicts and unsatisfactory relations between the international and the local authorities; every
effort would have to be made to minimize them by adequate provision in
advance for the practical needs of the situation.

Amid these cursory and somewhat confused efforts to balance various
American interests with respect to Taiwan, the Territorial Subcommittee
was more methodical. Under its aegis, Cabot Colville of the department's
Division of Political Studies prepared a study in May 1943 that provided
demographic, social, economic, and administrative background on Taiwan, and a section on its strategic importance (both its location and use
as a base for Japanese attacks in the southwest Pacific). The study also
presented four options for Taiwan's disposition: continuation of Japanese sovereignty, independence, internationalization (placing the island
under some international body), and restoration of Chinese sovereignty.
This latter option had two different approaches: restoration without
conditions and with "special arrangements in the interest of international security" (see Box 2.1 for the full text of the options section). In
assessing the four options, Colville considered fundamental principles
(especially those in the Atlantic Charter), the apparent ethnic Chinese
character of most of the population, the island's future economic vi-
ability, administrative and technical capabilities, ROC views, and security imperatives. He questioned whether the population of Taiwan had
the desire to remain a territory of Japan or any interest in becoming a
separate state. Lack of administrative and technical resources were obstacles to both internationalization and unconditional transfer to China,
and the ROC could be expected to oppose internationalization because

"the population of Formosa [was] Chinese in race and under Chinese sovereignty before 1895."[23]

This document was probably prepared for a meeting of the subcommittee that occurred on June 25. The subcommittee "accepted the thesis that Formosa should be returned to China, but some discussion took place as to the most suitable means of reserving for the United Nations the right to use naval and air bases on Formosa and the Pescadores. It was suggested that Formosa should be ceded in full sovereignty to China and that under a separate arrangement provision should be made for the use of the necessary bases. The fact was stressed that, in view of Chinese sensitivity to foreign control or supervision, it would be a grave error to make any reservations in the original retrocession of territory."[24]

In September 1943, the Far Eastern Division of the Military Intelligence Service, probably in the person of George Kerr, prepared a memorandum on political and economic issues regarding Taiwan. Unlike Kerr's effort the previous July, the new memo did set forth options on the island's future legal status, as follows:

- Outright return to Chinese rule, either as a part of Fujian Province, or as a separate province with full provincial status, or as a special area administered by a non-Formosan Government created by the Chongqing government.
- "Return to China with a reservation ('concession leased area') for joint use by the United Nations (including China)."
- "Administration under a Mandate arrangement jointly exercised by the United Nations having an interest in the Pacific, with China fully participating."

The September 1943 memorandum reiterated Taiwan's importance as a regional policing site and identified the southwestern part of the island as an ideal location for air and naval bases. But it also recognized that the ROC might object to such an outcome and suggested a face-saving approach to take account of Chinese concerns. Taiwan would be "returned to China" either at the end of hostilities on the island, or when Japan made a general capitulation, or at a peace conference. Thereafter, China would lease the southwestern part of the island either to the United Nations, in which China would be represented, or to a "joint Chinese-American administrative group." To reassure China about Allied intentions, the lease would run for a specific period of time. As to the rest of Taiwan, there was proposed an "autonomous Formosan-Chinese administration (as a Province of China) subject only to consultation and adjustment to needs of the leased area."[25]

The President Decides

These planning exercises, particularly the systematic approaches of the State Department's Territorial Subcommittee and the Military Intelligence Service, shed light on the conflicting priorities that underlay the decision on what to do about Taiwan. How to weigh the demands of an ally, even a weak one like China, against the apparent logic of the strategic situation in East Asia was a real dilemma, and American officials at the working level were indeed making an effort to grapple with competing priorities. True, they had relatively little time to spend on the future of Taiwan, and their understanding of the history of the island may not have been commensurate with the far-reaching consequences of the decisions they had to make. True also, the navy was pursuing its own institutional interests. But American officials were taking seriously the daunting and new responsibilities that the war had forced upon the United States.

What most of the participants did not know during their deliberations in the spring and summer of 1943 was that Roosevelt had already decided *in February at the latest* that Taiwan would be returned to China. Moreover, the Chinese government was informed of that decision by the end of March. The Taiwan decision did not, therefore, reflect the military's defeat in a bureaucratic struggle at the hands of the State Department (as George Kerr's account would later assert). Rather it reflected an exercise of presidential leadership for reasons other than the State Department's purported "continental" approach to Taiwan or Kerr's definition of America's "enlightened self-interest." It is not even clear that the president was aware that such a "battle of the memoranda" was occurring.[26]

Roosevelt may have come to an initial decision concerning Taiwan's fate as early as December 1942, when Owen Lattimore briefed the president on conversations he had had with Chiang before leaving China the previous month. Among the points that were likely conveyed was Chiang's desire that the island be returned to China. In a follow-up letter to Chiang on his briefing of FDR, Lattimore did not convey an explicit response to Chiang's proposal. But he did say: "The President wishes me to convey to you in the most cordial and sympathetic way that he feels that there is a basic similarity, indeed a basic agreement, between the way in which he is thinking about these major problems and the way you are thinking about them."[27]

The most definitive piece of evidence on FDR's decision appears in the files of Harley Notter, who was in charge of the State Department's planning effort. Among them is a file on "Talks with FDR," in which Notter sought to document contacts with the White House on his work. In that file there is the following entry: "February 22, 1943—Hull, Welles, Taylor, Isaiah Bowman, Pasvolsky went to White House in morning, waited 25 minutes but had to return in the afternoon. Conversation lasted 1 hour. President's ideas [after discussion of European territorial issues]: China should receive Formosa and Manchuria and there should be a trusteeship for Korea. France should lose Indo-China, but its disposition is a question."[28]

Over a month later, Roosevelt brought up Taiwan during the visit to Washington of Anthony Eden, the British secretary of state for foreign affairs. Eden's meetings with various American interlocutors featured a wide-ranging discussion of postwar arrangements. Taiwan came up on March 27 at a White House session that included Roosevelt, Hull, Welles, and Harry Hopkins on the American side and Eden and William Strang on the British side, plus the two ambassadors. In the discussion of East Asia, "the President suggested that a trusteeship be set up for Indochina; that Manchuria and Formosa should be returned to China and that Korea might be placed under an international trusteeship, with China, the United States and one or two other countries participating. . . . Mr. Eden indicated that he was favorably impressed with this proposal."[29]

Two days later, ROC Foreign Minister T.V. Soong sought a meeting with Under Secretary of State Welles to get a readout on the Eden discussions. Welles told Soong that Roosevelt had stressed to Eden that the U.S. government saw China as an indispensable part of the war effort and of the postwar international organization. Furthermore, U.S., U.K., and ROC views on arrangements in East Asia after Japan were "very much in accord." Formosa and Manchuria should be returned to China (with due regard for the Soviet Union's commercial interests in the latter), and Korea should be an independent country under a temporary international trusteeship. Asked about Hong Kong, Welles said that was an issue for China to raise with Britain.[30]

Thus, Roosevelt made the initial decision to return Taiwan to China perhaps by December 1942 and certainly no later than February 22, 1943, at a time when the rest of the government had not yet fully addressed the issue. The record of the discussions in the advisory committee and a survey of the department's papers from 1942 and early 1943 plus those of Secretary Cordell Hull reveal nothing to suggest that the State Department was even close to adopting a formal position on the issue by early 1943. Moreover, knowledge of FDR's decision was confined to a small circle of other Americans, most important, Hull, Welles, Hopkins, and Bowman. Maxwell Hamilton, chief of the State Department's Division of Foreign Affairs, betrayed no awareness of Roosevelt's action—or that Taiwan would even be an issue in the Eden meetings—when he sent forward a memo on February 27 regarding East Asia issues entailed in U.S.–U.K. relations. It also appears that Hull, Welles, and Isaiah Bowman allowed the discussions on Taiwan's future in the State Department's subcommittees to go on even though they knew that FDR had already made the decision. The only hint that anyone on any of the subcommittees knew that the issue had been addressed at high levels was a statement of the Far Eastern Division's H. Merrell Benninghoff in the Security-Technical Subcommittee on May 19 that "Manchuria, as Formosa, must be returned to China *because of our commitments* and because of historical factors."[31]

FDR's initiative concerning Taiwan was only a minor example of the incoherence in U.S. policy making during his presidency. The creation of institutionalized mechanisms for making decisions that reflected some measure of interagency consensus would not occur until later administrations. Conflicts between the War, Navy, and State Departments were endemic, with the Office of Strategic Services a new entrant. Moreover, Roosevelt fostered incoherence and bureaucratic rivalry in order to enhance his own power. The career diplomats, who might have expected to have the lead on postwar political arrangements, were often sidelined by other agencies. As Hugh Borton, a participant in the State Department's advisory committee, would later write, the similarity between the conclusions of the committees and the Cairo Declaration "was by chance, not design."[32]

FDR's Motivations

It is one thing to establish more precisely when Roosevelt made the initial decision concerning Taiwan's disposition. It is another to clarify *why* he did so and why he acted when he did. Some guesswork is required, but the answer appears to lie in a combination of factors: alliance management, FDR's strategic vision, and personal diplomacy.

Not a Case of Ignorance

At the outset, we can be certain that FDR *did not* choose to return Taiwan to China simply because he was unaware of other options, such as political independence, trusteeships with plebiscites, trusteeships without plebiscites, and so on. What is striking in FDR's discussions with Eden, for example, is the extent to which he drew on a range of modalities to resolve territorial issues. Even in East Asia, as we have seen, he suggested ultimate independence for Korea with an interim trusteeship and a trusteeship for Indochina. Outside of Asia, moreover, he suggested plebiscites in the Baltics (if only to give the appearance of popular consent to Soviet control); independence for

Serbia and a trusteeship for Croatia, to be followed by plebiscites in Croatia and Slovenia; and independence for Austria and Hungary, Syria, and Lebanon.

Generally, Roosevelt favored decolonization. He preferred international trusteeship for dependent peoples over national ones (the sort employed after World War I). He had a faith in the value of plebiscites to resolve issues. Had he wished to do so, he could have proposed a mechanism by which the people of Taiwan might choose their future. But he chose not to apply one to them in that case. The contrast with his choice on Korea, the other Japanese colony on China's periphery, is particularly striking. Yet his approach on Bessarabia may suggest something implicit in his proposal to Taiwan. Both he and Eden reportedly "agreed that Russia should have Bessarabia because it has been Russian territory during most of its history." By analogy, the belief that the residents of Taiwan were Chinese and that the island had been ruled by China before 1895—two recurring points in the State Department's planning exercise—would argue for returning it.[33]

As an aside, it should be noted that Chiang Kai-shek, like Roosevelt, was not unaware of different approaches to rule over non–self-governing peoples. In his November 16–17 conversations with Owen Lattimore, he demonstrated a flexibility to the rest of East Asia that he did not toward Taiwan (over which "China must recover full sovereignty"). He saw no way that Western colonial empires could be fully restored. Instead, he foresaw creation of an "interim order," followed by clear and fairly rapid movement toward independence. Korea, Japan's other colony besides Taiwan, should ultimately be independent but was not ready; it would require long-term "friendly interest and support" from the United States and China. Indochina should be independent, but was not ready for it. China could act as an "elder brother" until it was, but Chiang opposed the restoration of French colonialism or creation of a mandate. He made a special point of saying that China could make an "irredentist" claim to Indochina, since, he claimed, it had been a Chinese province during the Ming dynasty. But the ROC would not do so (in contrast to its claim for Taiwan, a province under the Qing).[34]

Alliance Management

Another possible explanation for the decision to return Taiwan to China is that Roosevelt believed it was necessary to mollify Chiang Kai-shek. To compensate for the relatively low priority given to the China front, the ROC was to be treated as a potential great power and provided with symbolic evidence of that status in order to maintain its commitment to the war effort. As evidence of a policy of compensation, scholars cite the ending of extraterritoriality and of the exclusion of Chinese immigrants, permitting Chinese officials to sit on the sidelines of military planning conferences, insisting that China be included in the Moscow Declaration of October 1943, inviting Chiang to Cairo, and accepting the ROC's territorial claims.[35]

It is certainly true that Roosevelt indulged Chiang Kai-shek. In retrospect, the president "seemed an infatuated captive of the myth that China under Chiang was one of the world's great powers and deserved to be treated as such." He had a rather misinformed empathy for the difficulties of Chiang's background and situation, as demonstrated in a letter he wrote to George Marshall on March 8, 1943, not long after he arrived at his Taiwan decision: "All of us must remember that the Generalissimo came up the hard way to become the undisputed leader of four hundred million people—an enormously difficult job to attain any kind of unity from a diverse group of all kinds of leaders—military men, educators, scientists, public health people, engineers, all of them struggling for power and mastery, local or national, and to create in a very short time throughout China what it took us a couple of centuries to attain. Besides that the Generalissimo finds it necessary to maintain his position of supremacy. You and I would do the same thing under the circumstances. He is the chief executive as well as the commander-in-chief, and one cannot speak sternly to a man like that or exact commitments from him the way we might do from the Sultan of Morocco." And, as Roosevelt told Eden, he "wanted to strengthen China in every possible way."[36]

It is certainly plausible that Roosevelt believed that his Taiwan initiative was an easy way to reward China for its contribution to the Allied effort and raise its morale. Yet it is probably not a sufficient explanation for his action. For Chiang, the nature and extent of American material assistance was a more telling measure of the costs and benefits of his American alliance than the promise of territory that did not appear particularly important in the key struggle between the Nationalists and the Communists. Indeed, just around the time that Roosevelt informed his advisers that he wanted Taiwan returned to China, it happened that he also had to arbitrate a major debate over strategy in the China theater. That was the fight between Stilwell and Chennault over when it was appropriate to use air power in the fight against Japan. Chennault, supported by Chiang and Hopkins, believed that an air campaign could begin immediately and would have a significant impact on the war. Stilwell, supported by Stimson and Marshall, argued that two tasks had to be accomplished first: creating a secure logistics channel through Burma to support Chennault's effort, and building stronger Chinese ground forces to protect his air fields. No later than February 19, Roosevelt decided in favor of Chennault.[37]

Whatever Roosevelt's motivation in taking his Taiwan initiative, there is no explicit evidence that it was a response to any immediate concern about China's commitment to the war effort. Early 1943 was not one of those times that Chiang conveyed warnings that China might drop out of the war. Chiang had sent Roosevelt a letter on February 7 concerning the air power debate, and it made no mention of a separate peace. There would be serious concern come May, when Roosevelt and Churchill met in Washington, and the former would again emphasize the importance of Chennault's effort in boosting Chinese morale and Chiang's fortitude. "The President made it plain that he wanted action now in China, which could only be by air power. He feared that China might collapse and did not think the continual Chinese calls for aid to be 'crying "wolf, wolf."'"[38] There was less sense of urgency during the China discussions in February. Roosevelt's consistent desire to provide political support to Chiang was probably a subconscious factor in his Taiwan decision but does not appear to have been the dominant factor.

Roosevelt's Postwar Vision

Of greater direct impact on Roosevelt's Taiwan decision was his personal and idiosyncratic vision for the preservation of international peace and security after the war. As Robert Divine and others have demonstrated, Roosevelt had little confidence that an international organization similar to the League of Nations would be up to the task, even if it had expanded powers. Although the State Department was working with just such a design in mind, the president moved in a different direction. To his mind, it was the great powers and not a global body that should keep the peace. Moreover, they were the only ones capable of doing so. This was the vision of the "Four Policemen": a condominium composed of the United States, Great Britain, the Soviet Union, and China that would ensure, by force if necessary, that no nation would have the ability to commit aggression. This concept would shape how at least Roosevelt would address the Taiwan question. That his subordinates might disagree—or think his ideas crazy—was immaterial. He dominated the policy-making process and tended to get his way on issues on which he felt strongly.[39]

The first evidence that Roosevelt was thinking in terms of this blueprint for postwar security came at the Atlantic Conference with Winston Churchill in August 1941, even before the United States had entered the war. Roosevelt objected to a paragraph in the draft declaration that called for an "effective international organization." He proposed as an alternative that the United States and Britain serve as an international police force for an undefined period of time. FDR's advisers challenged him on that point and he ultimately backed down somewhat, accepting in the text of the Atlantic Charter a commitment to a "wider and permanent system of general security." But he was adamant that the small nations would not be involved in this system, since it was only the great powers that had the resources and the will to fight.

From this seed, Roosevelt germinated the idea of the Four Policemen. He did so without consulting the State Department, which was developing plans for a more Wilsonian body. FDR next revealed his concept to Foreign Minister Viacheslav Molotov of the Soviet Union in May 1942. He dismissed as impractical a clone of the League and suggested instead that the United States, Britain, the Soviet Union, and possibly China would keep the peace. They would do this in part by disarming not only the Axis powers but friendly countries as well, and by acting to block aggression particularly through the use of air power. This system would remain in place for at least twenty-five years. This mode of peacekeeping and peace enforcement would be facilitated by controlling strategic valuable islands and colonial possessions, in some cases through trusteeships by the Big Four. In June Roosevelt told the king of Yugoslavia that "complete disarmament of the enemies was proposed; that there should be a force capable of imposing disarmament; that when any armament was undertaken, the nearest country should 'call a policeman,' which would promptly clear up the situation."[40]

Roosevelt returned to the Four Policemen project late in the year, as the tide began to turn in the Pacific with the victory at Guadalcanal. In a November conversation with internationalist activist Clark Eichelberger, FDR described his vision as previously formulated and added the ideas that the Four should engage in regular verification of disarmament of the other countries. If any nation secretly rearmed, the Great Powers should first carry out quarantines and then bombing. The president suggested that Eichelberger float these ideas as a trial balloon, confirming that his thinking had moved to a new stage (even though he was not ready to have the plan attributed to him).

It is not exactly clear when Chiang Kai-shek first heard of the Four Policemen scheme. Laughlin Currie, during his visit to China in August 1942, told him of Roosevelt's desire that China be one of the world's four great powers. Wilkie noted during his October visit that the United States, Britain, the Soviet Union, and China would play the leading role in the postwar world, but he himself betrayed doubt that the four would be able to avoid conflict among themselves, much less police the rest of the world. For his part, Chiang, out of a mistrust of Britain and the Soviet Union, argued for U.S.–ROC cooperation to preserve the peace in the Pacific.[41]

In his final conversation with Wilkie, Chiang floated an idea that was consistent with both his hope for close Sino-American cooperation and Roosevelt's idea. After stating that "coastal fortresses" like Lushun, Dalian, and Taiwan must be returned to China, Chiang said that he would "welcome the United States to participate in the construction of naval bases at these fortresses, and our two countries can jointly maintain and use these bases." He made a special request that Wilkie convey his proposal to American government leaders. It is not clear, however, whether Roosevelt got this message, since there are no records in the Roosevelt Library of any report by Wilkie to the president on his trip.[42]

Chiang again raised his offer of joint bases in his November 16 meeting with Owen Lattimore, the same session where he said that "China must recover full sovereignty in Taiwan & Northeast." According to Lattimore's notes, Chiang went on to say: "However, once this done, [China is] prepared, indeed anxious, to allow U.S. Chinese joint air & naval bases in both areas. This necessary to prevent recurrent Japanese imperialism, westward or eastward. No use checking them on one side only. They wld only spread in the opp. direction." Lattimore reminded Chiang of the American public's antipathy toward alliances and the political trouble that such a proposal might cause. Chiang took the point but said that "he was not proposing an alliance, nevertheless this suggestion is for the President's ear only, in the first instance." Lattimore asked whether the bases could include Britain or any other country; Chiang replied that they were to be "strictly Chinese-American."[43]

Once Lattimore briefed the president on Chiang's views, it was decided that there should be drafted for Roosevelt's approval a letter from Lattimore to Chiang that would summarize the president's thinking, including the Four Policemen concept. The draft, which was sent to FDR on December 18, can be read as a forward-leaning version of the president's thinking and a response to the views that Chiang had conveyed to Lattimore. It is worth quoting at length:

> Like you, the President is convinced that for the western Pacific from about the latitude of French Indo-China to about the latitudes of Japan, the principal major powers concerned will be China and America. After this war we shall have to think of China, America, Britain and Russia as the four "big policemen" of the world. . . . China and America have obvious qualifications as the most responsible powers in a large area of the western Pacific. In the northern part of the Pacific, however, where American territory approaches closely to Siberia, Korea, and Japan, it would be undesirable to attempt to exclude Soviet Russia from such problems as the independence of Korea.

The draft also discussed U.S.–ROC bases and made specific reference to the Lattimore-Chiang conversation of November 16. It read: "South of Korea the question of actual bases from which China and America might protect the peace of the western Pacific is one of those details which may well be left for later consideration. *The President is much impressed by your clear view that only bases in the two key areas of Liaotung and Formosa can effectively coordinate land, sea and air power for the long term prevention of renewed aggression*."[44]

Yet when Roosevelt reviewed the draft on December 22, he backed away from such an explicit and detailed statement of his own thinking. Although there is no evidence that the draft misrepresented his private plans, he may have decided that it was premature to convey these views to Chiang before he had shared them with Churchill. He altered the letter so that it purported to present *Lattimore*'s ideas on postwar East Asia as he had presented them to FDR, rather than the other way around. Moreover, the sentence about Formosa's use as a base was deleted. Even so, its inclusion in the draft indicates that Roosevelt was already thinking about the disposition of Taiwan, and as an element of the Four Policemen scheme.[45]

The concept was still on Roosevelt's mind the day after he reviewed the draft of the Lattimore letter. On December 23, he ordered his military staff to study how the idea of an international police force might be implemented. He assumed that such a force would be formed and wanted the Joint Chiefs of Staff to study where around the world air facilities should be created to enable the force to carry out its mission. The recommendations were to be made "without regard to current sovereignty" and would be the basis of U.S. demands at the peace negotiations after the war. FDR's request caused consternation in the military because they could not understand what he meant.[46]

Taiwan's place in Roosevelt's postwar strategic vision next surfaced in March 1943. Just before the Eden visit, the State Department's planning effort and Roosevelt's own thinking came together in a plan for an international organization that Under Secretary of State Sumner Welles submitted to the White House. It envisioned a three-tier structure: an assembly of all member nations, an eleven-nation executive council, and an executive committee of the Big Four with exclusive peace-enforcement powers. The Welles plan was presented to Eden on March 27 in the same conversation as FDR's proposal concerning Taiwan and the Manchurian Northeast. Five days before, Roosevelt had told Eden that "he thought that China might become a very useful power in the Far East to help police Japan" (Eden demurred). And on two different occasions, in discussing "strong points" from which the United Nations or U.S. and British forces would police the world, FDR mentioned Formosa and "the Harbor of Formosa." On the second occasion, he indicated that U.S. troops would "probably" be in Taiwan."[47]

Thus the documentary record is persuasive that by the end of 1942 Roosevelt was already contemplating the use of Taiwan as one of the strategic sites from which China and the United States would keep the peace in East Asia. This idea converged neatly with Chiang Kai-shek's offer of Taiwan as the site for a joint U.S.–ROC base, and one means of binding the United States to China after the war. We may infer that in FDR's mind it made no sense *not* to transfer Taiwan to China since he had decided that China was to play such an important role in realizing his personal vision for the preservation of international peace and security. That the return of the island to the ROC would buck up morale at a critical time was an added side benefit, and the fact that most of the population was Chinese may have been a supplementary rationale. Others—George Kerr and the Mont Tremblant conference participants—had contemplated using Taiwan as a base for postwar policing. But Roosevelt was the only one who had married that idea to a prominent strategic role for China, thus creating a more compelling reason to return the island to the ROC.

Roosevelt would later abandon the Four Policemen concept (although it was still very much in play at the time of the Cairo Conference). In effect, the United Nations Security Council became a combination of Welles's executive council plus the peace-keeping and peace-enforcement functions of the executive committee. The leadership role of the Big Four plus France was preserved in the veto power of the permanent members. Yet by virtue of Roosevelt's confidence in his own ideas, and because of his skill in keeping issues in his decision-making domain and out of the hands of the bureaucracy, the Four Policemen idea almost certainly shaped his approach to the subsidiary issue of Taiwan's postwar status.

The Madame's Visit

The last factor that influenced Roosevelt's decision on Taiwan—and when he made it—was February 1943 visit to Washington of Madame Chiang Kai-shek, Soong Meiling. She had come to the United States at the president's invitation, initially to get medical care. She left China in November 1942 and was accompanied by Owen Lattimore. On November 16, the same day that Chiang Kai-shek told Lattimore that Taiwan should be returned to China, he wrote a letter to FDR to thank him for facilitating the stay. He also said: "She knows my mind and heart as thoroughly as it is humanly possible for one person to understand those of another." Because of her medical treatment, it was not until February 17 that Madame Chiang arrived in Washington and proceeded to the White House.[48]

Most accounts of her U.S. tour emphasize either Madame Chiang's use of an idealized image of China in order to manipulate American opinion or her empress-like demands on those whom she expected to serve her. Less has been written on how she tried to change U.S. policy toward China, primarily because there has been little or no documentation about the substance of her meetings with Roosevelt and others. The White House made no records. The recollections of Harry Hopkins, Cordell Hull, and Sumner Welles reveal little detail. And so far, the diplomatic correspondence published on Taiwan concerning Madame Chiang's trip does not include reports on her conversations with the president.[49]

Yet neither the Madame's personality nor the paucity of records should blind us to her remarkable political ability. Although she was an outsider in a world of men, both in China and the United States, she still deployed considerable strengths to promote the interests of her weak country as she and her husband defined them. She overcame a considerable handicap to exert significant influence. Welles later remarked that "she knows precisely what kind of Far East of the future will best safeguard the permanent interests of the Chinese people." She was sufficiently persuasive with the public that rumors began to circulate (without foundation) that Roosevelt might shift the focus of American attention from Europe to the Pacific. Even FDR seemed entranced. To Eden FDR had "purred his satisfaction at Madame Chiang Kai-shek's description of Mr. Wilkie as adolescent and himself as sophisticated."[50]

It was no accident that both Madame Chiang and her husband focused on Roosevelt himself as they sought to influence American policy toward China. Undoubtedly, that was their cultural inclination as Chinese, and it was probably reinforced by their knowledge of FDR's sentimentality toward China, his hopes for the Generalissimo, and the way he ran his government. Cordell Hull for one recognized that she and other ROC officials were making repeated end runs around the State Department and that he was incapable of preventing his agency's marginalization. He also complained that "the President unfortunately permitted this condition to continue." Stanley Hornbeck would complain that *"everything* connected with Madame Chiang's visit has been handled *so far as the Department is concerned* by the White House or agents or agencies (not including this Department) upon which the White House has called for that purpose."[51]

Although Madame Chiang's top priority during her White House visit was to secure greater American material support for China's war effort, it is clear that postwar issues were also on her agenda. What is not so clear, because of scanty documentation, is exactly how she shaped his decision.

What we do know from the memoir of Harry Hopkins, FDR's chief foreign policy aide, is that she held meetings with Roosevelt on several occasions between her arrival on February 17 and her departure on February 28. The last conversation occurred late on the afternoon of the day she left. We know also that she sent Chiang Kai-shek a cable summarizing her discussions with FDR on February 28. One part of the report gave his response concerning military assistance. The other addressed territorial issues: "Concerning postwar questions, the Ryukyu Archipelago, Manchuria, and Taiwan should revert to China in the future. The sovereignty of Hong Kong should belong to China, but it might be designated a free port. Korean independence may be jointly guaranteed by the United States and China." We also know that the issue of joint bases was discussed, for she later reported that "Roosevelt expressed [word omitted] concerning your idea that the U.S. and Chinese navies will jointly use Dalian and Lushun [both on the Liaodong Peninsula] and Taiwan. He also said that once China had made sufficient preparations, the United States could then withdraw."[52]

Pending the further opening of the ROC wartime diplomatic archives, it is uncertain when precisely Madame Chiang first raised the disposition of Taiwan with Roosevelt. She certainly had the opportunity to do so before he met with his foreign policy advisers on February 22 and informed them that the island would be returned to China. If so, his statement to her on February 28 came after he had floated the proposal with his aides. That sequence is more plausible than the alternative explanation, that she herself did not raise the matter until February 28, and that he had coincidentally discussed it with his advisers six days before, while she was staying in the White House.

It seems unlikely that the Taiwan decision was motivated in any significant measure by a perceived need to buy China's continued participation in the war. Even though Madame Chiang was not completely satisfied with the American commitments she received to shift to an air strategy, she took pains to reassure the White House that China would stick with the war effort. In a February 27 conversation with Harry Hopkins, she "outlined her views at great length about the postwar world, the first burden of which was that we could be sure China would line up with us at the peace table," because of its confidence in FDR. That he and the Madame discussed both the return of Taiwan to China and the island's use as a U.S.–ROC base after the war demonstrates that his decision stemmed primarily from his postwar strategic vision, to some degree from the Madame's charming powers of persuasion, and less for reasons of alliance management.[53]

Recapitulation

To sum up the argument presented, let us restore a chronological focus to what has been primarily an analytical discussion.

In the fall of 1942, the ROC government formalized its demand that Taiwan be restored to China after the war. Foreign Minister T.V. Soong stated that demand publicly. Chiang Kai-shek conveyed it privately to men whom he believed were a direct channel to President Roosevelt (Wilkie and Lattimore). At the same time, Chiang offered Taiwan and Lushun as sites for joint U.S.–Chinese bases. Roosevelt received these messages in December 1942, at just the time that he began to operationalize his Four Policemen concept for preserving postwar security, a scheme in which China would be one of the keepers of the peace.

On February 17, Madame Chiang arrived in Washington and got extraordinary access to the president because she was staying at the White House. On February 18 she gave her two congressional addresses. It was no later than February 19 that FDR made his decision on the Stilwell-Chennault debate and tilted for the first time in Chennault's direction, which the Madame and Harry Hopkins supported. Also on February 19, FDR and the Madame held a joint press conference. Furthermore, during these few days, we infer, she reiterated her husband's position on the return of Taiwan and his offer of base rights.

On February 22, the president informed his senior diplomatic advisers of his decision that the island would be returned to China. Pending the opening of ROC archives concerning Madame Chiang's trip, we cannot be certain that her discussion of Taiwan's reversion with the president preceded his instructions to his aides on February 22. Yet it is the most compelling reason for him to do so at that particular time.

Five weeks later, Roosevelt informed Anthony Eden of his Taiwan proposal, to which Eden made no objection. Right after Eden left, Welles informed T.V. Soong of the decision concerning the island.

Cairo

Taiwan did not figure much in White House decision making in the months between the Eden meetings and the Cairo Conference. The State Department's advisory committee prepared its territorial recommendations, seemingly ignorant that the die was already cast as far as Taiwan was concerned. In June,

Roosevelt pruned the navy's February list of possible American bases in the Pacific, of which Taiwan had been one; a proposal submitted by the Joint Chiefs of Staff in November left out Taiwan. Also in June, however, FDR told Madame Chiang that he approved of U.S.–ROC *joint use* of Taiwan and the two northeast bases.[54] In the run-up to the Cairo Conference, FDR sent Patrick Hurley to Chongqing to get a reading on Chiang's views but territorial issues were not raised—probably because Chiang believed they were already resolved. Chinese planning documents for the conference did include the reversion of Taiwan and Manchuria, and independence for Korea as ROC goals.[55]

Around the same time, the president and his advisers discussed an agenda of China issues, in which Taiwan was addressed in a discussion of an item on "bases for mutual assistance" in preserving international security. Roosevelt announced that "the Chinese want Formosa." Harry Hopkins, probably alluding to Chiang's conversations with Wendell Wilkie and Owen Lattimore, observed that "if it was believed that Formosa would be an important place for a base, the Generalissimo would be glad to give base rights to the United States." Roosevelt agreed with Hopkins but observed that Chiang was unlikely to provide permanent base rights. There lurks in the transcript of the meeting the possibility that Roosevelt and Hopkins were announcing decisions of which the military was unaware. The key point is that the Taiwan question was viewed through the lens of postwar security planning.[56]

At Cairo, Roosevelt and Chiang discussed Taiwan at dinner on November 23, at which Hopkins, Madame Chiang, and Wang Chonghui were present. Based on a 1956 Chinese summary of the conversation, Roosevelt and Chiang "agreed" that Manchuria, Taiwan, and the Pescadores, "which Japan had taken from China by force must be restored to China." Chiang proposed, and Roosevelt agreed, that Korea should become independent, Taiwan's sovereignty should be restored, and the United States and China should help Indochina become independent. Consistent with Roosevelt's Four Policemen concept, the two presidents also agreed to work together to preserve regional security after the war, and Chiang suggested that the ROC would "place Lushun . . . at the joint disposal of China and the United States," and that each country would have joint use of other bases. Taiwan was not mentioned in the retrospective Chinese report of the conversation.[57]

The Taiwan decision was not completely cut and dried however. In discussions on the draft declaration, the British tried to avoid an explicit commitment that Manchuria, Taiwan, and the Pescadores be returned to China, on the grounds that there was no indication as to the disposition of other occupied territories (such as Malaya and Singapore). They suggested that the document merely say that those territories be abandoned by Japan. The

ROC delegation argued that such ambiguity would be inconsistent with the principle of antiaggression for which the war was being fought and render the declaration valueless. Averell Harriman weighed in on the side of the Chinese and the British backed down. A similar argument occurred over advocating independence for Korea. The British were no doubt trying to challenge the decolonizing tendencies of the United States; in the process they probably reconfirmed Chinese suspicions about British motives.[58]

It is worth noting that FDR's handling of Taiwan differed from his approach to Hong Kong. Although he suggested to Madame Chiang in February 1943 that the territory be a free port after its sovereignty reverted to China, and although there was a passing reference to U.S.–U.K. differences regarding Hong Kong during Eden's visit in March, Roosevelt apparently did not focus on the matter until the fall, six months after he had decided on Taiwan. In October, right before Hull's departure for the Moscow Conference, FDR suggested that the British might, "as a gesture of generosity," return Hong Kong, after which China might immediately declare Hong Kong a free port under international trusteeship. At Cairo, he raised the issue with Chiang, who suggested that he talk with Churchill. Chiang may also have agreed to make Hong Kong a free port. Roosevelt apparently did raise his idea with Churchill, but his brief report of the conversation made reference to the free port element but not a trusteeship. That FDR did not apparently consider a similar trusteeship for Taiwan perhaps reflects both his view that Taiwan had strategic importance whereas Hong Kong did not and his desire to avoid Churchill's ire on the subject of the British empire.[59]

Postscript: Planning for Occupation

Until at least October 1944, it was anticipated that the United States would seize and occupy Taiwan as part of the campaign against Japan. That being the case, the navy, to which the occupation was assigned, wished to retain a monopoly of control on the island as long as possible. Thus the State Department's country-and-area committee for East Asia decided in June that "it is envisaged that our military administration of civil affairs in Taiwan will continue until such time as Chinese sovereignty in Taiwan is restored." (Rejected were, on the one hand, an explicit statement that sovereignty would remain with Japan "until it was transferred by legal means," and, on the other, a proposal to carry out an early legal transfer of the island by a simple Allied occupation.) Also, it was decided, Chinese governmental functions would not begin on Taiwan until ROC sovereignty was accomplished. These plans became a dead letter when U.S. combat forces bypassed Taiwan and, later, Douglas MacArthur authorized the Nationalist military to accept the Japanese surrender on Taiwan. Yet they remain evidence of an inclination in some quarters to subvert FDR's fundamental intentions by manipulating implementation of the occupation to permit a prolonged American presence on Taiwan, even though it was a premise of those documents that Taiwan would be returned to China.[60]

Conclusion

Having reconstructed the Taiwan decision from the historical shards available to us, several features stand out. First of all, this was very much Roosevelt's decision. He came to his conclusion on the island's fate in late 1942 and early 1943, months ahead of any recommendation emerging from the methodical planning by agencies of the U.S. government. He did so, as far as we can tell, based on contacts between his personal representatives and high officials of the ROC government and on his own encounters with Madame Chiang, rather than on the diplomacy conducted by the State Department or recommendations by the military departments. Indeed, only a few officials in the State Department knew of this decision, whereas the ROC government was informed almost immediately. FDR's modus operandi regarding Taiwan was fully consistent with his general decision-making style.

Second, Roosevelt spent relatively little time on the disposition of Taiwan. Although it is impossible to be precise, it appears that he probably spent no more than a few hours over the course of a year, if that, on a decision that would dominate U.S.–PRC relations for the entire second half of the twentieth century. Such limited attention should not be surprising, since it was a very minor issue compared to the huge challenge of winning the war in both Europe and the Pacific, and since FDR was clear in his own mind about what should be done. The same was true of Chiang Kai-shek and Churchill. The time spent on the Taiwan question was a function of its perceived insignificance.

Third, no one in the U.S. government made the argument in 1942 and 1943 that the people of Taiwan were not Chinese and therefore that the island should not be returned to Chinese sovereignty. The only question raised was whether the ROC government had the capacity to govern the territory. This way of framing the issue was no doubt the result of a certain level of ignorance about Taiwan's reality. But it was consistent with one template that policy makers adopted for reducing the chance of future conflicts. That template, applied most in Europe, called for putting members of the same ethnic group or nationality together in the same country as much as possible.

Cases like the Sudetan Germans were to be avoided. There was another template, that of decolonization, whereby international trusteeship would be exercised over peoples under colonial rule until they were judged to be ready for self-government and independence.[61] There was, in effect, a decision not to place Taiwan in the same category as Korea or Indochina. Ironically, it had been the leadership of the KMT and the CCP that had viewed Taiwan and Korea in similar terms, and it was they who had to make the bigger conceptual leap in order to assert that the island belonged to China.

Fourth, and most important, all American policy makers both during the war and after agreed that Taiwan was important to the strategic posture of the United States in East Asia. They may have defined that value in different ways, with Roosevelt's definition the most idiosyncratic. Yet the island's use as a staging area for the Japanese attack on the Philippines had brought home the desirability of denying it to a hostile power after the war. All decision makers realized that there were other considerations that had to be weighed against Taiwan's strategic value, and it is understandable that different agencies came to different conclusions. FDR was weighing the same competing priorities as others; he just came up with a different answer. Chiang Kai-shek evidently had some appreciation of the president's thinking and offered joint bases on the island as a way of aligning China with America's strategic direction and solidifying U.S.–ROC postwar cooperation. It was only in the 1970s when a new strategic imperative came into play—forging U.S. and PRC cooperation in order to contain the Soviet Union—that the United States abandoned both the idea that Taiwan contributed to American security and the arrangements that came with it: diplomatic relations with the ROC, the mutual defense treaty, military installations on the island, and so on. In the process, the United States also dissociated itself from positions on Taiwan's status that were inconsistent with the Cairo Declaration.[62]

So, the record as we have it supports the view that President Roosevelt regarded the return of Taiwan to China as means of implementing his postwar security strategy and chose not to give the people of the island a voice in that outcome. That American decision makers regarded the natives of the island as Chinese, that Madame Chiang was an effective and attractive advocate for ROC views, and that the Taiwan decision might compensate for a lack of material assistance all reinforced that fundamental rationale. Without difficulty, Roosevelt later secured Churchill's and Stalin's agreement to that arrangement, and the victors of World War II disposed of this piece of territory as the victors had disposed of territory in previous wars.

Washington moved to consider other options (trusteeships, an independent Taiwan, a UN study) as ways of denying Taiwan to the PRC, again primarily for security reasons and not to promote popular sovereignty. It would be another five decades before, with the democratization of the island's political system, the people of Taiwan would secure more of a say over their destiny.

3

Difficult Dilemmas

The United States and Kuomintang Repression, 1947–1979

Nancy Bernkopf Tucker offers this judgment on the balance that Washington struck during the 1950s and 1960s between containing communism in East Asia and promoting democracy and political liberty on Taiwan: "The United States exerted influence over [Taiwan's] military, political, and economic affairs, providing financing, encouraging reform, and occasionally supporting activities that challenged the rigid control of the Kuomintang regime. Washington, however, valued the strategic potential of Taiwan too highly to risk undermining mutual confidence by insisting upon the kind of liberalization that America's principles and traditions in theory demanded."[1]

That the United States adopted this approach toward Taiwan should not be surprising, since it was how the United States tended to strike the balance in other "friendly" countries during the cold war. It was also consistent with the parallel tendency of American presidents in both the 1940s and the 1970s to ignore the views of the people of Taiwan as they made decisions on U.S. policy that had a fundamental impact on the future of the island.

Although Tucker's judgment rings true and is backed by some convincing evidence, she did not have the luxury of space to examine the fine detail of how the U.S. government responded—or did not respond—to the repression that the Kuomintang (Guomindang, KMT) regime inflicted on the people of Taiwan. The portions of her book that address domestic politics in Taiwan consume only eight short pages, and although one is inclined to agree with the conclusion, there remains a desire to know more. How in fact did American diplomats on the island and decision makers in Washington view and rationalize the abuses of human rights that came to their attention? How did they cope with the problems of freedom denied that fell into their laps? Did it ever occur to them that the Nationalist government could better maintain its hold on power and on the goodwill of the United States by opening up the political system than by keeping the lid screwed down—the counterintuitive insight that inspired Chiang Ching-kuo (Jiang Jingguo) in the 1980s?

Answering those questions is the focus of this chapter. To document the

U.S. response to tyranny on Taiwan we examine a series of cases that illuminate American definitions of the situation, the actions or inactions taken, and the rationales articulated. The cases are:

- The February 28 Incident;
- The "White Terror" of 1949–1952;
- The Lei Zhen case of 1960;
- The Peng Mingmin case of 1964;
- The Kaohsiung Incident of 1979.

The February 28 Incident

The most extensive English-language account of the February 28 Incident (abbreviated in Chinese to the numbers 2-28) is of course George Kerr's *Formosa Betrayed*. It describes in chilling detail the events leading up to the outbreak of the confrontation and the brutal means with which the Nationalist government brought it to an end. And Kerr has a secondary theme: the marked tendency of the U.S. consulate in Taipei and the State Department in Washington to adhere strictly to the norms of diplomacy and so not challenge the authority of Governor-General Chen Yi and his administration. For example, he recounts that three days after the initial incident a Taiwanese doctor came to the consulate with a dumdum bullet that had been fired into his office by a passing patrol. The doctor asked that the consul file protest with the government because the bullet was illegal under international law. "The Consul," Kerr reported, "took the position that this unfortunate incident was strictly an affair between two Chinese groups; the United States had no reason to take cognizance of trouble between a provincial governor and his people. This was China now."[2]

Kerr's moral outrage is the appropriate response to the ROC government's brutal suppression of the 2-28 uprising and to its denial of a Taiwanese political voice thereafter. In that respect, his basic account has been confirmed by subsequent appraisals. Yet *Formosa Betrayed* should not necessarily be taken as the last word on the American response to the tragedy. At the very least, Kerr's account should be checked against the contemporaneous documentary evidence of the time, including items prepared by Kerr himself.

The Taipei consulate was a small post with only three Americans employees: the consul, Ralph Blake; Kerr, who served as vice consul; and Robert Catto, a U.S. Information Service (USIS) officer. The post was, in Kerr's words, "in a schizoid state." Blake reportedly believed that his duty was to interact with the local authorities and tend to commercial matters; he "was not interested in people—trade, yes, but not people." (In fact, Blake was also responsible for the welfare of resident American citizens.) Catto's job was to create a good impression of the United States and its traditions, including the resistance to tyranny on which the country was founded. Not only did Kerr side with the USIS officer, he also had his own special perspective. He had lived in Taiwan before the war, had been opposed to Taiwan's return to China, and sympathized with the Taiwan people and their growing difficulties with "carpetbaggers" from the mainland. But the consulate's general guidance, as Kerr reminded the readers of *Formosa Betrayed* with caustic repetition, was, "This is China now." Thus, the seven million native Taiwanese were of little or no concern to the United States, and the consulate downplayed the growing tensions between mainlanders and Taiwanese in its reporting to the American Embassy in Nanjing. Kerr and Catto, on the other hand, believed "it was important to conserve America's high prestige and influence among the Formosans; the United States might need their goodwill one day."[3]

Kerr is no doubt correct in describing the conflicting views of the consulate's officers and the mixed messages that its different elements projected. Mixed messages would be a constant problem of postwar American foreign policy. Nor should we be surprised at the description of the consul's duties. These, most likely, constituted the charge he had received from the State Department at the time of his appointment. Kerr, to be sure, would have wanted to reconcile the consulate's conflicted agenda in favor of Robert Catto's ideals, but that was a judgment for Washington to make, both in terms of substantive direction and in providing the personnel to carry out the mission. In 1947, Washington's vision for its consular diplomats was still rather traditional and therefore limited.

The consulate's task was compounded by a special feature of postwar Taiwan: Taiwanese hoped and expected that Americans, particularly American diplomats, would save them from the misbehavior of their new rulers. "The expectation of American aid was a deeply emotional phenomenon; the Formosans had expected so much, and as things now stood (in 1946) some act on the part of the United States . . . was believed to be the only possible solution to local difficulties." As late as January 10, 1947, the consulate filed a report that described the tendency of Taiwanese to look to the United States as their salvation in light of looming civil war on the mainland. The American position, as Kerr described it, was indeed "awkward." The Taiwanese hoped the United States would help them "escape a new tyranny," but the consulate had neither the authority nor power to do so. Damping down Taiwanese expectations would be a necessary and challenging job.[4]

The February 28 Incident began with an altercation between agents of the Monopoly Bureau and a streetside female seller of cigarettes on the evening of Thursday, February 27, which resulted in the death of the woman.

Taiwanese demonstrated in Taipei the next day and the military responded with machine gunfire. Protests then spread all over the island. On Saturday, March 1, shooting continued even as Taiwanese leaders sought to engage Governor Chen Yi to bring the situation under control. On March 2, after continued negotiations between the government and Taiwanese leaders, and after having apparently tried and failed to move troops into Taipei, Chen agreed to begin talks with a Taiwanese committee to settle the incident. By March 5, the island was basically in Taiwanese hands though armed Nationalist soldiers were a continuing problem. On March 7, the Settlement Committee presented Chen Yi with their thirty-two demands. But unbeknownst to them and contrary to his own public promises, Chen arranged for reinforcements from the mainland. On the afternoon of March 8, troops began landing at Jilong (Keelung) and the real carnage of the 2-28 Incident began.

What was the Taipei consulate doing in this first week? Beginning some time on February 28, it transmitted a series of situation reports to the embassy in Nanjing that described the latest developments. Almost immediately, on the night of February 28, eleven mainlanders entered the consulate without permission, seeking refuge. They were allowed to stay, pursuant to regulations that permitted discretion when mob violence seemed imminent. Blake later was able to convince seven of them to return home. Then on the afternoon of Saturday, March 1, fifteen mainlanders from the Railway Bureau took refuge in the consulate. Later, seven more mainlanders climbed over the compound wall and Taiwanese in the street stoned the consulate. Blake sought the help of the authorities in removing his uninvited guests. Because the consulate was becoming a magnet, the embassy in Nanjing instructed Blake to "be strictly guided" by the circular on temporary refuge and asylum, and advised him that the situation "apparently involves large scale violence against masses of people which would not make feasible, even if desirable, discretionary sanctuary envisaged in Department's policy." He was told to urge the authorities to remove any refugees, which he did the same evening.[5]

On Sunday, March 2, the consulate checked on the locations of American citizens, a key responsibility in such an unstable situation. In addition, Kerr was working on a long report on the situation that was transmitted to the embassy the next day. The report described the events since February 27, the efforts of moderate Taiwanese leaders to gain control of the situation by working with the government, Chen Yi's apparent desire to improve his military position, the status of foreigners, the continued popularity of Americans, rumors of reinforcements from the mainland, and a warning that "if the Government fails to keep its promises there will be unlimited conflict throughout the island."[6] When he transmitted Kerr's report, however, Consul Blake sent a cover note that vouched for the veracity of the events reported but also questioned the style in which they were presented.

> In my opinion, however, the purposes of the Embassy and the Department might perhaps better be served by a more objective style of presentation of the facts being reported and the conclusions drawn there from, even though the sincerity behind the presentation cannot possibly be subject to the slightest question. It is accordingly recommended that this observation be borne in mind in the evaluation of this and possibly future mail reports on the same subject, which pressure of other urgent duties and maintenance of workable staff relationships make it impracticable for me to prepare or, where no factual inaccuracy occurs, to revise in large scale.[7]

On March 3 there occurred the incident with the dumdum bullet recounted above. This was one of three approaches by Taiwanese that day to seek official American help. The others were a request from the Settlement Committee that the United States "announce the [2-28] incident to [the] entire world"; and a petition to Secretary of State George Marshall, requesting a UN administration of Taiwan. Blake told the delegation from the Settlement Committee that "it is not Consulate's function to act as news dissemination agency and that it is in position only to transmit communications for U.S. Government to Embassy subject latter's decision regarding onward forwarding." In reporting the dumdum bullet request Blake stressed that he "fully realize[d] importance of not involving Consulate with either side in present struggle." The embassy quickly approved of his action on that case and the Settlement Committee's request. "Consulate [is] also instructed to continue to refrain from intercession either official or personal in such internal difficulties while reporting any further approaches of this character to Embassy." The consulate on March 5 did accept a letter from the Political Reconstruction Promotion Association with the request that the U.S. Embassy transmit it to Chiang Kai-shek.[8]

Despite this effort to maintain a correct neutrality, the consulate was not so impartial in its early policy recommendations. Seeing the intense conflict between Taiwanese and mainlander officials and hearing Taiwanese pleas for American help, it sent the following message to Nanjing on March 3: "After gravest consideration Consulate concludes only practicable solution would be immediate American intervention in its own right or on behalf of UN to prevent disastrous slaughter by Government forces if loosed on capital. . . . Then Government might yield to opportunity to be relieved of serious and continuing military liability during present mainland difficulties."[9] There is no record of a reply from Nanjing or Washington; the embassy did not even send the recommendation on to the department until March 6. Most likely, the suggestion was ignored. But it is hard to see how it would have been transmitted in the first place if Blake did not agree with it.

The consulate had a more immediate concern two days later, on March 5. It notified the embassy that the situation on Taiwan was developing quickly, with new rumors of troop shipments from the mainland. "If expected crisis develops it will come quickly. . . . Possible danger now [to the] Consulate anticipated not from Formosans but from reckless or unfriendly Government forces jealous of American popularity among people." The consulate asked that the embassy consider the evacuation of consular families while it was still possible, as well as asking for more foreign news coverage and a small U.S. military force for protection. (The Taipei office of the UN Relief and Rehabilitation Agency was also recommending the evacuation of its staff.) The embassy replied on the next day by saying that it had quickly requested that the "highest Chinese authorities" ensure full protection for Americans in Taiwan. It delayed a decision on evacuation for twenty-four hours, at which point the consulate was to provide a new assessment. It also reminded the consulate to remain neutral: "At this critical time you should be most careful to avoid any external appearance of prejudging the merits of present dispute or becoming a participant in it in any manner whatsoever. You will also realize that in this situation American officials must only look to the constituted authority, whose responsibility it is to afford you adequate protection." American officials depended for their safety and that of their countrymen on the very forces that had created the crisis in the first place.[10]

On the afternoon of March 6, the consulate reported that the situation was calmer and that the evacuation of unessential personnel was unnecessary. On March 7, Kerr sent in another long report that updated the current situation and analyzed the political forces at play. There was a military truce but some Taiwanese were arming in case the government brought in reinforcements. The Chen Yi administration was an empty shell and its control extended only to limited areas. The Settlement Committee had formulated moderate and realistic demands that represented a broad social consensus, and Chen Yi was reportedly willing to accept them. In addition to the Settlement Committee, which represented moderate opinion, underground elements were preparing for direct action should the negotiations between the government and the Settlement Committee break down. In addition, gangs made up of "rascals" were ready to make trouble. There was no evidence that Communists were behind the uprising.[11]

It is worth asking at this point what the U.S. government might have done prior to March 8, when the troops began arriving from the mainland, to prevent the disaster that occurred. The consulate's proposal for American intervention was obviously a nonstarter, not only because it received no response but also because it was too radical. The underlying assumption of the idea—that the ROC government would be happy not to have responsibility for Taiwan for awhile—does not seem credible given the clouds surrounding U.S.–China relations after the end of the Marshall mission only two months before.

A more sensible step does not seem to have been considered, even by the consulate. That was to urge the government in Nanjing not to send reinforcements to Governor Chen, and so put pressure on him to negotiate with the Settlement Committee. Such transfers were rumored in Taipei from the beginning of the crisis and the consulate made almost daily reports to the embassy of the possibility. To be sure, such an intervention would have been contrary to the neutral role that the embassy had mandated for the consulate and that Washington had endorsed by its silence. And to have been effective, the embassy would have had to take such an initiative in the early days of the crisis. To even ask the question today reflects 20/20 hindsight concerning the long-term impact of the suppression that was certainly not obvious at the time. That the option was not considered reflected perhaps the great stress under which American officials in Taipei were working and the distance from the crisis that all others kept.

Having missed at least the theoretical chance to forestall the violent denouement of 2-28, the United States could have little impact as the crisis moved toward a conclusion. The embassy sent an assistant military attaché to Taiwan from March 9 through March 11, partly, it appears, to assess the safety of Americans. Although he was severely constrained by his ROC government escorts (and knew it), he saw enough to conclude that "only real political and economic reform can quiet Taiwan unless tremendous military effort is made with additional reinforcements from mainland." He also reported that Americans would remain for the time being but the situation would be monitored for indications that an evacuation might be necessary.[12]

It was during the attaché's visit to Taipei that Kerr prepared a memorandum for the embassy on the implications of the island-wide repression. As he saw it, Chiang Kai-shek could make one of two choices. He could keep Chen Yi in power and so provoke long-term resistance by the Taiwanese that would cause economic ruin on Taiwan, make it a military liability for the government, and perhaps result in a Communist takeover. Or he could replace Chen with "a man of integrity, preferably a civilian," who could restore competent administration and make Taiwan an economic asset to China and a military and ideological asset to the democracies. Kerr without question hoped that Chiang would choose the latter option, and he recommended that the United States urge him in that direction, for its own interests and

for Chiang's. "If the Generalissimo were persuaded to replace General Chen
. . . he could win back the Formosan people to a willing and useful participation in Chinese affairs."[13]

Kerr's memorandum arrived at the embassy on March 11 or 12. It summoned him to Nanjing on March 17, perhaps because he had become too emotionally involved in the ongoing conflict. But Ambassador John Leighton Stuart may also have seen a value in Kerr's analysis and recommendations. Stuart regarded Taiwan as a prime example of all that was wrong in Nationalist China, a place where poor government had wasted an opportunity to use well the assets that the island represented. As he wrote on March 26, the "only hopeful signs" on the island "are the determined resistance of the islanders and the widespread criticisms of the Governor-General and his associates"—a view that Kerr no doubt shared. Although Kerr did not feel completely welcome in the embassy, he became Stuart's temporary adviser on Taiwan issues and in that capacity helped him make a significant démarche concerning Taiwan. And the target of this initiative was Chiang Kai-shek himself.[14]

As early as March 4, Chiang received an urgent appeal from the Taiwanese Association in Shanghai, calling on him to thoroughly investigate the 2-28 Incident. His initial inclination, apparently, was to support Chen Yi. And it is hard to conceive that the troops that began arriving in Taiwan on March 8 would have been transferred without Chiang's authorization. On March 10, Chiang spoke about Taiwan at the weekly KMT memorial service and generally supported Chen's side of the story. He also said that he had sent high officials to Taiwan to "help Governor Chen in settling this Incident." That was a reference to a delegation led by General Bai Chongxi and including Chiang Ching-kuo that arrived on the island on March 17. Then, five days later, the KMT's Central Executive Committee resolved by an overwhelming vote to censure Chen Yi and demand his resignation. Chen submitted his resignation on March 28 and Chiang accepted it on March 31.[15]

Ambassador Stuart believed that Chiang was the victim of bad information and wanted to do something about it. "I have been painfully aware of the discrepancy between more objective reports of what is happening in Formosa and those which reach President Chiang and influence his policy. In this and other issues I continually find myself tempted to exceed diplomatic propriety by assuming the role of a friendly unofficial adviser." As early as March 13, the embassy told Washington that it had worked indirectly to bring the facts of the "repression" to Chiang's attention. And on March 29, Stuart used the occasion of a meeting with Chiang to refer to events in Taiwan. When Chiang "insisted that this was not so serious as reported," Stuart offered to provide him a summary of reports that the embassy was preparing "especially for him." Chiang accepted the offer "with alacrity."[16]

Kerr therefore set to work on a memorandum that drew heavily on his previous reports and described the deterioration of governance and the economy that had occurred since the arrival of Nationalist troops and officials in 1945; the spontaneous protest that had erupted in response to the beating of the woman cigarette vendor; the efforts to reach a settlement of the issue; and the authorities' indiscriminate use of force both before and after the arrival of the first reinforcements on March 8. The memorandum warned that the perilous shape of the economy might create public support for communism that had not existed before, and that a policy of occupation would be very costly. At a couple of points, he played up the respect that the Taiwanese felt for Chiang: "However bitter their criticism of local administrative policy before these uprisings, there can be no question that the Formosan-Chinese have felt loyalty to the Central Government and toward the Generalissimo. Fifty years under Japanese rule had sharpened their sense of Chinese nationality and race. . . . For eighteen months Formosan-Chinese blamed the provincial administration and at the same time assured themselves that if the Generalissimo were made fully aware of conditions he would reform the system in effect on Taiwan." But Kerr went on to warn: "There may be a sullen peace achieved by military action, but it cannot be enforced." The alternative was to use Taiwan to earn "foreign credit for China." Economic rehabilitation and use of Taiwanese business talent was one necessity. The other was building a sound political and social administration.

> Now is the time to act. To encourage and ensure wholehearted effort the Formosan-Chinese must be allowed to take a larger part in government at all levels. Changes in personnel as well as in the structure of the administration must be thoroughgoing; it is felt that half-way measures and palliatives now will only postpone a larger repletion of the current protests against corruption, maladministration and autocracy in the provincial government. Formosa can be restored to its former high level of political allegiance and of economic production by prompt and fundamental reform.[17]

To Stuart, Kerr offered seven options—"degrees of intervention"—from good offices to promoting a UN trusteeship. Stuart chose only to offer good offices, and presented Kerr's memorandum to Chiang on April 18. Moreover, Stuart advocated the appointment of a civilian as Taiwan's new governor, as Kerr had strongly recommended in his March 10 memorandum. Stuart suggested that Chiang appoint T.V. Soong (Song Ziwen) but the latter declined. On April 22, Wei Daoming, former ROC ambassador to Washington, was appointed to succeed Chen Yi.[18]

To sum up, the U.S. government tried to assume a neutral and distanced stance at the outbreak of the 2-28 Incident, for the sensible reason that it did not wish to see the consulate become a magnet either for people fleeing violence or for political activists who wished to induce the United States into assuming a role in the dispute that was more than it was willing or able to perform. Moreover, the consulate's primary task was to see to the safety of American citizens. Still, it produced excellent reporting that was sent forward even though it might have been laced with more moral passion than was traditionally acceptable for diplomats. The consulate probably asked for too much when it proposed intervention but failed along with the embassy to consider an effort to block reinforcements. Once suppression by the military began on March 8, however, U.S. diplomats abandoned neutrality and undertook an effort to persuade Chiang and other high-level KMT leaders to undo the damage of the 2-28 Incident by appointing a civilian governor and undertaking economic and political reform that would foster political participation by the Taiwanese. George Kerr provided the embassy's definition of the Taiwan situation, a template that continued for the rest of the year.[19] In the aftermath of the Marshall mission, the initial stance was perhaps justified. But the post-March urging of reform was consistent with what became the dominant theme of U.S. policy toward the Nationalist government. The United States did not take sides within the Taiwan arena but sought to change the rules of the game by which politics was played.

Nonetheless, Stuart's hopes that civilian leadership on Taiwan could bring about a change for the better were soon dashed. A consulate report in early July noted that secret police activities were increasing not declining, and that the provincial government in Taipei had little or no control over military and civilian officials at lower levels. Disappearances had resumed, and army officers in central Taiwan were engaged in kidnapping. "Impression spreading that new civilian government powerless to control military or is giving it free rein." The populace's wait-and-see attitude toward the new leadership was giving way to muffled criticism. The gloomy situation was "providing willing listeners to Chinese Communist agents."[20]

The "White Terror"

The so-called White Terror that began in 1949 is less well known than the KMT's harsh response to the 2-28 protests (in part because there was no George Kerr to chronicle it), but it was just as brutal and more systematic. Indeed, a retrospective compilation of human rights cases from 1947 to 1991 shows that there were more cases between 1950 and 1954 (184) than all other years combined (162).[21]

Repression intensified on Taiwan after the Nationalists lost the Huaihai battle in late 1948. The government recognized that the mainland was lost and that Taiwan might in fact be its only retreat. It therefore took steps to consolidate control over what had hitherto been an arena of peripheral concern. That expectation became a reality as 1949 proceeded, and the central government and Chiang Kai-shek moved to Taiwan in December. The next challenge was an imminent invasion by the People's Liberation Army (PLA), and the regime believed it had to rid the island of threats from within. Communist agents were one concern, but "Taiwan Independence" elements were as well. Chiang Ching-kuo moved quickly to bring some coordination among the various intelligence and secret police agencies on the island.[22] According to one estimate, 10,000 people were interrogated in 1949 and over 1,000 executed. In 1950, the security forces pursued around 300 "spy" cases involving over 3,000 people.[23]

There was a sharp contrast between those two years in the American mission's reporting on domestic political developments. In 1949, it made few specific reports of government repression. There was one in February that spoke of a "trend to harsh police government marked in many actions." Another in August told of "almost daily public executions of disturbers of public order" and a "deteriorating social situation." Yet another in October referred to "evidence of the reported wholesale arrests by the KMT police of persons charged with Communism who in fact are not Communists but who are not ardent KMT members." Reporting in 1950, on the other hand, was much more extensive. The limited coverage in 1949 is understandable given an almost universal attention to the big picture: the KMT's declining fortunes on the mainland, the dislocations caused by more and more refugees, growing anxiety regarding the fate of Taiwan, and a shift in hopes about the United States, that it would save the island from communism.[24]

This is not to say that American diplomats on Taiwan had changed their view of KMT rule. In a response to a query from Washington on the subject at the end of 1949, the post was quite negative. "Nationalist Government has no popular support in Taiwan. . . . Taiwanese are politically inarticulate, unorganized and unpredictable. . . . Continued U.S. aid to unreformed KMT and supporting armies will delay or preclude Taiwanese self-expression and increase arguments of Communism. . . . Mass of Taiwanese hate KMT."[25] But with the Americans distracted, the regime could go about its dirty work unobserved.

As the end on the mainland grew near, Washington officials focused increasingly on whether and how to prevent the fall of Taiwan, and they regarded KMT repression as a secondary yet significant obstacle to achieving that objective. There was a working consensus in Washington that, on the one hand, keeping the island out of the Communists' hands would be strategically beneficial; but, on the other, U.S. forces were unavailable to carry out that mission and the KMT regime had the military resources to defend itself but was too corrupt and feckless to do so. Policy makers spent 1949 casting around for an approach that would square this circle. Early in the year they decided to pursue a policy of economic and diplomatic assistance contingent on reforms by the KMT authorities in Taipei to undertake reform, but simultaneously to maintain contacts with potential Taiwanese leaders who might be the core of an autonomy movement. Among the reforms desired was to "permit and encourage active Formosan participation in positions of responsibility in Government."[26] Yet no approach was made to Chen Cheng, the Taiwan governor, because he "appeared incapable of providing Formosa with the sort of liberal government which alone could ameliorate the hatred of Formosans of their Mainland rulers and in so doing build up political stability on the Island." On his return from a spring visit to Taiwan, Livingston Merchant proposed a policy of disassociation from the KMT regime, in part because it would deplete the store of Taiwanese goodwill for the United States.[27] Others proposed a UN trusteeship in order to "enable the people of Formosa to express their wishes as to their future status."[28] High-level remonstrance was considered again in July and then temporarily set aside.[29]

It was not until November 3, after most of the mainland had fallen that Consul-General John MacDonald visited Chiang to deliver the message that the United States was not going to send troops to defend the island and that, in view of the "previous misgovernment of Taiwan," its attitude toward the island would be contingent upon the government providing the people a "higher level of political and economic well being," which would in turn avoid unrest and meet "the legitimate aspirations of the population of Taiwan." Chiang was peeved by the reference to misgovernment but pleased that it was to him that the message was delivered, even though he had officially resigned as president.[30] One month later, Wu Guozhen, of whom the United States had a relatively good opinion, became governor of Taiwan Province and he named Taiwanese to head a majority of the departments of the provincial government.[31]

The situation began to stabilize after the turn of the year but the level of uncertainty and anxiety remained high. Then with the fall of Hainan in April 1950 and Nationalist withdrawal from the Chusan Islands in May, tensions increased even more on Taiwan and the drive to wipe out internal opposition intensified.

In this new situation, American diplomats on Taiwan sought to both promote reform and manage the expectations of Taiwanese who continued to regard the United States as the only way to save their homeland. Yet there was a clear contrast between Robert Strong, who served as consul-general during the first eight months of 1950, and Karl Rankin, who succeeded him, in the approach that each took to KMT repression and what the United States could and should do about it.

Strong was, in the later words of a colleague, "outspoken [and] . . . skeptical of the capabilities of the [government] to do any better and to hold out."[32] Under his leadership, the consulate reported more regularly on the KMT's repression than had been the case the year before:

- In February, he met with Han Liwu, minister of education, who expressed concern that the terrorizing activities of the secret police were degrading confidence in and support for the government rather than rooting out subversion.[33]
- In April, Yang Zhaojia, provincial commissioner of civil affairs, emphasized the bitterness that Taiwanese felt toward mainlanders, and the fear and oppression that still prevailed. Yang said he was regularly approached for help by relatives of individuals who had disappeared without trace and without legal proceedings.[34]
- In early May, Vice Consul Thomas Ainsworth prepared a memorandum on the scale of pro-Japanese sentiment, a major reason for which was Taiwanese resentment over KMT repression and the absence of the sort of due process that the Japanese colonial government had practiced.[35]
- Later in May, as the danger of a Communist invasion loomed, the consulate learned the regime was arresting more Taiwan Independence activists. "Arrests [are] being stepped up in [an] attempt [to] assure security of threatened areas."[36]
- By mid-July, the situation had deteriorated: "Campaign against Formosans continues but in fairness it must be said mainlanders resident here are also receiving rough treatment. Rate of executions has been stepped up. . . . Atmosphere in Formosa is bad. Fear of anything resembling free expression of opinion is general. Fear of arrest predominates in intellectual and official circles. . . . Persons with contacts with official Americans are suspect."[37]

Critical though he was of the KMT suppression, Strong was guarded in his conversations with Taiwanese, in part because that was what Washington required. In January, he urged some of these individuals to be realistic about their situation. There was no way of getting rid of the KMT and that "for the time being any hope for independence lay with Nationalists not with Communists, and thus measures designed [to] weaken Nationalists merely served [to] increase chances [of] Communist control." In July, Jiang Weiquan, a

Taiwanese vice minister of the interior, expressed the hope that the United States would urge the government to reform its dealings with Taiwanese. Strong informed the department that "I agree on this with Chiang but was not in a position to say so." The department endorsed Strong's approach with the independence activists. Moreover, it believed that if its diplomats had broad contacts with the Taiwanese, the ROC government would misunderstand and some Taiwanese might manipulate such contacts to improve their personal positions.[38]

How Strong managed this dilemma can be seen in his approach to two different groups of Taiwanese activists. The first was the Taiwanese Democratic People's Association (TDPA), whose organizer, James Chen, was eager to get U.S. support, since without it prospective members would "fear arrest since [the] Generalissimo [is] determined [to] wipe out all independent activities and his police were now very active." Strong was reluctant to get in the middle of a situation that was "viewed with suspicion by Chinese government," a stance that the State Department explicitly approved. Strong urged the organization to "stand on its own feet" and not depend on the United States. By early April it seemed that the regime might in fact allow the TDPA to form and Strong discussed the matter with Taiwan governor Wu Guozhen, a relative liberal on the KMT political spectrum. Strong stressed to Wu that he was not speaking on behalf of any particular Taiwan organization and was aware of the limitations and even mendacity of some Taiwanese activists, but he did offer a forthright critique of the government's repression of political activity and his rationale for why political liberalization would be in the regime's interest. His report to the department is worth quoting at length:

> U.S. Government in accord with tradition was interested in free-self-expression of all peoples and in achievement their legitimate aspirations; Taiwanese had certain local interests apart from mainland; they now had no political parties or other groups for expressing views or representing own interests; KMT had been dictatorship for long time and might not understand legitimate desires and needs this direction. Taiwanese were not in position overthrow Chinese Government by any means and both sides knew it; feeling of Taiwanese against mainlanders strong and deep-seated; if Chinese Government continued refuse permit them have their own political organizations, full and united resentment against mainlanders would continue and grow; on other hand if Chinese Government permitted political association, much of energy and combative spirit would be dissipated in internal squabbles which would draw some of attention from "evils" of Chinese Government; in the end three or four organizations might be created which would more or less represent political divisions among

Taiwanese; these would have legitimate role in provincial politics, would not be united against mainlanders, and would make good impression outside; Chinese Government should give up Soviet theory that it knows better what is good for Taiwanese than do they themselves; this is perfect opportunity for Taiwanese learn democratic procedures refused them by Japanese; Chinese Government only stood to gain.

The conversation ended with Wu apparently concluding that Strong was lobbying for the TDPA rather than making a general observation. Strong left unconvinced that even Wu understood "paramount necessity for Chinese Government cease [to] alienate self from people and permit people have organizations not completely controlled by KMT." Then with the fall of Hainan the TDPA disappeared from view.[39]

The other organization was the Formosa League for Re-emancipation (FLR), which was founded in Hong Kong by independence activist Thomas Liao. Its leading activist in Taiwan was Peter Huang, who came from Hong Kong in June 1949. His initial scheme was to mobilize support among Taiwanese and then provoke the government into a bloody crackdown in hopes of getting American backing for their cause. On several occasions, American diplomats sought to dissuade Huang from that course of action and he soon saw its futility. In early 1950, he got a job with the Joint Commission on Rural Reconstruction in order to make ends meet and to provide a cover for his political activities. His principal American contact, USIS officer David Osborn, became concerned for his safety and advised him to leave Taiwan. Huang stayed, however. The FLR was not touched in the roundup of Communists in February and March but could do nothing to increase its own political support. When the regime began arresting independence activists, Huang recognized the value of escape and even sought the consulate's help in getting transportation to Japan on a U.S. military ship or plane. Consul-General Strong did not think Huang himself believed he was in any danger and the matter was dropped.[40]

Huang was arrested on May 16, soon after the loss of Hainan. Eighteen of his colleagues were detained soon thereafter (ten were subsequently released). The consulate staff concluded that the FLR leaders were no threat to the government and Strong believed he should intervene in the case, which he saw as a "continuation of KMT intolerant police state methods which have consistently served to alienate population," and sought approval from the State Department. Washington immediately instructed him to approach the foreign ministry informally to get information on the charges, evidence, and outcome of the trial. Without questioning the judicial process, Strong was to suggest that the case had a bearing on the U.S. government's interest in fostering Taiwanese resistance to Communist subversion and in promoting good relations between the ROC government and the people. Strong did so and was told only that the charge was treason. Strong met with Wu Guozhen on June 12 and learned a bit more about the case. Wu acknowledged that the U.S. attitude had been noted.[41]

In early July, around the time that the American mission in Taipei was elevated to embassy status, Strong learned that the nine defendants still in custody had made full confessions and were awaiting release. Then in mid-month there was news that Huang had been sentenced to fourteen years in jail and the other eight to lesser terms. The State Department instructed Strong to raise the case again with Wu Guozhen on the same basis that he had with the foreign ministry, and say in addition that "provocative actions" (like these sentences) might cause Taiwanese hostility and confirm third countries' beliefs that the ROC government had lost support of the people. Wu was almost hostile when he received Strong's démarche and that U.S. "interference" in the case caused him trouble and made Chiang Kai-shek "incensed." Strong concluded that the government, uncertain about who the United States supported, felt that it must "show Formosans who is boss." Strong advised that any additional initiatives on the FLR case "might do more harm than good, unless strong position is taken." The Department endorsed Strong's actions as achieving the U.S. objective of making sure that senior officials were aware of the case.[42]

Washington reinforced Strong's démarches. In a letter to Wu Guozhen in August 1950, Dean Rusk, assistant secretary of state for Far Eastern affairs, stressed the importance that the United States placed on elected, representative government and on the protection of personal and political freedom. An unrepresentative government, he averred, could not remain effective for long. International organizations and the "free countries" were placing more emphasis in their foreign policy on human rights. "I need hardly mention to you the deeply adverse effect which reports of mass arrests and executions by extra-legal processes always have in this country."[43]

Robert Strong left Taiwan in August 1950 with few illusions. He believed that Taiwan was "on the downgrade" both politically and militarily. Criticism of the government was not tolerated and there was no real system of justice. Individuals who sought to contact the consulate risked their freedom in the process. The economy was improving but the political reforms undertaken by the regime would only have the effect of centralizing power in the hands of Chiang Kai-shek and Chiang Ching-kuo. "The result is a reign of terror, more silken than in other countries or in other times, but nevertheless in progress." Strong clearly believed that the KMT's repression could be counterproductive because it denied the regime popular support, and he was clear in his own mind what reforms the government should undertake to afford the Taiwanese better treatment and thereby shift their views of the government. Although he had been willing to voice his concerns to Nationalist officials on a very small number of specific cases, he also understood the dilemma facing the United States. If the United States were to really push political reform, he said, that effort would have to address larger issues as well and come with "positive assurance that in protecting Formosan interests we do not intend [to] unseat Chinese Government or challenge its authority here and will encourage Formosans [to] cooperate with Chinese government." And "any move by the U.S. to cut its ties with the Nationalist Government would have most serious repercussions and undo constructive measures previously undertaken."[44]

As Strong's time as consul-general came to an end, there was a warning signal for American diplomats responsible for Taiwan. General Douglas MacArthur made a brief visit to Taiwan on July 31 and August 1. Upon his return to Tokyo he told William Sebald, the State Department representative in his headquarters, that ROC officials deeply resented the attitude of "general hostility" on the part of American diplomats in Taipei. Soon, Senator Joseph McCarthy, fired by the idea that disloyal diplomats had contributed to American defeats overseas, would mount attacks on the State Department. That and the Nationalist government mobilization of American conservatives against its critics would give diplomats ample reason to shun Strong's example of hard-headed analysis and measured yet forthright remonstrance to the KMT authorities.[45]

Karl Rankin succeeded Strong in Taipei with the title of chargé d'affaires and he adopted a very different approach to the Nationalist government. Rankin had served mostly in Europe, including Greece at the time of the Communist threat there. He saw Taiwan as an asset in the global struggle against communism and he responded quickly to Nationalist requests for a better relationship, one that focused more on the positive. He would develop a reputation for transmitting reports that sought to paint a favorable picture concerning political conditions (even when the underlying factual analysis did not justify the rosy conclusions), and often sounded the alarm on weak ROC morale and the need to reassure it. He did not share Strong's view that KMT repression was undermining the government and therefore affected U.S. interests.[46]

This is not to say that the embassy stopped reporting the dark side of KMT rule. On a weekly basis, it sent reports on political, economic, and military developments, and regularly there was information on repression by the regime. A couple of examples will suffice:

- The secret police, the embassy reported in the fall of 1950, were taking no chances when it came to differentiating who was a Communist and who was not, and were unconstrained by any limits of due process. As a result of its arrests and executions, a climate of fear pervaded the island. Even reports that the Communist network had been wiped out did not create any confidence that the authorities would relax their efforts. It was only late in 1950 that Taiwanese started feeling brave enough to approach contacts at the embassy.[47]
- Local level elections started well, but fairly soon evidence of regime pressure and interference surfaced. An independent who won the race for Hualian magistrate was urged to join the KMT. According to the embassy: "Incident significant, if true, in that it would set pattern for intimidation in subsequent magisterial elections thereby vitiating benefits of elections which in themselves so far free."[48]

In late 1952 and early 1953, the embassy prepared two downbeat reports on Wu Guozhen's plan to enhance the role of local government. It concluded that the impact of this effort, designed to impress both the Taiwanese populace and the United States, was likely to be more cosmetic than real. Local officials still had very little authority, and the central government understood clearly that to truly expand the power at the local level while the Taiwanese populace was so alienated would undermine its own power and so the primary goal of mainland recovery. And, the embassy warned, "there exists the possibility . . . that over a period of time the practice of the form without the substance may result in a disillusionment with the whole democratic process itself."[49]

Yet this reporting did not in any way change Rankin's views on the low priority of political freedom and democracy as objectives of U.S. policy. He saw his main job as fostering Taiwan's economic development and cooperation between the United States and ROC military in order better to pursue the American goal of containing communism. He sent in a series of cables to Washington, most of which he reproduced in his memoir, that taken together convey his case against promoting changes in the Taiwan political system (a project that often was referred to by the code word "reform").

First of all, the United States should keep its eye on the ball. Taiwan was important for its contribution to the strategic fight against communism. "We should not lose sight of the fact that reform is of immediate consequence to us only in so far as it contributes to the fulfillment of our primary policy . . . [and] must not be allowed to prevent effective cooperation between governments in attaining our more tangible and urgent objectives."[50]

Second, what the United States needed from the ROC government was effectiveness. "Giving support to subversive minorities or publicly castigating that government in a manner liable to lessen its prestige" would likely not bring commensurate gains in effectiveness and should be avoided. Within those parameters, Washington might seek "improvement of the political posture of the Chinese government . . . such as to gain greater popular support for that government both in Formosa and on the Chinese mainland."[51]

Third, the United States should pursue quiet diplomacy. Except under very exceptional circumstances "any and all criticism, direct or implied, [is] to be conveyed privately to the appropriate persons and not made the subject of public statements or press interviews."[52]

Fourth, the political situation in Taiwan was not so bad by comparison, and was getting better. "In considering the need for political improvement on Formosa it is important also to recognize the considerable progress which has been recorded in the past two or three years, largely on Chinese initiative. Popular elections, the inclusion of a majority of Formosans in the civil service, improvements in court procedures, and the attainment of a degree of law and order probably unequaled elsewhere in Asia yet without significant restrictions on freedom of movement, all give evidence that the Chinese government is evolving into something better. Certainly this is very different from the straitjacket of communism." (And certainly this judgment contrasted with the embassy's reporting on political conditions.)[53]

Rankin was a bit ahead of his time. His perspective was not completely shared by officials of the Truman administration like Dean Rusk, who had placed at least some emphasis on human rights. But the Korean War reduced the threat of a PRC invasion and so the need for "reform." Moreover, it produced other issues that consumed the U.S.–ROC relationship. The Eisenhower administration would soon endorse his views on the need to accommodate to authoritarian regimes that supported U.S. strategic objectives, as did the KMT's friends in Congress. To be sure, Rankin never asserted that political repression was an asset, and he was prepared to admit that "the shortcomings of the government of the Republic of China . . . are an open book." But he felt that those defects should be made an issue only when doing so involved "an overriding American interest"—which in his view it never did. Otherwise, criticism would only weaken the ability of the United States to achieve its objectives. Rankin's version of hard-headed realism did, nonetheless, require some level of denial, something he demonstrated most clearly in a speech that he gave in Taipei in May 1952. In speaking of the implications of the fight against communism in Greece, he said, without a trace of irony, that he was "convinced that a regime which could exist only by terror and the denial of human rights was essentially not only inefficient but weak."[54]

Interlude: Taiwan's Political System and the
Mutual Defense Treaty

During January 1955, the members of the U.S. Senate in executive session conducted an extensive review of Taiwan policy. The focus, of course, was the mutual defense treaty that the United States and the ROC had signed in December 1954 and that had been submitted to the Senate for its advice and consent, and the Formosa Resolution that the administration formulated to take account of the offshore islands. Much of the discussion of these two measures concerned their precise terms, global strategy, military operations, and whether the United States was changing its view on sovereignty over Taiwan or giving a blank check to Chiang Kai-shek. That Taiwan was more than a piece of geography was often lost in the exchanges between senators and Secretary of State John Foster Dulles and senior military officers. But here and there, political considerations surfaced as well.[55]

The key argument that the administration offered for the treaty and the Formosa Resolution was that the island of Taiwan was one link in the island chain that stretched from Japan down to Australia. In the message that President Eisenhower sent concerning the resolution, he asserted that the security of East Asia was contingent upon Taiwan and the Pescadores remaining in "friendly hands." In unfriendly hands, they would "seriously dislocate the existing, even if unstable, balance of moral, economic, and military forces upon which the peace of the Pacific depends. It would create a breach in the island chain of the Western Pacific that constitutes, for the United States and other free nations, the geographical backbone of their security structure in that ocean." Elaborating on the point, Admiral Arthur Radford, chairman of the joint chiefs of staff, said that the loss of Taiwan would "outflank" the U.S. position in both Okinawa and the Philippines.[56]

Taiwan domestic politics affected this geopolitical design in several different respects. First of all, there was the fact that the ROC government was "strongly anti-communist" in ideology. More important, excluding Taipei from the East Asian defense architecture might be taken as a signal that Washington wished to preserve the island as trade-goods for a deal with the PRC. That would be "damaging to the morale and prestige of the Republic of China and . . . [reflect] on the integrity and honor of the United States itself."[57] Ambiguity over whether the United States would help defend Taiwan and the offshore islands would undermine morale, the factor that Chiang Kai-shek frequently stressed as his greatest point of vulnerability. Chiang "has a great problem," reported Admiral Radford, "to maintain the loyalty of his whole organization under conditions that may seem perfectly hopeless." If the United States were to undermine mainlanders' hope for a return home, "we may destroy the morale of the troops." Communist sympathies on the island might begin to flourish. And were the PLA to mount a campaign against Taiwan, Dulles warned, Taiwan morale might crumble absent a demonstration of American resolve and "you could have a very rapid disintegration in the position of the free countries all along that offshore island chain."[58] Thus the U.S. strategic position depended, according to the administration, on its ability to help preserve the legitimacy of Chiang's regime.

Not all senators were taken in by this line of argument. Some forced Dulles to acknowledge that there was "some resentment and friction" in the early days of Nationalist rule and that Chiang had been reelected as president by a legislature (actually the National Assembly) composed of people elected on the mainland (and hence unrepresentative of the people on Taiwan).[59] The sharpest challenge, the only one that clearly reflected a Taiwanese point of view, came from Senator Wayne Morse of Oregon. He got Dulles to admit that "the Nationalists" were a minority on the island and that the Taiwanese had no voice whatsoever in choosing their government. He read a letter he had received from "a very prominent Formosan" who asked Morse to investigate the KMT's "totalitarian despotism" and deprivations of human rights. Morse then stated his reservation about a treaty with a government "foreign to the native Formosans, one against whom many of them apparently would like to instigate a revolt, because they hate the Nationalist Chinese as much as they do the Communists."[60]

Dulles had a two-part answer on balancing security and human rights interests concerning Taiwan, as explicit an explanation of the Eisenhower administration's approach as we are likely to get:

> There is no doubt, I would say, but what the governments in that part of the world in the main do not conform to our ideals of democracy and bills of rights and the like, and if we only associate ourselves by treaty with those who do conform to our own standards we would be in very exclusive company. I do not myself believe that there is at the present time any general unrest in Formosa. There was in the beginning . . . when they first came over there, there was quite a sharp clash between the native people and the some 2 million that came there. That is not surprising. Those are pretty well ironed out and since that time there has been no evidence of any particular discontent on the part of the people of Formosa.[61]

Dulles ignored, of course, the effectiveness of KMT repression in suppressing popular dissent, but Morse did not pursue the issue.

The Lei Zhen Affair

Lei Zhen was a liberal mainlander and a former KMT official. He was first editor and then publisher of the *Free China Fortnightly*, which regularly criticized KMT rule and the idea that the goal of returning to the mainland justified restrictions of political freedoms. He was arrested on September 4, 1960, after having taken steps to form an opposition party along with a number of Taiwanese politicians. After a one-day trial, Lei was convicted of sedition and sentenced for ten years; three colleagues received lesser sentences. In response, the U.S. government did not question the arrest or the trial per se but repeatedly stressed to Taiwan officials the serious blow to Taiwan's image that the case represented, and in effect warned against further arrests. One reason it pursued this quiet diplomacy was a new factor in the diplomatic equation—and an omen of things to come. That was the effort of Lei's daughter to lobby members of Congress, who in turn prodded the Eisenhower administration to take action.[62]

The year 1960 was one of some political turmoil in Taiwan. It was the year in which Chiang Kai-shek's current term as president would expire and he would either seek another term or retire. Contrary to the hopes of some, Chiang opted to stay for another term and named Chen Cheng as his vice president. When the National Assembly convened in February to ratify this decision, a group of KMT "revisionists" tried and failed to amend the constitution to strengthen the provisions of initiative and referendum. Simultaneous with the stand-pat attitude in the KMT, dissident politicians laid the foundation for an opposition party, which was illegal under the temporary provisions for the "period of national mobilization for suppressing communist rebellion." During local elections in April, there emerged "a chain of organization" among non-KMT candidates. Then on May 19, the day before Chiang was to be inaugurated, over seventy opponents of the KMT, including Lei Zhen, issued a statement that called for cooperative efforts among the minor parties and independents prior to middle-level elections in November, under the banner of the Forum for the Improvement of Local Elections (FILE). The nascent opposition drew strength from a couple of statements by Chen Cheng that he favored a multiparty system, and from events in Korea, where student demonstrations brought down the long-time regime of Syngman Rhee and the United States encouraged a return to democracy. Taiwan dissidents approved of the American intervention while KMT officials, remembering U.S. pressure for reform before 1949 and suspicious that it supported an opposition party, warned against diplomats giving any hint of encouragement lest it provoke instability.[63]

The embassy understood the need for "circumspection" but it also understood its obligation to report honestly. Indeed, the political reporting from this period is extensive and its description of Taiwan politics rings true. In an early 1960 report on recent local-level elections, for example, U.S. diplomats wrote that it was difficult to judge whether the KMT had succeeded in its effort to project a new, more progressive image "since most voters had no real choice." Still, all American officials were conscious of the limits of U.S. influence. As Edwin Martin, who was then serving in the department, told a Presbyterian missionary visiting from Taiwan, tense Taiwanese-mainlander relations were "a very difficult problem for an outside government to deal with, since it was an internal matter about which the GRC [Government of the Republic of China] had expressed extreme sensitivity."[64]

By 1960 *Free China Fortnightly* was already on somewhat thin ice with the government. In addition to its gadfly criticisms of KMT rule, in 1958 it had called on the United States to provide "political aid" to Taiwan in addition to economic assistance. And it had been the target of allegations that it received funding from the Asia Foundation, which, it was said, was the same as getting support from the U.S. government. But those purported transgressions were nothing compared to Lei Zhen's overt political activities in the summer of 1960.[65]

In mid-July, FILE leaders began to organize at local levels, with a view to establishing the new party in the fall. At meetings in central and southern Taiwan, Lei set forth a program of ending the KMT's dominance over the island's political and social institutions. The Taiwan Garrison Command soon began to exert pressure on FILE, which itself was experiencing conflicts among its putative leaders. Then on August 28, Lei, Gao Yushu (former mayor of Taipei), and Li Wanju sought to reassure the public that the new party would be anti-Communist and would not be a purely Taiwanese organization. They also announced the party's name: the China Democratic Party. At that point, the security services urged Chiang to act preemptively to stop the new party from becoming a reality. A week later Lei was arrested. On September 13, Chiang Kai-shek categorically told a group of American reporters that Lei had knowingly harbored a Communist agent—thus sealing Lei's fate if it had not been sealed before. The Taiwan Garrison Command issued an indictment on September 27, asserting that charge and another, that articles in *Free China Fortnightly* were seditious. The trial was held on October 3 and the ten-year sentence was handed down on October 9.[66]

From the day of the arrest, the embassy in Taipei reported developments on a daily basis but generally did not seek to influence events. The policy action for the U.S. government occurred in Washington, where members of Congress bombarded the State Department about the case. The first letter came from Representative Charles Porter of Oregon and was dated September 5, the same day that the *New York Times* reported Lei's arrest. It was Lei's daughter, Emily Dequan Lei Wang, who had contacted Porter. The representative minced no words. "I protest these arrests and ask that you take appropriate action to persuade Chiang to drop these charges." Porter reminded the department that U.S. assistance kept Chiang in power and that the cases of South Korea and Turkey demonstrated "the despotic excesses of U.S.-sponsored governments finally led to rebellions." He was clear what the United States should do: "If we don't stand up for democracy, who will?"[67]

At first the department's response was tepid. Assistant Secretary for Congressional Affairs William Macomber quickly wrote Porter that this was an internal Chinese affair that should be left to Taiwan's courts but that the department "had no reason to believe that Mr. Lei will not be given a fair trial." Deputy Assistant Secretary John Steeves made the same argument on September 10 when he met with Emily Wang and Representative Porter. Lei's daughter countered with doubts about the fairness of a military trial, or whether her father would get a trial at all. By now, the department understood it had a problem on its hands and laid out for the embassy its rationale for a more aggressive approach. "Embassy will appreciate that regardless merits of GRC's case against Lei under Chinese law his arrest bound to have adverse political and psychological repercussions both in U.S. and abroad so far as GRC concerned which will tend to be magnified by any irregularities which might occur in GRC's handling of case." The department indicated it would soon take up the case with ROC Ambassador Ye Gongzhao.[68]

That meeting occurred on September 13, between Ambassador Ye and Assistant Secretary for Far East Affairs Graham Parsons. Earlier on the same day, the department had received worrisome news from Taipei about rumors of the imminent arrest of Gao Yushu and Li Wanju, who seemed determined to go ahead with plans for the new party. Because they were Taiwanese, the embassy predicted that their arrest would "arouse [the] Taiwanese, who so far seem surprisingly little exercised over Lei arrest." The embassy agreed that the United States should convey "advice" to the ROC government on the negative impact that the arrests were having on international opinion, but thought this message was better conveyed in Washington than Taipei. And right before the Washington meeting, an ROC embassy officer asked his American counterpart to ensure that Parsons not pull any punches, so that Ye would have "ammunition for a strong report to Taipei." Parsons issued all the requisite disclaimers about internal affairs but then proceeded to "convey our concern" about the Lei case and its impact on the U.S. ability to support the ROC's international position. He referred to Lei's past reputation, the sympathy that Americans have for movements that seek to secure their human and civil rights, the congressional concern that Lei would not get a fair trial, the impact in other countries on which Taiwan depended, the poor timing of the arrests on the eve of the UN General Assembly and before the U.S. presidential election, and the damage that further arrests would do (for example, strengthening the belief that the Taiwan government's target was not seditious behavior but formation of an opposition party). Ye accepted that the timing was bad and offered only a modest defense of the government's actions.[69]

Two other things happened on September 13. First, Chiang issued his public judgment on Lei, effectively denying him due process. And Senator Harrison Williams (of New Jersey), contacted by Emily Wang, sent a telegram to the Department to protest Lei's arrest. Ms. Wang would continue her campaign, sending letters to President Eisenhower, Secretary of State Christian Herter, and other executive branch officials. She sought Eleanor Roosevelt's assistance and that of Senators Clifford Case, J. William Fulbright, Warren Magnuson, Estes Kefauver, Prescott Bush, Lyndon Johnson, John Stennis, Joseph Clark, plus Representative Clement Zablocki, and others. The State Department was kept busy preparing replies to all these letters, and soon focused on the impact of the Lei case on the ROC's image.[70]

On September 30, the State Department sent a message to the embassy in Taipei that took a new tack on the Lei case. With the events in South Korea very much in mind, Washington expressed a worry that Chiang Kai-shek might make the same sort of repressive mistakes that Syngman Rhee had made and so undermine political stability on Taiwan. Moreover, it noted, "any GRC policy of freezing [the] political status quo would conflict directly with [the] long established U.S. policy objective of working toward responsible representative government capable of attracting growing support [of the] people [of] Taiwan." In this one instance at least, the Eisenhower administration saw a conflict between Chiang's authoritarian system on the one hand and American values and strategic interests on the other. It instructed Ambassador Everett Drumright to present the U.S. attitude on what had happened in Korea as a way of intimating U.S. concern that Chiang might go down the same road.[71]

A week later Drumright responded. The ambassador was conservative and anti-Communist by political temperament, so it was no surprise that he shot back a cable that took issue with Washington's suggestion. Taipei officials did not misunderstand the U.S. approach in South Korea, he wrote. They simply disagreed with it, believing that the United States had encouraged the opposition to Rhee and so aggravated the political situation and put South Korea at risk. Drumright himself thought a comparison with South Korea was not apt. Taiwan's economy and government administration were better; the KMT regime was not as heavy-handed as Rhee's; and there were local elections. There was no effective political opposition for the simple reason that Chiang was determined to prevent one, as he amply if regrettably demonstrated in the Lei case. Taiwanese politicians were "unprincipled opportunists" in any case. "There is a conscious effort in train to broaden

Taiwanese representation in [the] Central Government [and a] slow but continuing progress in [the] area of human rights"—as evidenced by the freedom enjoyed by the *Free China Fortnightly* itself. Slow, steady progress was being made in the direction of representative government. Moreover, U.S. strategic interests were at stake. "We have known all along that a free political atmosphere is an unattainable goal if we want [a] stable, militarily secure Taiwan to deter [the] Communists and preserve our peripheral defenses. . . . We really have no alternative in terms of our own security but to continue [the] policy . . . to work with Chiang and [the] KMT. Neither [the] world situation nor objective conditions here permit [the] luxury of [a] free organized opposition."[72]

Although Drumright's assertions about the progress occurring on Taiwan were optimistic, and although his subordinates saw a lot wrong with the way the KMT was running Taiwan, to his credit he did not censor their reports. As noted above, political reporting was consistently sound. And as recently as September 29, the embassy had sent in a report on Taiwan's civil and military judicial systems that cited the Lei case as a good example of using the courts to stifle political dissent. Nor were embassy officers reluctant to restate Washington's view on the implications of the Lei case for the ROC's image. An embassy officer did so to a deputy secretary-general of the Kuomintang the day before Drumright sent his message back to Washington. But clearly, Drumright's assessment of the stakes involved and what the United States could or should do about it was somewhat different from that of Washington or his own staff.[73]

Washington was unwilling to let the issue drop. Not only were members of Congress continuing to raise the issue as the Taiwan judicial process moved through the trial and appeal phase and to press the department to make a public statement. There were also genuine concerns about the speed at which the trial had occurred (creating the impression that Lei had been railroaded); the fact that it occurred in a military court; the mild character of the *Free China Fortnightly* articles if judged by any standard other than a Taiwan one; the loss of *Free China Fortnightly* as an anti-Communist beacon that had credibility because it was the outspoken standard; the easy inference that Lei was arrested to stop the formation of an opposition party and the continuing concern that his colleagues might be arrested. Steeves raised all of these points with Ambassador Ye on October 24, and Ye was fairly critical of his government's handling of the case, confiding he had urged Chiang that Lei not be tried in military court. Ye expressed appreciation for the "judicious" manner in which the United States had conducted itself, promised that he would report the conversation faithfully, and asked that Drumright be instructed to convey similar points to the foreign ministry.[74]

The next day the department did just that. It instructed Drumright, "unless you perceive objection," to reiterate at a high level the points made in Washington and convey that the administration was "seriously concerned" about the impact the Lei case was having on American opinion. Specifically, the repercussions "will be even more serious if similar action [is] taken against other opposition leaders, especially Taiwanese." Drumright did not meet with Foreign Minister Shen Changhuan until two weeks later, on November 8, and it is not clear how much of the administration message he delivered. He did report Shen's effort to defend the arrest and he offered his judgment about Taipei's future course. "I believe it is unlikely that the Government will move to undo what has happened. I think it doubtful whether Lei can expect leniency. I think it is almost certain that he will not be allowed to resume political activity." Whether Drumright raised what for Washington was the critical issue—further arrests—is completely unclear from the report of the meeting.[75]

Drumright showed his colors once more in a report of a conversation he had with Hu Shi on November 15. It was Drumright who saw progress in some of the steps that the ROC government had taken while Hu was skeptical that they represented significant change. The ambassador believed that the government thought it was confronting "the question of survival or destruction"—and may have even agreed with that analysis. Hu found it hard to comprehend the KMT's "ruthlessness." Tellingly, one of the Washington readers of this cable made the following marginal notation: "Who's representing who?"[76]

On November 24, a Taiwan court rejected Lei's appeal and the State Department decided it was time for another démarche. Lei had no further legal options available so that the only avenue was executive clemency. Livingston Merchant, under secretary for political affairs and the officer who had been sent in mid-1949 to explore alternatives to Chiang, met with Ambassador Ye and urged that Chiang give "serious consideration" to a reduction or remission of Lei's sentence. "Such an action would uphold the dignity of Chinese law and at the same time demonstrate that the law can indeed be tempered with mercy. This in our judgment would be in line with the highest Chinese traditions." Ye offered Merchant yet another defense of the arrest and trial, but promised to convey the U.S. views.[77]

Almost simultaneously, Washington replied to Drumright's October cable that objected to use of the Korea analogy. The department accepted many of his points, for example, that political liberalization should not be sought "at the expense of security and stability." But it reached a different conclusion: "that these objectives may actually be jeopardized unless steps are taken in good time to prevent an explosion such as took place in Korea." And it questioned the view that over the long term "a considerably freer political atmosphere and a stable, militarily secure Taiwan" were incompatible. The animosity between mainlanders and Taiwanese was not abating, and the former's repression of the latter could lead to a political explosion. And there were questions as to the true degree of Taiwanization in administrative agencies. Most important, the regime's handling of the Lei Zhen case had "seriously damaged its reputation among some of the most important people in the Congress and among some of the staunchest supporters of the GRC in the United States." In the State Department's view in effect, U.S. interests—including strategic interests—would be served by "measured and steady progress" toward representative and democratic government.[78]

Thereafter, the case wound down and American attention receded. Chiang did not reduce or remit Lei's sentence, even after a number of Taiwan figures, led by Hu Shi, submitted a petition for a special pardon in February 1961. But neither did the authorities detain prominent Taiwanese politicians associated with him. If American policy had any success during this incident, it was in urging restraint on further arrests. On February 26, 1961, embassy officers met with Gao Yushu, Lei's associate, and learned that for a variety of reasons (a dearth of "bold leadership," lack of mainlander participation, withdrawal of some important Taiwanese support, lack of money), inauguration of the China Democratic Party was indefinitely delayed. They also heard a stronger than usual appeal for American assistance: "Your Revolution could not have succeeded without France's help. Ours cannot succeed without your assistance." Yet Gao, like other Taiwan dissidents, would be disappointed. Some in the U.S. government understood intellectually that political repression on Taiwan, as in South Korea, could undermine the internal stability on which the American security posture depended. But Everett Drumright was a significant exception and his heart was not in the démarches that the State Department instructed him to deliver. Washington officials also understood clearly the practical damage that the Lei case did to their effort to preserve Taiwan's tenuous international position and it was on the grounds of the ROC's reputation that they made their appeals to Chiang for moderation. And they had allies among Nationalist diplomats in that remonstrance. In the end, however, Drumright was correct; Chiang saw in Lei Zhen too great a challenge and chose to disregard American views.[79]

Peng Mingmin

Peng Mingmin was a Taiwanese from Kaohsiung, born in 1923, the same year as Lee Teng-hui. He received some higher education in Japan and returned to Taiwan right after the end of World War II. He witnessed the various ways in which the island's new Nationalist rulers alienated the local population. At the time of 2-28, his father was a public figure in Kaohsiung but went into seclusion after he was almost killed by the local garrison command. In school in Taipei, Peng kept his head low and graduated in 1948. He became an instructor at National Taiwan University (NTU) and later had the opportunity to study aviation law in Montreal and Paris, one of the few Taiwanese allowed to go to university abroad. He returned to Taiwan and NTU in 1954, gradually moved up the academic ranks, and was chosen for special diplomatic projects. But he realized at a certain point that the regime was using him for propaganda purposes, to demonstrate that there were intelligent Taiwanese who supported the government. He became increasingly politicized in the early 1960s and impatient with playing the government's game.

Peng had come to the U.S. embassy's attention and was included in a number of social and other gatherings. In talking with American diplomats he bitterly and emotionally criticized KMT rule and denied that it had brought any benefit to Taiwan. In early 1963, he even handed over a paper that laid out his point of view. Peng also criticized the United States for supporting the KMT "dictatorship" and urged it to exert pressure on the ROC to make political concessions to the Taiwanese.[80]

In 1964 Peng and two younger colleagues (Xie Zongmin and Wei Daoming) got tired of private discussions and hit on the idea of making a public proclamation attacking the KMT, advocating reform, and asserting the rights of the Taiwanese. Peng seemed to believe naively that the only thing needed to bring about change was someone to speak the truth. Once the draft was completed,

> We were exhilarated, flushed with a sense of success, but conscious that now we were on a dangerous path. Life seemed to have taken on a new meaning. The obstacles in our path were dwarfed by the magnitude of the effect we hoped this manifesto might have upon the lives of ten million Formosans and upon the refugees living among us. Every thoughtful man and woman on the island was aware of some of these problems. We sought now to bring the picture into sharp focus. We would define the issues for them or at least help the individual clarify his problems by defining them. If our manifesto generated debate in every community, it would prepare the way for popular support for any overt attempt to break up the party dictatorship and destroy the stranglehold of the secret police system.[81]

The fall of 1964 was probably not the best time to challenge the KMT, since it had faced real or perceived probes of its power from a variety of sources. In November 1963, there was the coup against President of South

Vietnam Ngo Dinh Diem, with intimations of American complicity. Early in 1964, France had established diplomatic relations with Beijing, the first major European country to do so since 1950. In April, there was a minor revolt by armored units. In June, independent candidates had won election to four out of the island's twenty-one mayor and magistrate seats. Most embarrassing for the KMT was the victory of Gao Yushu as mayor of the capital city of Taipei, whom other non-KMT politicians reportedly then approached about forming a new political party. Taiwanese members of the Taipei city council were being obstreperous, which reflected "a muted restlessness among Taiwanese . . . in other parts of the island." Also in the summer, the police mounted a drive against "undesirable elements" (mainly hooligans). Fall would bring the annual tension concerning its UN membership, which Beijing's explosion of a nuclear device would only heighten.[82]

So Peng probably miscalculated the regime's tolerance of the challenge that he planned to pose, and its omnipresent eyes and ears were his undoing. The printer that Peng hired to publish the declaration betrayed him and his confederates, and they were arrested on September 20, 1964.

The embassy got word of the arrest ten days later, and was under the impression that Peng would be charged with inciting violence and plotting the overthrow of the government. It sought information from foreign ministry officials, American journalists, and Peng's academic colleagues. ROC diplomats did not have any information about the case in the early days but promised to get some. NTU president Qian Siliang informed the embassy that he was in contact with Peng's family and the authorities, and speculated that punishment would not be too serious. Xu Zuoyun (Hsu Cho-yun), on the faculty of NTU, confirmed the impression that Peng was involved in subversive activity and noted that he had alienated many of his colleagues for various reasons. Gao Yushu conveyed surprise that Peng would engage in subversion. When the embassy's political counselor told him that Peng had printed pamphlets that "in the local context would be considered subversive," Gao opined that Peng had acted recklessly.[83]

On October 23, the Taiwan Garrison Command announced that it was holding Peng, Xie, and Wei on charges of "sabotage." The next day, the embassy recommended to Washington that, in light of the announcement and Qian's information on Peng's condition, there be "no approach to GRC either by embassy or department pending further developments." For the embassy, this was a case to avoid.[84]

The State Department would soon take a different view. Word of Peng's arrest quickly stimulated American academics, including John King Fairbank and Henry Kissinger, to contact Washington on his behalf. Senator Frank Church was the first of several members of Congress to write the State

Department. The department was concerned that unless the ROC handled the case with "special care" for the "impact on influential segments of public opinion abroad," there would be an "adverse impact" on the ROC's international image just at the time when the United States was defending its membership in the United Nations. In addition to its raising the case with the ROC ambassador in Washington, the department instructed the embassy to "raise matter with GRC in manner it deems appropriate and effective." Two days later Ambassador Jerauld Wright spoke with Foreign Minister Shen, who termed the case a "serious matter" and promised to provide full information.[85]

Two weeks later, with no letup in enquiries, the department asked for the embassy's assessment of whether the arrest presaged a deteriorating political climate on Taiwan and stricter limitations on academic freedom. On November 28 the embassy responded that it did not but did note the anxiety the regime felt because of the PRC's nuclear explosion and its UN campaign. Pending more information from the foreign ministry, "all information we have been able to obtain so far indicates Peng was involved in advocating overthrow of government and that security authorities therefore had no choice but to arrest him."[86] Then the department became worried that Peng might be executed for his offenses, but after a series of communications was able to ascertain that this was unlikely.[87]

Finally, on December 4, Cai Weiping, director-general of the foreign ministry's Department of North American Affairs, briefed the embassy on the case. He asserted that the pamphlets that Peng, Xie, and Wei had prepared revealed "Peng's advocacy [of] overthrow of government by violent means, [his] intent to discard the constitution and intent to establish a rebel organization for purpose forceful upset of government." The embassy officer reiterated the U.S. concern about the impact on the ROC's image and expressed the hope that "the public aspects could be handled in [a] way [to] minimize adverse circumstances." In that same vein, he also asked about how the ROC embassy in Washington would respond to enquiries.[88]

Then in late December, the embassy began to hear a different side of the story. NTU professor Xu Zuoyun had previously accepted the government's charge that Peng was engaged in subversion, based on reading a copy of the purported pamphlet. More recently, he had read a version (closer to the truth) that indicated that Peng did not in fact call for violent overthrow of the government but instead had criticized government leaders and policies. Xu told American diplomats that "he personally agrees with all of these statements and could fully support Peng in such a program." He had concluded that the other was a fabrication, but understood that the original "would still subject the author to arrest, particularly with the open attacks it contained on the top leaders."[89]

It was a mark of the diffidence with which the embassy approached the case that it never, based on the available records, sought to secure a copy of Peng's original pamphlet to verify for itself which version was correct. Given the concern about the ROC's international image, it might have seen a value in knowing whether the KMT had created a public-relations trap for itself. But it lacked that level of curiosity. And, as the State Department wrote John King Fairbank in early December, "we do not consider it appropriate for the United States Government to attempt to inject itself into a case which is under investigation by the Chinese government." Washington would only "informally apprise" Taipei of the concern that the case had provoked among American China specialists.[90]

Nor did the Peng case impede visits by senior Taiwan officials to Washington. In January 1965 Chiang Ching-kuo, newly installed as minister of national defense, expressed interest in such a trip, and the embassy endorsed it, on the grounds that the visit would "dispel to some extent unfavorable image many Americans have had of him in past." (With good reason; it was Chiang's subordinates who had charge of the Peng case.) The State Department demurred temporarily but approved a low-key visit after another appeal by the embassy (the visit took place in September). Similarly, in February Taipei requested that Foreign Minister Shen visit Washington. That was also approved. But the briefing papers prepared for high-level meetings at best suggested that Taiwan's domestic situation be linked with the need to maintain the ROC's positive image, and at worst expressed fatalism about the durability of the KMT regime.[91]

Some American diplomats' reticence may have stemmed from concern that *they* were becoming parties to the Peng case. In late January, the embassy reported word that Peng's confession may have sought to implicate U.S. officials, particularly Deputy Chief of Mission Ralph Clough. It reviewed the contacts that its officers had had with Peng over the past several years and what he had said to them. It also noted that the regime "has long been suspicious of the Embassy's contacts with the Taiwanese." Then in early February, Chiang Ching-kuo himself provided the embassy with a copy of the indictment against Peng. He also conveyed a subtle warning: "he said that Peng had admitted being influenced by many Americans, but this had been left out [of the indictment] so as not to arouse anti-American feeling." The Garrison Command may have been more paranoid than the embassy knew. Peng recounts in his memoir that his interrogators had the following line of questioning: "'Who is behind you?' 'How many?' 'What foreign organization?' 'You have foreign financial support. The American government must be behind this!' 'We know that the American government has special units in all countries to overthrow governments they don't like. Syngman Rhee, Diem, for example, and now the Generalissimo?'"[92]

To its credit, the embassy provided a fair analysis of the indictment. It commented: "the evidence as given in the indictment appears only to prove that Peng and his colleagues conspired to prepare and print a pamphlet. . . . The indictment does not include any quotes from the pamphlet . . . nor does it specify the language employed in 'inciting the masses' and advocating 'overthrow of the government.' Consequently, it is unclear to what extent Peng and the others actually advocated violence against the government." And around this time the embassy took up a death sentence handed down in the case of John Liao, brother of long-time independence leader Thomas Liao, to remind the government of the impact that an execution would have on its image. But the embassy maintained its distance from the judicial process, and it did not, as far as can be determined, object to the allegations that it was somehow complicit in Peng's activities.[93]

The trial occurred at the very end of March. The embassy declined a government invitation to send an observer to the trial, another sign of the lengths to which it would go to dissociate itself publicly from the case. Its report gave the regime some credit for attending to public relations, by making sure Peng had a lawyer and allowing his supporters to talk to the media. It noted that the prosecution had presented enough information to demonstrate that the pamphlet was "subversive in the local context, if only by its strong criticism of President Chiang," and so to eliminate suspicions that Peng had been totally framed. But the embassy also concluded that the government had failed in a substantive sense to make its case. The prosecution did not quote Peng's pamphlet and "no solid evidence seems to have been produced which proves the charge in the indictment that Peng some time in 1964 advocated that Xie and Wei 'join with him in an attempt to overthrow the government.' Moreover, it appears there was no explicit call for violence or revolution but implicit calls for 'use of extreme methods to change the government.'"[94]

On April 2, the court handed down the sentences: eight years each for Peng Mingmin and Xie Zongmin and ten years for Wei Daoming. Within two months, the regime was searching for a basis on which it could release Peng and so end the image problems the case had brought on. Peng sent an expression of repentance to Chiang Kai-shek and freedom of a sort came on November 3.[95]

There was a postscript to the affair. After Peng was released, he chafed under the constant surveillance and deflected efforts by Chiang Ching-kuo and others to co-opt him again. An application to study abroad was rejected. Finally, in frustration, he fled Taiwan in January 1970. Suspicions about American involvement with Peng resurfaced. A bomb destroyed the Tainan office of the USIS, and there were strong suspicions that it was set by people in or connected to the KMT government who were not happy with the United

States. The embassy, in turn, was not too friendly to an American missionary couple that had had contact with Peng before his escape. And a few months later, when it appeared that Peng might try to settle in the United States, the ROC ambassador, Zhou Shukai, urged the State Department to deny him entry because the World United Formosans for Independence (WUFI) had claimed Peng as its leader. When Peng applied for a visa at the U.S. embassy in Stockholm at the end of July, the consul fenced with Peng over whether he would engage in political activities, whether he would lend his name to any organization (i.e., WUFI), and the relevance of his "criminal record." In the end, Peng received his visa.[96]

Peng later wrote that he had been under the impression that the U.S. embassy had "preserved a discrete silence" concerning his case. That is a fairly accurate description. The United States was less aggressive in the Peng case than it had been with Lei Zhen's. There were expressions of concern about the impact on the ROC's image, but they were relatively mild (perhaps because Peng did not have an ally in the United States as Lei did in his daughter). The embassy consistently characterized Peng's words and actions as "subversive in the local context," even after it learned that the regime had mischaracterized what Peng had said. That may have been a characterization that fit the political realities of Taiwan in 1964, but it sets a pretty low standard for what constitutes subversion. The embassy apparently never tried to secure a copy of Peng's pamphlet and chose not to send an observer to the trial.[97]

As in the Lei case, it was the State Department that showed the stronger concern about the impact of the case on the ROC's image, in part perhaps because Washington was more sensitive to the political implications of losing Taipei's seat at the United Nations, and so struck a different balance between strategic equities and political imperatives. In addition, the embassy certainly worried about regime allegations that it itself was tied to Peng, to the point, apparently, of offering no rebuttal. This desire to keep a distance from dissidents no doubt stemmed from the long-standing concern that opposition politicians would try to manipulate the U.S. government into supporting them. This concern was manifest in November 1966, when oppositionist Guo Yuxin invited Ambassador Walter MacConaughy to a dinner with other non-KMT politicians. When the embassy learned that Peng was invited, it suggested this might "place the Ambassador in a somewhat embarrassing position." Guo then removed Peng from the guest list.[98]

The embassy also appears to have accepted the KMT monopoly of power as an immutable fact of life. This was clear in its annual political and economic assessment, which was transmitted in the middle of the Peng affair and concluded that, "there was little likelihood of evolution towards a more viable political structure of offering the Taiwanese a larger role in the central government or party."

> U.S. efforts to influence the situation, except those of an indirect and long-term nature, are unlikely to have much effect and could easily be counterproductive unless managed with great discretion. GRC security authorities are showing increasing sensitivity toward Embassy contacts with Taiwanese. Furthermore, there is a feeling in high quarters, reflected from time to time in the press, that the U.S. has an inadequate understanding of Asian peoples and that well-intentioned U.S. attempts to influence the internal politics of Asian nations are therefore likely to do more harm than good in terms of overall free world interests.

What is striking about the Peng case is how little geopolitical considerations were raised as a reason to not act. Perhaps by 1964 that was a factor that did not need to be stated. Yet there were other factors that had come to the fore. Preserving the ROC's seat at the United Nations had become the primary objective of Washington's Taiwan policy, and KMT repression complicated that effort. In addition, Washington's perception of the ROC's strategic value may have declined in 1962 when Chiang Kai-shek began making preparations to take military action on the mainland and it had to block him. Increasingly, the embassy's rationale for not challenging KMT repression was the reality of KMT dominance. The "local context" had become the basis on which to decide what was subversive.[99]

Finally, there is the impression, reading between the lines, that the embassy did not have much respect for Peng. This reflects, fundamentally, a philosophical disagreement over the utility of making overt challenges to a hegemonic regime. Peng had the perhaps naive belief that speaking the truth might shock the authorities into bringing about some sort of change. American diplomats believed that the power realities would render any challenge a fool's errand. Embassy officers also betrayed, by reporting stories that Peng had a less than sterling personal character, an implication that he was not the noble political figure he pretended to be. They came to believe, as well, that he had something of a martyr complex. Soon after Peng was released, he began to circulate articles explaining his behavior. The embassy's assessment: "Peng appears to be deliberately courting re-arrest, since his activity in distributing what are by local standards incendiary and clearly actionable articles cannot long escape notice of the authorities."[100]

Aside: The Views of American Diplomats

From 1963 to 1968, American political scientist Douglas Mendel sought the views of U.S. Foreign Service officers about KMT repression and U.S. policy.

Their response for public consumption was identical to that expressed by John Foster Dulles almost a decade before: "If we were to adopt such a policy [of denying aid to undemocratic allies], we would not only lose many friends and allies, but we would also withdraw support from many countries that need it in order to maintain their independence. . . . There is an important degree of freedom of action, of press criticism, and of participation by the people in elections for the provincial government." One Washington-based diplomat suggested that the regime had reason to jail Peng Mingmin because he tried to distribute antigovernment leaflets. Others credited Chiang Ching-kuo with eliminating corruption or noted that the United States would be blamed by someone whatever stance it took.

On the other hand, Foreign Service officers serving in Taiwan and talking in private had a different outlook. They tended both to know more about local conditions, having traveled all over the island, and to sympathize more with the Taiwanese. They were less likely to defend the regime, and were prepared to acknowledge the regime's harsh treatment of the native population and their aspiration for independence. They also held out the prescient hope that sooner or later mainlanders who controlled the KMT would have to accommodate the Taiwanese majority.[101]

Interlude: Diaoyutai and the Political Reform Movement

The political ferment of 1971–73 was something of a turning point on Taiwan. It began as a nationalist protest movement by students and intellectuals in response to the transfer of administrative control over the Diaoyutai islands from the United States to Japan, in connection with the reversion of Okinawa. Fed by the journal *Daxue zazhi*, it soon became an unprecedentedly public demand by intellectuals for a reform of the rigid political system that had allowed such defeats to happen. The authorities allowed such dissent (a latter-day form of Confucian remonstrance) partly because the dissenters were by and large educated and also because a rising Chiang Ching-kuo wished to create political leverage to carry out his goals of broadening the regime and making it more responsive to popular concerns, all still within the confines of one-party rule. Thereafter, liberalization and then democratization occurred by fits and starts, but the direction was emerging. Only the speed and the degree of rearguard repression were uncertain. This episode was a turning point also in the sense that henceforth opposition Taiwanese— not intellectuals like Lei Zhen, Peng Mingmin, and the writers in *Daxue zazhi*—would form the primary pool of political activists.[102]

Ironically, the best U.S. government analysis of this movement, one that emphasized Chiang Ching-kuo's use of it to improve his image with Taiwanese and young people and gain leverage over conservatives, was done not in Taipei by the embassy but in Washington by the State Department's Bureau of Intelligence and Research. The embassy, on the other hand, downplayed the significance of the demands for political reform. Its reporting generally emphasized the island's political quiescence and Chiang Ching-kuo's effective control. The report that focused directly on the *Daxue* group had the telling title "The Intellectual Fringe." Although the report granted that the movement might be seen as a hopeful sign, its assessment of its significance— and of the U.S. response—was decidedly downbeat. "Because of a credible external threat, and a monopoly of power by the authorities of the GRC and KMT—coupled with tacit support of a USG occupied with greater concerns and unwilling to try to mold Taiwan's political institutions—it is difficult to assign any serious significance to a small band of idealistic reformists. Premier Chiang Ching-kuo operates a stable and effectively controlled province. Under such circumstances, few know or care about a small minority's search for freedom in a country whose citizens are better off, economically and even politically, than most of the world's peoples. It would appear therefore that only a sharp shock derived from internal or external forces could make their advocacy amount to more than idealistic carping at a carefully managed show."[103]

The Kaohsiung Incident

The Kaohsiung Incident occurred on December 10, 1979, UN Human Rights Day. It was the result of a different kind of Taiwan politics—more mass based, more public, and more confrontational. Chiang Kai-shek's hard authoritarianism during the 1950s and 1960s, in which the costs of political activism were so high that few would risk it, was evolving into Chiang Ching-kuo's softer authoritarianism, with a series of cycles of regime relaxation, opposition testing, opposition overreaching, regime repression, and relaxation again. The Diaoyutai episode of 1971–73 was one of those cycles; 1979 was the relaxation phase of another. But whereas elites, including mainlander elites, mounted the Diaoyutai challenge (as they had during the Lei Zhen and Peng Mingmin episodes as well), it was an increasingly mass-based opposition monopolized by the Taiwanese *dangwai* (people outside the party) that led the campaign that culminated in the Kaohsiung Incident. The incident also demonstrated the new configuration of American influence: a combination of the Executive Branch acting quietly and members of Congress trying to work more publicly.

As with the leaders of the Diaoyutai movement, the opposition in 1979 used a diplomatic disaster to its advantage, in this case the U.S. severance of diplomatic relations with Taipei. What, the *dangwai* asked, was the ROC when even the United States no longer recognized it as the government of China? Had not the KMT lost its entire legitimacy and its rationale for denying majority rule on Taiwan? Still forbidden to form a party, the opposition mobilized under the cover of one of its magazines, *Formosa*. It set up branch offices of the publication around the island and became the organizational framework of a political rival to the KMT. The *dangwai* conducted mass activities around the island to generate support for its candidates in future elections. Birthday parties were not illegal, so the *Formosa* network held birthday parties that thousands of people attended. To be sure, this type of challenge to the regime posed the risk of a crackdown, but the *dangwai* believed the opportunity for political gains made it a risk worth running.

The opposition's growing aggressiveness intensified a debate within the KMT over how to handle the Taiwanese. On the one hand were reformers who thought that the regime had no choice but to continue a strategy of coopting Taiwanese politicians and businessmen, of allowing some measure of political debate, and of using elections at least as a barometer of the public's evaluation of government performance. On the other side were conservative forces that wished to maintain the KMT's monopoly and saw no reason to accommodate to Taiwanese demands. Included in this group were the security services whose job it was to limit opposition activity and so preserve stability. In the middle was Chiang Ching-kuo, who had used the security services as his initial power base and who believed that he still had to defer somewhat to party elders who were his long-time associates or his father's cronies. It had been Chiang himself who had embarked on the cooptation and gradual liberalization strategy early in the 1970s, stimulated by an emerging counterintuitive insight that the way to preserve the KMT's hold on power was to open up the political system. By 1979, the end of the official U.S. relationship gave him a new reason for pursuing a reformist path.[104]

In early December, *Formosa* sought permission to conduct both a mass rally and parade in Kaohsiung on the evening of December 10. The Garrison Command rejected the request but the opposition decided to go ahead anyway. Chiang Ching-kuo, employing a more sophisticated approach to riot control, ordered the police not to retaliate even if the demonstrators beat them. The local garrison command belatedly agreed to the rally but not to the parade and received a pledge from the rally chairman, Huang Xinjie, that the affair would be peaceful.

A critical question, debated to this day, is whether the security forces enlisted members of gangs with which it was allied to join the crowd and provoke violence. The government charged later that the demonstrators intended all along to attack the police. Some observers, in contrast, believe that even if violence was not planned, the nature of the situation made some sort of spontaneous eruption all but inevitable. U.S. officials serving in Taiwan at the time concluded that the security services did use agents provocateurs, based on reports that none of the individuals shown committing violent acts in pictures taken by the authorities were part of the *dangwai*.[105]

In the event, opposition speakers energized the crowd and *dangwai* activist Shi Mingde proceeded to lead some of the demonstrators on a march, breaking through police lines. Individuals who followed him attacked members of the nearby security forces and a police station, and a hitherto peaceful rally turned into a violent confrontation.[106]

In contrast to the modest U.S. responses to previous instances of KMT repression, the Carter administration's role in the Kaohsiung Incident was much more aggressive and intrusive. The working assumption of that response was that Chiang Ching-kuo, unlike his father, was committed to opening up the political system. He wanted liberalization to occur gradually and without jeopardizing stability, but he wanted it to occur. Thus at a meeting of the KMT Central Committee that occurred on the morning of December 10, hours before the rally in Kaohsiung was to begin, Chiang declared that "developing the basics of democracy" would be the party's goal. U.S. officials feared that political confrontation would undermine Chiang's reformist agenda because it would play into the hands of more radical elements in both the regime and opposition, including the conservatives in the KMT whom Chiang felt that he had to accommodate. Progress depended on the ability of moderates in each camp to manage conflict and take the concerns of the other side into account.[107]

By 1979, of course, the United States no longer had an embassy in Taiwan. Pursuant to the normalization agreement with the PRC and the Taiwan Relations Act, the U.S. unofficial relationship was conducted through the American Institute in Taiwan (AIT), with a headquarters in Washington headed by David Dean and the Taipei office led by Charles Cross. Publicly, American officials suggested that the AIT could not interfere in Taiwan human rights cases because of the absence of diplomatic relations. That was actually a deception, designed to provide greater freedom of action, for the AIT was very much an actor in the Kaohsiung drama.[108]

American involvement had begun even prior to the incident. A couple of days before December 10, an American diplomat had a dinner that brought together figures from both the opposition and the government. The message for the opposition individuals was that December 10 was the worst possible time to hold a rally because the Central Committee meeting was an occasion when Chiang was more exposed than usual to the old guard within the KMT. The *dangwai* leaders present got the message and endeavored to turn off the rally, to no avail. And the American calculation of intra-KMT dynamics proved correct. The AIT learned after the incident that conservative party elders were very happy about having successfully tricked the opposition through a *kurouji*—literally a trap with bitter meat, or gaining sympathy through deliberately becoming the victim. Chiang was now under the gun, and he decided that a major crackdown and arrest of *dangwai* leaders was necessary in order to maintain unity within the KMT between conservatives and reformers and to deter future confrontations. It appeared that the government had won a propaganda victory because of its seemingly restrained behavior.[109]

After the arrests there was "alarm" in Washington about the degree of the repression and concern that Taiwan's interests and image in the United States would suffer if the incident were mishandled. Heightening that concern were the quick appeals from the Taiwanese-American community and their friends in Congress. At play were several decisions facing the Taipei government. Would further arrests be made? Would trials occur in civilian or military courts? Would they be open or closed? Would the death penalty be sought for the most serious cases (a matter of particular concern)? And which categories of people would be charged? That is, would the authorities focus on the individuals who actually committed the violence or on the leaders of the *dangwai*?[110]

The AIT pushed privately on all of these questions. It stressed the need for restraint and for open, civilian trials. The AIT's Charles Cross, for example, told the government that the *dangwai* was not that strong, that the authorities had a good case, and that they should not overreact. Although the AIT did not argue on behalf of any individual in order to avoid creating the impression that specific *dangwai* individuals were "working for the United States," it did urge that the prosecutors charge those whom cameras recorded committing acts of violence and it argued against the death penalty.[111]

In pushing this agenda, the AIT had two principal channels. The first and most regular was a dialogue with an intimate of Chiang Ching-kuo, on whom Chiang relied to get a clear understanding of American views, and whom the AIT used to convey its views. The other was David Dean, head of the AIT's Washington headquarters, who had developed a good personal relationship with Chiang during a previous tour on the island and whom Taiwanese-Americans in Washington lobbied to go to Taiwan to show American concern. He made the first of several trips to Taipei in January 1980. Chiang assured him that the matter would be managed sensibly, that most of the trials would take place in civilian, not military, courts, and that no one would be executed.[112]

And administration officials had a new weapon. That was the increased salience of human rights in U.S. foreign policy, driven by groups and individuals who sought every chance available to level public criticism at repressive governments like the ROC. (As we shall see in a later chapter, this trend was the result of a complex set of factors, both generally and with specific application to Taiwan.) American officials could point to the criticism from members of Congress and human rights groups as evidence of how Taipei's handling of the Kaohsiung Incident was harming its reputation and so reducing its support. The fact that these attacks were public—unlike the more private .efforts of Lei Zhen's daughter—only magnified their impact. The only way to blunt this criticism, U.S. officials would argue to Taiwan leaders, was to exercise restraint.

Pressured on all sides, Chiang in the end was only partially responsive to American appeals. Moderate *dangwai* leaders were not detained. Some cases were moved from military to civilian courts. Military trials occurred in public. As Chiang assured Dean, the death penalty was not sought. But Chiang also approved prosecution of individuals clearly associated with the *dangwai* and not those who had committed the violence. (The regime's rationale was that the former had created the climate for the actions of the latter. The real reason, some suspect, is that the people who committed the violence were the bait in the *kurouji*.)[113]

It happened that the State Department was required early in 1980 to issue its annual report on human rights practices around the world. It was in the fall of 1979 that the AIT would have had to send in a draft of its report for Taiwan, but there was enough time to incorporate information on the Kaohsiung Incident. The report's account of the events of December 10 was balanced, citing the denied permit, the marchers' penetration of police lines, the subsequent arrests and closure of opposition magazines. It cited conflicting statistics regarding injuries, and so left open which side committed the most violence. It did not discuss the possibility that gang members had acted on behalf of the security forces. It mentioned accusations that those arrested had been tortured but claimed that there was no independent verification of the charges (more credible information would emerge during the trials). The report cited the views of unidentified commentators that the sedition charges were more severe than the incident itself warranted. It concluded that the regime's response could reverse an improvement in the political climate that had occurred in prior months, and noted that overseas Taiwanese were particularly concerned.[114]

The Kaohsiung Incident took on a whole new character in late February. On February 28, the twenty-third anniversary of the 2-28 Incident, armed men entered the home of Lin Yixiong, one of the eight leading defendants, and killed his mother and two twin daughters and severely wounded another child. Some American officials suspected that the murders were the work of a criminal gang, and Chiang's leading American biographer documents the existence of an alliance between such gangs and the security services and cites rumors that Chiang Ching-kuo's own son may have instigated the attacks. The Lin murders put a human face on the Kaohsiung Incident that it did not previously have. The crime, which the AIT protested, intensified the criticism from the Western press and human rights groups.[115]

The Lin murders created a special problem for the AIT because the authorities detained an American academic, Bruce Jacobs, and showed some inclination to charge him with the crimes. The AIT aggressively warned the government away from an attempt to get itself off the hook by shifting the blame to Jacobs. Had they done so, there would have been a sharp American reaction. Still, the AIT exerted its influence privately, in order not to add to the problems that Chiang already faced.[116]

The trials for the key defendants—those charged with sedition—began on March 18 and lasted for one week. Foreign observers were present, including an AIT officer (in contrast to the Peng trial when the embassy declined an invitation). On April 18, verdicts were announced for those tried in March: life in prison for Shi Mingde, fourteen years for Huang Xinjie, and twelve years for the other six. Given the perceived weakness of the government's case, the verdicts confirmed the view that the ROC was using the judicial system to suppress dissent. Six days later, the authorities arrested the Reverend Gao Junming, the head of the Presbyterian Church in Taiwan, and nine other Presbyterians who had sheltered Shi Mingde. That brought the American churches into the picture and gave critics of the KMT a new ally. The foreign outrage grew in early June when a military court sentenced Gao Junming to six years in jail and his comrades to lesser terms. As Jay Taylor concludes, "what had started out as a political coup for the KMT and the government had turned into a victory for the democratic movement."[117]

With the trials over, the American effort shifted to cleaning up the mess as soon as possible. AIT officers and other American officials met on a regular basis with relatives and associates of those convicted. Any time there was a basis for early release from prison (medical parole, for example), they made an appeal. Progress was slow, however. Gao Junming was not released until 1984, and Shi Mingde, the last of the sedition defendants, was not released until 1990.

Thus, the administration worked actively behind the scenes to moderate the Taiwan government's response, in order to save it from itself. As Cross wrote in his memoir, the AIT's "pressure" on the government was conducted "steadily, quietly, and without threats." David Dean recalled later that Taipei had no doubt that this was a major issue in the U.S.–Taiwan relationship.[118] Believing still that Chiang Ching-kuo wanted to open up the Taiwan political system, the AIT sought to prevent conservative forces in the KMT from binding him to a permanent policy of repression.

The results, however, were mixed. On the positive side of the ledger, the trials were open, the death penalty was avoided, and the *dangwai* and political reformers in the KMT were able to return to fight another day. On the negative side, the authorities ignored American entreaties to try the individuals responsible for the violence (for good reason); the Kaohsiung Incident remained a sticking point in U.S.–Taiwan relations for almost a decade; and the security services did not give up their tendency toward independent action.

Conclusion

The American diplomatic response to the Kaohsiung Incident demonstrates the sort of aggressive and sustained effort that the United States could mount if it chose to do so. Officials were proactive in late 1979, trying to avoid an explosive confrontation. After the event, they urged the ROC government through channels that reached right to Chiang Ching-kuo to respond with restraint on a variety of issues. And they maintained quiet pressure on the regime to release prisoners.

To be fair, our account has demonstrated that the United States did not take a completely see-no-evil stance in other episodes of major human rights abuses by the KMT. In 1947, despite the general rule that China's internal affairs were off limits, Ambassador Stuart decided that the carnage of the 2-28 Incident could not be ignored. He therefore remonstrated with Chiang Kai-shek and may have been responsible for the appointment of the relative moderate Wei Daoming as governor. In the late 1940s, when U.S. policy makers believed that KMT rule itself was undermining the U.S. interest in denying Taiwan to the PRC, American diplomats approached several Nationalist leaders to urge general "reform" and more enlightened treatment of specific cases, with the underlying goal of making KMT rule more palatable to the Taiwanese majority. During the Lei Zhen affair, the State Department understood the arrest would undermine its campaign to keep Taiwan in the United Nations, and it warned Taipei against detaining even more dissidents. The Peng case fostered the same anxiety.

In some of these cases, therefore, at least some American officials had recognized that Nationalist policy would either damage the ROC's image or even hurt U.S. interests. But their responses tended to be on the margin, tentative, and short-lived. On balance, the United States accepted KMT authoritarianism on Taiwan as a given for the first three decades after the take-over in 1945. But did that acceptance reflect more an absence of American will than a lack of leverage?

To be sure, there was a considerable capability gap. Before the 1970s,

American diplomats faced significant obstacles to improving its human rights practices even when it might have seen some reason to do so. The reasons that it was possible to exercise some leverage after the Kaohsiung Incident provide a useful point of reference for understanding why it was less possible to do so before. First, Chiang Ching-kuo was a less stubborn leader than his father had been. He had already recognized that the KMT regime would have to be more responsive to the Taiwan populace if it wished to survive, and reformist advisers were encouraging him to go further. Political reform was no longer a dirty word and Taiwan was already a more open political system. Second, American diplomats had better access to Chiang Ching-kuo than they had had to his more remote father, and so were able to exert influence more effectively. Third, the ROC was arguably more dependent on the United States at the time of the Kaohsiung Incident than it had been when previous episodes occurred. Taiwan's diplomatic space was shrinking. The security guarantee of the mutual defense treaty had disappeared. And finally, the strength of the Taiwan lobby, which had worked to protect Chiang Kai-shek, had waned. Indeed, as we shall see in a later chapter, Congress was raising the salience of human rights in American foreign policy and some members were criticizing Taiwan publicly. This convergence of factors gave the United States more leverage in 1979–80 than it had in 1947, the early 1950s, 1960, and 1964.

Chiang Kai-shek's harsher and more rigid and ideological approach to dissent had another consequence for American intervention. That is, even if the United States concluded that it was in its interest to try to save the KMT regime from its worst political abuses, not only would it be unlikely to succeed but a belief on the part of Taiwan oppositionists that the United States might come to their defense would increase the likelihood that they would run excessive risks in challenging the regime. American diplomats, therefore, faced a moral dilemma. Even if they sympathized with the aspirations of Taiwan dissidents and admired their courage, was it not irresponsible to encourage them to act when there was a near-certain probability that they would lose their freedom and suffer horribly as a result, regardless of how much the United States might encourage the ROC government to exercise restraint? Thus George Kerr spoke of the "awkward" position of the United States that was created in 1946 by excessive Taiwanese expectations that it would save it from Nationalist rule. And once the 2-28 Incident began, the Taipei consulate had reason to avoid becoming a magnet for Taiwanese refugees. During the White Terror, Robert Strong was guarded in his contacts with Taiwanese, in part because he did not want them to claim American support as a tool in furthering their domestic political agendas. During the Peng Mingmin affair, the U.S. embassy thought that Peng was naive about the regime he was challenging and had something of a martyr complex. Moreover, it became very concerned that his confession might have implicated U.S. officials.

Still, even though it probably would have been quixotic to challenge Chiang Kai-shek's hard authoritarianism and be seen by Taiwan dissidents as doing so, the fact remains that before the late 1970s the United States clearly did not believe that such a challenge was appropriate. It never became a central premise of U.S. policy that the denial of human and political rights so threatened U.S. interests that it was necessary to try to change the nasty status quo. Or, to put it differently, American policy makers never felt strongly that movement toward a free and democratic Taiwan—letting the people have a political voice—would so strengthen relations with the island that it was worth putting high on the policy agenda. A detailed examination shows clearly that mitigating the regime's repressive behavior was not a salient issue for American policy. As Taiwan came to play an increasing role in the containment policy of the United States in the 1950s, Washington did exert significant leverage on Taipei in the military and economic arenas. But it saw little incentive to give priority to promoting political liberalization on the island or even criticizing or reversing the worst excesses of KMT rule, even though arguably the ROC was more dependent on the United States than the other way around. To do so, Karl Rankin and others believed, would only reduce Taipei's "effectiveness" and so undermine American strategic objectives. Everett Drumright believed that the United States had to work with Chiang Kai-shek in order to preserve its own security, and that it could not afford the luxury of greater political freedom on Taiwan. Reinforcing this policy perspective was the political danger posed by the ROC's friends in Congress, who deterred the State Department from being too critical of KMT rule or from trying to change it.

By the 1960s, however, American officials were less likely to use a strategic rationale for the low priority placed on limiting abuses by the Nationalist state and encouraging political freedom for the Taiwanese majority. The main reason for only limited intervention in episodes like the Peng Mingmin affair was more pragmatic. The regime was simply too strong and too determined to stamp out dissent. U.S. diplomats did make the case that it was in the ROC's own international interests to show restraint, and these efforts may have helped at the margin. But that did not alter the basic fatalism. It was not until the late 1970s, when the KMT under Chiang Ching-kuo had begun the slow, gradual process of political reform and Taiwan's dependence on the United States increased, that the opportunity for greater American leverage began to emerge.

4

The Status of the ROC and Taiwan, 1950–1972

Explorations in United States Policy

In the history of U.S.–Taiwan relations, the dates January 5, 1950, and February 22, 1972, are bookends of a sort. On the former date, Harry Truman asserted that the United States "has no predatory designs on Formosa *or any other Chinese territory*," and his secretary of state, Dean Acheson, said, "When Formosa was made a province of China, nobody raised any lawyers' doubts about that." That is, Taiwan was a part of China. Moreover, Truman and Acheson made clear that the United States would do nothing to prevent a Communist takeover of the island. That in turn would spell the end of the government of the Republic of China (ROC) that had fled there, leaving the People's Republic of China (PRC) as the only government of China. On February 22, 1972, over twenty-two years later, Richard Nixon told Zhou Enlai, "Principle one. There is one China, and Taiwan is a part of China."[1]

But for most of the time in between those two sets of authoritative statements, the government of the United States pursued a different course: to gain acceptance of the idea that there were, or might be, more or less equal political entities on each side of the Taiwan Strait. To say that the United States pursued a "two-China policy," to use the usual shorthand, is hardly a novel conclusion. It has been the staple of scholarship on U.S.–China relations for decades. Robert Accinelli, for example, traces the process by which the concept moved to the center of American diplomacy during the 1950s. Nancy Bernkopf Tucker nicely outlines John Foster Dulles's evolution toward an "awareness of the need to deal with both Chinas." Scholars from the PRC have assembled evidence from American sources to make their case that Washington pursued a deliberate strategy from 1950 on to deny it control over Taiwan and to preserve the Chiang regime.[2]

Washington's "two-China" effort was often defensive in motivation: a means to keep Taiwan out of the PRC's hands; to justify coming to the island's defense; to preserve the ROC's position in the United Nations; to mollify Taipei's American supporters, and so on. It manifested itself in a variety of ways, some of them rather subtle. For example, to dictate to Chiang Kai-shek that his armed forces could not undertake operations against the mainland without U.S. consent was to deny, in effect, Chiang's fundamental premise that this remained a civil war. For the United States to conduct talks with PRC representatives at the ambassadorial level, no matter how fruitless, was to acknowledge the de facto existence of the Beijing government and confer some minimal legitimacy upon it.

This chapter does not seek to explore all the many facets of U.S. policy during these two decades. Rather it focuses more narrowly on the series of substantive rationales that Washington policy makers devised to justify the proposition that there was a political entity on each side of the Taiwan Strait, and on what happened to those ideas as they were processed within the U.S. government. It focuses very much on the views of senior U.S. policy makers, which were the American views that counted most. We also examine how these ideas fared in the conduct of foreign relations. In particular, we address the responses of the ROC government on Taiwan to U.S. views, for it had the most to gain or lose should they become the basis of international action. The following episodes most clearly display American proposals and ROC responses:

- the neutralization of Taiwan at the beginning of the Korean War;
- the 1950 proposal for a UN study commission on Taiwan;
- the Japan peace treaties;
- the U.S.-ROC mutual defense treaty;
- the proposal for a renunciation of force;
- the challenge to the ROC's UN seat that emerged in the late 1950s and had to be faced in 1961, 1964, and 1966; and
- the expulsion of the ROC from the United Nations in 1971.

As will become clear, Washington's policy rationales actually addressed two different issues. The first concerned the nature and status of the governing authorities that ended up on the island: the Republic of China. The second was the postwar disposition of the territories of Taiwan and the Pescadores and whether they had been returned to the state called China. Moreover, there was more variation in the evolution of U.S. policy than is usually thought. Which issue was addressed at any point in time depended on the challenge faced by U.S. policy makers. Taiwan's status tended to get more attention in the early years of the period under study, when denying the island to the PRC was the priority. The nature of the ROC got more attention from the mid-1950s on, with the beginning of the ambassadorial talks and the need to defend that government's international status. There were, moreover, different and competing ideas about the ROC. The near constant throughout this period was Chiang Kai-shek's rigid adherence to principle in the face of American pragmatism and creativity.

The Truman Administration

Prelude to the Korean War

From late 1948 on, the mood in Washington concerning Taiwan and the Nationalist government was increasingly pessimistic. There was little confidence that Chiang Kai-shek's armies could defend the island against the People's Liberation Army (PLA), and although the loss of the island would significantly undermine U.S. interests, policy makers decided it was not worth the deployment of U.S. forces and military aid to the Nationalists to reverse the tide. The dominant view was that the Communists would sooner or later take the island and the United States would have to recognize their government as the new government of China.[3]

Yet there were other voices that argued against accepting a full Chinese Communist Party (CCP) victory. There were proposed three different ideas for denying Taiwan to the PRC, each with a different legal rationale. The first was that Taiwan really still belonged to Japan and that the Nationalist government had been given only administrative responsibility for the island in 1945, not title. Thus, ownership of Taiwan would be determined only during the peace negotiations with Japan. This approach was shared by General Douglas MacArthur and, briefly, by George Kennan. Kennan urged that the authority of MacArthur's command over the island be reasserted, if necessary by using U.S. forces to eject Chiang.[4]

The second idea was to engineer a UN trusteeship for Taiwan. The premise behind this proposal was that Taiwan had been a colony of Japan that had not legally been returned to China and whose people had the right first to international stewardship and then to self-determination like other dependent peoples. The precondition of a trusteeship was getting rid of the Kuomintang (KMT) government, and the State Department explored that option in the spring of 1949. Acheson dispatched a special envoy to Taiwan to determine if there was a viable indigenous Taiwan independence movement that Washington could manipulate into demanding UN intervention at the expense of the KMT (there was not). At another point that year, George Kennan suggested that Washington get another Asian nation to propose a UN trusteeship for the island.[5]

The third idea, floated in a National Security Council draft paper of October 25, 1949, proposed that there were two Chinese states, one Communist and the other non-Communist, one on the mainland and one on Taiwan. The United States, it was argued, should not recognize Beijing as the sole government of China but consider seeking diplomatic relations with both. (By inference, this view accepted that the territory of Taiwan was not in legal limbo but belonged to one of these Chinas.)[6]

As creative as these ideas were, none was ever seriously pursued and the Truman administration soon accepted the hard reality that the Communist victory was certain and would probably extend to Taiwan. On January 5, 1950, Truman and Acheson made the statements cited at the beginning of this chapter. Both made clear that the United States considered Taiwan a part of China and that there would be no support for the ROC government or intervention in "a civil conflict." There would be no "lawyers' arguments" designed to forestall a Communist takeover.[7]

Then in late spring the trusteeship proposal gained new life, resuscitated by Dean Rusk, the new assistant secretary of state for Far Eastern affairs. The fall of Hainan in May and the resulting panic in Taipei had energized Rusk to find a way to save Taiwan. He was aided in that effort by John Foster Dulles, who had become Acheson's special adviser for the Japanese peace treaty but who offered views on other issues besides. In May Rusk proposed a policy of neutralization, denying Taiwan to the PLA but also blocking Nationalist forces from attacking the mainland. Dulles made this proposal because he thought the West had to take a stand against Communist expansionism and that Taiwan was a good place to make that stand because "its status internationally is undetermined by any international act and we have at least some moral responsibility for the native inhabitants." Rusk therefore proposed to Acheson that the United States neutralize Taiwan, first by blocking military action both against and from Taiwan (à la MacArthur), and second by insisting that Chiang request a UN trusteeship. There is no evidence, however, that Acheson responded to the Rusk proposal.[8]

The Korean War and the United Nations, Round I

The beginning of the Korean War reshuffled the Taiwan deck. At the Blair House meeting on the evening of June 25, Acheson proposed that the Seventh Fleet be ordered to the Taiwan Strait to prevent attacks by either side against the other. In effect, he was calling for neutralization. He also proposed that "the future status of Taiwan might be determined by the UN"— with a trusteeship certainly being one form of such determination. Truman, perhaps with MacArthur in mind, added, "or by the Japan peace treaty." The next evening, Truman extended that idea by suggesting (echoing Kennan?) that consideration be given to "taking Formosa back as part of Japan" and putting it under MacArthur's command. He also noted the need to "lay a base for our action in Formosa." Then on June 27, Truman made his famous statement announcing the deployment of the Seventh Fleet to the Taiwan Strait. In addition, he said that "the determination of the future status of Formosa must await the restoration of the security in the Pacific, a peace settlement with Japan, or consideration by the United Nations." In effect, the administration had packaged together elements of various policy proposals that had been floating around for more than a year. But it abandoned the most radical idea that had been at play: removing Taiwan from Chiang Kai-shek's control.[9]

The ROC government objected quickly and publicly to the U.S. position. On June 28, Foreign Minister Ye Gongzhao made the following statement: "That Taiwan is a part of the territory of China is generally acknowledged by all concerned Powers. The proposals of the United States of America . . . should in no way alter the status of Formosa as envisaged in the Cairo Declaration, nor should it in any way affect China's authority over Formosa." That same evening Ye also told Robert Strong—who had been elevated to chargé d'affaires of the U.S. mission when the ROC moved its capital to Taipei in December 1949—that his government was concerned about the reaction on Taiwan to Truman's statement, particularly the part about a UN role. The worry, Ye said, applied both to mainlanders and their "dream of returning to mainland" and to the native Taiwanese and their interpretation of Truman's statement. But Taipei did not pursue the issue, probably because it had reason to believe that the United States would again find the ROC a useful ally. As ROC Ambassador Wellington Gu Weijun (Ku Wei-chun) told Dulles, "the [Korea] action as a whole was so magnificent that possible lack of refinements should be overlooked."[10]

Even as Washington sought to keep the *island of Taiwan* out of Beijing's clutches with its new formulation, it maintained a diplomatic distance from the *Nationalist government*. A policy document regarding Taiwan and China, drafted in August 1950, was quite explicit:

> It is not in the interest of the U.S. to restrict its freedom of action by indefinite commitments to the Chi auths on Formosa as to our future policy. Specifically, we should make no long-range commitments about continued recognition of the Nationalist Govt as the Govt of China, about the Chi seat in the UN, or, particularly, about U.S. support for attempts by the Nationalist Govt to return to the mainland. This does not mean that we may not continue to recognize the Nationalist Govt and support it in the UN; it does mean that our policy shld be based solely on overall U.S. interests and not upon commitments for the Chi Nationalist Govt impairing our freedom of action.[11]

This aloof approach was reflected in the level of U.S. diplomatic representation in Taipei. Washington chose not to replace John Leighton Stuart, who was still nominally the American ambassador to China but had suffered a stroke in late 1949. After the Korean War began and the Seventh Fleet began patrolling the Taiwan Strait, Washington saw the need to upgrade its representation and transferred Karl Rankin, then consul-general in Hong Kong, to Taipei to replace Strong as chargé d'affaires with the higher personal rank of minister. Rankin asked that he have the personal rank of ambassador in order to enhance the political effect of his appointment but Washington refused, saying that Truman's June 27 statement "was based on military factors, without prejudice to political considerations." The United States did not wish to bolster the ROC's position too much.[12]

During the summer of 1950, American policy makers had to defend the U.S. intervention in the Taiwan Strait in the UN arena. It therefore sought to cast the question of Taiwan's future as an international issue and not an internal Chinese matter. That would strengthen its case for having neutralized the island militarily and reduce the political differences with its allies over whether to admit the PRC into the UN. The means to achieve these objectives was a proposal to the General Assembly to form a commission to study the Taiwan question. The initiative soon died for a variety of reasons, but what is important here is the substantive rationale behind the proposal and the ROC reaction.

The primary focus of that rationale, at least in internal discussions, was the need to protect the rights of the population of the island. On July 28, Acheson instructed the U.S. ambassador to Britain, Lewis Douglas, to ask Foreign Secretary Ernest Bevin whether "democratic countries [are] not entitled to question the turning of Formosa over to such [a] regime [the PRC] without consulting Formosans or applying principles of UN Charter applicable to dependent peoples." He was also to note the unsatisfactory record of the KMT regime on Taiwan. Washington knew that London would counter by raising the Cairo Declaration of December 1943, which declared the intention to return Taiwan to the ROC and which London felt weighed more heavily in the balance. So Acheson also told Douglas to respond that the Soviet Union had violated its commitments at Cairo and that the PRC was an animal very different from the ROC, which was the Chinese party at the Cairo conference. Two months later, in his speech to the United Nations General Assembly, Acheson asserted that "the problem of Formosa and the nearly 8 million people who inhabit it should not be settled by force or by unilateral action." In light of the "international interest" in the matter, he urged that the UN General Assembly study the problem "under circumstances in which *all* concerned and interested parties shall have a full opportunity to express their views."[13]

John Foster Dulles also offered a fully developed set of views in an October 23 conversation with Acheson that is worth reviewing at length. Dulles began by stressing the special responsibility that the United States bore concerning Taiwan because of the issue's link with the Japan peace treaty, which would "formally remove Formosa from Japanese sovereignty," and because the United States was the chief occupying power in Japan. However the treaty disposed of Taiwan, it should "*contribute to peace and stability in the Pacific area and [to] the welfare of the people*." The United States, Dulles said, should neither cast doubt on Cairo and Potsdam nor take the position that Taiwan should not be returned to China at some point. Still, the PRC government was not in power at the time of Cairo and Potsdam, and "it certainly is not clear that the people of Formosa desire to be placed in subjection to that government."

Dulles then suggested four points that the United Nations should consider prior to a final decision under the peace treaty. First, it should assess whether the assumption at the time of Cairo and Potsdam—that the people of Taiwan wanted to be returned to China—was still valid. That assessment was particularly needed in light of the nature of the Beijing regime and because "United Nations Charter undertakings . . . override an inconsistent arrangement" (i.e., Cairo and Potsdam). Second, even if Taiwan was to be returned to China, there should be some arrangement for autonomy, reflecting "the oft-expressed desire of the Formosan people for a measure at least of self-government," and "consistent with the Charter conception with reference to non-self governing peoples." Third, free trade between Taiwan and Japan should be preserved, in light of past economic integration. And fourth, the UN might consider permanently neutralizing Taiwan (whatever the ultimate political solution) and sending a peace observation commission to deter a breach of the peace.[14]

Several features of Dulles's approach are worth noting. First of all, he emphasized the Japan peace treaty as the proximate mechanism for addressing Taiwan's disposition. Second, Cairo and Potsdam were relevant not because Allied leaders had decided the island's fate, he said, but because of the presumption at the time that Taiwanese wanted to revert to Chinese rule. Third, the principles of the UN Charter might supersede the intentions set forth in Cairo and Potsdam. And finally, there was no discussion of the ROC claim that Taiwan had indeed been returned to China and that it remained the legitimate government of the island. The reason for that latter omission became clear four days later, when Dulles met with the ROC's permanent representative to the UN, Jiang Tingfu. Dulles presented a formulation that was to shape his approach toward Taiwan for the remainder of his career: "The Chinese Nationalist Government must see the disadvantage of the United

States adopting the position that Formosa was a part of China[,] which would mean that neither the United States nor the United Nations could do anything in what would be a purely civil war." International action to defend Taiwan was only possible if its legal status was cloudy.[15]

Unlike Truman's statement of June 27, which received only a mild reaction from the ROC government, Washington's United Nations initiative, made public in late August, stimulated Taipei's attention. ROC officials consistently opposed the idea that the United Nations would take on the Taiwan issue at all, and offered several ancillary points that spoke to the island's status. On August 30, Ambassador Jiang told Warren Austin, U.S. permanent representative to the UN, that the American assertion that Taiwan's status was undetermined was tantamount to saying that "Formosa was not a part of China and that [the] Nationalist Government was now 'a government in exile.'" Foreign Minister Ye told Rankin that UN action might lead to a trusteeship or plebiscite that might oust the ROC government. A few days later, Ye urged the United States to end the uncertainty caused by the UN initiative and state "definitely that [the] future status of Formosa must await [the] peace settlement with Japan."[16]

The UN commission idea failed because the State Department was not able to craft it in a way that satisfied all the parties concerned, including the ROC and its American supporters. And this was the last time that the U.S. definition of Taiwan's status was so focused on the need to give the people of the island a say over their own destiny.[17]

Japan Peace Treaties

The political identity of Taiwan and the ROC came up in another way during 1951 and 1952, in the negotiations of the Japan peace settlement between Japan and the victors of World War II. This is a long and complicated story, but as it unraveled three basic questions emerged. First of all, which China, if any, would be represented at the San Francisco peace conference? Second, if neither China participated, would Japan sign a separate treaty with one of them? And third, how would the peace treaty deal with Taiwan? That is, would Japan actually transfer title to Taiwan and the Pescadores to another party, and if so, which one? The first two questions bore on the status of the ROC; the third was relevant to the territory of Taiwan.[18]

Different countries had different views on these issues, but initial answers emerged by the late spring of 1951. On the first question, Britain originally wanted the PRC to represent China at the peace conference, whereas the United States was opposed. In the end, they agreed that neither "China" should attend. On the second question, Britain initially thought that Japan should not sign a treaty with either Chinese government, but both London and Tokyo eventually agreed that an accord with the ROC was acceptable. It was also understood that in that treaty the ROC would make commitments only for the area under its control, not for all of China. On the third question, the United Kingdom had initially favored having the treaty cede Taiwan to "China," but under pressure it soon accepted the American proposal that Japan renounce title to Taiwan without assigning it to any other party.[19]

Again, what is relevant for this exercise is the substantive rationales offered to justify the American approach.[20] Two issues were at play: the status of the ROC government and the disposition of the territory of Taiwan.

Concerning the former, Dulles had to respond to British concerns that including the ROC in the treaty process would make impossible future dealings between Tokyo and the PRC. Dulles expressed his own view that "the civil war in China had resulted in fact in a division of China's sovereignty," and that the "National Government assuredly possesses some elements of China['s] sovereignty as member of UN and [as] *de facto* authority [on] Formosa." Based on international law, Dulles said, it would be possible for Japan to deal with the ROC but still develop relations later with the part of China under Beijing's control. As we shall see, this "divided country" approach would reappear in Dulles's handling of China policy.[21]

Dulles took a different tack with the ROC government. Taipei was of course unhappy at its exclusion from the San Francisco conference, because it had wanted to receive confirmation of its status as the government of China, as well as its sovereignty over Taiwan. It expressed this opposition in its confidential comments on the treaty draft, and Chiang Kai-shek went so far as issuing a public statement on June 18, 1951, that denounced the ROC's exclusion from the conference. In response, Dulles told Ambassador Gu it was inappropriate legally for the ROC to sign the treaty for "China" because it lacked the authority to bind the whole of the Chinese population. The United States would encourage Japan to sign a separate peace treaty with Taiwan, he said, but only if Taipei could come up with a formula that confined its treaty obligations to the area that was actually under ROC control. (The ROC would not present a draft "scope of application" clause until October, and ultimately the treaty applied to "all territories which are now and may hereafter be under the actual control of" the ROC.)[22]

Interestingly, the Office of the Legal Adviser in the State Department objected to Dulles's interpretation of international law. It asserted that because the United States still recognized the ROC, it was for the U.S. "the instrumentality which represents the historical state of China." Rejecting Dulles's view that the ROC could not bind all of China, the office believed that the

ROC could speak de jure for the entire country through treaties even though it could not enforce de facto the obligations in territories under Communist control. The legal adviser also objected to Dulles's idea that China's sovereignty had been divided. Despite these objections, there is no evidence that Dulles paid them much heed. He persisted in his view that the ROC could not speak for all of China and wrote that his divided sovereignty idea was merely "metaphorical."[23]

Those were Dulles's rationales concerning the *status of the ROC*. On the question of *Taiwan's status*, he again had to steer a course between the ROC and Great Britain. Taipei's view, of course, was that Taiwan and the Pescadores were "historically, ethnically, legally, and in fact a part of Chinese territory." All that was pending was "the formal act of finalization." The ROC also resisted a proposal in an early draft of the treaty that the status of the islands would be settled by the United Nations or by the United States, United Kingdom, Soviet Union, and China. It was successful in that latter effort and was prepared to accept Dulles's ultimate solution that Japan would renounce title but not transfer it.[24]

To the British, Dulles emphasized other reasons for a minimalist approach to Taiwan in the treaty. He laid these out in a conversation with the British ambassador to the United States on April 12, 1951, and they were similar to the points he had made to Acheson six months before in the context of the UN study commission. Dulles said, first, that he did not want the treaty to negate "all international concern" concerning the territory (in part because that concern served to justify the American policy of neutralization). Second, he feared that if the treaty said that Taiwan should be returned simply to "China" (as the British wanted), there might be controversy later on regarding which China was intended. Specifically, Japan might indicate one China now and another one later. Dulles went on to reiterate other elements of U.S. policy. Taiwan should not be turned over to a Communist regime without "some attempt being made to determine the desires of the people on that island." In any future disposition, he said, Taiwan should perhaps be given substantial autonomy, should maintain its special economic relationship with Japan, and be required to be internationally neutral.[25]

Scholars have suggested that this statement by Dulles reflects his inclination toward a two-China policy.[26] Yet this is a misreading that conflates the twin issues concerning U.S. policy (Taiwan's status and the nature of the ROC). Dulles did accept that the ROC was the government that the United States recognized and that held China's seat at the United Nations, and he knew it had a place in the heart of American conservatives. But his focus in this case was on the fate of Taiwan, and he still wished to preserve at least in theory the right of the people on Taiwan to have some say in their future. He continued to regard the island as a former dependent territory and not as a predetermined possession of either the PRC or the ROC.

Yet the ROC–Japan treaty with its associated scope-of-application provision did create for the first time a formal, if still de facto, link between the ROC government and the territory under its jurisdiction. Foreign Minister Ye sought to make the best of the matter when he addressed the Legislative Yuan on the treaty: "Formosa and the Pescadores were formerly Chinese territories. As Japan has renounced her claim to Formosa and the Pescadores only China has a right to take them over. In fact, we are controlling them now and undoubtedly they constitute a part of our territories. However, the delicate international situation makes it that they do not belong to us."[27] That Taipei's American supporters insisted on a separate treaty between Japan and the ROC did enhance the heretofore limited status that the United States had accorded the ROC government. On the other hand, the ROC's exclusion from the peace conference undercut its claim to be the government of all of China, and the partial disposition of the territory of Taiwan and the Pescadores denied it title to about the only territory that it controlled. And it was only through the efforts of the United States that Beijing had been blocked from representing China at the peace conference. Taipei's position was still tenuous.

After the Korean War began, therefore, the Truman administration pursued a fairly consistent approach toward the legal issues surrounding the ROC government and the territory of Taiwan. It adopted a policy of diplomatic distance toward the ROC. It continued recognition and diplomatic relations and preserving the status quo in the United Nations, but only because these steps were a response to political pressure from the ROC's supporters in the United States. Chiang's American friends were thus his best defense against U.S. policies that he did not like, as became very clear when it came time to negotiate the Japan peace treaty. His influence was indirect but not inconsequential.

With respect to Taiwan, the administration took the position that the island was not yet a part of China, in order to justify the policy of neutralization and to avoid creating any legal pretext for a PRC takeover. Taiwan was an issue of continuing international concern and its people should have some say in their future. If this meant that the United States would not recognize ROC ownership of the island even as it recognized that government, so be it.

There is no evidence, however, that the Truman administration sought actively to create a political reality that was consistent with its definition of Taiwan's status and the ROC's limbo position—in effect, a Taiwan state. Its approach was more tactical expedient than strategic design. And over time, of course, the facts on the ground created more and more obstacles to a one-China, one-Taiwan solution. These included the KMT's tight internal control and its resolute opposition to letting the island's population decide its fate; the new strategic imperative created by the Korean War; and the Defense Department's growing stake in a Taiwan relationship. This dead-end and the Republican victory in November 1952 would steer U.S. policy in a new direction.[28]

The Eisenhower Administration

"Unleashing Chiang Kai-shek" is usually regarded as the most significant China initiative of the early Eisenhower administration. For our purposes, however, the more important initial step was the appointment of Karl Rankin as ambassador to the ROC in early February.[29] Since the summer of 1950, Rankin had been chargé d'affaires in Taipei, and the Truman administration's failure to name an ambassador was a subtle suggestion that it viewed the ROC government as a less than permanent fixture of the East Asian scene. Eisenhower's action endowed Taipei with greater legitimacy and permanence. In addition, formal internal policy statements of the Eisenhower administration stated as U.S. objectives "continued recognition and support of the Chinese National Government on Formosa as the Government of China and the representative of China in the United Nations and international bodies, and continued efforts to persuade other nations to adopt similar positions." Note the contrast between this statement and that of the Truman administration in the summer of 1950 that warned against any long-term commitments to the ROC that might limit American freedom of action. (Note also that the 1953 statement did not address the question of Taiwan's legal status and how to resolve it.)[30]

Even more revealing of the Eisenhower administration's approach to the status of Taiwan and the ROC was the crafting of the mutual defense treaty, which was signed in late 1954 and ratified in early 1955. Like the Japan peace treaty, this is a long and complex story that only needs to be summarized to provide a context for a discussion of shifting U.S. views on the ROC and the island of Taiwan.

The ROC began asking for a bilateral defense treaty soon after Eisenhower took office. The administration put Taipei off until September 1954, when the PRC shelled Jinmen. Beijing had undertaken that action to deter a formalization of the U.S. defense commitment to Taiwan, but it only drove Washington faster in that direction. Even so, the Eisenhower administration still had to address two issues before it committed itself to the defense of Taiwan. The first was Taipei's intention to continue some level of military conflict with the PRC, which was consistent with its theory that the civil war with the Communists had not ended. Washington did not want to assume the obligation of defending the ROC against a PRC attack that Taipei had provoked through its own actions. Second, the United States was concerned about the vulnerability of the offshore islands. It did not want to get into a war with the PRC over the islands (especially if it would have to use tactical nuclear weapons and if the Soviet Union might intervene). Washington was able to satisfy these concerns in the course of the negotiations on the treaty. Taipei accepted that the treaty area relevant to the U.S. security guarantee was Formosa and the Pescadores only, and committed in a private side communication that the Nationalist military would not undertake any major offensive military action without American consent.

Yet the security of the offshore islands remained a problem. Although Washington did not want to be legally obligated to defend the offshore islands, it recognized that its credibility and morale on Taiwan would be at stake if they were to fall to the PRC. Moreover, Dulles believed that the president lacked the statutory authority to come to the islands' defense even if it were decided it was in the national interest to do so. He could not apply to the offshore islands, which had always been part of China, the argument he used concerning Taiwan and the Pescadores (that their legal status was not determined). Hence, U.S. actions to defend them would be tantamount to intervention in a civil war. One response to this conundrum, formulated in the fall of 1954 and kept in reserve for months thereafter, was to secure a ceasefire resolution in the United Nations and so make the offshore islands a matter of international concern (Operation Oracle). But the situation became more complex in January 1955, when the PLA captured Yijiangshan, one of the northernmost offshore islands. Washington devised a three-pronged response. It pressured Taipei to withdraw its forces on the now very exposed Dachen islands. It got Congress to pass a resolution authorizing the president, in effect, to defend the offshore islands if he determined that their loss would have a bearing on the security of Taiwan and the Pescadores. And it reassured Chiang Kai-shek that at least temporarily the United States would defend Jinmen and Mazu, the most important offshore islands.[31]

These events are interesting for our purposes as a window, first and foremost, on American thinking about Taiwan and the ROC and secondarily on the views of the Nationalist government.

First, there is no question that by concluding a defense treaty Washington had strengthened the position and prestige of the ROC government. It was now part of the hub-and-spokes security relationship that the United States had created in East Asia and included Japan, South Korea, the Philippines, Thailand, and Australia and New Zealand. This was a far cry from the late Truman administration's policy of distance. On the other hand, for the United

States to require that it approve any major offensive military action by the Nationalist army was inconsistent with the ROC's view that it was a lawful government trying to regain control of "bandit"-held territory, and Taiwan diplomats spent a considerable amount of time trying to limit that obligation. In addition, by confining the U.S. defense obligation to Taiwan and the Pesdacores, the treaty further strengthened the association between the ROC government and those territories alone. That association indirectly undermined the Nationalists' theory that it was more than the government of those islands. In addition, Taipei fought to secure a stronger, public commitment from Washington to defend the offshore islands. In the end, Chiang accepted both limits because formalizing American support took higher priority.[32]

Also in conflict with the Nationalists' view of itself was the unchanged U.S. position that Taiwan and the Pescadores were a piece of unfinished legal business, left over from the war against Japan. Dulles's view, as conveyed to Britain and New Zealand was that the islands had not been ceded by Japan to China, and that "the U.S. as a principal victor over Japan has an interest in their ultimate future" and did not want them to come under the control of a hostile power. Eisenhower deftly referred to the islands' undetermined status in his message to Congress requesting the Formosa resolution. "Since the end of Japanese hostilities in 1945, *Formosa and the Pescadores have been in the friendly hands of our loyal ally, the Republic of China*. . . . The United States and the friendly Government of the Republic of China . . . have a common interest that Formosa and the Pescadores should not fall into the control of aggressive Communist forces." The implicit message: the ROC government did not "own" the only territory that the United States was bound to help it defend. Dulles pushed this idea further in talking with India's foreign minister, Krishna Menon, and Burma's prime minister, U Nu. To them he claimed that the United States could exert a legal claim to Taiwan because it had defeated Japan and Japan had merely renounced title over Taiwan.[33]

Taiwan's uncertain legal status was a subject of recurring interest in the closed sessions of the Senate Foreign Relations Committee of early 1955 that considered first the Formosa resolution and then the defense treaty. Senators were particularly concerned that the treaty would somehow convey title to the Nationalist government. Some senators were concerned that such an action, even implicit, might give the PRC a stronger claim over the islands at some later date. Liberals worried that it would legitimize KMT control over the Taiwanese population. On several occasions Dulles reiterated the administration's view that the Japan peace treaties had renounced title over Taiwan but not transferred it, that the ROC was in some sense an "occupying power," that the United States itself had a "residual right" by virtue of its status as victor over Japan, and that the current conflict impinged too much on U.S. security interests to be considered merely a civil war. In these private sessions, however, Dulles introduced a new idea: that the ROC's claim to Taiwan and its ability to perfect its title under international law would improve over time. As in common law, he said, "even if you are a squatter, if you squat long enough, you end up by having title." At another point, Dulles said, "I do not think that today the title is perfect in the Republic of China, but it has a better claim to sovereignty than any other nation has." But he assured senators that the treaty per se did not make Taiwan's legal status any less undetermined than it was before. Just to reinforce the point, the Senate Committee included the following statement in its report on the treaty: "It is the understanding of the Senate that nothing in the treaty shall be construed as affecting or modifying the legal status or sovereignty of the territories to which it applies."[34]

Taipei had been relatively quiet on the status-of-Taiwan issue through the negotiations on the treaty. Foreign Minister Ye had tried to delete any suggestion that the treaty confined the ROC's sovereignty to Taiwan and the Pescadores and sought a reference in the preamble to the general sovereignty over all the territory of China, all to no avail. When in February 1955 the U.S.–U.K. position on Taiwan's undetermined status became known on Taiwan, however, Chiang immediately responded. In a public comment on the UN ceasefire resolution that could apply equally to the long-standing American view, he criticized "some foreign observers" who "say that the status of Taiwan has not been determined." He cited the Cairo and Potsdam declarations and their acceptance by Japan. "Therefore," he went on, "when Japan surrendered, the Government of the Republic of China repossessed Taiwan and Penghu [i.e., the Pescadores] and constituted them as Taiwan Province. Since that time, Taiwan and Penghu have regained their status as an integral unit of the Republic of China. In the San Francisco Peace Treaty and the Sino-Japanese Peace Treaty, Japan renounced her sovereignty over Taiwan and Penghu, thereby completing the process of restoring these areas to our country." Aside from this public statement, however, Chiang made no other challenge to the U.S. position and there was no diplomatic follow-up.[35]

Ambassadorial Talks; Renunciation of Force

Until the conclusion of the mutual defense treaty, the Eisenhower administration's strategic outlook did not depart radically from the course set after the beginning of the Korean War. Washington continued to regard the PRC as the main threat to peace in the region, an unpredictable actor that should be contained at every turn and certainly be denied any legitimacy. The alliance with the ROC government and close cooperation with the Nationalist military were means to achieve the goal of containment. Taiwan's undetermined legal status justified international concern for its security. True, the ROC had a very different objective (retaking the mainland), and U.S. policy caused anxiety among its European allies. Yet to avoid a conflict over Taiwan, the administration saw no alternative to pure deterrence, and it set about creating the legal foundation for such a policy while taking into account the unique problems posed by the offshore islands and Taiwan's uncertain title. In no way did Washington believe that the PRC might contribute to a more peaceful environment.

Then in the spring of 1955 American thinking changed, with significant consequences for the U.S. approach to the ROC and for Taipei's response to American policy. In effect, Washington began to base U.S. policy on the possibility that Beijing might become part of the solution to tensions in the Taiwan Strait and not simply the source of the problem. At least, it was thought, the United States should challenge Beijing to be something other than a troublemaker. Motivating this new departure was both the general acceptance of the PRC as a permanent fact of international life and the dawning realization that the United States might have to fight a war with China over the offshore islands *and* use nuclear weapons to defend both them and U.S. credibility. American policy makers also understood that the islands had no military value. Memories of Dien Bien Phu, where the French had staked their whole position in Indochina on the defense of a mere outpost, were still fresh.

In early April 1955, therefore, Eisenhower and Dulles began a search for a way to better protect Taiwan and U.S. interests. Their first attempt was a proposal to Chiang Kai-shek that he radically reduce or withdraw his forces on the islands in return for a more robust defense of the Taiwan Strait and Taiwan itself. Chiang quickly rejected the idea, but a second option popped up almost immediately. This was Zhou Enlai's offer on April 23 to hold negotiations with the United States. Washington responded positively to Zhou's offer. And among the issues that Eisenhower wanted on the agenda were a ceasefire in the Taiwan area and a PRC renunciation of the use of force—evidence that he thought Beijing might actually contribute to regional stability.[36]

This of course was not the first time that the United States had held talks with the PRC. The "ambassadorial talks" that would begin in August upgraded the level and expanded the agenda of discussions already under way. Nor was it the first time that a renunciation of force had been raised. Yet the United States was clearly moving into uncharted territory. Instead of relying on the United Nations to secure a ceasefire regarding the offshore islands only, it was pursuing a *general*, *bilateral* agreement with the PRC that would commit each side not to use force, including in the Taiwan area, and it almost succeeded.[37]

The idea for such an agreement and the mere fact that the United States was its prime mover naturally raised profound concerns in Taipei, because it undercut the stronger political position that the ROC thought it had achieved through the mutual defense treaty. Also, the ambassadorial talks heightened Beijing's position as an interlocutor of the United States and so raised questions about how Washington viewed the status of the PRC regime. And for the United States to suggest something new about the status of the PRC was to call into question Taipei's own belief that it was the sole legal government of China. Thus began the ROC's critique that the United States was pursuing a two-China policy. In response, Washington had to define with more precision how it perceived the PRC, and, by implication, how it defined the ROC.

Actually, Taipei's concern about a two-China trend began as early as the fall of 1954 in the context of a proposal for a UN ceasefire resolution, which raised similar concerns. At that time, Jiang Tingfu, the ROC's permanent representative to the UN, complained that a ceasefire would amount to a truce that froze the status quo; "this would tend to condition the UN to a two-China concept." In January, Ambassador Ye said that the UN effort would give the PRC de facto status, and he asked that Washington repudiate the "two-China concept" and reaffirm its opposition to UN membership for the PRC.[38]

Even at this early stage, Dulles was willing to respond to Taiwan concerns about a two-China trend, and he laid out in preliminary form the conceptual framework with which he would later justify his efforts to engage the PRC bilaterally on a renunciation agreement. In a conversation with Ye in February, Dulles admitted that "there are two Chinas in the sense that there are two contending Chinese forces, and two rival Chinese Governments." They were parties to a continuing civil war. The United States recognized "the existence of the Chinese Communist regime as a fact, just as we recognize the fact of the existence of Communist regimes in East Germany, North Korea, and North Vietnam." On the other hand, Washington did not extend them diplomatic recognition nor regard them as lawful governments. The United States hoped for reunification of all four countries "under non-Communist Governments."[39]

This then was the "divided country" template that Dulles had first surfaced in 1951 and would apply to the China-Taiwan situation for the rest of his time as secretary. In his mind, there were not two Chinese states but one divided China with two governments. The United States recognized the ROC government on a de jure basis and acknowledged de facto the existence of the PRC. Nor was division necessarily a permanent state of affairs; unification would not be ruled out. Dulles would later apply to China some of the details of the U.S. approach for Germany, Korea, and Vietnam. In October 1955, for example when Foreign Minister Ye raised the possibility of the

PRC's pushing for a political settlement of the Taiwan Strait issue, Dulles replied that "we would maintain that the principles we advocate for other partitioned countries should be applied uniformly. We might propose free internationally supervised elections for China, including the Mainland, such as have been proposed for other divided countries."[40]

In the ROC's eyes, it was one thing for the United Nations to insert itself into the Chinese civil war. It was quite another for the United States to do so. That Washington was holding talks with Beijing in the first place and referring to the "People's Republic of China" in public statements was bad enough, for it legitimized the illegitimate. What was worse was the talks' shift in emphasis from technical issues like repatriation to an agreement on a mutual force renunciation in the Taiwan area, which, Taipei concluded, transgressed its "rights, claims and essential interests," something Washington had said it would avoid. Substantively, the ROC asserted that a renunciation of force constituted a de facto recognition of Beijing and was convinced that "a 'Two Chinas' concept was now inescapable." Taipei of course opposed any suggestion that it was not the sole, legal government of China, and any denial of its "right to deliver Chinese people from tyranny." For the United States to suggest to Beijing, as it did, that it objected primarily to the *way* it pursued its Taiwan claims would, Taipei thought, merely encourage those claims. Washington offered a rather narrow response to these stern démarches by saying that a renunciation of force would neither prejudice Taiwan's interests nor imply any recognition of Beijing or affect the ROC's UN membership.[41]

Dulles's effort to secure a renunciation-of-force agreement in the ambassadorial talks failed but he pursued the same goal from a different direction in the wake of the offshore islands crisis of 1958.[42] This came after the crisis subsided when, on a quick visit to Taipei, he tried to convince Chiang to unilaterally renounce the use of force against the mainland. Chiang resisted renunciation mightily because, in his mind, it was tantamount to the acceptance of two Chinas. Dulles countered by offering his divided-country definition of the situation. He told Chiang that "there exist four countries in the world which are divided by Communist efforts: China, Korea, Viet-Nam, and Germany. In three of these countries the situation has been dealt with in such a way that there is some confidence of no resumption of fighting. Only in the case of China is there no armistice." Dulles urged Chiang to announce, in effect, his side of an armistice in order to put the onus on Beijing. (He also argued that the UN tide was running against the ROC, in part because it engaged in provocative military actions against the PRC; renouncing offensive operations would improve Taiwan's international image.)

In the end, Chiang conceded enough to satisfy Dulles by saying that the ROC would stress political means as it pursued the goal of mainland recovery.

But Dulles remained defensive about ROC criticism. In a memo written after his departure from Taipei, Dulles asserted that a divided-country model "did not involve a 'two China' policy" because the United States and many other countries recognized the "free government" (the ROC) as the only lawful one and only dealt with the PRC on a de facto basis. Note, however, that in the joint communiqué that Dulles had negotiated, the United States recognized the ROC not as the government of China but only as "the authentic spokesman for Free China and of the hopes and aspirations entertained by the great mass of the Chinese people." (Note also that none of this changed the U.S. position on Taiwan's undetermined status.)[43]

United Nations, Round II

If the dilemma posed by the offshore islands had stimulated Eisenhower and Dulles to pursue a bilateral renunciation-of-force agreement with the PRC (and, as a result, more clearly enunciate the divided-country concept), the shifting balance of power in the United Nations led other American officials to push in an explicit two-Chinas direction. For example, in February 1957, Robert Bowie, director of the Department of State's Policy Planning Staff and one of Dulles's valued in-house advisers, argued that PRC membership in the United Nations was inevitable and that the United States should accommodate itself to that reality. Bowie proposed a two-China solution whereby Beijing and Taipei would be UN members in their own right and where safeguards were put in place to preserve the integrity of the new "Republic of Taiwan." This was the first proposal at a senior level to move toward a separate Taiwan state and to clearly negate the claim of the ROC that it was the government of all of China. It resurfaced at a National Security Council (NSC) meeting late in the month with a proposal for an "acceptable general settlement" to protect an "independent Taiwan" and avoid spending increasing political capital to preserve the ROC's UN membership. But Dulles rejected this challenge by saying that "there was no point whatsoever in the argument that we must make some kind of bargain with Communist China in order to save Taiwan." Beijing, he said, would be on the defensive so it was unnecessary to make concessions. There would be several more efforts along these lines during the late Eisenhower administration but none of them went anywhere.[44]

Dulles's response—and its tactical focus—obscured a more supple approach. Indeed, he on several occasions indicated that he anticipated Beijing's becoming an accepted member of the international community along with Taipei. In a book published after the Communist victory in 1949 and before the outbreak of the Korean War, Dulles had set an extremely low standard for PRC membership in the United Nations—that Beijing "prove its ability to govern China without serious domestic resistance." In a July 1955 conversation with India's foreign minister, Krishna Menon, he indicated that it was Beijing's international behavior that blocked U.S. recognition and UN membership, not any immutable legal principle. (This could not simply be a case of telling Menon what he wanted to hear. Because India at this time fancied itself as a go-between for Washington and Beijing, Dulles could only assume that his observation would reach the PRC government.) In the fall of 1958, Dulles admitted to the British foreign minister, Selwyn Lloyd that it would not be possible to keep Beijing out of the United Nations forever and again offered the nonideological view that the PRC's bad behavior was the major obstacle to membership, not the absence of a right to join. During his Taipei trip in October, moreover, Dulles rather offhandedly floated a new idea concerning the PRC and the UN. He asked whether it should continue to be treated as a credentials matter (that is, concerning which government had the best claim to China's seat) or addressed as a new-member issue (whether Beijing met the qualifications for membership as another state). Ambassador Ye objected to the idea because it was too close to two Chinas. The idea seemed to disappear, but in fact a seed had been planted that would flower two years later. Clearly, even Dulles understood that the UN situation was accelerating Washington's need to define the PRC and the ROC in a way that would preserve the latter's presence and avoid a neuralgic issue in American politics.[45]

Our discussion of the Eisenhower administration has focused on the role and thinking of John Foster Dulles because he dominated both China policy and the U.S. definition of the ROC and the island of Taiwan in both the Truman and Eisenhower administrations. As he moved from special adviser to secretary of state, he ended the policy of distance toward the ROC that had prevailed under Truman, a move that was no doubt welcomed by the Republican Party. He also set aside the emphasis he had previously placed on respecting the wishes of the people of Taiwan (again, perhaps, an accommodation to political reality). Despite these shifts, Dulles did not abandon his belief that policy had to have a basis in international law. He did not change the view that the legal status of Taiwan had yet to be determined, as most clearly demonstrated in his secret testimony to the Senate Foreign Relations Committee. His lawyer's mind would not permit a U.S. security commitment to Taiwan and the Pescadores if they were defined to be a part of China. The only qualification to this view was his closed-door observation that the ROC's claim to Taiwan and the Pescadores might be perfected over time (again, a very lawyerly argument).

The most interesting aspect of Dulles's approach was his denial, on several occasions, that he was pursuing a two-China policy. Obviously, he recognized the need for some contact with the Beijing regime, and the spring 1955 shift in U.S. policy to engage China on issues of war and peace in East Asia was a significant development. In a foreign policy sense, therefore, Dulles moved toward a two-China policy. And that conceptual shift and the looming problem of the United Nations forced Washington to think about the PRC and the ROC in new ways. Still, Dulles rejected both Taipei's allegation that the United States was pursuing a two-China policy and the proposals of some U.S. officials that he move to one. His template, he asserted, was that of a divided country. In his mind, there was one Chinese state with two contending governments. Moreover, one of those governments (the ROC) was more deserving of international recognition as the only lawful government. That did not rule out dealing with the PRC on a de facto basis. And it did not foreclose the possibility, which he stated implicitly in public and more explicitly in private, that the PRC could establish the legality of its government by changing its behavior. For its part, Taipei was increasingly anxious that the United States was undermining its international position through its contacts with the PRC and its pursuit of a renunciation-of-force agreement. But as long as the ROC's UN membership remained in abeyance, American intentions were not really put to the test. That comfortable state of affairs would soon change.

The Kennedy and Johnson Administrations

United Nations, Round III

The Kennedy administration could not be complacent about the ROC's position at the United Nations. A moratorium on discussion of the China seat, which had avoided discussion of the issue during the 1950s, was no longer viable. To make matters worse, a number of newly independent African countries swelled the ranks of countries in the General Assembly sympathetic to the PRC. So merely to avoid the ROC's exclusion required greater effort. Kennedy himself was worried about the domestic political consequences of Taipei losing its seat. He feared that Eisenhower, who had offered generally to be supportive on foreign policy, would come out of retirement if he reversed past policy on China. Making matters worse was Chiang Kai-shek's resistance to any deviation from the principle that the ROC was the sole legal government of China. His attitude was more important because any U.S.-devised solution to the UN problem would require his consent. Chiang had been willing to accommodate somewhat on the mutual defense treaty because he was getting something he wanted. On the UN seat, however, he faced the prospect of losing his legitimacy as he understood it.[46]

The conceptual work on the UN problem had actually been done in late 1960 within the Far Eastern Bureau of the State Department. A set of memoranda were prepared for Dean Rusk, whom Kennedy had named secretary of state, that laid out the policy problem and analyzed options for solving it. The working assumptions were that support for a moratorium was unsustainable and that a variety of political and procedural reasons made the formal enactment of a two-China solution difficult, if not impossible. Nonetheless, the United States should promote such a solution because it would command greater support than the prior strategy of simply keeping the PRC out. In addition, it was argued, Beijing would certainly reject such a formula and therefore bear the onus for its own exclusion. The chief obstacle, of course, would be convincing Chiang Kai-shek that such a tactical approach was necessary to ensure the ROC's inclusion.[47]

Two substantive approaches for a two-China ploy were offered. The first was an elaboration of the new-member idea that Dulles had floated in Taipei in October 1958, which perhaps had germinated in the Department of State in the interim. As detailed in a paper written by William Sullivan, there were several elements. First, the General Assembly would pass a resolution declaring that the ROC "is an original *and continuing* member of the United Nations, that it has lost control over major portions of its territory, that the People's Republic of China (PRC) has established itself as a government in that former territory, that the PRC has the attributes of sovereignty and that, subject to the provisions of Article 4 of the Charter, the PRC *is eligible for membership in the United Nations.*" Regarding the Security Council, a charter amendment would change the name of the Security Council seat that Taipei had occupied from "Republic of China" to "China" and would create a seat for India; the ROC would choose not to occupy the China seat since it could not act on behalf of the Chinese people; and the United States would not veto the arrangement. Finally, it was expected that a number of countries would establish diplomatic relations with the ROC.[48]

The second conceptual approach to the Taiwan/UN issue had as its core idea the successor-state theory, "that the 1945 country of China has been succeeded by two States—one large and one small—and that these have both, automatically, succeeded to membership in the General Assembly." This contrasted with the prevailing theory that the issue was one of representation, that is, which of the two rival governments had the right to represent a single Chinese state. It was also different from a focus on membership—whether the PRC met the qualifications for admission to the United Nations, which tended to ignore the relationship of the two governments to the Chinese state.

Under the successor-state theory, two options were presented. The first was that the China that was a UN charter member had now become the PRC and the ROC, and that the governments of each should be seated. The second option was that the Beijing government would represent the PRC state and the Nationalist government would represent a Republic of Taiwan. However, "this alternative would be based on an articulated or tacit premise that Taiwan (consisting of Formosa and the Pescadores) had become one of the successor States to the original Republic of China."[49]

The issue of the legal status of the territory of Taiwan and the Pescadores— as opposed to the status of the ROC—was addressed only at one point in these documents. One policy analyst noted that some might argue that there could not be a Taiwan state as a successor state to the ROC because the island's legal status was undetermined. More practically, he reminded readers that the status-not-determined view was a "legal argument (advanced for political reasons)"; hence, "we might infer hypothetically that if any of the above solutions to the China/Taiwan issue were universally acceptable, that would constitute acceptance of the view the ROC government and that government alone possessed the title to Taiwan and the Pescadores." By implication, moreover, the United States could extend a security guarantee to a separate Taiwan state without intervening in a civil war.[50]

The late 1960 policy papers thus offered new rationales for a *substantive* solution to the UN contest, rationales that add two sets of answers to the questions of the nature of the ROC government and the legal status of Taiwan. Based on this conceptual foundation, Washington began three efforts, one in the Kennedy administration and two during the Johnson administration, to secure such a substantive solution, even though it understood that such an approach would be difficult because it would be opposed by Taipei and Beijing. And in all three cases, the United States ended up abandoning those efforts in favor of a *procedural* way out of the problem: that China representation was an "important question" that required a two-thirds vote for approval.[51]

Early in the 1961 episode, different bureaus within the State Department disagreed on which course of action to take. The Far East and International Organizations Bureaus favored the new-state proposal, whereas the policy planning council advocated the successor-state approach. The latter argued that securing ROC agreement to the new-state option would use up all of Washington's political capital and leave none for other priorities (e.g., securing Nationalist withdrawal from the offshore islands). Moreover, it would create domestic political difficulties. The two bureaus argued in reply that it would be impossible to get Chiang to abandon the offshore islands. Nor was there any chance that Taipei would accept the successor-state formula, "which envisages automatic seating of Communist China" and would probably stimulate an ROC walkout. The domestic political costs of such an outcome would be much greater than the new-member option, under which the United States could still oppose PRC entry.[52]

By spring, the Kennedy administration approached the ROC and Great Britain on its new ideas. With Taipei the discussion was rather general, but with London there was a full discussion of the various options. But on the same day that Kennedy and the British prime minister, Harold MacMillan, were discussing "Chirep," a cable arrived from Taipei that reduced the prospects for a novel solution. Chiang wrote Kennedy that the ROC could not accept a two-Chinas or any other arrangement that would "affect the character of the Republic of China's right of representation in the United Nations. There is no room for patriots and traitors to live together" (in Chinese, *hanzei buliangli*). Washington continued to urge ROC diplomats to seriously consider both the new-member approach and the successor-state option, but both were deemed unacceptable because of their two-China character. Rusk reported to the president on May 26 that it was unlikely that any sort of two-China approach would gain Taipei's approval. But he suggested a marriage of the two approaches to secure consensus within the administration.[53]

At least to this point, therefore, the Kennedy administration pursued more of a two-China policy than had John Foster Dulles. Dulles had held to the idea that there was only one Chinese state. It was divided, to be sure, with two contending governments, but it was still one Chinese state. In contrast, the Kennedy administration argued that this one state—China—had become two states: the PRC and the ROC (the Republic of Taiwan option had fallen off). In contrast to Dulles, moreover, the Kennedy administration was more inclined to accept the idea that Taiwan and the Pescadores did belong to the ROC.

Yet the United States still got nowhere with Chiang on its approach. A June 21 cable from Taipei reported that he "regarded U.S. proposals advanced thus far . . . as not only ineffectual but as a plan to bring about a 'two Chinas' arrangement in the UN. GRC [Government of the Republic China] would have no part of such proposals and would withdraw from UN rather than be party to them." One month later, Rusk threw in the towel on a substantive solution to the problem and recommended the procedural way out that had been anticipated in the memoranda he had received seven months before, that the United States seek a vote in the General Assembly that the China representation question was an "important question" that required a two-thirds vote for passage. In addition he proposed that the United States support a Swedish proposal to study the issue. Kennedy was not sure about the latter idea but went along.[54]

Meanwhile, another looming UN problem threatened to undermine the position of the ROC. The Soviet Union was pushing the admission of Outer

Mongolia. Taipei vigorously opposed such a move because it held to the view that Outer Mongolia was still a part of China, and it threatened to exercise its veto. In return, Moscow threatened to veto the entry of Mauritania. Washington feared that Mauritania's exclusion would cripple African support for preserving the ROC's membership and it pleaded with Chiang not to exercise the veto. Chiang stubbornly held to his position until early October when Kennedy agreed to make a public statement that said that the United States "has always considered the GRC the only rightful government representing China" and would continue to oppose the PRC's entry into the UN. In addition, Kennedy pledged privately that the United States would exercise its veto if necessary to keep Beijing out of the United Nations. Chiang had wanted Kennedy to make the latter pledge publicly, but Rusk opposed it because that would undermine the important-question and study-commission tactics.[55]

Once Kennedy made this veto commitment, the chance of any two-China approach during his administration fell to zero, at least in the United Nations. Chiang's rigid attitude and the perceived threat posed from the right by Eisenhower and other Republicans minimized the president's maneuvering room. True, Kennedy suggested a more flexible approach in his last press conference when, asked about the PRC trade embargo, he replied, "When the Red Chinese indicate a desire to live at peace with the United States, with other countries surrounding it, then quite obviously the United States would reappraise its policies. We are not wedded to a policy of hostility to Red China." Dulles had signaled that same pragmatic, nonideological approach during the Eisenhower administration. Roger Hilsman repeated it in his Commonwealth Club speech after Kennedy's death, in an attempt to test how hostile to the PRC the American public actually was. Yet the prospects for change remained limited as long as Chiang Kai-shek was wedded to a policy of hostility, which he was.[56]

United Nations, Round IV

With the UN General Assembly looming in the fall of 1964, Washington officials again debated how to preserve the ROC's membership. The first offering came in the form of a national policy paper drafted by Joseph Yager of the State Department's Policy Planning Council. He noted that more and more countries believed that both the PRC and the ROC should be seated in international organizations. He warned that if an organization merely invited Beijing to join, Taipei might respond by walking out. Washington, he counseled, should continue "to urge on the GRC the merits of a pragmatic, as opposed to a rigidly doctrinaire, approach to the Chinese representation problem." Yet Yager opposed having the United States itself adopt a two-China policy, because it would undermine stability on Taiwan, offend patriotic Chinese, end the ROC's value as a diplomatic counterweight to Beijing, and perhaps open the door to a deal between the KMT and the CCP.[57]

Others soon weighed in. In October James Thomson on the NSC staff suggested, as part of a broader recommendation, that the United States acknowledge a de facto recognition of Beijing and modify its containment policy, that it hold the line in the UN General Assembly in 1964 but move over the next year to a "one-China, one-Taiwan" seating arrangement. Thomson indicated that "if we play our cards right—and if the Chinats don't commit political suicide—we might even succeed in shifting the onus for Peking's continued exclusion to the Chicoms." In November, Harlan Cleveland, assistant secretary of state for international organization, predicted that the United States faced ultimate defeat if it tried to keep the PRC out of the UN. He proposed a two-Chinas solution, in which Beijing would become "the senior one of the two Chinas" and take the Security Council seat. Regarding the seat in the General Assembly, Cleveland offered the two mechanisms previously suggested: admission of the PRC as a new member; and two successor states to the China that had signed the UN Charter. He noted that the latter device had been used to accommodate the breakup of the United Arab Republic.[58]

Those calling for change had their hands strengthened by Canada, which indicated its support for dual membership. At a White House meeting on November 15, Adlai Stevenson, the U.S. permanent representative to the United Nations, argued that the choice was between Taiwan's exclusion and a two-Chinas approach that the PRC would reject. The other option was creation of a study group, which Taipei opposed. Then Rusk reframed the issue. He warned against giving the appearance of weakness by giving in to the pro-PRC trend. That impressed President Lyndon Johnson, who decided to make no change in tactics.[59]

In the end there was no vote in 1964 because of a financial crisis at the UN and there the matter stood for two more years. In the 1965 round the U.S. mission to the United Nations was worried about the outcome and urged the study commission as an alternative to the important-question gambit. But the State Department was more optimistic and was proved right in the end.[60]

United Nations, Round V

The contest in 1966 was a different matter. Johnson was restless about China policy in general and the UN representation issue in particular. Mid-level officials who feared that the tide was turning mounted an effort to shift policy. The first step came as William Bundy, assistant secretary of state for Far Eastern affairs, prepared to travel to Taipei. He and Joseph Sisco, assistant secretary of state for international organizations, sent a memo to Rusk asking that he authorize Bundy to warn Taipei that the UN situation was unsustainable and that an alternative be considered that would bring Beijing in without excluding Taipei. Rusk rejected any floating of a two-Chinas option but did agree to alerting the ROC leadership to the trend. Bundy did so but got no immediate response.[61] The next initiative came in April from Arthur Goldberg, who had succeeded Stevenson at the United Nations. He concurred that "we'll go down to defeat if we pursue our present posture," and advocated that Washington pursue a two-Chinas approach in the knowledge that Beijing would reject it and that Taipei was the real problem. He also suggested a high-level group to develop policy.[62]

In response to Goldberg's overture, Sisco on April 27 submitted a comprehensive memorandum that laid out the options for the United States. Sisco assumed that any PRC admission to the General Assembly should be part of a two-Chinas approach, and that it would be possible to persuade Taipei to go along. The proximate goal should be to "place the onus" on Beijing for its exclusion. In what would be the most exhaustive discussion of the issue during the Johnson administration, Sisco laid out six options:

- Propose a General Assembly resolution recognizing that there were two successor states to China's seat, both of which should be represented in the Assembly. If Beijing rejected the declaration, its seat would remain open.
- Form a study committee. Sisco feared that this approach was unmanageable and might lead to the PRC's taking China's seat or to a one-China, one-Taiwan solution.
- Extend a mandate to the Secretary General or the General Assembly president to explore a two-China solution with Beijing and Taipei.
- Resort to the International Court of Justice.
- Continue current policy with active lobbying.
- Stick with the present strategy but stop lobbying.

Sisco believed that none of the three latter options would adequately promote U.S. interests. As far as tactics were concerned, Sisco believed that the United States could either take the initiative to try to bring Taipei around or just stand aside and let others bear the responsibility for the issue. He urged that Rusk convene a meeting of relevant State Department officials in order to prepare a recommendation for Johnson.[63]

Goldberg chimed in three days later in a message to Johnson in support of the successor-state option. He included a couple of different draft resolutions to exemplify his approach, each of which noted that the ROC was the only recognized government of China at the time the UN Charter was signed; that Beijing and Taipei had for many years since exercised government authority or control over their respective territories; and that the two should be seen "as successors of the state signatory to the [UN] charter." He also asked that he be permitted to engage the Canadians as a possible sponsor, as a way of redirecting their impulse to get the PRC admitted. Rusk did not immediately respond and Walt Rostow, now national security adviser, was cautious. He worried about the reaction both in Taiwan and in the United States. He recalled the Kennedy veto pledge.[64] But in mid-May, Rusk reached consensus with Goldberg and sent a position paper to Johnson. He agreed with his advisers that the traditional approach was not sustainable, and, in a major personal departure, concurred that a two-China solution was far better than admission of the PRC at the ROC's expense, particularly since Beijing would not agree to the former. He recommended that the administration "discuss these tactical problems with the Republic of China in Taipei in an attempt to get them to stand steady, rather than withdraw from the UN, if parties other than the United States develop a 'two Chinas' tactic." The substantive basis for such an approach was that "the GRC has a right to representation in the UN," essentially a successor-state justification without calling it that. Rusk also asked that discussions begin with the Canadians on the matter.[65]

Little happened until the summer, because Rusk wanted to "make [the] major pitch on this new tactic" himself during his July trip to Taipei. Bundy and Sisco previewed for Taiwan diplomats American concern that traditional tactics would not work. Walter McConaughy, the new ambassador to the ROC, made a similar presentation to Chiang Kai-shek on June 30 and urged that Taipei not "act impulsively or out of any sense of outrage," but stand fast and let the PRC exclude itself. McConaughy did not, however, discuss the substance of a new resolution. Chiang refused to accept the American viewpoint. He held that if the United States merely held firm and reined in the Canadians that would be enough. He also asserted that accommodating to PRC entry would violate the fundamental principle "that there be no truckling, surrender, or compromise with a rebel regime." Chiang again cited the formula of the Three Kingdoms strategist, Zhuge Liang: *hanzei buliangli* (no room for patriots and traitors to live together). The ROC would walk out before letting Beijing have a seat. The only hope that McConaughy could offer Washington was that Chiang might walk out when the PRC actually took its seat, not in response to a vote to seat them.[66]

In light of this situation, Rusk chose not to table the two-Chinas option when he arrived in Taipei in early July. He and Foreign Minister Wei Daoming disagreed over prospects for the General Assembly vote, and Rusk repeated his more pessimistic outlook to Chiang. But the latter "replied he had already given his views to Amb McConaughy" and the United States should stand its ground.[67] Thus was derailed the effort led by Sisco and Goldberg to put a two-China option on the agenda of U.S.–ROC diplomacy. They had succeeded in winning Rusk over to their side, a signal achievement. But Chiang stopped the initiative in its tracks and so Rusk decided to stick with past tactics.

Then in early November, the Canadian government decided to recommend that the president of the General Assembly undertake a study on the China representation issue, with terms of reference that suggested that both Beijing and Taipei should get seats. Moreover, Ottawa would abstain on the Albanian resolution, which might lead to more defections from the ROC. Washington quickly decided to support a more neutral study commission if necessary as a way of sidetracking the Canadians (it was too late for the two-China option).[68]

Selling this pragmatic and defensive tactic to Taipei was not so easy, and the ROC position vacillated wildly. On November 10 Foreign Minister Wei told McConaughy in Taipei that the ROC would consider pulling out if the study-commission gambit succeeded; the United States should pressure Canada. Five days later in Washington, Wei was more moderate and was willing to go along if the preamble to the resolution was not prejudicial. "GRC basic policy," Wei said, "is to overthrow Chicoms and recover mainland and therefore GRC is opposed to any form of two Chinas." Then on November 21, McConaughy was told that Chiang had decided that Taipei *would* walk out the same day that a study commission was authorized. McConaughy saw Chiang on November 23 and reported Rusk's surprise and dismay at this reversal. "You will have given Peking a major victory. . . . The U.S. would be most deeply disturbed by a radical action on your part." Chiang asserted that "any" study commission implied the existence of two Chinas. The United States could "arrange" the defeat of the Canadian initiative and so "reassure the GRC of the friendship and motives of the U.S." It took a letter from Johnson to finally bring Chiang around.[69]

The ultimate outcome was better for the ROC than expected. Not only was the Albanian resolution defeated and the important question passed, the PRC's friends engineered a resounding defeat of the study commission resolution. Still, there were bruised feelings in Taipei. The Foreign Ministry made sure that McConaughy knew that had the ROC walked out, as Chiang was inclined to do, it would announce that the "GRC cannot allow itself to be sacrificed on the altar of appeasement."[70] The Americans could preach the importance of tactics and pragmatism and use muscle when necessary, but Chiang preferred his absolutist principles. He used them as weapons to constrain his U.S. allies, and he wielded them well.

During the last two years of the Johnson administration, American offi-cials had no new or significant initiatives concerning Taiwan's international status, nor were they compelled to formulate any. China's allies in the UN could make little headway as long as the Cultural Revolution turmoil contin-ued. By 1968, U.S. officials tended to agree that a two-China outcome was most appropriate. Bundy made a speech to the Cincinnati World Affairs Coun-cil in mid-February 1968 that made clear that the U.S. government did not deny Beijing's existence and was prepared to deal separately with it and Taipei. Simultaneously, Rusk had come to a two-China conclusion. He sent a memo to the president that acknowledged that Washington "for all practical purposes deal[s] with Peking and Taipei as if they were separate states. This is a direction to which our policies have been taking us for 15 years and it is probably in our interest to work gradually toward at least a tacit acknowl-edgment of this reality by both." From Taipei, McConaughy warned that a U.S. approach that regarded the PRC and ROC "as separate political entities, each controlling certain territory" would feed suspicions and resentment in Taipei. But Thomas Shoesmith, head of the ROC desk in the State Depart-ment, argued for a time-buying strategy. Change on both Taiwan and the mainland would create circumstances conducive to a two-China or one-China, one-Taiwan outcome. Such a strategy, with its associated approach to the ROC and Taiwan, was a sensible adaptation to existing realities. Broader geopolitical trends would soon transcend those realities.[71]

The Nixon Administration

United Nations, Round VI

As Richard Nixon and Henry Kissinger charted a bold new course for Ameri-can China policy—to make common strategic cause with Beijing against Moscow—they threw overboard past approaches to both the ROC and the legal status of Taiwan. As noted at the beginning of this chapter, Nixon told Zhou Enlai, "Principle one. There is one China, and Taiwan is a part of China." Nixon also said "There will be no more statements made—if I can control our bureaucracy—to the effect that the status of Taiwan is undetermined," and that, "we have not and will not support any Taiwan independence move-ment."[72] Because of Nixon's anti-Communist credentials, he was less con-strained by American conservatives and Chiang Kai-shek. Even so, before the ROC's expulsion from the United Nations in October 1971 (a conse-quence of the China opening) and Nixon's trip to the PRC in February 1972, Nixon and Kissinger had to go through the motions of protecting Taipei's interests, if only to guarantee the success of secret diplomacy.

Again, the arena was the United Nations. In 1969, the United States had engineered an easy victory on the important-question vote (71–48). In July 1970, Secretary of State William Rogers had already warned Nixon that the United States would soon have to shift in tactics and offered "dual representation" as an option. And in October, the White House offered a shift in policy emphasis: "The U.S. opposes the admission of the Peking regime into the UN *at the expense of the Republic of China*." The vote in November showed that the tide was turning. The important-question margin was only 66 to 52, and for the first time a majority had voted to seat the PRC and expel the ROC (two-thirds was required at that point). As more and more countries established diplomatic relations with Beijing, every new vote estimate for the 1971 General Assembly session indicated that the ROC would be expelled if there were not a change in tactics. The State Department therefore began work on a plan to prevent that outcome. It recommended an emphasis on the principle of universality and a dual-representation proposal: that the PRC should enter the United Nations but the ROC should not leave. The most difficult issue was how to handle China's seat on the Security Council.[73]

On March 23, Secretary Rogers received a memorandum in support of the universality–dual representation strategy. But it did not base the proposal on divided-country or successor-state concepts, as had previous administrations.

> The resolution should avoid definition of the legal, political or geographic status of the two Chinese entities; it should take no position on whether Taiwan is or is not a part of China. A resolution which does not require a decision on these points and is based squarely on *de facto* realities will least affront the claims of Peking and Taipei and will have a greater chance of success in the General Assembly. With respect to the Republic of China's claim to be the sole legal government of China, our public position should be that this is a question to be decided peacefully by the parties concerned. Our public position on the legal status of Taiwan should be that it remains not yet finally determined and that we believe the future relations of Taiwan to the Mainland is a question to be decided peacefully by the parties concerned. . . . In order to afford the best protection to the Republic of China, its status as a UN member should be confirmed without reference to its claim to be the sole government of China, or to any other geographic or political definition. Once such a resolution is adopted, we can legitimately argue that the matter has ceased to be one of which entity represents China, and that the Republic of China has been confirmed as a member in its own right independent of any particular geographic or political basis, and therefore can be expelled only through the operation of Article Six of the Charter requiring a (vetoable) Security Council recommendation and a two-thirds majority in the General Assembly.[74]

Although the State Department deliberately avoided a definition of the legal status of the two Chinas, the approach it recommended had more in common with the divided-state concept. The memorandum defined the universality concept to mean that "all *de facto* governments which for long periods have effectively controlled significant territory and population would enjoy representation in the UN," and the divided countries of Germany, China, Korea, and Vietnam were the most prominent examples of such *de facto* governments. Moreover, as a later memorandum reported, the legal adviser of the United Nations had told the department that if "successor state theory" were applied to the case of China, one of the two would have to enter as a new member (and so be subject to a Security Council veto). Indeed, the State Department's whole approach was to treat this as an issue of representation and not one of membership, that is, that both the PRC and the ROC have the right of representation (thus the term, dual representation).[75]

Why did the department take the view, as expressed elsewhere in the briefing memorandum, that the United States should "avoid language which states or implies a judgment . . . either that Taiwan is a part of China or that it is a separate sovereign entity"? Several answers were given later in the package. First, the position outlined above was most consistent with the stance Washington had taken publicly and in the ambassadorial talks. Second, there was no great pressure to change the position. Third, to say that Taiwan was a part of China would "weaken politically and legally the basis of our defense commitment to the GRC," a restatement of the view espoused by Truman and Dulles. Fourth, to take the position that Taiwan was an independent entity would offend both Taipei and Beijing, the latter because Beijing would take it as an indication that the United States intended to "maintain Taiwan permanently as a U.S. military base." Notably lacking from the list of rationales was the idea that the people of Taiwan should have a say in their fate. Indeed, to say that the parties concerned should decide the status of Taiwan in a way biased the result, since at that time both Beijing and Taipei took the view that the island had been returned to China.[76]

Unlike previous American efforts to find a pragmatic solution to the ROC's UN problem, this one was not blocked by Taipei. Through an extended process of persuasion, State Department officials were able to convince Taiwan's diplomats that the outlook was so dire that Taipei had to accept dual representation if it wanted to remain in the United Nations. These diplomats then managed to convince Chiang Kai-shek and Chiang Ching-kuo that the ROC's interests were better served by mounting an active defense than by abandoning the battlefield (a reversal of the principle of *hanzei buliangli*). True, Taipei tried to hold onto the "important question" gambit and was very unhappy when it became clear in the summer of 1971 that the ROC could retain its seat in the General Assembly only if Washington signaled other countries that it would accept the PRC's replacing the ROC in the Security Council. In the end, however, even Chiang Kai-shek came around.[77]

It was the Nixon White House, of course, that undermined the State Department's initiative. By the spring of 1971 Nixon and Kissinger had already made important progress on their opening to Beijing. The State Department officials who toiled assiduously to fashion a UN strategy to preserve the ROC's UN seat against lengthening odds were unaware of the White House diplomacy that would alter the context of their work. For example, the department spokesman made a statement reiterating standard policy on Taiwan's undetermined status on April 28, one day after Nixon had received an invitation from Zhou Enlai to send an emissary to Beijing. In mid-July, just when the effort to cultivate pragmatism in Taipei was bearing fruit, Kissinger was in Beijing telling Zhou that the United States did not support two Chinas, one China and one Taiwan, Taiwan independence, and would make no further statements that Taiwan's status was undetermined. Kissinger allowed the State Department's effort to go forward, in part because it deflected the department's attention from the main game. But he and Nixon also undermined the campaign to save Taipei's seat, first by delaying a decision to begin the effort until after Kissinger returned from the PRC and then by scheduling his second visit during the very period when George Bush, the U.S. permanent representative to the United Nations, lobbied aggressively but in vain to save Taipei's seat.[78]

Conclusion

Several points of interest spring from this review of American China and Taiwan policy during the 1950s and 1960s. First, to simply say that the United States was pursuing a two-China policy in those two decades only scratches the surface of a more complex phenomenon. Washington did have diplomatic relations with Taipei and dealt with Beijing on a de facto basis for reasons of national interest. Moreover, in the 1960s it sought to create a mechanism that would facilitate Beijing's entry into the United Nations while preventing Taipei's expulsion. Yet more precision is required in describing how the United States adjusted its substantive approach to the two sides of the Taiwan Strait to respond to changing circumstances. On the one hand, two issues were really at play: the legal status of the territory of Taiwan and the Pescadores; and the nature of the Republic of China. On the other, American policy makers applied very different templates to the two Chinese governments and to their relationship to the Chinese state. John Foster Dulles used the concept of divided country and the Kennedy and Johnson administrations preferred the successor-state idea.

To recapitulate the chronology:

- In 1950 the Truman administration adopted the position that the status of Taiwan had yet to be determined in order to provide legal justification for neutralizing the Taiwan Strait and defending the island against a Communist attack. Internationalizing the Taiwan issue also motivated its proposal for a UN study concerning the island. At the same time, Washington maintained a diplomatic distance from the ROC. Rapprochement with the PRC was politically out of the question. In 1951, in preparing the Japan peace treaty, Dulles engineered a solution that excluded both the ROC and PRC from the peace conference, ended Japanese sovereignty over Taiwan and the Pescadores without transferring it to any other party, and restricted the application of the separate Japan–ROC peace treaty to the territory under Taipei's control. Throughout this period, the United States placed considerable emphasis on the need to take into account the views of the people of the island about their future.

- In the first two years of the Eisenhower administration, the status of the ROC in U.S. policy increased significantly. Washington elevated the chief of mission in Taipei to ambassador in February 1953 and agreed eighteen months later to conclude a mutual defense treaty with the ROC. Yet it held to its position that the legal status of Taiwan had yet to be determined, in order to fortify the view that an American defense of Taiwan was internationally justified and not intervention in a civil war. At the same time, Washington insisted that it approve in advance any significant offensive operations against the mainland (even though Chiang Kai-shek saw the conflict as a civil war). Concern for the views of the people of Taiwan disappeared as a rationale for U.S. policy.

- In the spring of 1955 Eisenhower and Dulles concluded that the chance of the United States' having to defend the offshore islands with nuclear weapons was still too high, in spite of the alliance. Taking advantage of Zhou Enlai's offer of talks, they sought to engage Beijing to secure a mutual renunciation of force in the Taiwan area. For Dulles, China was like Germany, Korea, and Vietnam, a divided-country situation (one country with one legitimate government and one de facto regime) that should be stabilized by some sort of armistice. In the end, he was relatively unsuccessful, securing a semirenunciation of force from Chiang only. Yet he denied that he was promoting a two-China outcome. Implicitly he also rejected Chiang's view that the PRC was by definition a bandit regime that had no legitimate role in the international community. It was rather its behavior that excluded it.

- During the 1960s, the main challenge to U.S. policy makers was the politically charged possibility that the ROC might be ejected from the United Nations. The Kennedy and Johnson administrations relied on the procedural device of the important question to block efforts on Beijing's behalf. But there was growing support for a new substantive approach, that the ROC and PRC were not two contestants for the UN seat of a divided China but rather two states that had succeeded the China that had signed the UN charter. Under this approach, Taiwan's legal status would no longer be an issue because it would belong to the state that ruled Taiwan.

- The Nixon administration—or at least its State Department—faced the same UN problem but came up with a different solution. It basically returned to the idea that there was one China that had two governments, each of which deserved to be represented in the United Nations. But it deliberately avoided a detailed legal rationale, and it reaffirmed the undetermined status of Taiwan as a basis for continuing the defense commitment to the ROC.

Even though the details of American policy are more complex and varied than has been thought heretofore, the bottom line is basically the same. Through several administrations, Washington sought to promote U.S. interests and manage the politics of China policy by promoting the idea that there were, or might be, more or less equal political entities on each side of the Taiwan Strait. However, and this is our second observation, it was thwarted in that effort by the resolute opposition of Chiang Kai-shek. Prior to 1971, by which time the game was already lost, Chiang criticized any proposed arrangement that he felt created two Chinas, and he refused to cooperate in achieving it. And he was fortified in that opposition by the leverage exercised by his supporters in the American political system, as exemplified most vividly by Eisenhower's threat to Kennedy to come out of retirement if the latter undercut the position of the ROC. Chiang was quite skillful in a tactical sense in opposing Washington's pragmatic proposals to save the ROC's UN seat. What he lacked was strategic vision regarding the trend of international politics.

Yet Chiang's resistance to U.S. policy was not constant over time or equal as to substance. Although Taipei consistently differed with Washington on the legal status of Taiwan, saying that it had been returned to China, this was not an issue that exercised Chiang. Taipei's protests on this point have a rather pro forma quality to them. Perhaps Chiang and his subordinates believed that possession was nine-tenths of the law, which Dulles indirectly acknowledged in 1955. More important in the early 1950s, when this issue was more salient, was the growing American security commitment to and cooperation with the ROC. Taipei was getting a lot—a superpower ally on which to depend and one that it might even manipulate—so it had less incentive to engage in legal quibbling.

Chiang focused more on how American policy affected his own leadership of the anti-Communist struggle and the relative political status of his government and the PRC. His objections were rather episodic prior to 1955: anger that the ROC was denied a seat at the San Francisco peace conference and resentment that Washington insisted on prior approval of any offensive actions, which deprived him of the political and military initiative. But his opposition became more constant and single-minded after that. He believed that both the ambassadorial talks and the maneuvering to preserve the ROC's UN membership were wrong because they legitimized the immoral regime in Beijing. For Chiang, the moral character of a regime was the fundamental criterion for its existence and membership in the international community. He appears to have taken quite literally the principle *hanzei buliangli* (there is no room for patriots and traitors to live together), and ascribed a moral character to his own government. Thus he had a hard time understanding that there were any benefits from pragmatism if the result was to confer status and morality on "traitors" in Beijing. It was only in 1971, when the ROC realized that disaster loomed, that it gave up its focus on status and morality and opted for pragmatism.

In July 1971 the ROC vice foreign minister, Yang Xikun (Yang Hsi-k'un), offered a sketch of Chiang's political outlook that is useful in understanding both his opposition to American pragmatism through the 1960s and his yielding to it in 1971. "He [Chiang] appreciates the need for a greater measure of flexibility, and is not an absolutely hide-bound traditionalist. But he is proud of his race, his country, its past, and his government. He has a deep sense of obligation to all Chinese, including of course the mainland people. National humiliation is difficult for him to accept. He is sentimental and has a high moral standard reflected in a distaste for compromising principle for the sake of expediency."[79]

There is a tragic irony for Taiwan in Chiang's resolute adherence to his *hanzei buliangli* doctrine. If he had accepted American proposals for some kind of dual presence in the United Nations for the PRC and the ROC earlier than he finally did, Taipei might still be represented in international organizations today. Beijing's campaign to replace Taipei as the government of China in the eyes of the world succeeded in large measure because Chiang viewed his adversaries—and himself—through an ideological lens. This would be his most lasting legacy to Taiwan.

Afterword

With the normalization of relations between the United States and the PRC in December 1978, the American quest for an arrangement that treated the governments in Beijing and Taipei more or less equally seemingly came to an end. Washington recognized the government of the PRC as the sole legal government of China, an act that had profound consequences for the ROC's membership in international organizations, where "China" was the name of the seat over which the two sides had contended. The United States established diplomatic relations with Beijing and committed to conducting its relations with "the people of Taiwan" on an unofficial basis, which was less than the PRC had had with a liaison office from 1973 to 1979. But Washington maintained a somewhat ambiguous position on the status of the island of Taiwan, saying only that it "acknowledged the Chinese position that there is but one China and Taiwan is a part of China." Moreover, consistent with past policy, the United States stated its expectation that the Taiwan issue would be "settled peacefully by the Chinese people themselves." The Taiwan Relations Act (TRA), which supplemented the position of the Executive Branch, authorized continued arms sales to Taiwan, even though the island was claimed by the PRC, with which the United States had diplomatic relations. And, in an echo of past efforts at internationalization, the TRA declared that it was U.S. policy "to consider any effort to determine the future of Taiwan by other than peaceful means, including by boycotts or embargoes, a threat to the peace and security of the Western Pacific area and of grave concern to the United States," and it held open the possibility that the United States might come to Taiwan's defense if it were attacked. When the August 1982 communiqué on arms sales raised concern in Congress that Washington had changed its position on Taiwan's sovereignty, it extracted from the Executive Branch a statement that "the United States government takes no position on Taiwan's sovereignty. We regard this as a matter to be determined by the Chinese people on both sides of the Strait."[80]

U.S. relations with Taiwan today are far more robust in substance than they are in form. There is an elaborate and institutionalized interchange through an unofficial but governmentally authorized mechanism. Washington has richer ties with Taipei on an unofficial basis than it does with many countries with which it has diplomatic relations. Taiwan, for example, is one of the United States' major customers for defense articles and services. Washington's commitment to come to the island's defense in event of attack has become less and less ambiguous.

So is there a sense, despite protestations to the contrary, that the United States today has a "two Chinas" or "one China, one Taiwan" or, most generally, a "two entities" approach? To put it differently, which template from the 1950s and 1960s best reflects current policy and practice? If the form of relations is the criterion, then Washington clearly follows a one-China policy, for it has diplomatic relations with Beijing and unofficial ties with Taipei and does not support the latter's membership in international organizations for which statehood is a prerequisite for entry. If substance is the norm, then the United States clearly pursues a two-entities approach, one in which its ties with Beijing and Taipei are each significant but in different ways. The PRC wins out in form but Taiwan in substance.

Compared to past templates, this two-entities approach has elements of each but is not fully consistent with any one. To say that the United States acknowledges the Chinese position that there is one China and Taiwan is a part of China is to tilt toward the divided-country conception, since historically Beijing and Taipei shared the view that Taiwan was a part of China and unification should occur at some point (they only disagreed on the terms). And Washington most certainly deals with Beijing on a de jure basis and with Taipei on a de facto basis, the reverse of the pattern in the 1950s and 1960s. Yet the United States has been careful not to endorse unification as an ultimate goal (as Dulles did at one point), or any formula for unification. Any substantive outcome is good as far as Washington is concerned as long as it is reached peacefully. And with the authority of the Taiwan Relations Act, the United States still reserves the right to intervene should the PRC attack Taiwan (thus legalistic concerns that this is a civil conflict have waned).

The successor-state template is the one that is probably least consistent with the current U.S. approach. True, some have argued that the Taiwan Relations Act actually treats Taiwan as a state and mandates support for its membership in international organizations. But that appears to be an overinterpretation of the language of the act. Nonetheless, Washington would not oppose a cross-strait outcome that accorded statehood to the governing authorities on Taiwan. And it has never made a substantive challenge to Taipei's claims that it is a state.

In recent years, the United States has also returned to the essence of the dependent-territory template, that the people of Taiwan should have a say in their future. As President Clinton put it in early 2000, the Taiwan Strait issue should be resolved peacefully and with the assent of the people of Taiwan. Washington, unlike Beijing, has accepted the consequences of Taiwan's democratization for cross-strait relations.

There is another irony in all of this. During the 1990s, Taiwan's leaders, facing the prospect of negotiations with Beijing, offered versions of each of the three templates that the United States had pursued in the 1950s and 1960s. In 1991, as Taipei abandoned the view that it was the only Chinese government and renounced the use of force, new concepts of the ROC's relationship to China surfaced. The most obvious was the divided-country concept. As Lee Teng-hui put it in 1998, "There is one divided China. . . . China must be reunified." Also more salient in the 1990s was the idea that the ROC had existed since 1912, that it was, in effect, a still-existing successor to the Qing dynasty. The successor-state template gained sharper definition with the position that the ROC had jurisdiction only over the islands of Taiwan, Penghu (the Pescadores), Jinmen, and Mazu, and with Lee's announcement in July 1999 that cross-state relations were a special state-to-state relationship. That is, perhaps Taiwan was a state. And finally, Taipei has become increasingly insistent that the island's people must approve any changes in Taiwan's status.

In effect, the United States was most creative in its conceptions of both the ROC and Taiwan at the time that Chiang Kai-shek was the most opposed to any scheme that in his eyes undermined the position that the ROC was the sole legal government of China. By the 1990s, when Taiwan came around to seeing the value of such ideas, the United States would no longer promote them.

5

The "Sacred Texts" of
United States–China–Taiwan Relations

Whenever the leaders of the United States and the People's Republic of China (PRC) meet, they discuss Taiwan. And they perform a ritual that is designed to reassure each other and their respective publics that fundamental interests are being preserved. Chinese leaders insist that the United States must strictly comply with the principles of the "three communiqués" concerning Taiwan if U.S.–PRC relations are going to be sound. American leaders respond that, of course, Washington will adhere to the three communiqués. They also reiterate the U.S. "abiding interest" in a peaceful resolution of the Taiwan question. And they sometimes reaffirm a commitment to the Taiwan Relations Act (TRA).

At the center of this ritual are the founding documents of the U.S.–China–Taiwan triangle. They are the Shanghai communiqué, concluded in February 1972 at the end of President Nixon's visit to China; the joint communiqué on the normalization of U.S.–PRC relations announced in December 1978; the Taiwan Relations Act that Congress passed in March 1979; and the U.S.–PRC communiqué on arms sales to Taiwan concluded in August 1982. Let us leave aside the curious phenomenon of two countries' regulating their relationship by continual reference to documents that are now twenty to thirty years old, and simply note that hardly anyone ever reads the texts of these documents anymore, either fully or carefully. There is some focus on the core sentences concerning Taiwan, but never on the larger textual context. So observers are only vaguely aware of the principles on which Beijing regularly demands compliance, and to which the United States reaffirms adherence. Similarly, few understand what the Taiwan Relations Act says and what it means.

This chapter explores these four "sacred texts" and what they say about the Taiwan Strait issue. For each document, we shall examine both the process by which it was drafted and the content of the final product. For the three communiqués, we shall also look at the ancillary texts and statements that were issued around the same time, and at variations in the English and

Chinese texts. The focus is very much on the texts themselves, less on the details of the negotiating process that preceded the documents, the political and diplomatic context that surrounded them, or broader U.S. policy toward the PRC and Taiwan.[1] It would be a mistake, of course, to regard these texts as the sum total of the U.S.–PRC–Taiwan relationships. Context is all important. But it would also be an error to treat them as trivial ciphers. The communiqués and the TRA were concluded at key points in the relationship, and represent the crystallizations of the policies and intentions of the leaders and governments that remain a baseline for current activity. Moreover, it goes without saying, although the three communiqués focused on Taiwan, they were negotiated without consulting either the government or people of the island.

The Shanghai Communiqué, February 1972

Crafting the Document

There was never any question that Richard Nixon's visit to China would result in a formal communiqué. That was the proper instrument to mark such a momentous occasion—"the week that changed the world," as he hyperbolically described it. Moreover, Nixon and Mao Zedong could not ignore the sources of division and conflict that had accumulated over the past twenty-five years, even as they sought to maximize their shared geopolitical advantage.

The past estrangement was so profound that even the character of the document to be developed was at issue. Starting in late summer 1971, John Holdridge of the National Security Council staff developed a draft modeled on the bland statements released after the trips of other foreign leaders to Beijing. Henry Kissinger presented this draft or something like it to Zhou Enlai when he visited Beijing in October 1971 to advance the Nixon trip. On Mao Zedong's instructions, however, Zhou rejected the American approach. Mao wanted the document to set forth fundamental bilateral differences. When Zhou presented a draft along those lines Kissinger quickly perceived the benefits of frankness. Each side could reassure its allies and domestic constituencies that past principles had not been abandoned. Misunderstanding born of ambiguity would be avoided. With the basic approach agreed upon, there began a multiday drafting exercise.[2]

Even as each side stated its own views, they sought to take into account the other's stance. Kissinger insisted that "the language of the disagreements had to be compatible with the occasion. . . . We would not accept language that tended to put us on trial or to humiliate an American President even if it was clearly labeled as the Chinese point of view." At one point, Zhou dropped two sentences that described the PRC position on a certain issue because they would be too offensive to an American audience. Still, Kissinger's memoir suggests that the joint effort had a certain asymmetry. The American side struck a moderate tone but had to encourage the Chinese to soften their harsher formulations.[3]

How specifically to address the Taiwan issue was more complicated, since the PRC saw it as a civil war in which the United States had intervened for almost three decades. Zhou reported that Mao wanted more than just conflicting formulations; he wanted Washington to renounce its ties to Taipei altogether. Kissinger refused the demand but had ideas on how to talk about the issue that would ensure the success of Nixon's visit. Zhou demanded a renunciation of the American position of the previous two decades, that the status of Taiwan was not determined, and instead sought to secure an affirmation that it was a part of China. In a meeting on October 21, Kissinger made an initial breakthrough, reportedly by drawing on a 1950s State Department planning document. He told Zhou, in a statement that was apparently prepared in advance: "I want to formulate my answer with some precision. . . .We do not challenge the fact that all Chinese maintain that there's only one China and that Taiwan is part of that China. And therefore we do not maintain that the status in that respect is undetermined." The two sides then proceeded to exchange a number of drafts of the communiqué. Chinese officials writing their side's first draft adopted Kissinger's formulation to describe the *American* position concerning Taiwan. And, at a later meeting, they got the Americans to insert the point that Taiwan was a province of China. To describe the *Chinese* position in the communiqué, Beijing proposed to reiterate the standard PRC view that it was the sole legal government of China, that Taiwan was a part of China, that resolving the Taiwan issue was an internal matter, and that Beijing was opposed to activities that created two Chinas, one China and one Taiwan, Taiwan independence, and so on. Kissinger accepted all those points in China's statement of its position.[4]

The one matter on which it was not possible to settle on final language in October was the U.S. security relationship with the island and that was deferred until the Nixon party arrived in Beijing on February 21. The disagreement was over how the Taiwan Strait issue would be resolved—peacefully or not—and the conditions under which U.S. troops would be withdrawn. The American position was that the United States would reaffirm its interest in a peaceful solution of the Taiwan question and state as an objective the withdrawal of U.S. troops, *conditioned or premised* on a peaceful solution and an easing of regional tensions. The PRC position was that the United States should commit unconditionally to withdrawing its troops and merely *express the hope* of a peaceful resolution.[5]

After many hours of trying to resolve these issues as a single package, Kissinger proposed to split them. The ultimate withdrawal of U.S. forces would be premised on a peaceful solution, while the nearer-term reduction of American personnel would be linked to the reduction of regional tensions (a code word for Vietnam). The PRC vice foreign minister, Qiao Guanhua, rejected any sort of conditionality but did suggest substituting the word "prospect" for "premise." Kissinger felt that "prospect" reflected enough of a positive Chinese commitment to justify agreement. Also at this point the Chinese side agreed to a change in the U.S. formulation on Taiwan's status: from a "province" of China to a "part" of China.[6] As far as Nixon, Kissinger, and the PRC government were concerned, the communiqué was complete.

At this late stage, the State Department members of Nixon's delegation got their first look at the document. They recommended a number of changes, even though they knew the Chinese Communist Party (CCP) Politburo had already given its approval. For example, Marshall Green, assistant secretary of state for East Asian affairs, objected to a statement in which the United States affirmed its security treaties in East Asia but failed to mention that with Taiwan. On this point, Qiao agreed to dropping the overall statement and to accept vaguer language on the U.S. relationship with Japan and South Korea.[7]

Interpretation

As Kissinger stressed in his memoirs, the Shanghai communiqué was unusual in the annals of diplomacy. It made a virtue out of divergent views, so that both sides could emphasize what they had in common but each could say that it stuck to its principles. He also asserted that the Nixon trip and the Shanghai communiqué "put the Taiwan issue in abeyance, with each side maintaining its basic principles," as they pursued their common strategic interest in containing the Soviet Union.[8]

Box 5.1 rearranges the Taiwan portion of the text of the communiqué so that the views on specific topics are placed side by side. It also rearranges the various PRC views on Taiwan so that the sequence is the same as in the analogous U.S. section.

At first glance, the section on Taiwan appears similar to an earlier section on issues like Korea and South Asia. That is, conflicting points of view are

Box 5.1
The Shanghai Communiqué

China (rearranged)	*United States (as in original)*
The Taiwan question is the crucial question obstructing the normalization of relations between China and the United States;	
The Government of the People's Republic of China is the sole legal government of China: Taiwan is a province of China which has long been returned to the motherland;	The United States acknowledges that all Chinese on either side of the Taiwan Strait maintain there is but one China and that Taiwan is a part of China. The United States does not challenge that position
The Chinese government firmly opposes any activities which aim at the creation of "one China, one Taiwan," "one China, two governments," "two Chinas," an "independent Taiwan," or advocate that that "the status of Taiwan remains to be determined."	[and therefore disassociates itself from any formulae or outcomes inconsistent with that position]*
The liberation of Taiwan is China's internal affair in which no other country has the right to interfere;	It reaffirms its interest in a peaceful settlement of the Taiwan question by the Chinese themselves.
and all US forces and military installations must be withdrawn from Taiwan.	With this prospect in mind, it affirms the ultimate objective of the withdrawal of all US forces and military installations from Taiwan. In the meantime, it will progressively reduce its forces and military installations on Taiwan as the tension in the area diminishes.

*See Henry Kissinger, *White House Years* (Boston: Little Brown, 1979), and John H. Holdridge, *Crossing the Divide: An Insider's Account of Normalization of U.S.–China Relations* (Lanham, MD: Rowman and Littlefield, 1997).

arrayed. If one examines the side-by-side presentation in Box 5.1, however, a different type of interaction is obviously at play. That is, the PRC was the *demandeur* and the United States was on the defensive.

Beijing categorically stated its views on six issues: the significance of the Taiwan issue; whether it is the government of China; whether Taiwan is a part of China; the unacceptability of various formulae, such as two Chinas;

how the Taiwan issue is to be resolved; and the fate of U.S. forces and military installations on Taiwan.

On the first issue, the PRC stated that the Taiwan question was "the crucial question" obstructing U.S.–PRC normalization. For its part, the United States implicitly accepted the point by making no companion statement of its own. Which begs the question: why should Washington have accepted Beijing's definition of the situation?

The second, third, and fourth issues can be treated as a package. Beijing stated that "the Government of the People's Republic of China is the sole legal government of China: Taiwan is a province of China which has long been returned to the motherland. . . . The Chinese government firmly opposes any activities which aim at the creation of 'one China, one Taiwan,' 'one China, two governments,' 'two Chinas,' an 'independent Taiwan,' or advocate that 'the status of Taiwan remains to be determined.'" The PRC was thus denying any legitimacy to the Republic of China (ROC) government and asserting that Taiwan was and had been a subordinate part of China. Also, it rejected the various proposals that the United States and others had considered or promoted since the Communist victory in 1949 in order to deny the island of Taiwan to the PRC and preserve the rival ROC government.

The American statement on Taiwan was simultaneously artful, subtle, misleading, and somewhat confused. It read: "The United States acknowledges that all Chinese on either side of the Taiwan Strait maintain there is but one China and that Taiwan is a part of China. The United States does not challenge that position." The most cited problem with the first sentence was to whom on Taiwan it applied. Did it apply only to people on the island who regarded themselves as Chinese? If so, it probably captured only a minority of the population because there was a significant portion of the population who after decades of Kuomintang (KMT) repression subjectively identified themselves politically as Taiwanese, not Chinese. (That same repression, of course, made it impossible to know how many people did so.) If the term "all Chinese" was meant to refer to people on Taiwan who were objectively Chinese in a social and cultural sense, then it would have captured just about all the island's residents. But then the views that were attributed to them were incorrect. If the population had been allowed to express their views, a good portion would have disagreed with the proposition that there was one China and Taiwan was a part of China.

The explanation is that the phrase "all Chinese on either side of the Taiwan Strait" was not to be taken literally but was probably a term of art to refer to the two governments. This was a circumlocution made necessary by the fact that the United States recognized the ROC but was negotiating with the PRC, which it did not recognize. But Nixon and Kissinger hoped to use the fact that both the Beijing and Taipei governments agreed that there was only one China to allay PRC suspicion that the United States was pursuing a two-China approach. At the same time, they avoided the issue of which of the two regimes was the sole legal government, on which China had stated its firm position.

The confusion in the U.S. statement concerns the precise way it discussed Taiwan's relationship to the state called China. Grammatically, the sentence that begins "The United States acknowledges" can be broken into two equivalent statements: "The United States acknowledges *that* all Chinese on either side of the Taiwan Strait maintain there is but one China" and "The United States acknowledges *that* Taiwan is a part of China." The two relative clauses beginning with "that" are each objects of the verb "acknowledge." Such a reading would be significant, for it would in fact be the strongest public U.S. statement ever on Taiwan's legal status, and the closest to the PRC's own view.

But is that what was really meant? Or was the statement that "Taiwan is a part of China" one of the points on which both sides of the strait agreed, rather than something the United States acknowledged (despite the clumsy sentence construction)? The Chinese version of the passage appears to attribute the Taiwan clause to Chinese on both sides of the strait. To confirm that judgment, I consulted native Chinese speakers who are well educated and knowledgeable about U.S.–PRC relations. They stated that the meaning of the Chinese text is that Taiwan's being a part of China was something that Chinese on both sides of the strait maintain, not something that the United States acknowledged. My informants stuck to that interpretation even when the contrary one was suggested.

The other problem with the grammatically correct version of the sentence is how then to interpret the next "does not challenge" sentence. What exactly is "that position" that the United States in the next sentence does not challenge? If we were to judge that the *United States* had acknowledged that Taiwan was a part of China, then why would it need to then not challenge its own position? By this logic, what is not challenged can only be the agreed Chinese position that there is only one China and that Taiwan is a part of it. Still, the formulation is awkward.

Part—or perhaps most—of the confusion stems from the process by which the passage was drafted. The early drafts discussed in October 1971 included the following statements: "The United States acknowledges that all Chinese on either side of the Taiwan Strait maintain there is but one China. The United States does not challenge that position." It is clear here that what the United

States does not challenge is the cross-strait consensus on one China. At one point during the October discussions, however, the clause "and that Taiwan is a province of China" was inserted at the end of the first sentence. It is more than conceivable that no one noticed that the addition rendered unclear the object of the verbs "acknowledge" and "does not challenge." It is also plausible that the Chinese officials who asked that the Taiwan section be added did not understand the intricacies of relative clauses and which verb was operative. Viewed from this perspective, it appears that the grammatically correct interpretation of the U.S. position was inadvertent. But for American negotiators to have missed the confusion that might be created on such an important an issue was not a trivial oversight.[9]

Let us assume, therefore, that Kissinger in fact intended to attribute the statement on Taiwan's status to the people or governments on both sides of the strait and not to the United States. We must still determine the significance of the U.S. statement. What does it mean for Washington not to challenge something that it acknowledges, particularly when it had taken a contrary position for the previous two decades? Does it in fact represent an American acceptance that Taiwan was a part of China?

We may approach the text itself from four directions. The first is the U.S. side's near blunder in talking about Taiwan's status. When the February 1972 discussions began, the text of the U.S. position referred to Taiwan as a "province of China." That was changed to "part of China" at Kissinger's request at the last minute. If the United States had referred to Taiwan as a province of China and then later on recognized the PRC as the sole legal government of China, it would have been tantamount to saying that Taiwan was a part of the PRC (since the governing authorities of a province cannot be a sovereign government). That Kissinger corrected the error only at the last minute, again, suggests either a lack of attention to drafting detail or an inclination to acknowledge Chinese sovereignty over Taiwan. Either way it was almost a serious mistake.[10]

The second textual consideration is to ask why the sentence, "The United States does not challenge that position" was necessary in the first place. To have not made that statement would certainly have preserved a larger measure of ambiguity, since Washington would then have only been acknowledging a factual situation. To make the statement, therefore, appears to be an affirmative move by the United States in the direction of China's position. The answer to the question appears to lie in the intense pressure that Zhou Enlai applied on Kissinger to accept China's definition of the Taiwan situation. In both the July and October 1971 meetings, Zhou insisted that the United States accept five propositions if it wanted to normalize relations with China: that the PRC was the sole, legitimate government representing the Chinese people; that Taiwan was an inalienable part of China; that the United States did not support a two-Chinas or one-China, one-Taiwan policy, or the Taiwan independence movement; that it no longer regarded the status of Taiwan as undetermined; and that the United States would not let Japan intervene in Taiwan as it withdrew. As discussed above, Kissinger used the "all Chinese . . . does not challenge" formulation as a direct yet still ambiguous response to Zhou's demands.[11]

The third consideration of the text of the communiqué per se has to do with the thesaurus of diplomacy as it applies to the words "does not challenge." One can position that term on a spectrum of words and phrases that reflect a gradation of views, ranging from "accept" on one end to "reject" on the other. Right in the middle is "takes no position." The issue here is where "does not challenge" fits on that spectrum. Arguably it is less than "accept" and more than "takes no position," suggesting again a modest bias in the direction of a U.S. acceptance of Chinese sovereignty over Taiwan.

The fourth textual consideration stems from a comparison of the English and Chinese texts. Although Kissinger reports in his memoirs that English was the controlling text, ironically the Chinese text left the more ambiguous meaning. His aide, Richard Solomon, concluded that regarding Taiwan, "the Chinese version conveys even less of a sense of U.S. acceptance of the PRC view that the island is Chinese territory than does the English. It more strongly conveys the idea that we do not wish to get involved in a debate regarding the Chinese position on Taiwan," which suggests that the English text left more of a sense of accommodation to Chinese views.[12]

So far, we have focused on clues that we can draw from the text itself on the U.S. position on Taiwan's legal status. And the picture is ambiguous. Although there are signs that Washington had accepted the Chinese position, they could well have been the result of faulty drafting. Nor, arguably, did they leave the Chinese side with a clear impression of a change in U.S. policy. Greater clarity is present, however, when it comes to the private statements of U.S. leaders.

Nixon, in his first small-group meeting with Zhou on February 22, 1972, stated U.S. agreement with Zhou's five principles (thus reaffirming Kissinger's commitments). He said that Zhou could count on them "no matter what we say on other subjects." Nixon's first two statements concerned Taiwan's status: "Principle one. There is one China, and Taiwan is a part of China. There will be no more statements made—if I can control our bureaucracy—to the effect that the status of Taiwan is undetermined. Second, we have not and will not support any Taiwan independence movement."[13] In Nixon's mind, therefore, the island belonged to China and senior PRC leaders knew that was his position. And both Nixon and Kissinger repeatedly suggested that administration policy went beyond American public statements (the communiqué, for example).[14]

This conclusion is made stronger by a revelation by John Holdridge in his memoirs. He reported that the American government "does not challenge" the statement applied not only to the position maintained by Chinese on both sides of the Taiwan Strait but also to China's opposition to five types of activities: creating one China, one Taiwan; one China, two governments; two Chinas; an independent Taiwan; or advocating that the status of Taiwan remains to be determined. The apparent logic is that the cross-strait consensus (which the United States acknowledged and did not challenge) is fundamentally inconsistent with these activities, which deny the unity of China. Chinese on both sides of the strait could not, for example, maintain there was one China and then advocate two. By not challenging the consensus, the United States was therefore implicitly dissociating itself from its own past positions. The linkage is clear with respect to the last point in the carefully crafted statement that Kissinger made to Zhou in October 1971: "We do not challenge the fact that all Chinese maintain that there's only one China and that Taiwan is part of China. *And therefore we do not maintain* that the status in that respect is undetermined." As we also know, the Chinese side was pushing the United States to dissociate itself as explicitly as possible from those positions. If Holdridge's recollections are correct, he points to a hidden hinge in the Shanghai communiqué between the Chinese view of what it would not tolerate and the U.S. statement of what it would not do.[15]

On the other hand, it appears that China itself did not interpret the communiqué as a fundamental shift in U.S. policy concerning Taiwan's status. The best available interpretation can be found in a comprehensive history of the Taiwan issue in U.S.–China relations by Su Ge, who for many years has had close connections with the PRC Foreign Ministry. His account of the drafting of the Shanghai communiqué does note that Vice Foreign Minister Qiao Guanhua, with whom Kissinger negotiated during the Nixon trip, asserted that the United States had recognized that Taiwan was a part of China. But Su himself does not claim in his analysis of the communiqué that it represented an American acceptance of the Chinese position. Although Su's account is retrospective, it would be surprising if he did not make that claim if in fact the Chinese government believed it.[16]

The fifth issue addressed in the Taiwan section of the communiqué was how the Taiwan issue was to be resolved. As usual, the PRC position was categorical: "the liberation of Taiwan is China's internal affair in which no other country has the right to interfere." For its part, the United States reaffirmed "its interest in a peaceful settlement of the Taiwan question by the Chinese themselves."

Thus, the two sides took mutually contradictory positions. "Liberation" in the Chinese lexicon is a political outcome that may be legitimately achieved by violence. The United States asserted that it had a national interest in a nonviolent outcome. Zhou did tell Nixon privately that Beijing had "self-confidence" that it could deal with Chiang Kai-shek "peacefully." That was hardly a commitment, and the language of the communiqué itself gave no hint of self-restraint.[17]

Three things are worth noting about the formulations in the communiqué. The first is a translation issue. In the relevant statement of the American position, the Chinese text used the word *guanxin*—usually translated "concern"—as the verb for which a peaceful resolution of the Taiwan issue is the object. But the word in the English text was "interest." Arguably, the term "interest" is stronger than the word "concern," and has the connotation of an objective or situation in which the United States had a significant stake, and impairment of which would govern its future behavior. The Chinese text suggests a weaker U.S. reaction to a nonpeaceful resolution of the Taiwan issue than does the English text.

Second is the substantive asymmetry between the Chinese and American formulations as stated. The PRC side focused on the nature of the conflict— that it was an internal affair—and said nothing about what means it would use to resolve it. But quite implicit in its characterization of the conflict as a civil war was that it possessed the right to use force. The U.S. side did not speak directly to the nature of the conflict but did appear to lean toward the Chinese view on the matter when it spoke of a peaceful settlement "by the Chinese themselves." Even if the United States was merely choosing to be silent on the nature of the dispute, to do so represented an implicit shift in approach. This is because since 1950 Washington had justified its interest in a peaceful outcome—and its attendant security role—by defining the Taiwan situation as a matter of international concern, and thus not as a civil war. It had deliberately linked its definition of the situation and its efforts to prevent a nonpeaceful settlement. Now the United States took no explicit position on the nature of the conflict, and so weakened its assertions concerning a peaceful resolution. (Note, moreover, the problem created by the phrase "by the Chinese themselves"; which people on Taiwan are involved?)

This American silence on this point is all the more interesting when we link it up with a part of the communiqué that appears to have nothing to do with Taiwan at all (which demonstrates, by the way, the importance of looking at this document as a whole). That is the section in which the two sides agree to apply to their bilateral relationship the five principles of peaceful coexistence, including respect for sovereignty and territorial integrity and noninterference in the internal affairs of other states. By even implying that the United States regarded the Taiwan issue as an internal affair, in which therefore it had no right to interfere, it undercut its stated interest in a peaceful solution, *and*, to go back to the earlier discussion, strengthened the suggestion that it saw Taiwan as a part of China.[18]

The sixth Taiwan issue in the communiqué was the question of the withdrawal of U.S. troops and installations from Taiwan. As recounted above, Kissinger did try to link that withdrawal to a peaceful settlement of the issue. But in the end, the linkage was indirect and implicit. The Chinese position, based on its historical position that U.S. forces had "occupied" China's territory of Taiwan, was categorical: all forces and installations "must be withdrawn." The United States had a two-part position. First, U.S. forces would be unconditionally reduced as "tension in the area diminishes"—a reference to Vietnam. Second, with the "prospect" of a peaceful settlement "in mind," it "affirms the ultimate objective" of withdrawing all forces and installations.

Here we must consult our diplomat's thesaurus again, and distinguish between three different concepts. The first is that of contingency, as conveyed by the words "condition" or "premise," which Kissinger tried and failed to apply to a peaceful settlement. The second concept is hope, which, as applied to a peaceful resolution, is what China suggested be the basis for the U.S. withdrawal. The third is credible expectation, which is conveyed by the word "prospect." The three concepts vary in terms of sequencing and level of certainty. In the case of contingency, the United States would withdraw its troops from Taiwan only after it was absolutely certain that the dispute would be resolved peacefully. In the other two cases, withdrawal would more likely come first and the level of certainty of a peaceful outcome would be lower, but with greater certainty for a credible expectation than with a hope. So Nixon and Kissinger were willing to adopt a middle position, in return for which they made, it should be noted, the rather vague commitment of reaffirming the ultimate objective to withdraw troops. And when Nixon returned to the United States, he asserted a linkage that was at odds with the words of the Shanghai communiqué. "With respect to Taiwan, we stated our established policy that our forces overseas will be reduced gradually as tensions ease, and that our ultimate objective is to withdraw our forces as a peaceful settlement is achieved." This could reflect an understanding of the word "prospect" that connotes conditionality, but it also could be a rationalization for an

American audience. Indeed, Nixon and Kissinger would continue to seek some commitment of peaceful PRC intent, but more as a temporary solution to a political problem rather than a substantive guarantee.[19]

To sum up, did the Shanghai communiqué in fact allow each side to stick to their principles on Taiwan while pursuing their common strategic interest in containing the Soviet Union, as Kissinger asserted? It is certain that the U.S.–PRC rapprochement did complicate Moscow's geopolitical position in a significant way. And China did not change its basic principles on the island's legal status and how the matter would be resolved. Mao and Zhou had only relaxed their prior insistence that the matter be resolved before bilateral relations were improved. In return, however, the United States did four things. First, it subtly tilted in the direction of Beijing's position that Taiwan was a part of China. This tilt was more pronounced in private conversations than in the communiqué. Mao and Zhou may have taken those statements more seriously, in part because they placed great stock in the statements of leaders like Nixon and also because Kissinger had stressed the importance of drafting the communiqué in a way that would not alarm the American public. But the tilt was still present. Second, the United States suggested that Taiwan was a Chinese internal affair, in which it also pledged it would not interfere, thus undermining its past rationale for defending the island (that it was a matter of international concern). Third, it subtly dissociated itself from Taiwan outcomes that China opposed. And finally, it made a commitment to withdraw substantial military forces and installations from Taiwan as regional tensions declined, and declared an "ultimate objective" of ending its military presence on the island based on the expectation that Beijing would settle the issue peacefully rather than a guarantee that it would.

To be sure, Nixon restated the need for a peaceful solution in his first public statement on returning to the United States. He also sought to convince Zhou that a PRC pledge of peaceful intent would help him in managing political problems back in the United States. Yet considering all that the United States had given away to secure strategic cooperation with Beijing; considering the many examples of faulty drafting; and considering Washington's willingness to remain silent sometimes when Beijing asserted its own position, to claim that the United States "maintained its basic principles" on the Taiwan issue is somewhat disingenuous.[20]

The Normalization Communiqué, December 1978

Every time the PRC and another country established diplomatic relations, they issued a communiqué to mark the event and state the terms of the transaction. So it was inevitable that Beijing and Washington would do so when the time for normalization arrived. And given the U.S. relationship with Taiwan, such a document would be more complex than that for any other country. The Carter administration would have to tackle a number of politically and substantively difficult issues: the future U.S. political relationship with Taiwan; the legal status of the island and its relationship to the Chinese government that the United States was recognizing; and the U.S. security relationship with Taiwan, including the problems not addressed in the Shanghai communiqué—the defense treaty and the future of arms sales. The normalization communiqué would differ from the Shanghai communiqué because the problems to be solved were more difficult and because it would be the charter document for the new U.S.–PRC relationship.

But the normalization communiqué was different in two other ways. First of all, the Carter administration used the necessity of this document as an instrument in conducting the negotiations. In the summer of 1977, it had a draft ready to jump-start normalization in the event Beijing was on the same substantive wave-length as Washington. A year later, the United States presented a draft for the deliberate purpose of testing PRC seriousness.

Second, the normalization communiqué was supplemented more systematically by other statements: written documents in the name of each government and oral statements by the two top leaders, President Carter and CCP chairman Hua Guofeng. The communiqué itself was part of a large and deliberately constructed package. We know this because one account of normalization refers to Assistant Secretary of State Richard Holbrooke's review of the "communiqué and the accompanying documents." Moreover, there is evidence that each side showed the text of its unilateral statement to the other side.[21] Yet for all the analysis of the negotiations leading up to normalization, no attention whatsoever has been paid to these ancillary documents and why they were necessary.

Box 5.2 presents these various statements in a novel way. It first presents those elements of the communiqué in which the two governments spoke together—areas of consensus. It then lays out in two columns the statements that each government makes for itself. It does so on an issue-by-issue basis and irrespective of the document in which the statements appear. Quotations from the communiqué itself are in boldface. Those from the written statements are in italics. And extracts from the oral statements by the two leaders are in regular typeface.

Drafting—and Using—the Text

Jimmy Carter came into office determined to recognize the PRC as the government of China. All that remained to be decided were the precise terms of

Box 5.2
The Normalization Communiqué and Associated Documents (text from communiqué in **bold**; from written statements, *italics*; from leader statements in regular typeface)

Joint Statements

The United States of America and the People's Republic of China have agreed to recognize each other and to establish diplomatic relations as of January 1, 1979. . . .
The United States of America and the People's Republic of China reaffirm the principles agreed on by the two sides in the Shanghai Communiqué and emphasize once again that:

- **Both wish to reduce the danger of international military conflict;**

- **Neither should seek hegemony in the Asia-Pacific region or in any other region of the world and each is opposed to efforts by any other country or group of countries to establish such hegemony;**

- **Neither is prepared to negotiate on behalf of any third party or to enter into agreements or understandings with the other directed at other states. . . .**

- **Both believe that the normalization of Sino-American relations is not only in the interest of the Chinese and American peoples but also contributes to the cause of peace in Asia and the world.**

The United States of America and the People's Republic of China will exchange Ambassadors and establish Embassies on March 1, 1979.

PRC Statements	*U.S. Statements*
As of Jan. 1, 1979, the People's Republic of China and the United States of America recognize each other and establish diplomatic relations, thereby ending the prolonged abnormal relationship between them. This is an historic event in Sino-United States relations.	*As of January 1, 1979, the United States of America recognizes the People's Republic of China as the sole legal government of China. On the same date, the People's Republic of China accords similar recognition to the United States of America. The United States thereby establishes diplomatic relations with the PRC.*
As is known to all, the Government of the People's Republic of China is the sole legal government of China and Taiwan is a part of China.	**The United States of America recognizes the Government of the People's Republic of China as the sole legal government of China. Within this context, the people of the United States will maintain cultural, commercial, and other unofficial relations with the people of Taiwan.**

Box 5.2 *(continued)*

The Government of the United States of America acknowledges the Chinese position that there is but one China and Taiwan is a part of China.

The question of Taiwan was the crucial issue obstructing the normalization of relations between China and the United States. It has now been resolved between the two countries in the spirit of the Shanghai communiqué and through their joint efforts, thus enabling the normalization of relations so ardently desired by the people of the two countries.

The establishment of diplomatic relations between China and the United States is a historic event. It opens up broad vistas for enhancing understanding and friendship between the two peoples and promoting bilateral exchanges in all fields. It will also contribute to peace and stability in Asia and the world as a whole.

The United States believes that the establishment of diplomatic relations with the People's Republic will contribute to the American people, to the stability of Asia where the United States has a major security and economic interest, and to the peace of the entire world.

On that same date, January 1, 1979, the United States of America will notify Taiwan that it is terminating diplomatic relations and the Mutual Defense Treaty between the United States and the Republic of China is being terminated in accordance with the provisions of the Treaty. The United States also states that it will be withdrawing its remaining military personnel from Taiwan within four months.

In the future, the American people and the people of Taiwan will maintain commercial, cultural, and other relations without official representation and without government diplomatic relations.

The Administration will seek adjustments to our laws and regulations

Box 5.2 *(continued)*

to permit the maintenance of commercial, cultural, and other non-governmental relationships in the new circumstances that will exist after normalization.

As for the way of bringing Taiwan back to the embrace of the motherland and reunifying the country is entirely China's affair.

The United States is confident that the people of Taiwan face a peaceful and prosperous future. The United States continues to have an internal interest in the peaceful resolution of the Taiwan issue and expects that the Taiwan issue will be settled peacefully by the Chinese people themselves.

It is the common aspiration of all the Chinese people including our compatriots in Taiwan to accomplish the great cause of reunifying the country with Taiwan returning to the embrace of the motherland. ... We hope that our compatriots on Taiwan will join all other Chinese people ... in making further contributions to the cause of reunifying China.

Paragraph two of the joint communiqué which I announced just now says: "The United States of America recognizes the Government of the People's Republic of China as the sole legal government of China. Within this context, the people of the United States will maintain cultural, commercial, and other unofficial relations with the people of Taiwan." In our discussions on the question of the commercial relations, the two sides had differing views. During the negotiations the US side mentioned that after normalization it would continue to sell [a] limited amount of arms to Taiwan for defensive purposes. We made it clear that we absolutely would not agree to this. In all discussions the Chinese side repeatedly made clear its position on this question. We held that after the normalization continued sales of arms to Taiwan

---

Box 5.2 *(continued)*

*by the United States would not
conform to the principles of the
normalization, would be detrimental to the peaceful liberation of Taiwan and would
exercise an unfavorable influence on the peace and stability
of the Asia-Pacific region. So
our two sides had differences
on this point. Nevertheless,we
reached an agreement on the
joint communiqué.*

*At the invitation of the US
Government, Teng Hsiao-p'ing,
Deputy Prime Minister of the
State Council of the PRC, will
pay an official visit to the United
States in January 1979, with a
view to further promoting the
friendship between the two
peoples and good relations
between the two countries.*

---

the bargain and the timing of the event. The Carter administration had inher-
ited the commitments of its predecessors on how key issues would be addressed and the text of a draft communiqué, and Carter reportedly felt a
general obligation to abide by those commitments.[22]

The first step in the process was Policy Review Memorandum 24 (PRM
24), completed in June 1977. Therein, Carter's advisers recommended that
the United States establish diplomatic relations with Beijing and terminate
ties with Taipei, including the defense treaty and the U.S. military presence
on the island. In effect, PRM 24 proposed that, based on past commitments,
the United States accept the three conditions for normalization that Beijing
had enunciated during the Ford administration.[23]

President Carter accepted these recommendations, but insisted that
Beijing provide three assurances of its own—in part, no doubt, to help him
blunt domestic opposition to normalization. The first was that the United
States would continue to sell arms to Taiwan. Second, the "people of the
United States" would continue cultural, economic, and other relations with
"the people of Taiwan" on an unofficial basis. (The phrases in quotation
marks were terms of art to refer to the two governments.) Third, at the time
of normalization, the United States "could make a unilateral, uncontested

statement concerning its expectation that the Taiwan issue would be settled peacefully." Thus Carter had abandoned at the outset any hope that he could induce Beijing to make its own unilateral statement of peaceful intent.[24]

Carter was sufficiently eager and proactive on China policy that he instructed Secretary of State Cyrus Vance to reveal the full U.S. position when he visited Beijing in August. Vance also carried with him a draft recognition communiqué that could be the basis of further negotiations if the PRC responded positively. In the event, he chose to present a tougher U.S. position, in part because he knew that securing ratification of the Panama Canal treaties would be enough of a political challenge for the administration over the next few months. He also told PRC foreign minister Huang Hua that "it would be necessary for U.S. government personnel to remain on Taiwan under an informal relationship." And he put the PRC on notice that the United States would have to make a statement about the peaceful resolution of the Taiwan issue, which it expected the PRC side not to contradict. In the end, he did not table the draft communiqué because the Chinese vigorously rejected the suggestion about U.S. government employees on Taiwan.[25]

A period of limbo ensued until national security adviser Zbigniew Brzezinski's May 1978 trip to Beijing. He indicated to his Chinese hosts that Washington was prepared to accept the PRC's three requirements. He also stated that Washington would make a peaceful-resolution statement that it expected Beijing not to contradict. He recommended that the two sides begin normalization discussions and the PRC agreed. In June, Brzezinski, in order to avoid protracted negotiations, suggested that the U.S. side "lay out our position more comprehensively, perhaps through the device of submitting a draft normalization communiqué." Leonard Woodcock, head of the U.S. Liaison Office in Beijing, was charged with conducting the negotiations, and on July 5, he proposed to Huang Hua that they begin by addressing four issues: the post-normalization U.S. presence on Taiwan; "our statements on the occasion of normalization"; U.S.–Taiwan trade after derecognition; and "a joint communiqué and the modalities of normalization." (Note that two of the initial items for discussion concerned documents, plural: the communiqué and associated statements.) Woodcock was instructed to unfold the U.S. position gradually in order to probe the Chinese reaction at every point. Security issues—the most sensitive—were to be reserved until later in the process. Yet there is no indication that either side tabled a text during the summer.[26]

After successfully brokering the Camp David agreement between Israel and Egypt in September, Carter was eager to push forward on China. On September 19, he met with Chai Zemin, the new head of the PRC Liaison Office in Washington, and told him that the United States would insist on two things: making a unilateral statement at the time of normalization on a peaceful resolution of the Taiwan issue, which Beijing would not contradict; and selling carefully selected weapons systems to Taiwan that would not be threatening to China. Huang Hua gave a response to Vance on October 2 by rejecting any residual security relationship. Brzezinski and his China adviser, Michel Oksenberg, decided that the only way to show that the administration was serious was to table a draft communiqué. Carter agreed on October 11, and Woodcock submitted the first draft in early November. Brzezinski reports that Chinese officials later told him that Beijing indeed drew the intended conclusion from Woodcock's action.[27]

The next step, according to Jimmy Carter's memoir, came in late November 1978. Washington sent Woodcock a final draft, "including the exact wording of three provisions which I knew would be difficult for the Chinese to accept": termination of the treaty, a unilateral statement on peaceful resolution, and continued arms sales. Deng Xiaoping responded with a draft that, in Carter's words, "contained unacceptable language concerning our future relations with Taiwan." Washington stuck to its text, Carter says, because it knew that the newly preeminent Deng was ready to enter the negotiations.[28]

Note, however, that the very three points that Carter's account says were in "the final draft" did not in fact appear in the final text of the communiqué itself. The original American intent was to address as many issues as it could in the communiqué itself. As Carter suggests, this was not possible. The solution was to use the communiqué to cover the easier points and to move all other issues to the ancillary statements. Each side, therefore, would speak to those matters in a way that it felt appropriate while coordinating those statements wherever possible.[29]

Deng and Woodcock met to discuss the communiqué and other documents on December 12 and almost came to closure. Woodcock informed Deng that the United States intended to terminate the treaty in accordance with its terms rather than abrogate it. As a result, the treaty would remain in effect until the end of 1979. In response, Deng asked that Washington sell no arms to Taiwan during that period. Woodcock soon conveyed Carter's agreement to that request, but only with respect to new obligations, and not to spare parts and systems in the pipeline.[30] Then at the last minute, there was concern that Beijing did not understand that arms sales to Taiwan would continue, and indeed thought they would be terminated. So Washington sent Woodcock in one more time to dispel any confusion. He repeated the president's formulation of September 19 but said that U.S. officials would publicly discuss the issue only if asked. Deng was reportedly furious, saying that China was absolutely opposed to continued arms sales. He agreed to go ahead with normalization only after Woodcock suggested that the subsequent transitional period would permit solving problems left over from history. But Deng did reserve the right to return to the issue and asked that arms sales be secret (Washington replied that the latter request was not feasible).[31]

Interpretation of the Text

The joint communiqué itself had three major purposes. The first was to announce the joint decisions to extend mutual recognition and establish diplomatic relations as of January 1, 1979, and to establish embassies in each other's capitals on March 1. The second was to reaffirm and reemphasize principles established in the Shanghai communiqué. Third, the United States made several unilateral statements relevant to Taiwan. The elements relevant to the first purpose—recognition and so on—are factual and straightforward and require no discussion. Of more interest are the statements concerning the other two.

Regarding the reaffirmation of principles from the Shanghai communiqué, what is remarkable are the principles that are *not* reiterated. In the 1972 document the two sides pledged to apply to their bilateral relations the five principles of peaceful coexistence, including those of respect for sovereignty and noninterference in internal affairs. We argued above that the latter principle strengthened the impression that the United States agreed that Taiwan was an internal affair. The normalization communiqué, however, does not reaffirm it. Now that omission could be a function of the deadlock on arms sales (which was the main evidence of interference). But it could also reflect an American desire to distance itself from those principles and so reassert the idea that Taiwan would remain, even after normalization, a matter of international concern. I am inclined to believe the latter.[32]

Concerning the third issue—Taiwan—the Carter administration did three things *in the communiqué*. First of all, it recognized the government in Beijing as the sole legal government of China, thus ending the view that the government in Taipei possessed that status, and, by use of the word "sole," dissociated itself from a two-China solution. Furthermore, Washington pledged that, "within this context, the people of the United States will maintain cultural, commercial, and other unofficial relations with the people of Taiwan." (The term "other" was understood by the United States to include arms sales.)

Most interesting was the formulation in the English text concerning Taiwan's legal status—whether the island belonged to the state called China. Above, we noted that elements of the Shanghai communiqué suggested that the United States was tilting toward the view that the island was a part of

China. And we know that Nixon in private made an explicit statement to that effect. The drafting of the normalization communiqué was cleaner than the Shanghai document, stating that "the Government of the United States of America acknowledges the Chinese position that there is but one China and Taiwan is a part of China." The text is clear, removing the ambiguity that sloppy drafting had introduced into the Shanghai communiqué. Note in particular that what the United States acknowledged was "the Chinese position," not "China's position" nor "the PRC position." Moreover, there was no discussion of the outcomes that China opposed that the United States did not challenge in the Shanghai communiqué. There is no suggestion in the English text that Washington itself accepted the view that title over Taiwan belonged to China. It merely acknowledged the Chinese position.

However, this shift in the communiqués is somewhat less significant than it might appear, for Brzezinski during his May 1978 trip to Beijing had reaffirmed "Nixon's five points," one of which was that the United States accepted that Taiwan was a part of China. To be sure, the points in a communiqué are a more significant expression of U.S. policy than the assurances of a national security adviser. Still, the formulation in the communiqué did not contradict Brzezinski's statement. Whether President Carter reiterated that statement during Deng's visit to Washington in early 1979 is an interesting question.[33]

The alert reader will have noted the reference to the *English* version of the text. That is because the Chinese text on the Taiwan question is not a precise equivalent of the English one. The verb in Chinese—*chengren*—is properly translated "recognizes" rather than "acknowledges." The object of that verb is *Zhongguo de lichang*—"China's position"—and not the deliberately vague "Chinese position" of the English version. Recall, moreover, that in both the English and Chinese versions the United States "recognized" the government of the PRC as the sole, legal government of "China." The inference in the Chinese version is that the United States recognized the PRC's position that Taiwan was a part of China.

Even in Chinese, however, the statement is a bit odd. An accurate English translation of the Chinese version is: "The Government of the United States recognizes China's position that there is but one China and Taiwan is a part of China." But the formulation that would most favor Beijing would be "The Government of the United States recognizes that there is but one China and Taiwan is a part of China." There is a subtle difference here (between recognizing a fact and a position about that fact), one that might devalue the purported power of the word *chengren.* Still, Beijing might well say that this is a distinction without a difference. Moreover, it would probably claim that the Chinese text is controlling.

Experts have come to conflicting conclusions about what all this means. On one side are those who stress continuity between the Shanghai communiqué and the normalization communiqué and believe that the United States was saying basically the same thing about the status of Taiwan in each document. They write off the differences between the two to sloppy drafting in the former and better construction in the latter. On the differences in translations between the two texts of the normalization communiqué, they point to the Carter administration's assertion that the English version of the normalization communiqué was controlling. For example, "acknowledge" trumps *chengren* and "Chinese position" outweighs *Zhongguo de lichang*. And, according to this point of view, the essential and unchanged *American* position was that Taiwan's status had yet to be determined. Washington had acknowledged the Chinese position on the issue but not announced its own.[34]

The contrary point of view is that something changed. That is, Washington had made a legal undertaking that it recognized that Taiwan was a part of the state called China. American assertions about the English text being controlling were just a subterfuge, and the Chinese text could and should be used to clarify ambiguities in the English. And for these experts, the Chinese text is very clear. The United States recognized the PRC as the government of China, and it recognized China's position that Taiwan was a part of it. QED.

Su Ge's history of the Taiwan issue in U.S.–China relations leans toward the former interpretation. As in the case of the Shanghai communiqué, he does not suggest that China believes that a significant change in the U.S. position on Taiwan's status occurred as a result of the normalization communiqué.[35]

There is a third explanation for these differences in translation, aside from the rush and fatigue of the negotiations. That is, each side allowed the other some terminological leeway in order to satisfy its substantive or political concerns. Washington accommodated China's desire for greater clarity in the Chinese text and Beijing allowed the United States to state a more ambiguous position in English. Like the issue of arms sales, perhaps, this was a problem that would take care of itself as the PRC and Taiwan resolved their differences.

If cross-strait differences were not quickly reconciled, however, such flexibility would sow the seeds for future trouble. If unification did not take place quickly, as was the case, the two sides could argue over whether the United States had acknowledged PRC sovereignty over Taiwan at the time of normalization. Beijing could say that it had and Washington could say that it had not. As long as there were sufficient shared interests to mute this matter, neither capital had an interest in exploiting the underlying disagreement. But if there were too few interests to share, then Beijing's temptation to assert its position would be irresistible. This was a scab that would never go away, easily scratched whenever there was a temptation to do so.

Ancillary Statements

As suggested above, ancillary statements became an essential part of the normalization bargain because the two sides could not agree on how to address certain key issues in the joint communiqué. Most significant in this regard was the U.S. security relationship with Taiwan, which had been the most difficult part of the negotiations of the Shanghai communiqué and had obstructed normalization during President Ford's term.[36] Indeed, this portentous issue, so central to PRC concerns about sovereignty and so neuralgic in the American political system, was not addressed at all in the charter document of the U.S.–PRC relationship. In the end, the two sides took care of it in ancillary documents and adopted the approach of the Shanghai communiqué, each stating its views in its own way while taking into account the other's concerns.

In their respective written statements, each side reiterated the facts concerning recognition and the establishment of diplomatic relations, and each pointed to the promise that normalization held for regional peace and stability. The PRC repeated some of the "principled" positions that it had expressed in the Shanghai communiqué on the Taiwan issue. For example, it reasserted that the PRC was the sole, legal government of China, that Taiwan was a part of China, and that the Taiwan issue was the "crucial issue" obstructing normalization.[37] Then it made what in retrospect is a rather remarkable statement: "It [the question of Taiwan] has now been resolved between the two countries in the spirit of the Shanghai communiqué and through their joint efforts."[38]

The United States used its unilateral statements for two purposes. The first was to outline the steps it would take in bringing about normalization. It pledged to meet Beijing's three conditions: breaking diplomatic relations with Taiwan; withdrawing U.S. military personnel and facilities; and terminating the defense treaty (but according to its terms). In its written statement, as in the communiqué, Washington pledged to conduct its relations with "the people of Taiwan" on an unofficial basis. In the written statement it said it would seek changes in domestic law to facilitate the new relationship.

The other purpose to which the Carter administration put its statement was to address Taiwan's future, particularly its security. The written statement asserted that "the United States is confident that the people of Taiwan face a peaceful and prosperous future. The United States continues to have an interest in the peaceful resolution of the Taiwan issue and expects that the

Taiwan issue will be settled peacefully by the Chinese people themselves."
President Carter's oral statement reiterated that expectation and tied it to the
relevant U.S. statement in the Shanghai communiqué. He added, "I have
paid special attention to ensuring that normalization of relations between our
country and the People's Republic will not jeopardize the well-being of the
people of Taiwan."

This was the "unilateral statement" by which the administration coped
with the PRC's refusal to make its own commitment of peaceful intent. Washington had received a commitment that Beijing would offer no overt contradiction, and indeed there was no immediate Chinese restatement of a refusal
to renounce the use of force. On the other hand, Beijing did address the issue
more subtly in its written statement by saying that, "As for the way of bringing Taiwan back to the embrace of the motherland and reunifying the country, it is entirely China's internal affair." This formulation was similar to the
principle that Beijing had enunciated in the Shanghai communiqué ("the liberation of Taiwan is China's internal affair in which no other country has the
right to interfere"). Saying that this was China's internal affair was also a
coded way of reserving the right to use force.[39]

Hua Guofeng entered this dialogue on Taiwan's security in his press conference. He emphasized that Beijing had repeatedly made clear that it could
not agree to continued U.S. arms sales to Taiwan, and that such sales were
inconsistent with the principles of normalization, the goal of "peaceful liberation," and with promotion of regional peace and stability. "Nevertheless,
we reached an agreement on the joint communiqué." Hua needed to explain
to his domestic audience why Taiwan would still have a security lifeline to
the United States, particularly since the written PRC statement had asserted
that "the question of Taiwan," the crucial obstacle, "has now been resolved."[40]

How significant was the U.S. unilateral statement? Did it—and the PRC's
lack of a direct rebuttal—represent an implicit renunciation of the use of
force? Or was it simply the Carter administration's way of dealing with political opposition to normalization in the United States? And did the PRC in
fact not contradict the statement? The Carter administration placed considerable emphasis on the formula after normalization and Carter himself remained
convinced of its significance (as displayed in a conversation with me twenty
years later). Yet there is evidence that American policy makers saw the use
of force question not so much as an issue of principle but as a domestic
political problem. Kissinger had emphasized the need for manipulating American public opinion when he sought a PRC nonforce pledge. Vance in August
1977 referred to the "negative reaction in the United States" that various
PRC statements on liberation by force evoked. Brzezinski took the same
approach in May 1978. He acknowledged that the resolution of the Taiwan

issue was a Chinese problem but then sought Chinese help for Carter. "We have certain domestic problems and certain historical legacies which we will have to overcome. These are complex, difficult, and in some respects very emotional issues. That is why we will have to find some formula which allows us to express our hope and our expectation regarding the peaceful resolution of the Taiwan issue." Nowhere was there an indication that this was a foreign policy problem rather than a domestic political one.

The PRC side approached the matter in a similarly instrumental fashion. Deng replied to Brzezinski in May 1978 that "each side could express its own opinion. The Chinese would say that how and when they liberated Taiwan was an internal problem to be solved by the Chinese themselves. We [the United States] could express our views." In reply, Brzezinski accepted the idea of two statements but noted they could not be in *direct* contradiction (that is, they could indirectly contradict each other). Right after normalization, Deng held a press conference in which he not only reiterated that Taiwan was an internal affair but said also that Beijing would not renounce the use of force. As to Carter's expectation that the matter be resolved peacefully, Deng said that China would "take note" of it.[41]

Arguably, the approach of the normalization documents to the use of force against Taiwan did not constitute a solution to the underlying problem. The United States could claim—as was done later in the Taiwan Relations Act— that normalization was premised on the expectation of a peaceful solution. But the thrust of the PRC statement on the issue was that the United States could expect all it wanted, but this was Chinese business and Chinese business alone.

And yet I would argue that there is another unilateral PRC statement at the time of normalization that should be added to the written government statement and Hua Guofeng's press conference. That is the January 1, 1979, statement on Taiwan by the Standing Committee of the National People's Congress (NPC). We know that this document was in the works in early December, because Deng told Woodcock about it during their December 12 meeting. And it is possible that Deng had intended to make that statement public on the original target date for announcing normalization (January 1). If that were the case, then the NPC statement would serve as a positive response to the Carter expectation. That the NPC statement was not proclaimed on December 15 is readily explained by the fact that it was only on December 14 that the two sides agreed to advance the normalization announcement to the next day.[42]

The NPC statement reflected a new and more political approach to the Taiwan Strait issue. This can be seen not only in the word used to describe the outcome: the goal now was the "reunification of China" rather than the "liberation of Taiwan." But it was not just words alone. Specific steps and proposals were also included.

- Beijing announced the end of the every-other-day ritual bombardment of the offshore islands and proposed discussions to end the state of confrontation between the two sides "so as to create the necessary prerequisites and a secure environment for the two sides to make contacts and exchanges in whatever area."
- The PRC proposed to open cross-strait trade, transportation, postal links, travel, and exchanges.
- The Beijing leadership pledged to "take present realities into account . . . and respect the status quo on Taiwan and the opinions of people in all walks of life there and adopt reasonable policies and measures . . . so as not to cause the people of Taiwan any losses.

Thus were sowed the seeds of the one-country, two-systems formula for solving the Taiwan Strait question. To be sure, the government and people of the island have never accepted this approach. Yet the NPC statement reflects Deng's decision to search for a political solution to the issue so that military force would not be necessary. Although Beijing would continue to reserve the right to use force against Taiwan, shifting the focus of its efforts to the terms on which China would be reunified politically was a significant step forward, one that was generically consistent with the "expectation" of the United States.

In sum and substance, we can conclude that the Carter administration *fully* satisfied only one of its original conditions for normalization: to continue cultural, economic, and other relations with "the people of Taiwan" on an unofficial basis. On the other two, the results did not completely meet U.S. hopes. On arms sales, Washington asserted its intention to continue arms sales but at least some in Beijing were under the impression until the last minute that arms sales would cease. In the end, China disagreed with the U.S. position and Deng therefore reserved the right to reopen the issue, which happened in 1981.[43] On the use of force against Taiwan, the United States announced its expectation of a peaceful solution. The PRC did not directly contradict that statement but did so implicitly; it also soon declared a new, political approach to "reunification."

The Taiwan Relations Act, Spring 1979

The third "sacred text" to be examined was not a joint communiqué between the executive branches in Washington and Beijing but an act of the U.S.

Congress. Even for an unofficial American relationship with Taiwan after normalization, legislation was necessary to create the legal authority for its conduct and institutions. But the members of Congress used that necessity to express themselves concerning Taiwan's security and arms sales. They did so partly because they believed that the normalization approach to those issues was inadequate, partly because they resented what they saw as failure to consult by the administration, and because the White House understood that Congress would want to make its own contribution to normalization. Yet those congressional actions were less than meets the eye.

Crafting the Act

The Carter administration had anticipated early on the need for legislation to facilitate unofficial relations with Taiwan. For example, loans from the Export-Import Bank, guarantees from the Overseas Private Investment Corporation, and sales of enriched uranium for power reactors are restricted by law to friendly countries, a status that Taiwan would arguably cease to have after derecognition. There were more than sixty treaties and agreements between the United States and Taiwan whose status after normalization was a question mark.

So one month after Cyrus Vance's visit to Beijing in August 1977, Richard Holbrooke, assistant secretary of state for East Asia, tasked Harvey Feldman, director of the Office of ROC Affairs, with preparing alternative arrangements. In secret, Feldman was to create a system "whereby all essential U.S. ties with Taiwan could be maintained, but in the absence of any official American office." At this stage, Feldman conceived of an organization in Taipei that would have no official name but that would carry out the same functions as did the existing embassy. He recognized that this organization would need a Washington-based counterpart office and that there would have to be some way to detach government officials to serve in the Taipei office. Thus was born what was to become the American Institute in Taiwan (AIT).[44]

In November 1977, Feldman set aside his work because the Carter administration was focused on other issues. Then one year later the effort resumed. Feldman and Lee Marks, the senior deputy legal adviser in the State Department, jointly chaired a group that drew up the text of the bill that served as the basis for the Taiwan Relations Act.[45]

Once the administration's bill was introduced, it was subject to the regular legislative process. It was referred to the committees of jurisdiction: House Foreign Affairs and Senate Foreign Relations. Those bodies then developed their own texts, which were based on the administration version but which also addressed concerns from inside and outside the Congress. Some members had introduced legislation that sought to remedy the absence of provisions on Taiwan's security. American businessmen offered suggestions to ensure that private, commercial relations with Taiwan would continue unimpeded. These concerns found their way into the TRA.[46]

The two committees considered these bills in markup sessions, where members had the opportunity to offer amendments, in order to deal with remaining problems or to weaken or toughen the committee texts. Once the bills were reported out of committee in late February, a similar process occurred on the floor of the House and Senate. The House passed its version on March 13 and the Senate on the next day. Then a House–Senate conference committee, made up of senior members of the two committees of jurisdiction, considered the amended bills in order to reconcile the differences between the two. The work of the conference committee was reflected in the report it sent to the House and Senate, which approved the report on March 28 and 29, respectively. Throughout this process, the Carter administration worked behind the scenes with its allies on Capitol Hill to remove restrictive language if possible and block efforts to impose constraints on its freedom of action.

Interpretation

To provide, twenty-plus years after the fact, a blow-by-blow account of the Congress's consideration of the bill that became the TRA would exceed both the limits of space and the reader's interest.[47] Instead, we shall begin by comparing the administration bill and ultimate TRA, in order to demonstrate the areas of congressional interest and to suggest that Congress made adjustments only at the margins. Then we shall provide a longer analysis of the security sections of the TRA plus the sections on international organizations and the application of laws, in order to demonstrate that the legal impact of the TRA is less than is often claimed.

A comparison of the bill introduced for the administration and the act that ultimately became law reveals several categories of changes.[48] Most of the changes were additions; Congress regarded the initial bill as incomplete but not inherently defective. Some of the emendations were fairly technical in nature. For example, members sought to ensure that the absence of diplomatic relations did not infringe Taiwan's legal rights and obligations in U.S. courts nor affect its ownership of property. (The latter protection was particularly important with respect to Twin Oaks, which had been the official residence of Taiwan's ambassador.) They also wanted to ensure that state or local law did not impede the work of the American Institute in Taiwan, and that it would be exempt from taxes.

Other changes were more substantive, but even here there were a variety of concerns. Of greatest significance were the provisions concerning policy issues like Taiwan's security, its membership in international organizations, and human rights, some of which will be discussed below. Second, Congress imposed several reporting requirements to ensure oversight of the implementation of the Taiwan Relations Act. Third, members sought in three areas to make explicit what was implicit in the administration's bill. In the section concerning the continued application of U.S. laws and programs to Taiwan, it made specific reference to activities under the Atomic Energy Act, the continued application of the Immigration and Naturalization Act, and Taiwan's eligibility for the programs of the Overseas Private Investment Corporation. It "approved" the continuation in force of treaties and agreements with Taiwan unless otherwise terminated. The enacted TRA was more specific concerning the activities that the American Institute in Taiwan was authorized to undertake, particularly in the consular area. And the final bill "requested" the Executive Branch to allow the Taiwan counterpart organization to the AIT to have the same number of offices in the United States as there were consulates before normalization and "authorized" the president to grant privileges and immunities to the personnel of the Taiwan organization.[49]

These provisions were not inconsistent with the thrust of the Executive Branch's draft. Some might argue that they were unnecessary and marginal in their impact. Indeed, provisions whose operative verbs were "approved," "requested," and "authorized" had no binding impact. The additions were less significant than they appear. Yet given the mistrust that Congress felt toward the administration because of the latter's failure to consult broadly before the normalization decision and given the concerns of businessmen involved in U.S.–Taiwan trade, it was perhaps inevitable that Congress would chose clarity over vagueness on how it felt the new relationship with Taiwan should be conducted.[50]

The security section of the TRA is composed of a declaration of policy, in subsections 2 through 6 of section 2(b), and provisions concerning the implementation of policy, section 3.[51]

Some of the policy statements are consistent, to some extent, with the statements of the administration. Subsection 2 declares that peace and stability in the Western Pacific are in the interests of the United States, but then goes on to say that they are matters of "international concern" (that is, not just an internal affair of China). Subsection 3 expands on the administration's stated "expectation" of a peaceful resolution, by saying that the normalization decision clearly rests on that expectation (i.e., there is an explicit linkage). Subsection 5 pledges continued provision of defensive arms (an issue the administration had addressed only on an if-asked basis).

Subsections 2(b)(4) and 2(b)(6) plus section 3(c) go further than the administration by creating something of an analogue to the defense treaty, which was to lapse at the end of 1979. The three elements of this analogue were as follows:

- It was U.S. policy to consider any effort to determine the future of Taiwan by other than peaceful means, including by boycotts or embargoes, a threat to the peace and security of the Western Pacific area and of grave concern to the United States.[52]
- It was U.S. policy to maintain the capacity of the United States to resist any resort to force or other forms of coercion that would jeopardize the security, or the social or economic system, of the people on Taiwan.
- In the event of a threat to the security or the social or economic system of Taiwan (as well as a resulting danger to the United States), the president was "directed" to inform Congress promptly. The president and Congress were to determine, "in accordance with constitutional processes," the appropriate U.S. response.[53]

It is important to distinguish the ways in which this package of provisions exceeded or fell short of the defense treaty (the relevant provisions are placed side by side in Box 5.3). On the positive side, whereas the treaty spoke only of armed attack, the TRA expands the number of contingencies that might trigger a U.S. response ("any effort . . . other than peaceful means, including by boycotts or embargoes"). Moreover, the TRA built in a stronger role for Congress than was explicitly stated in the treaty.

However, the TRA was deficient in a couple of important respects. Most important, the provisions concerning triggering PRC actions and the maintenance of capacity to resist coercion were only statements of policy, whereas the treaty had binding force. Experts on legislative construction note that when statements of policy are expressed as facts—rather than as prescriptions for action—they have no such binding force.[54] Moreover, the treaty stated that an attack on one party would be regarded by the other party as a danger to its own peace and safety, and not just a matter of grave concern. Also, the treaty was more definite that the party not attacked "would act to meet the common danger." The TRA only states a U.S. policy of having the capacity to resist coercion against Taiwan, not an explicit commitment to use that capacity. Of course, the treaty's reference to constitutional procedures left open the possibility that

Box 5.3
The Taiwan Relations Act and Taiwan's Security

Mutual Defense Treaty	Taiwan Relations Act
Each Party recognizes that an armed attack in the Western Pacific Area directed against the terri-tories of either of the Parties would be dangerous to its own peace and safety . . .	Sec. 2 (b) It is the policy of the U.S. (4) to consider any effort to deter-mine the future of Taiwan by other than peaceful means, including by boycotts or embargoes, a threat to the peace and security of the West-ern Pacific area and of grave con cern to the U.S.; . . . [and]
and declares that it would act to meet the common danger . . .	(6) to maintain the capacity of the United States to resist any resort to force or other forms of coercion that would jeopardize the security, or the social or economic system, of the people on Taiwan.
in accordance with its consti-tutional processes.	Sec. 3 (c) The President is directed to inform the Congress promptly of any threat to the security or the social or economic system of the people on Taiwan and any danger to the interests of the U.S. arising therefrom. The President and the Congress shall determine, in accordance with constitutional processes, appropriate action by the United States in response to any such danger.

Congress might block an administration's desire to respond. Yet the bias of the treaty is on the side of action; that of the TRA is less clear-cut.

Constitutional scholar Richard Pious goes so far as to conclude that, "in operational terms, the United States has no real commitment to the security of Taiwan, or even to its 'social and economic system.' What it has, accord-ing to the terms of the Act itself, is a process by which the United States may recognize and act upon its own security interests. That is all the Taiwan Re-lations Act requires."[55]

On arms sales, the TRA prescribes the following:

Sec. 3 (a) In furtherance of the policy set forth in section 2 of this Act, the U.S. will make available to Taiwan such defense articles and defense services in such quantity as may be necessary to enable Taiwan to maintain a sufficient self-defense capability.

(b) The President and the Congress shall determine the nature and quantity of such defense articles and services based solely upon their judgment of the needs of Taiwan, in accordance with procedures established by law. Such determination of Taiwan's defense needs shall include review by U.S. military authorities in connection with recommendations to the President and the Congress.

By way of background, it is useful to consider the original House and Senate positions that were eventually reconciled into the above provisions. The House said that the United States will make available to Taiwan conventional defense articles and services "of modern technology in such quantity as can be effectively utilized for Taiwan's defense." Furthermore, the House "required" the Executive Branch to ensure that arms-sales decisions be made without regard to PRC views and include a review by U.S. military authorities. The Senate stated that the United States "will assist" Taiwan to "maintain a sufficient self-defense capability" by providing arms of a defensive character.

The compromise that emerged from the conference melded elements of these two positions.

- Concerning the objective of U.S. arms sales, the House agreed to the Senate position: maintenance of a sufficient self-defense capability. That was a more general standard than the idea of effective utilization. It was also more vague.
- Concerning what should be transferred, the Senate accepted the House's use of the phrase "defense articles and services," which is a term of art used to refer to any security assistance. In the process, the Senate gave up the more specific reference to "arms of a defensive character (which was closer to the Carter administration's pledge to the PRC), and the House abandoned the phrase "of modern technology," not a trivial concession.
- Concerning the process by which arms-sales decisions would be made, the Senate accepted the House's language with a couple of modifications. It dropped a direct prohibition on considering the PRC's views, but left an implicit reference ("The President and the Congress shall determine . . . based solely upon their judgment of the needs of Taiwan"). It also incorporated the phrase "in accordance with procedures established by law," which, as we shall see, was a significant change.

Reading between the lines, the conference committee's abandonment of the phrases "of modern technology" and "effectively utilized" and its retreat to the term of art "defense articles and services" reveals Congress's *initial* purpose: to legislate U.S. arms-sales policy and constrain the flexibility of the Executive Branch. Indeed, at the time that Congress was drafting the TRA, many members wanted the legislation to state explicitly what the United States should supply to Taiwan. According to the late Senator Jacob Javits, key members of the House and Senate, angered by the minimal reference to arms transfers in the administration's draft bill, advocated "provisions that would . . . have committed the United States to automatic large-scale transfer of military equipment."[56] In the end, that was not done and Congress retreated to vaguer formulations about what Taiwan should receive.

Moreover, the two provisions enacted have less impact than they seem to on the surface. Take first of all the initial part of section 3(a). In U.S. legislative practice, if Congress wishes to require an action by the executive, it uses the word "shall." To say that "the United States will make available to Taiwan such defense articles and defense services" represents less a mandate for action than it does a statement of intention.[57]

Second, there is a substantive ambiguity concerning what precisely the United States should provide Taiwan. The policy statement in section 2(b)(5) of the TRA and the Carter administration's pledges to Beijing refer to defensive weapons. Section 3(a) of the TRA speaks of defense articles (as noted, a term of art) that ensure a self-defense capability for Taiwan. Yet there is a case to be made that if the island were attacked the most effective defense would be attacks on air, missile, and naval bases on the Chinese mainland, which would require weapons of a tactical offensive capability.

Third, as noted, the requirement that U.S. government decisions on arms sales to Taiwan be based solely on the executive-congressional judgment of the needs of Taiwan was written in order to exclude a PRC voice in such decisions (as was specifically addressed in the House bill). What Congress may have forgotten—or not known in the first place—was that Beijing had reserved the right to reopen the arms transfer issue. Consequently, this provision was in potential jeopardy from the moment it was enacted.

Fourth, there is no indication either in the legislation itself or in the accompanying documents and statements (the legislative history) to clarify how the U.S. government should go about deciding, in a substantive sense, what Taiwan's needs were. Obviously, U.S. sales to Taiwan would vary tremendously depending on the criteria used to gauge its requirements. For example, the U.S. judgment might be based on PRC intentions, on PRC capabilities, or on both. Similarly, what Washington might be willing to provide would vary according to how much weaponry it expected Taiwan to produce on its own and purchase elsewhere. And Taiwan's needs for military hardware would be an inverse function of the probability of a political settlement—which would reduce the need for arms.

Finally, there is an ambiguity in the arms transfer provision of the TRA about the respective decision-making roles of the executive and legislative branches. The wording "the President and Congress shall determine" weapons transfer to Taiwan suggests a greater than normal congressional role. That was certainly what Taiwan's friends in Congress thought. At a House Foreign Affairs Committee hearing on November 8, 1979, Representative Robert Lagomarsino told Deputy Secretary of State Warren Christopher, "As the [TRA] states . . . this body and specifically this committee take a direct interest in the nature and quantity of arms sold to Taiwan and intend to be a full partner in any decision made on this matter."[58]

However, the statement "the President and Congress shall determine" is balanced—and probably negated—by the phrase "in accordance with the procedures established by law."[59] According to congressional staff members who worked on the TRA, there was no effort to establish extraordinary procedures for decisions on Taiwan arms sales. Moreover, a General Accounting Office report on the TRA concluded that the act "as written does not give Congress a voice in determining Taiwan's defensive arms needs earlier in the decision-making process" than otherwise required by law.[60] These are references to the Arms Export Control Act, which requires that the Executive Branch *inform* Congress of arms sales very late in the process (only after a letter of offer and acceptance was issued) and even then only for transfers above a certain value.

Recall that the phrase "in accordance with the procedures established by law" was not included in the House version of the bill, which is the only one that addressed the decision-making process. By including this phrase, Congress was taking itself out of that process, and giving the Executive Branch substantial discretion regarding what Taiwan's needs were and what specific weapon systems to provide. Moreover, Congress took itself out of the loop in a manner that violated at least the spirit and probably the letter of its own legislative rules. A House–Senate conference is not supposed to go beyond the limits set by the bills that each house passed, and any compromises should remain within those limits. Since the House in its provision did not address the applicability of existing law for arms-sales decisions concerning Taiwan, the conference was technically not in a position to do so. Why it made such a significant change has never been clarified, but it is reasonable to speculate that the administration encouraged its allies in Congress to undercut their own institution and that they did so.

In short, the TRA does not *mandate* the sale of arms to Taiwan because it is not self-enforcing in either a substantive or procedural sense. In drafting the TRA, Congress failed to make clear the meaning of the phrase "necessary to enable Taiwan to maintain a sufficient self-defense capability" and retreated on the issue of how Congress was to be a decision-making partner with the executive. Having passed a law that reaffirmed the administration's existing prerogatives concerning arms sales, Congress would have to assert itself politically if it wished to influence what defense equipment Taiwan received.[61]

Friends of Taiwan have made claims about two other parts of the TRA that exceed an objective reading of the text. The first has to do with the application of U.S. law to relations with Taiwan. Section 4(a) dictates that the absence of diplomatic relations or recognition shall not affect the application of the laws of the United States to Taiwan, and that U.S. law shall apply as it did before normalization. Section 4(b)(1) says that "whenever the laws of the United States refer or relate to foreign countries, nations, states, governments, or similar entities, such terms shall include and such laws shall apply with such respect to Taiwan."

The argument is made that these provisions constitute acknowledgment by the United States that Taiwan is in fact a country or nation and that its governing authority is a state under international law. That is a stretch for two reasons. First, the purpose of these two provisions is technical, not substantive. It is to provide clear guidance on whether Taiwan is eligible to participate in U.S. government programs as authorized by Congress. If a law, such as the Arms Export Control Act, refers to a "friendly country" as the recipient of U.S. security assistance, is Taiwan eligible? These provisions open doors for Taiwan but do not by themselves confer the status of country or state under international law. The second reason is more practical: that these provisions were based on the draft bill provided *by the administration.* Its objective was to preserve the substance of relations with Taiwan on an unofficial basis, and not to confer a recognition of statehood through the back door.

The second claim concerns section 4(d): "Nothing in this Act may be construed as a basis for supporting the exclusion or expulsion of Taiwan from continued membership in any international financial institution or any other international organization." It is asserted that at least the spirit of this provision is that the United States should take affirmative action to support Taiwan's entry into international organizations. Yet a close reading of the text itself does not justify that conclusion. Note first of all that the focus of this provision is Taiwan's "continued membership" in international organizations. That is, it arguably concerns organizations of which Taiwan was a member at the time the TRA was passed. Second, the provision does not order the Executive Branch ("the President shall . . .") to do anything. It simply absolves the TRA, and by implication the Congress, from any responsibility in Taiwan's expulsion from international organizations ("Nothing in this Act may be construed as a basis for supporting . . ."). Again, there is the hint that Congress thought it should address this issue, but ended up doing so in a way that had no legal effect.

The Arms Sales Communiqué, August 1982

It will be recalled that at the time of normalization, the Carter administration had firmly stated its intention to continue arms sales to Taiwan and the PRC had just as firmly stated its view that Carter's intention was unacceptable. Deng Xiaoping reserved the right to reopen the arms-sales issue at a later time, and his determination to do so was probably heightened by passage of the Taiwan Relations Act, the pending possibility of U.S. sales of the F-X fighter to Taiwan, Ronald Reagan's campaign statements before the election of November 1980, and mounting internal attacks on Deng's policies around the same time.

Deng had a clear-cut perspective on the role of arms sales in resolving the Taiwan issue. As he expressed it in his fractious December 15 meeting with Woodcock, if Taipei continued to get arms from the United States, it would have no incentive to negotiate. If Taipei refused to negotiate, then Beijing would have to use force. Thus if the United States wanted the Taiwan issue resolved without force, it should deny Taipei the means to defend itself. (Likewise it mattered little to Deng whether U.S. arms were offensive or defensive; it was transfers of any kind that were the problem.) This logic was no doubt grounded in traditional Chinese statecraft and in the Communist Party's experience in the civil war. Force was unnecessary in situations like the early 1949 siege of Beiping once the Nationalist armies under ROC general Fu Zuoyi lost all hope. It ignores the possibility that Taiwan would negotiate only when it had a certain sense of security.[62]

National reunification was one of Deng Xiaoping's three major objectives, and in his mind U.S. arms sales were a key obstacle. He set out to remove it and the August 1982 communiqué was the end result of his effort.

Crafting the Document

Deng's campaign began with Secretary of State Al Haig's trip to Beijing in June 1981. Deng told him that arms sales had to end or relations would suffer. The demand became sharper and more specific in the fall, when Premier Zhao Ziyang met Reagan in Cancún and Foreign Minister Huang Hua met with Haig in both Cancún and Washington. Zhao offered good news, that Beijing was about to announce a new initiative on unification (the nine-point formula of Marshal Ye Jianying). Huang provided the bad news: "In order to lay to rest the issue of American arms sales to Taiwan, . . . the United States must specify the period of time over which it intended to sell arms to Taiwan, undertake that sales in any given year would not exceed the level of the Carter years, and indicate that sales would decline year by year and then cease." In Washington, Huang reiterated the need for the United States to set a date by which arms sales would end. Haig rejected both that demand and Huang's allegation that the United States was trying to create two Chinas. But he did agree to Huang's suggestion of negotiations on the issue and, to the surprise of his staff, pledged that arms sales would not increase in quantity or quality, and would be less than the highest level reached during the Carter administration. Reagan reportedly approved that formulation, and talks began in December.[63]

It was during the January 1982 visit to Beijing of John Holdridge, now assistant secretary of state for East Asia, that the United States tabled a draft communiqué on the arms-sales issue. The draft was composed of "a list of principles" that Reagan had approved and that Washington "believed could form the basis of a joint communiqué settling the Taiwan question once and for all." Holdridge told PRC officials that the United States hoped to conclude the negotiations by the time of the tenth anniversary of the Shanghai communiqué in late February, but no later than August, the time at which a key arms-sales notification would have to be made to Congress. He also informed Beijing that Washington would not sell the F-X fighter to Taiwan but that it would replace aging or worn-out items in Taiwan's air inventory to maintain its defenses at current levels.

As far as substance was concerned, the draft communiqué included Haig's October pledge that U.S. arms sales would not exceed the highest levels of the Carter administration in quality or quantity. It also reiterated the Carter commitment that only defensive weapons would be sold (an element that later dropped out). But the draft also linked future reductions to China's continuing the policy of not using force to reunite Taiwan with the China mainland. There was no reference to a "date certain" for cutting off arms sales because, Holdridge said, the TRA mandated that sales should be based on Taiwan's needs, hence the linkage to PRC policy. In the weeks that followed, new drafts of the communiqué were exchanged, but progress was slow because the PRC rejected the linkage to nonuse of force, on the grounds that this was an internal affair.[64]

Vice President George H. W. Bush's May trip to Beijing accelerated movement toward a compromise. At this point, there began the exploration of a link between the existing PRC declaratory policy and U.S. arms sales. In advance of the visit, Reagan sent letters to Zhao Ziyang, CCP General Secretary Hu Yaobang, and Deng Xiaoping. All three letters had a sentence saying the United States "fully recognizes the significance" of the January 1979 statement and the Ye nine points. Holdridge claims in his memoir that this amounted to a "linkage of sorts" between arms sales and peaceful reunification. In the Zhao letter, moreover, Reagan said "We would expect that in the context of progress toward a peaceful solution, there would be a decrease in the need for arms by Taiwan." Need, of course, is the TRA criterion governing arms-sales decisions. Bush himself did not push the negotiations beyond this point, except to pledge that the TRA could and would be implemented in a manner consistent with the normalization communiqué. Deng did not budge from his demand that the United States set a date for the end to arms sales. But the vice president may have convinced Deng that the Reagan administration wanted to resolve the issue. In any event, the PRC presented a new draft soon after Bush's departure.[65]

On June 29, Haig resigned as secretary of state. In one last effort, he urged Reagan to lean in the direction of ending arms sales but the president refused. Given Haig's relatively pro-PRC stance, his departure reduced the U.S. inclination to make more concessions. Indeed, when the draft of the communiqué was circulated at this point among a wider circle of policy makers, they sought to toughen it. For example, in Haig's memoir, a key sentence of the draft reads "The United States does not seek to carry out a long-term policy of arms sales to Taiwan and affirms the *ultimate objective* of ending arms sales to Taiwan." In the final version, the second clause does not appear. On July 14, Ambassador to China Arthur Hummel presented the U.S. "final offer," with a warning that the notification for the F-5E sale was imminent. The next day, the PRC abandoned its demand for a date certain. The endgame had begun and drafts flew between the two capitals on a daily basis.[66]

Although a number of significant points remained unresolved, the Reagan administration knew that it now possessed relatively greater leverage. Beijing sought a U.S. commitment to "phase out" but Washington refused. PRC negotiators wanted the United States to say that arms sales would "progressively decline" but Washington only agreed to use the term "reduce gradually" in the English version; the Chinese version is closer to the Chinese desire. Beijing tried to clarify how the United States would set the baselines for the quantity and quality of future sales. Washington refused and informed PRC negotiators that it would take inflation into account and reserved the right, if it were not possible to provide replacements to Taiwan because they were no longer in American inventories, to provide a qualitatively superior one. The

United States tried to get the PRC to say that its "peaceful policy" was irreversible but soon backed off. Washington did insist on a connection between the PRC declaratory policy and U.S. arms sales; the PRC accepted use of the phrase "Having in mind the foregoing statements of both sides" as the link. The two sides agreed on a final text on August 16, and the State Department drafted the supplementary statement that Reagan issued at the same time that the communiqué was released.[67]

Interpretation

Of the three communiqués, the 1982 document is the one whose substantive logic is the most focused. The Shanghai communiqué made a virtue out of the disagreements between Beijing and Washington. The normalization communiqué was more instrumental, both codifying the American acceptance of the PRC's conditions on Taiwan and reasserting fundamental interests concerning a peaceful settlement. Examined carefully, the text of the 1982 communiqué contains a structure that is more integrated than its predecessors and a logic that is more explicit.

John Holdridge, the architect of the 1982 communiqué, asserts that by the end of the negotiations, "each side had moved very close to the position desired by the other." China stuck to its position that Taiwan was an internal affair but made explicit reference to its "fundamental policy" of seeking peaceful reunification. The United States interpreted the term "fundamental policy" to mean "unchanging and long-term," and thus felt justified in making a pledge to reduce arms sales. Holdridge concludes: "Beijing's commentary to the contrary notwithstanding, we did achieve a form of linkage between Chinese adherence to a peaceful reunification policy and U.S. actions." Conversely, a change in China's policy would affect U.S. arms sales to Taiwan.[68]

Let us set aside the question of whether the United States *or* the PRC has faithfully and strictly abided by the terms of the communiqué. After all, it is more a political statement of mutual restraint than an arms control agreement, since the terms were never defined. As pledges of mutual restraint, the document did shape the actions of the two capitals for a significant period of time. But there is more going on in the text itself than the sort of convergence and linkage that Holdridge claims.

The communiqué begins with several statements that purport to establish the factual background. The first paragraph reiterates the U.S. statements in the normalization communiqué that recognized the PRC government as the sole legal government of China and acknowledged "the Chinese position" that there was one China and Taiwan was a part of China. It also states that "the two sides agreed" the people of the United States would maintain commercial, cultural, and other unofficial relations with the people on Taiwan. All that is perfectly true, but with two qualifications. First, the Chinese-language version of the 1982 communiqué, like the 1979 document, permits the interpretation that the United States acknowledges the *PRC's* position—rather than the more ambiguous "Chinese position"—that Taiwan is a part of China. Second, the normalization communiqué did not speak of an agreement on unofficial relations with Taiwan; instead, the United States made a unilateral pledge to that effect. The revision suggests implicitly that Beijing is party to the agreement and so has a say in what constitutes acceptable U.S.–Taiwan relations (for example, whether or not arms sales were included in the word "other").

The second paragraph provides more factual background and also states the problem the communiqué is designed to address. That is, the issue of arms sales to Taiwan "was not settled in the course of negotiations. . . . The two sides held differing positions, and the Chinese side stated that it would raise the issue again following normalization." Furthermore, the two sides recognized that the matter "would seriously hamper the development of United States-China relations." They therefore held further discussions, beginning with the Reagan–Zhao meeting in Cancún.

This account is a skewed version of history, written from Beijing's point of view. Such an account ignores the fact that Carter directly informed Chai Zemin in September 1978 that arms sales would continue, and that the negotiations on normalization proceeded anyway. It also overlooks that Deng asked only for a moratorium on arms sales during the period that the U.S.-ROC defense treaty would remain nominally in effect but not, by implication, thereafter. The impasse became obvious when Woodcock, under orders and at the last minute, made it absolutely clear to Deng that sales would continue. Moreover, all American accounts of the negotiations say that Deng "reserved the right" to reopen the issue, not that he committed to doing so. On Deng's visit to Washington, he restated his opposition to arms sales but asked Carter to show restraint.[69] (Obviously, the Chinese government view of the events of late 1978 may be different from that of the United States, but that is no reason to accept its formulation.) Also, American accounts indicate that the Reagan–Zhao meeting ended before the arms-sales issue was discussed. Finally and most egregiously, why should the United States accept the point that not resolving the arms-sales issue "would seriously hamper the development of United States–China relations"? Just because Beijing thought so was no reason for Washington to agree.

The third paragraph states the principles that should be the basis for a solution to the problem. Specifically, "respect for each other's sovereignty and territorial integrity and non-interference in each other's internal affairs constitute the fundamental principles guiding United States–China relations." The 1982 communiqué notes that these principles were confirmed in the 1972 and 1978 documents. Moreover, "both sides emphatically state that these principles continue to govern all aspects of their relations."

These principles of course have appeared before. They were indeed a part of the Shanghai communiqué and the two sides agreed to apply them to their "mutual relations." But it is patently false that they were "confirmed" in the normalization communiqué (their absence was probably deliberate on the U.S. side) and that they therefore somehow "continue" to be applicable. True, they did appear in the Shanghai communiqué and one might justifiably ask which of the first two documents takes precedence, since one contained the principles and the other did not. Arguably, the normalization communiqué should, since it came later and since it governed the establishment of diplomatic relations. In short, for the United States to have restored these principles in the 1982 communiqué, and for it to have joined the PRC in "emphatically" stating that they "continue to govern all aspects of their relations" constituted a major concession by the Reagan administration, all the more so in light of the reiteration of the U.S. acknowledgment of "the Chinese position" that Taiwan was a part of China.

With both factual background and basic principles now misstated, the communiqué lays out, as in the Shanghai precedent, the positions of each of the two sides. The fourth paragraph presents the PRC position: that Taiwan is China's internal affair and that China has promulgated a "fundamental policy" of striving for peaceful reunification through the January 1979 message to compatriots in Taiwan and the nine-point proposal of September 1981. This paragraph has two purposes. The first is to reiterate the PRC view that, in effect, the United States has no right to meddle in the Taiwan issue, since it is internal and since the United States has "emphatically state[d]" that it will be guided by the principle of noninterference. The unstated corollary is that U.S. arms sales are a form of unacceptable interference. The second purpose is to establish that PRC intentions are consistent with the U.S. expectation that the matter be resolved peacefully.

But note the calculated way in which Beijing stated its position. First of all, it carefully described its goal as "*striving* for peaceful reunification." Pregnant in that phrase is the idea that reunification on a peaceful basis might not be possible despite PRC efforts and through no fault of its own. As Deng had indicated to Carter in January 1979, the mainland would be justified in a resort to force if Taiwan refused over a long period to negotiate. And, as we have seen, Deng regarded U.S. arms sales as a major disincentive for Taipei to negotiate.[70]

Second, Beijing did not offer a wholly new undertaking in the communiqué but merely referred to the 1979 and 1981 statements as evidence of its "fundamental policy." Those were good statements of intentions, but they did not necessarily provide a sufficient basis for restrictions on arms sales. The 1979 document was remarkable for its use of the word "reunification" for the first time (as opposed to "liberation") and the end of the ritualized shelling of the offshore islands. But the word "peaceful" did not even appear. The 1981 statement did include the word in its title and was more detailed in its proposal for reunification but it did not address security issues at all. Moreover, the word "peaceful" has a limited meaning in Beijing's lexicon—the absence of force. The intense coercion that brought the fall of Beiping in 1949 was peaceful because Fu Zuoyi gave up without a fight, in part because he lacked the means to do so. By analogy, restricting arms to Taiwan would make Taipei more pliable.

Third, there is a minor problem in the translation of the phrase, "fundamental policy," on which Washington placed so much emphasis as justification for its own commitments on arms sales.[71] The Chinese version is *dazheng fangzhen*. The word *fangzhen* refers to policy at the level of general principle or, simply, to principle (in contrast to *zhengce*, specific policy). The term *dazheng* (literally "great politics" or "great governmental affairs") is odd because it does not appear in any of the most common Chinese dictionaries published before the communiqué.[72] The word for "fundamental" that a second-year Chinese-language student would have offered is *jiben*. Indeed, the best Chinese term of this sort that would convey *in substance* the PRC undertaking the Reagan administration *claimed* to have secured is probably *jiben fangzhen yu zhengce*: fundamental general principles and specific policies. The presence of the obscure term *dazheng* suggests that Beijing actually wished to avoid making such a commitment, at least in Chinese. For the English text, it permitted words that helped Washington make its case.

The communiqué continues with the statement of the U.S. position. It begins with a series of contextual statements concerning:

- its recognition of the importance of U.S.–PRC relations;
- its disavowal of infringing on Chinese sovereignty, territorial integrity, or interference in Chinese internal affairs, of pursuing a policy of "two Chinas" or "one China, one Taiwan";
- its "understanding and appreciation" of the PRC's policy of striving for peaceful reunification as evidenced by the 1979 and 1981 statements; and

- its belief that the "new situation" regarding Taiwan provides "favorable conditions" for settlement of the arms-sales issue.

Each of these statements is peculiar. The first puts the United States in the position of supplicant, both because the PRC has not itself stated its appreciation of the importance of U.S.–PRC ties and partly because both sides had already acknowledged that failure to solve the arms-sales issue would hamper their relationship. The second sentence is redundant because the U.S. side already "emphatically stated" that the sovereignty, territorial integrity, and noninterference principles would govern "all aspects of their relations." The last part of this sentence (rejecting a two Chinas or one China, one Taiwan policy) has no antecedent in the text and is a response to an implied accusation that Washington was pursuing just such a policy.[73] The third sentence, through the use of the words "understands and appreciates," conveys a rather obsequious attitude toward PRC policy, as if that was all that was necessary to justify the U.S. undertaking on arms sales. The final sentence arguably exaggerates the newness of the situation by imputing more significance to Beijing's policy than is warranted.

Also significant is the statement that the United States *did not* make. Nowhere does it "reaffirm its interest in a peaceful settlement of the Taiwan question by the Chinese themselves," as in the Shanghai communiqué, or state its "expectation" that the matter will be resolved peacefully, as in Carter's normalization statement. Insisting on the inclusion of text along these lines *in the communiqué* would seem justified. The PRC had secured the reinclusion of the sovereignty and noninterference principles, which had been dropped in the normalization communiqué. Also, the 1982 document was about arms sales, and some reiteration of U.S. expectations would seem justified. Instead, the Reagan administration was willing to address the use-of-force issue merely by acknowledging the PRC proposals (Reagan did reiterate the U.S. expectation in his own statement released at the time of the communiqué).

Moreover, this whole paragraph seems unnecessary to the key bargain of the 1982 communiqué, that the United States would show greater restraint on arms sales in light of the PRC's stated policy of striving for peaceful reunification. If this paragraph had been left out, it would take only minor stylistic adjustments for the document to fully capture that purpose. Why therefore was it included? Without access to the negotiating record, a definitive explanation is not possible. But the only sensible reason is that Beijing wanted the communiqué to do more than state this basic bargain. By its substance, the paragraph achieved a second purpose important to the PRC: to secure an implicit admission by the United States that it had acted in a manner inconsistent with the principles underlying their relationship and oblivious of Beijing's generous approach to the Taiwan issue.

Thus the underlying meaning of the 1982 communiqué and its rather curious tone become clear. Beijing wished to use this document not just to establish a loose bargain of mutual restraint concerning Taiwan's security. It also wished to establish its moral superiority and to extract what amounts to a confession from the United States, a reaffirmation of the principles that it believed should guide the U.S.–PRC relationship, and an American commitment to act properly in the future. That is brought home in the first sentence of the next paragraph: "Having in mind the foregoing statements of *both sides.*" That is, the American undertaking would be premised not just on the PRC's affirmation of its policy, which is what American observers usually stress, but also on its own "reaffirmation" of past principles and its appreciation for PRC policy.

The American commitment on future actions had three elements. First was a denial on any intent of a long-term arms-sales policy. Second was capping the quality and quantity of Taiwan arms sales at the post-normalization level. Third was a gradual reduction of weapons sold, "leading over time to a final resolution."

This terminal phase is intriguing because the term "final resolution" is so vague. Does it mean an end of arms sales or resolution of the Taiwan issue? The PRC claimed the former, and the United States the latter. But there was a further gloss on the matter. The United States "acknowledged" ("recognized" in Chinese) China's consistent position regarding "the thorough settlement of this issue." Moreover, the two sides pledged to "adopt measures and create conditions conducive to the *thorough settlement* of this issue." To what do the words "this issue" refer? The communiqué applies the English words "issue" and "question" to both the arms-sales question and the broader Taiwan issue (the Chinese term *wenti* is used for both). But they apply in four cases to the arms-sales matter and twice to Taiwan more generally. Implicitly, therefore, the United States tilted a bit more than it admitted in the direction of ending arms sales. This was another case of statements that were unnecessary for the basic bargain but gave the PRC politically useful text without Washington's getting anything in return.[74]

Unilateral Statements

As soon as the 1982 communiqué was released, Washington and Beijing each issued unilateral statements to provide their perspective on it (extracts are presented in side-by-side form in Box 5.4). Where the statements

Box 5.4
The August 1982 Communiqué and Associated Documents

Communiqué: Joint Statement

In the Joint Communiqué on the Establishment of Diplomatic Relations on January 1, 1979, issued by the Government of the United States of America and the Government of the People's Republic of China, the United States of America recognized the Government of the People's Republic of China as the sole legal government of China, and it acknowledged the Chinese position that there is but one China and Taiwan is a part of China. Within that context, the two sides agreed that the people of the United States would continue to maintain cultural, commercial, and other unofficial relations with the people of Taiwan. On this basis, relations between the United States and China were normalized.

The question of United States arms sales to Taiwan was not settled in the course of negotiations between the two countries on establishing diplomatic relations. The two sides held differing positions, and the Chinese side stated that it would raise the issue again following normalization. Recognizing that this issue would seriously hamper the development of United States–China relations, they have held further discussions on it, during and since the meetings between President Ronald Reagan and Premier Zhao Ziyang and between Secretary of State Alexander M. Haig, Jr., and Vice Premier and Foreign Minister Huang Hua in October 1981.

Respect for each other's sovereignty and territorial integrity and noninterference in each other's internal affairs constitute the fundamental principles guiding United States–China relations. These principles were confirmed in the Shanghai Communiqué of February 28, 1972, and reaffirmed in the Joint Communiqué on the Establishment of Diplomatic Relations which came into effect on January 1, 1979. Both sides emphatically state that these principles continue to govern all aspects of their relations. . . .

In order to bring about, over a period of time, a final settlement of the question of United States arms sales to Taiwan, which is an issue rooted in history, the two governments will make every effort to adopt measures and create conditions conducive to the thorough settlement of this issue.

The development of United States–China relations is not only in the interests of the two peoples but also conducive to peace and stability in the world. The two sides are determined, on the principle of equality and mutual benefit, to strengthen their ties in the economic, cultural, education, scientific, technological, and other fields and make strong, joint efforts for the continued development of relations between the governments and peoples of the United States and China.

Box 5.4 *(continued)*

In order to bring about the healthy development of United States–China relations, maintain world peace, and oppose aggression and expansion, the two governments reaffirm the principles agreed on by the two sides in the Shanghai Communiqué and the Joint Communiqué on the Establishment of Diplomatic Relations, the two sides will maintain contact and hold appropriate consultations on bilateral and international issues of common interest.

Parallel Statements

Communiqué

PRC	United States
The Chinese Government reiterates that the question of Taiwan is China's internal affair.	The United States Government attaches great importance to its relations with China, and reiterates that it has no intention of infringing on Chinese sovereignty and territorial integrity, or interfering in China's internal affairs, or pursuing a policy of "two Chinas" or "one China, one Taiwan."
The Message to Compatriots in Taiwan issued by China on January 1, 1979 promulgated a fundamental policy of striving for peaceful reunification of the Motherland. The Nine-Point Proposal put forward by China on September 30, 1981, represented a further major effort under this fundamental policy tostrive for a peaceful solution to theTaiwan question.	The United States Government understands and appreciates the Chinese policy of striving for a peaceful resolution of the Taiwan question as indicated in China's Message to Compatriots in Taiwan issued on January 1, 1979 and the Nine-Point Proposal put forward by China on September 30, 1981. The new situation which has emerged with regard to the Taiwan question also provides favorable conditions for the settlement of United States–China differences over the question of United States arms sales to Taiwan.
	Having in mind the foregoing statements of both sides, the United States Government states that it does not seek to carry out a long-term policy of arms sales to Taiwan, that its arms sales to Taiwan will not exceed, either in qualitative or in quantitative terms, the level of those supplied in recent years

Box 5.4 *(continued)*

since the establishment of diplomatic relations between the United States and China, and that it intends to reduce gradually its sales of arms to Taiwan, leading over a period of time to a final resolution. In so stating, the United States acknowledges China's consistent position regarding the thorough settlement of this issue.

Unilateral Statements

PRC

United States

The joint communiqué reaffirms the principles of respect for each other's sovereignty and territorial integrity and noninterference in each other's internal affairs as embodied in the Shanghai communiqué and the joint communiqué on the establishment of diplomatic relations between China and the United States. Both sides also emphatically state that these principles continue to govern all aspects of their relations. That is to say, the question of U.S. arms sales to Taiwan must be settled on these principles.

Arms sales will continue in accordance with the [Taiwan Relations] Act and with the full expectation that the approach of the Chinese government to the resolution of the Taiwan issue will continue to be peaceful.

The U.S. side has committed that, as the first step, U.S. arms sales to Taiwan will not exceed, either in qualitative or in quantitative terms, the level of those supplied in recent years since the establishment of diplomatic relations between the two countries, and that they will be gradually reduced, leading to a final resolution of this issue over a period of time. The final resolution referred to here certainly implies that U.S. arms sales to Taiwan must be completely terminated over a period of time. . . .

Arms sales will continue . . . with the full expectation that the approach of the Chinese government to the resolution of the Taiwan issue will continue to be peaceful.

In the joint communiqué, the Chinese government reiterates in clear-cut terms its position that "the question of Taiwan is China's

We attach great significance to the Chinese statement in the communiqué regarding China's "fundamental" policy; and it is clear from our

Box 5.4 *(continued)*

internal affair." The U.S. side also indicates that it has no intention of infringing on Chinese sovereignty and territorial integrity, or interfering in China's internal affairs, or pursuing a policy of "two Chinas" or "one China, one Taiwan." The Chinese side refers in the joint communiqué to its fundamental policy of striving for peaceful reunification of the motherland for the purpose of further demonstrating the sincere desire of the Chinese Government and people to strive for a peaceful solution to the Taiwan question. On this issue, which is purely China's internal affair, no misinterpretation or foreign interference is permissible.

It must be pointed out that the present joint communiqué is based on the principle embodied in the joint communiqué on the establishment of diplomatic relations between China and the United States and the basic norms guiding international relations and has nothing to do with the "Taiwan Relations Act" formulated unilaterally by the United States.

The "Taiwan Relations Act" seriously contravenes the principles embodied in the joint communiqué on the establishment of diplomatic relations between the two countries, and the Chinese Government has consistently been opposed to it. All interpretations designed to link the present joint communiqué to the "Taiwan Relations Act" are in violation of the spirit and substance of this communiqué and are thus unacceptable.

statements that our future actions will be conducted with this peaceful policy fully in mind. The position of the United States Government has always been clear and consistent in this regard. The Taiwan question is a matter for the Chinese people, on both sides of the Taiwan Strait, to resolve. We will not interfere in this matter or prejudice the free choice of, or put pressure on, the people of Taiwan in this matter. At the same time, we have an abiding interest and concern that any resolution be peaceful. I shall never waver from this *fundamental* position.

Regarding future arms sales to Taiwan, our policy, set forth clearly in the communiqué, is fully consistent with the Taiwan Relations Act.

Box 5.4 *(continued)*

Needless to say, only by strictly observing these principles in dealing with the existing or new issues between the two countries will it be possible for their relations to develop healthily.

The U.S.–China Joint Communiqué issued today embodies a mutually satisfactory means of dealing with the historical question of U.S. arms to Taiwan. This document preserves principles on both sides, and will promote the further development of friendly relations between the governments and peoples of the United States and China. It will also contribute to the further reduction of tensions and the lasting peace in the Asia/Pacific region.

accompanying the normalization communiqué manifested textual disagreement within conceptual consensus, the 1982 statements reflected rather fundamental conceptual conflict. More than the other two communiqués, this one immediately prompted different interpretations of what the text meant. Among the points of divergence were the following:

- On the rationale for the reduction of U.S. arms sales, the PRC statement asserted that the arms-sales issue was governed by the principles of respect for each other's sovereignty and territorial integrity and noninterference in each other's internal affairs, that the communiqué had reaffirmed these principles, and that they "emphatically" would continue to govern all aspects of their relations. Furthermore, the Chinese side asserted that its policy of peaceful reunification was an "internal affair" and that "no misinterpretation or foreign interference is permissible." President Reagan's statement said that arms sales would continue with the full expectation that the PRC approach would continue to be peaceful, and that Washington attached great significance to PRC statements on its "fundamental policy."
- On the meaning of the term "final resolution," the Chinese statement asserted that it "certainly implies" that arms sales would end over a period of time. Reagan's statement applied the word "resolution" only to the Taiwan issue in general and Holdridge's congressional testimony denied that a termination date had been set.
- On the relationship of the communiqué to the TRA, the PRC statement said that any linkage between the two was a violation of the communiqué

and therefore unacceptable. Reagan, however, stated that U.S. policy as set forth in the communiqué was fully consistent with the TRA, in accordance with which arms sales would continue.

The United States had two other ancillary statements. The first was a set of assurances that were conveyed to the government of Taiwan in advance of the communiqué's release. These were proposed by Taiwan's representative office in Washington, in the expectation that they would guide future U.S. relations with the island. The Reagan administration agreed, and they were transmitted to Taiwan in July and to Congress in August. The United States pledged that it had not agreed to set a date for ending arms sales; had not agreed to hold prior consultations with the PRC on arms sales; had not agreed to revise the Taiwan Relations Act; had not altered its position regarding sovereignty over Taiwan; would not play any mediation role between Taipei and Beijing; and would not exert pressure on Taiwan to enter into negotiations with the PRC. In offering these "six assurances," Washington sought not only to allay Taipei's anxiety regarding the focus of the communiqué (arms sales) and its concern that Washington's overall Taiwan policy was moving in a direction that undermined Taiwan's fundamental interests, but also to manage the political fallout from the communiqué, both in Taiwan and Congress.[75]

The second American commentary on the 1982 communiqué occurred in the hearings that Senator John East called to consider whether the communiqué —an Executive Branch initiative—had on its terms negated or superseded the arms-sales provisions of the Taiwan Relations Act, an act of Congress. In the end, Senator East's subcommittee on separation of powers chose to avoid a constitutional conflict. It concluded that although the language of the communiqué was inconsistent with the TRA, and although the administration had not offered clear and consistent accounts of the communiqué and its legal implications, it still had "repeatedly articulated an interpretation of these policy statements that is generally consistent with the Taiwan Relations Act." In addition, in answer to questions submitted by the subcommittee, the State Department provided an important legal position on whether Taiwan was subject to PRC sovereignty: that is, the U.S. government took no position on Taiwan's sovereignty. That was a matter to be resolved by the two sides of the strait.[76]

The American policy makers who negotiated the 1982 communiqué deserve some sympathy, particularly if one keeps the broader context in mind. Even though they may have exaggerated the strategic value of China, the relationship with the PRC was important at the time for anti-Soviet and other reasons. Without question, it was in the commercial and humanitarian interest of the United States that Deng Xiaoping continue his reform agenda and improve the welfare of the Chinese people. Moreover, Haig, Holdridge et al. did not create the controversy over Taiwan arms sales. It was a product of the 1980 campaign and the expectations that candidate Reagan fostered on both sides of the strait. And it was also fueled by Deng Xiaoping's skewed understanding of the relationship between military power and negotiations, and his total misunderstanding of the dynamics of election politics. Focusing on the text, however, it is hard to avoid the conclusion that the United States gave away too much for the sake of harmony with its obstreperous partner. Having contributed to the flaws of the Shanghai communiqué, Haig and Holdridge were willing to accept those flaws and more in the 1982 document—to the point that it was infused with a moral asymmetry uncommon in diplomatic documents—in order to get the United States out of the jam in which Ronald Reagan had placed it.

Conclusion

These four documents remain interesting and revealing even decades after their completion. To the extent that they are read today at all, the focus is usually on key passages, usually concerning Taiwan. But there is no attention to other parts of the documents to which those passages are linked (the hidden hinges), or to comparisons of specific issues from one document to another (as in the different versions of the TRA, and between the 1972 and 1982 communiqués on the one hand and the 1978 one on the other). Nor is notice given to *where* important issues are addressed (in the communiqué itself or the accompanying documents), or to the issues that are not addressed when they probably should be, or to the degree to which each side took account of the political needs of the other in crafting the texts. Also ignored are differences in tone, from the unapologetic enunciation of conflicting positions in the Shanghai communiqué (with the PRC side being more strident), to the spare instrumentalism of the normalization document, to the moral asymmetry of the 1982 effort. It is only through this kind of *explication de texte* that such subtleties emerge. In the process, we see revealed the push and pull of the negotiations, the conflicting political priorities that the struggle over words exposes, and the occasional sloppiness that creeps in when negotiators are under pressure and too close to their work.

Our review of how the three communiqués were crafted demonstrates that three different U.S. administrations had a similar approach to negotiations. That is, they made major concessions to the PRC up front and then tried to get Beijing to yield on issues important to Washington. Thus, in the

Shanghai communiqué, Kissinger told Zhou Enlai much of what he wanted to hear on the Taiwan question in July 1971, offered language on Taiwan's status in the October discussions, and at some point accepted PRC language on the five principles of peaceful coexistence without considering the implications. Then he had to scramble at the last minute to secure acceptable language on Taiwan's security. In the normalization discussions, the Carter administration accepted Beijing's requirements on termination of the formal U.S. relationship with Taiwan, and chose to rely on a unilateral statement on peaceful resolution of the Taiwan question that Beijing more or less did not challenge. On the arms-sales communiqué, the Reagan administration accepted almost immediately the idea of a cap on arms sales and soon accepted the idea of reductions geared to future PRC behavior. But the PRC was very grudging in the linkage it would allow to its approach to Taiwan.

These "sacred texts" are not, of course, the sum and substance of the U.S.–PRC–Taiwan relationship. Yet they do serve as important points of reference and, in the case of the TRA, a number of instructions to the Executive Branch. The commitments that they embody are not trivial. If the United States were to act in ways that were obviously contrary to the commitments in the communiqués, the PRC would no doubt consider changing the relationship. If, for example, Washington recognized and set up diplomatic relations with the government in Taipei, Beijing would probably break relations with the United States. If, contrary to section 3(c) of the TRA, the president failed to inform Congress that Taiwan was under threat from the PRC when it clearly was, Congress might well undertake action to bend the president to its will. These documents create at least a set of constraints on Washington's and Beijing's behavior.

As important, or perhaps more important, than the words in the three communiqués is whether the U.S.–PRC relationship is serving the interests of the two countries. If either Beijing or Washington (or both) acts in ways that in some way conflict with the fundamental interests of the other, it matters little whether it is otherwise observing the tenets of the three documents. If the Congress concluded that the Executive Branch was pursuing a course that was dangerous to Taiwan, it would matter little if the administration was acting within the guidelines of the TRA. On the other hand, if the United States chose to take an action that was arguably inconsistent with one of the communiqués but Beijing was otherwise satisfied with the benefits of the relationship, it might overlook the transgression. The same tolerance is true of the Congress.

Beijing's fixation on the three communiqués does present a curiosity. No other government has sought to so anchor a foreign policy relationship in a set of documents, particularly texts into which it sought to infuse such a clear moral component. We can only speculate on the answers. The emphasis on words in traditional Chinese culture surely must be one reason. The moral component of Chinese statecraft is a likely second. Most important, probably, is China's substantial relative weakness vis-à-vis the United States. The three communiqués and the principles that they contain serve as an instrument with which the PRC can try to control the behavior of the United States, a stronger power. For example, the U.S. statement in the 1982 communiqué that the principle of noninterference in internal affairs would govern "all aspects" of its relations with China becomes a rhetorical weapon that Beijing can use to object to a variety of American actions that it does not like, such as complaints about the PRC's human rights record. That Beijing seeks to use documents and their principles to restrain Washington is perhaps one reason that there were no communiqués after 1982.

Power asymmetries are also at work in the relationship between Congress and the Executive Branch. Congress transformed the draft of the Taiwan Relations Act in order to constrain the administration from jeopardizing Taiwan's security and well-being. Here too, the effort did not necessarily succeed, for the act's words say less than meets the eye, and verbs and qualifiers become all important in determining how binding a particular provision is on the Executive Branch. The sections bearing on Taiwan's security (arms sales and the defense commitment) become less legal requirements than statements of political commitment that need constantly to be renewed. Unless Congress continues to define what it believes the TRA means in constantly changing circumstances, the Executive Branch will provide its own definition.

Yet the greatest power asymmetry concerns the parties that were most affected by the three communiqués but did not have a seat at the negotiating table. These were the ROC government and the people of Taiwan. The government of the United States in three different administrations made commitments to the PRC that bore on the status of the Taipei government and on the long-term fate of the island's people, with little or no consultation with the former and at best modest concern for the latter. Based on our analysis, Kissinger and Nixon tilted in the direction of accepting the PRC view that Taiwan was a part of China, and barely avoided making serious mistakes in getting to that conclusion. All three administrations waited until late in the negotiating process to address the issue of the PRC's use of force and got very little for their efforts. Any reassurance for Taiwan came after the fact. (In the case of one manifestation of reassurance, the TRA, there was a somewhat different dynamic. Congress enacted provisions that seemed on the surface to strengthen Taiwan but did not in fact do so in a legal sense.)

The American undertakings in the three communiqués were of course Washington's to make, based on its definition of its interests. And there was a strategic value to the rapprochement with China that Nixon began, Carter completed, and Reagan preserved. (One may ask, of course, which side had most to gain from the alignment, which side therefore possessed the greater leverage, and which side got the better of the bargain.) As we have seen in the previous chapter, moreover, Chiang Kai-shek did not help the ROC's cause by his rigid adherence to principle in the face of changing power realities. The problem, of course, was that the people over whom Chiang and his son ruled had no voice whatsoever in the process and were left at the mercy of the American negotiators. It is interesting to speculate, counterfactually, whether the United States would have acted differently had the democratization of Taiwan already occurred at the time that Washington and Beijing negotiated the three communiqués. That Taiwan is a democracy today is perhaps another reason that there have been no communiqués since 1982.

6

Congress Gets into
the Taiwan Human Rights Act

Through the early 1970s, as we have seen, the United States paid only limited and sporadic attention to the Republic of China (ROC) government's human rights practices. By and large, reforming Taiwan's political system was not on the U.S. agenda because other goals were more important. Moreover, when human rights was an issue it was one between the U.S. Executive Branch and the Taiwan Executive Branch. There were, of course, instances when American members of Congress showed an interest in the subject. Wayne Morse raised questions during the Senate's consideration of the mutual defense treaty in 1955 and Lei Zhen's daughter mobilized congressional support in 1960. But those interventions tended to be private and limited in duration.

The year 1977 represents the beginning of a new trend. This was the year of the first congressional hearing on human rights in Taiwan, the first time that the issue was discussed publicly and at length. The session was convened in June by Representative Donald Fraser (D-MN), chairman of the Subcommittee on International Organizations and Movements of the Committee on International Relations. It was the beginning of a halting process by which selected members of Congress changed the role of their institution in U.S.–Taiwan relations and so changed the game when it came to human rights. To be sure, the ROC's friends in Congress opposed this development but they could not stop it. And because some in the Taiwan leadership understood the need for political reform, they would point to external criticism as one reason Chiang Ching-kuo should begin the process of liberalization. In the end, congressional pressure alone was far from sufficient to bring about democracy in Taiwan, and it was not even the most important factor. Without pressure from reformist elements within the Kuomintang (KMT) and *dangwai* (people outside the party) confrontation from without, nothing would have happened. Yet American congressional criticism of the KMT was not trivial.

Nor was that criticism inevitable. In retrospect, three things happened that made it more likely. First was the increasing salience of human rights as an issue in American foreign policy during the 1970s. Second was a decision by the Taiwanese-American community to pursue a congressional strategy. Third was the right combination of institutional power and personal initiative by one member of Congress.

Background

The Rise of Human Rights

The Fraser hearing on Taiwan was only one of a large number that he convened, using the power of his subcommittee chairmanship in order to push the human rights issue higher on the agenda of U.S. foreign policy. Indeed, he had held close to a hundred hearings by the time of the session on Taiwan. Fraser's rationale was simple: "Protection of human rights is essentially the responsibility of each government with respect to its own citizens; however, when a government itself is the perpetrator of the violations, the victim has no recourse but to seek redress from outside his national boundaries. Men and women of decency find common cause in coming to the aid of the oppressed despite national differences. Through their own governments and international organizations, they have both the opportunity and responsibility to help defend human rights throughout the world. . . . The human rights factor is not accorded the high priority it deserves in our country's foreign policy. . . . [Yet] consideration for human rights in foreign policy is both morally imperative and practically necessary."[1]

Supporting Fraser's challenge to the policy status quo was the emergence of a large number of human rights nongovernmental organizations (NGOs) in the United States. Some had their roots in churches, whose missionaries witnessed the repression of other governments firsthand. Others focused on specific countries. Still others sought to rectify specific types of ills (thus Amnesty International addressed the problem of prisoners of conscience). After years of lobbying the United Nations, these groups come to conclude that the U.S. government should be the target of their activism, since it was powerful and the United Nations was not. Moreover, they believed, the American government was part of the problem because of its association with authoritarian governments. As a result, the NGOs came together and formed a coalition that sought allies in Congress like Fraser and Tom Harkin (D-IA). The groups provided like-minded members with information to expose human rights abuses overseas and supported their efforts to legislate restrictions on U.S. policy.[2]

The campaign to raise the salience of human rights was in part a political reaction to the *realpolitik* emphasis of the Nixon-Kissinger approach to world affairs, best exemplified in Kissinger's statement during his confirmation hearings for the post of secretary of state: "I believe it is dangerous for us to make the domestic policy of countries around the world a direct objective of American foreign policy. . . . The protection of basic human rights is a very sensitive aspect of the domestic jurisdiction of . . . governments." Congressional anger was only reinforced by the failure of the Nixon and Ford administrations to carry out enacted human rights legislation as Fraser and others thought they should.[3]

One specific fruit of this legislation was the State Department's annual report on human rights in countries around the world. In the early years, the individual reports were fairly brief. The one concerning Taiwan for 1976, for example, was only two pages long. But it provided enough information for the intelligent reader to know at least in capsule form that the people of the island lacked civil liberties and representative government.[4]

Yet this new emphasis on idealism over realism in American foreign policy did not necessarily mean that Taiwan would become a focus of American attention, for the NGO groups and their congressional allies made a strategic decision to focus on countries where the United States had military bases and gave substantial amounts of military and economic assistance. This made a certain sense because Congress was better able to influence policy when money had to be appropriated. But it was still a controversial step because it had the effect of sometimes leaving out Communist countries like the Soviet Union and China.[5]

Taiwan fit awkwardly into Fraser's set of priorities. True, the strategic rationale for tolerating KMT repression was losing its power. Richard Nixon and Henry Kissinger had made a radical reassessment of the strategic role of China, and concluded that the People's Republic of China (PRC) was no longer an adversary that might threaten U.S. interests in East Asia (the template of the 1950s and 1960s) but a potential partner in the containment of the Soviet Union. That being the case, Taiwan became less and less a geopolitical asset and more and more a domestic political inconvenience and there were thus fewer reasons to overlook the KMT's abuse of human rights. On the other hand, the Fraser emphasis on military aid and bases might have argued for ignoring the human rights situation on the island because by the mid-1970s the United States gave little aid to the ROC and had only a small military presence on the island. Moreover, the ROC still had a strong reservoir of support in the Congress, from the large number of members who wanted to protect Taipei as Washington moved to establish diplomatic relations with Beijing. Shining the light of publicity on the KMT's authoritarian regime was for them the wrong way to treat an embattled friend.

The Taiwanese-American Community

Another necessary condition for Congress's attention to human rights on Taiwan was stimulation from Taiwanese-American immigrants, the domestic constituency for whom it was the most important issue. Yet they took their time and made a false start before emphasizing a congressional strategy.

Taiwanese came to the United States in the 1950s and 1960s as students and most chose for political and economic reasons not to return to their homeland. As they put down roots, they also created organizations—Formosan Clubs—to foster group solidarity through social, cultural, and community welfare activities. Clubs around the country united in 1960 to form Formosan Clubs in America, which later evolved into the Taiwanese Association of America (TAA).

In 1955, Taiwanese in Philadelphia formed an explicitly political group, Formosans for Free Formosa (FFF). This group allied with the independence organization in Japan led by Thomas Liao, which was then the core of the overseas independence movement. In the early 1960s, under the leadership of history professor Chen Yide (Edward I-te Chen), FFF became a national organization named United Formosans for Independence. It soon combined with other like-minded groups to form the United Formosans in America for Independence (UFAI). Chen was part of a generational shift in the leadership from the older figures like Liao to students and young professionals, a shift that Liao's defection to the KMT in 1964 only accelerated. The UFAI network's main political activity seems to have been sponsoring demonstrations against the ROC government and in favor of an independent Taiwan.[6]

The next stage of organization came in January 1970 when, under the leadership of Cai Tongrong (Trong Chai / Ts'ai T'ung-jung), independence groups around the world joined together to form the World United Formosans for Independence (WUFI). (Cai was a native of Jiayi [Chiayi], one of the places where KMT repression was the worst after the 2-28 incident. Cai was in fifth grade at the time, and his teacher disappeared after actively opposing the Nationalist military.) WUFI sought to "organize the masses in Taiwan" in order to bring about a free, democratic, and independent Republic of Taiwan. It preferred to use peaceful means but would not rule out a "resort to armed struggle" as long as the KMT regime continued to use violence.[7]

UFAI, WUFI, and their supporters still faced a dilemma over how active to be in the United States. To some extent some activity was necessary. Holding demonstrations in American cities would bring publicity to the cause and mobilize its supporters. WUFI activists, for example, chained themselves to the gate at the United Nations in 1970 and 1971 in order to protest consideration of the Taiwan issue. There were American organizations with which Taiwanese could ally and movements from which it could learn. Amnesty International adopted Taiwan prisoners of conscience. The movement against the Vietnam War was a source of sympathy and ideas about political action. And beginning in the late 1960s there was a significant emphasis on what Taiwanese called "external affairs," seeking to influence the United States government, including Congress.

A key figure in congressional lobbying in these early days was Chen Longzhi (Chen Lung-chu). A native of Tainan and a lawyer by training, Chen had come to the United States in 1960 when he was twenty-five years old. He earned a law degree from Yale and then stayed at the university to collaborate with Harold Lasswell. The two wrote a book on Taiwan's representation at the United Nations, which earned Chen the label of traitor from the KMT regime.[8] Chen was drawn into UFAI and later WUFI, and was made responsible for external affairs because his Yale connections gave him a special entrée to Congress. He started with the office of Senator Abraham Ribicoff (D-CT), who gave him introductions to others like Senators Jacob Javits and John Sherman Cooper, and Representatives Donald Fraser, Morris Udall, and Jonathan Bingham. Chen was able to build a small, core group of members of Congress who shared his views. At his request, Representative Fraser put a statement in the *Congressional Record* and spoke to a Taiwanese rally at the Lincoln Memorial. As spokesman for WUFI, Chen also sought to secure media coverage for his cause. Yet resources were limited, and many Taiwanese feared to go public because of surveillance by the ROC security services.[9]

Parallel to Chen's lobbying, others in WUFI were more interested in fostering an opposition movement *in Taiwan* and engaging in direct political action against the KMT. This wing of WUFI operated clandestinely and sought to influence and manipulate the chapters of the Taiwanese Association of America. Two events would expose the contradiction between influencing American political institutions like the Congress and more direct attacks on the KMT. The first was the attempt in April 1970 to assassinate Chiang Ching-kuo outside the Plaza Hotel in New York City by Peter Huang Wenxiong (Huang Wen-hsiung), a WUFI member who was studying at Cornell. Although WUFI was cleared of any involvement as an organization in the attack, its association with Huang would give it an image problem for years. Chen Longzhi was unaware of the plot and so was caught off guard and immediately undercut. Senator Javits had been planning to introduce a resolution calling for self-determination for Taiwan, but quickly abandoned the effort. The resort to violence depleted sympathy for the Taiwanese cause.[10]

The second event was the ROC's departure from the United Nations. There ensued a debate within WUFI over whether "external affairs" was useful anymore. The clandestine wing of the organization successfully argued for a much greater focus on direct action and so each member had to choose whether he would continue the cause. Chen Longzhi decided at that point that it was better to work as a scholar than as a politician. Efforts to bring change in Taiwan by exerting influence in the American political system atrophied.[11]

Ironically, it was the attempt by ROC security services to monitor dissent *in the United States* in order to protect Nationalist orthodoxy that pushed new cohorts of Taiwanese-Americans to reenter the American political arena. Surveillance of Taiwanese students by agents of the KMT regime was not new, having begun in the 1960s. But it intensified in the early 1970s because of the attempted assassination of Chiang Ching-kuo; the Diaoyutai movement, which stimulated pro-PRC and pro-ROC students on American campuses to action and sometimes conflict; and the Nixon opening to China with the attendant prospect that the United States might abandon Taiwan.

In view of these developments, Taipei's security services stepped up surveillance—and sometimes intimidation and harassment—of Taiwanese students and activists on most major campuses and among community organizations. This effort was no doubt successful to some degree, in part because it was virtually ignored by the policy and counterintelligence agencies of the U.S. government.[12] But in the long run it backfired. It made more likely a decision among Taiwanese-Americans to move beyond their exile organizations and enter the political system, and to supplement or replace direct action in Taiwan with the exertion of leverage on American foreign policy. Taiwanese would, in a way, pick up where Lei Zhen's daughter had left off in 1960 and Chen Longzhi did in the early 1970s.

Yet that decision really did not come until 1982. In the mid-1970s, it was the initiative of Taiwanese individuals in the Washington area alone, not pressure from the broader community, that led Fraser to focus on Taiwan. Several of them, including Chen Tangshang (Mark Tan Sun Chen), approached Fraser's staff aide, John Salzberg, to acquaint him with the situation in their homeland. Simultaneously, Fraser's office received correspondence referred to it by Senator Alan Cranston (D-CA). Representative Fraser sent a letter to ROC Ambassador to the United States James Shen in March 1977 inquiring about the concerns, only to receive a propagandistic reply. In April, Salzberg traveled with a congressional delegation to Taiwan where he had an unproductive meeting on those same cases at the Taiwan Garrison Command. But without these two initiatives, the subcommittee might not have paid any attention to Taiwan at all.[13]

The hearing occurred two months later. The hearing report makes clear that the session had a number of features that would be repeated in later sessions. The State Department witness, in this case Burton Levin, sought to emphasize the ways that Taiwan was changing for the better. And if the basis of comparison was the late 1940s and early 1950s, when many foreign service officers like Levin were exposed to Taiwan, he was right; the situation had improved. But there was another standard, international norms, and James Seymour of New York University testified to all the ways in which the human rights situation in Taiwan did not meet that standard. He also mentioned the surveillance of Taiwan students on American campuses and warned that an ROC agent was even photographing the people who sought to attend the hearing. There were also competing Chinese and Taiwanese witnesses, some criticizing the government and some defending it. There was a letter from Senator Barry Goldwater that also defended the practices of the ROC government (which may have been responsible for stimulating the letter in the first place). And the hearing report included the March exchange of letters and the account of Salzberg's meeting at the Garrison Command. All the indicators of underground political combat were there.

But the hearing also placed on the public record, in an authoritative way that had never been seen before, extensive details of the practices of the Taiwan government. Perhaps because the Carter administration placed a higher priority on human rights as an objective of U.S. policy than had its predecessors, Levin offered candid responses to questions that Fraser had posed and made the following points:

- The police and security services at times used torture, harsh treatment, and psychological pressure on detainees.
- The government engaged in surveillance and harassment of the families and associates of those who opposed its basic policy.
- There were several hundred political prisoners, most of whom should be considered prisoners of conscience and whose average sentence was around ten years.
- Martial law gave the government broad powers to try a variety of crimes in military courts, to limit freedom of speech, political assembly, freedom of the press, and to prohibit strikes. Most human rights abuses had a legal basis in martial law.
- People suspected of sedition (including opponents of the regime) were detained, often incommunicado, for long periods of time without being charged or tried.
- The substance of due process in military trials was lacking.
- Elections for the legislature and national assembly did not give any possibility of representative government for the people of the island.

The Taiwan Relations Act

As significant as the 1977 hearing was both substantively and symbolically, the initiative was not sustained. Representative Fraser left the House of Representatives the next year to run for the Senate, and none of his colleagues immediately picked up the ball. The KMT's friends in Congress still held sway and most attention focused on the impact on the ROC of the Carter administration's policy toward China.

One member of Congress found the situation in Taiwan increasingly compelling. That was Jim Leach, who represented a district centered in Davenport, Iowa. A liberal Republican, a graduate of Princeton and the Johns Hopkins University School of Advanced International Studies, a former Foreign Service officer, and independently wealthy, Leach was first elected in November 1976. He had first learned about Taiwan's checkered history at Princeton and knew that the KMT was ignoring the democratic ideals that Sun Yat-sen had set for it (ideals that could still be a standard with which to judge the KMT). After taking office, he learned that a member of his staff, Cynthia Sprunger, had grown up in Taiwan as the daughter of Mennonite missionaries. Like the Presbyterians, the Mennonites focused their work on the Taiwanese majority and the two denominations had close relations. In the first half of 1977, at her father's request, Sprunger arranged a meeting between Leach and a Taiwanese Presbyterian clergyman living in England. He would be the first of a long line of Taiwanese visitors who sought out Leach's sympathy and support. Washington-area Taiwanese-Americans often accompanied these visitors. Some of them became regular interlocutors and provided Leach with information about current developments on Taiwan. But it was members of the Presbyterian Church, the largest independent organization on the island, who made the strongest initial impression.[14]

The normalization of relations between the United States and the People's Republic of China at the end of 1978 offered a new opening for Leach and other congressional critics of KMT repression. They sought to use the congressional drafting of the Taiwan Relations Act (TRA)—Congress's only contribution to the new policy toward Taiwan—to assert a priority for human rights in future United States policy. The leaders in this effort were Senator Claiborne Pell (D-RI), who had become sensitized to the aspirations of the Taiwanese majority as early as World War II, Leach, and Representative Donald Pease (D-OH), another human rights advocate. As Leach put it during the House floor debate, normalization had deprived the KMT of any lingering legitimacy and the only way to restore it was to seek the consent of the governed. Taiwanese-Americans worked with this group, testifying at a hearing that Pell chaired in early February, where they called on the U.S.

government to pressure the KMT government in Taiwan to improve human rights. They also lobbied other members.[15]

Yet the attempt to give a new priority to human rights and representative government on Taiwan was an exercise in frustration. What began as a legislative effort to require the American Institute in Taiwan (AIT) either to proactively promote these objectives or at least monitor progress toward them was progressively watered down by congressional friends of the ROC government and by the administration's allies. On the Senate side, Pell's original provision stated that "the Institute shall (that is, *must*) take all appropriate steps to strengthen and expand the ties" between the people of the United States "and those individuals and entities on Taiwan that are representative of the majority of the people on Taiwan"—that is, the Taiwanese majority. However, Senators Charles Percy and Jacob Javits convinced Pell to alter the provision before Senate consideration so that it merely "authorized" the AIT (that is, *permitted* it) to strengthen and expand ties with "all the people of Taiwan." It did further authorize the AIT to promote full human rights for "all the people of Taiwan" and to provide sufficient personnel and facilities for that purpose. But the committee report elaborated that this did not constitute a license to intervene in Taiwan's internal affairs, to favor any one particular group on the island, or to get involved in Taiwan's international status. Clearly, Pell's original intent had been deflected.[16]

There was a similar setback on the House side. Testifying at a hearing, Leach had urged that language be included requiring the AIT to monitor the level of political freedom, but he did not strike a responsive chord. Then during the markup of the legislation in the House Foreign Affairs Committee, Pease offered the text of the Pell amendment but it was rejected on a voice vote. On the House floor, Leach made a long statement that detailed the antidemocratic features of KMT rule and endorsed the Pell language in the Senate bill. Yet no one offered the Pell language as an amendment during the regular period for doing so. It was only at the very end of floor consideration that Representative Edward Derwinski (R-IL) used a legislative maneuver (namely, a motion to recommit with instructions) to insert language on human rights. Derwinski was a centrist but he was also a friend of Leach— the two served on the House Post Office and Civil Service Committee—and he reportedly was concerned that liberal support for the TRA was weak. With the support of both the Democratic and Republican leadership, he therefore offered this language at the very last minute in order to ensure a large bipartisan majority for final passage. His text was close to what was eventually adopted.[17]

In the House–Senate conference to reconcile differences between the two bills, Pell made an attempt to preserve his already watered-down text authorizing the AIT to include human rights on its agenda. The House side stood firm, with staff advising members that the Senate language would be seen as "a slap" at the Taiwan government and a mandate for AIT activism on Taiwan's internal affairs. The language in the bill as sent to the president read as follows: "Nothing contained in this Act shall contravene the interest of the United States in human rights, especially with respect to the human rights of all the approximately eighteen million inhabitants of Taiwan. The preservation and enhancement of the human rights of all the people on Taiwan are hereby reaffirmed as objectives of the U.S."

The conferees strengthened the Derwinski provision at the margin. He had referred to the president's policy (not to "the interest of the United States"), to the inhabitants of Taiwan (not to "all" the inhabitants). He had referred only to the "preservation" of human rights as a U.S. "commitment," rhetorically less than the final product. Yet despite these enhancements, the provision is quite weak, perhaps a device to give token satisfaction to members like Pell and Leach without having a tangible effect. The first sentence is rather empty, since there was no other part of the act that arguably did contravene the U.S. interest in human rights. The second sentence merely reaffirmed an objective for which historically little effort had been exerted and concerning which the TRA did not require any sort of action. The Taiwanese who hoped for specific provisions that would strengthen the AIT's role in promoting human rights in Taiwan and their friends in Congress were disappointed.[18]

Congress and the Kaohsiung Incident

As we saw in a previous chapter, the U.S. Executive Branch worked actively behind the scenes to moderate the Taiwan government's response to the Kaohsiung Incident. One reason that the administration's response was more aggressive and more sustained than had been the case in previous episodes of major human rights abuses by the KMT was the role of Congress.

Congress had been out of session when the incident occurred, and although members' offices had already begun to receive letters, it was not until early February that there was an opportunity for focused attention. That came in a House hearing convened jointly by the subcommittees on Asian and Pacific affairs and on international organizations. There were three sessions of this hearing between February 4 and 7, and Taiwan came up in two of them. On February 4, Richard Kagan, a history professor at Hamline University in Minnesota, testified solely regarding Taiwan. Representative Jim Leach testified on February 6, again only on Taiwan. Administration witnesses mentioned Taiwan briefly and factually in their statements on the whole region.

Unfortunately for critics of the Taiwan government, the focus of the hearing was not on the situation in individual countries but the process by which the State Department prepared the human rights reports and whether that process yielded an accurate picture. Kagan's testimony did cover the Kaohsiung Incident, including the assertion that the government had instigated the riot, and he did call for a suspension of arms sales to Taiwan. But most of his statement addressed the subcommittees' questions concerning process.[19]

Representative Leach's testimony did focus on the Kaohsiung Incident, and he warned that harsh sentences for the defendants would have "profound consequences for the future stability of Taiwan and for U.S.–Taiwan relations." He called for open trials in civilian courts and a spirit of clemency. He expressed the hope that responsible trials would remove the obstacles to the emergence of a democratic system, which, he repeated, was the best foundation on which the government might base its legitimacy. He did not call publicly for the administration to do anything. He expressed support for arms sales but warned that Americans would become increasingly uncomfortable if repression comes to characterize Taiwan's political system. The testimony was politely received and followed by a couple of questions but Taiwan was ignored for the rest of the hearing.[20]

Yet Leach's public testimony was only the tip of an iceberg. Because he was sincere and serious, administration officials met with him on a regular basis to discuss developments. Because he both reflected the outrage that some in America felt and held out the hope for political reform in Taiwan, U.S. officials could cite him as a reason for Taipei to show restraint. Leach played an important role in the administration's response to the incident. His public concern strengthened its private efforts.

The verdicts in the sedition trials became the focus of a set of congressional hearings in June and July before the House Subcommittee on Asian and Pacific Affairs. Administration witnesses characterized the events of the previous six months as "setbacks toward liberalization" but that the long-term trend was in the "healthy" direction of greater political participation by all elements on Taiwan. They said they were watching carefully the KMT's actions against the Taiwan Presbyterian Church; and that the AIT was informing Taiwan officials about U.S. views and of events on the island that had "disturbed" members of Congress, churches, and other American groups. Leach took the lead in calling for clemency for those convicted and making the case that "increased sharing of political power with the native Taiwanese is essential for continued political stability on the island." He also called for support of a resolution he had introduced that echoed his views and appeals. The subcommittee convened another hearing on July 30. Leach testified again and was joined this time by William P. Thompson, stated clerk of the American

United Presbyterian Church. Most of their criticism was directed at the actions of the KMT government, and Thompson made a point of praising the work of the AIT. They made no requests for specific action by the Executive Branch. The only point of discord between Leach and the administration was a disagreement over the significance of the open trials and of the regime's bringing Taiwanese into the government.[21]

The Kaohsiung Incident's most lasting impact was on the Taiwanese-American community. Previously ambivalent about the value of working through the American political process, individuals and groups around the country threw themselves into a campaign of letter writing, with a focus on members of Congress and the administration. For example, when Cai Tongrong met with a staff person in Senator Edward Kennedy's (D-MA) office about the incident in early January 1980, the latter urged Cai to have Taiwanese send letters to Kennedy. Cai unleashed a flood of letters, which prompted Kennedy to meet with Cai in February and make a public statement on the eve of the first trials. That campaign continued into the spring and stimulated letters supporting the ROC government. In early May, AIT received 812 letters or cards opposing the verdicts and 334 defending them.[22]

It was the Taiwanese Association of America (TAA) that provided the main organizational network for mobilizing such activity. The TAA was primarily a social and cultural organization but politics was only just below the surface, so TAA chapters were a willing vehicle for mobilization of people by Cai. They had provided the manpower for demonstrations in the Washington, DC, area, and individuals in the local TAA chapter had lobbied Congress at the time of the TRA.

There were other organizations, of course, and some expanded their role in the politicized atmosphere of 1980. One was the publication, *Taiwan Communiqué*, founded by Gerrit van der Wees, a Dutchman, and his Taiwanese-born wife, Mei-chin. They lived in Seattle and became interested in the human rights situation in Taiwan in the mid-1970s, and had links to the Japan-based International Committee for the Defense of Human Rights in Taiwan, run by Lynn Miles. In mid-1979 they began to disseminate a newsletter similar to Amnesty International's urgent-action memoranda. "Galvanized" by the Kaohsiung Incident, they became part of a Taiwanese lobbying effort in the Seattle area. In December 1980 they decided to make their newsletter a full-fledged publication, and *Taiwan Communiqué* became the principal, regular English-language periodical advocating self-determination for the people of Taiwan, with a publication run until 2003. More important, it became a key part of the foundation of the Taiwanese lobbying effort in the United States in the 1980s.[23]

The Limits of Congressional Influence

The Kaohsiung Incident also illustrates how hard it is for members of Congress to energize their institution to play a role in foreign policy, at least on the issue of human rights. Jim Leach was an ideal champion of that cause when it came to Taiwan. He was committed, principled, and able to articulate why it was in the KMT's own interest to move toward a more open political system. He was willing to work with the administration to pursue a common goal. Still, in light of the ultimate result, he had only a modest impact. His resolution, which assumed the best about Chiang's intentions and stated its appeals in very moderate language, died in the subcommittees to which it had been referred. Although he had a strong case, in the context of the U.S. Congress Leach was a voice crying in the wilderness. And he chose to modulate that public voice to accommodate somewhat the calculations of the administration's Taiwan experts, who were pursuing a medium-term strategy when it came to political liberalization.[24]

Scholars of Congress's role in foreign policy tend to emphasize the relative advantages that the Executive Branch possesses, such as control over information, broad areas of constitutional discretion, and so on. Some authors look at the legislative scorecard and become cynical about Capitol Hill's willingness to challenge the president. Stephen Weissman argues that there is a congressional "culture of deference," a set of norms, attitudes, customs, and institutions that has led Congress—and especially its members who oppose Executive Branch policy—to "substantially cede its fundamental constitutional role in foreign policy." Barbara Hinckley goes further to assert that the supposed conflict between the branches is largely an illusion, an illusion that is encouraged by the participants. "We . . . find agendas filled with highly selected debates and symbolic issues, with demands for reports that are not read and tough restrictions with built-in escape provisions. The two branches support each other in this symbolic display, staging dramatic last-minute compromises or complaining about each other's usurpation or meddling."[25]

Yet explaining the relative role of Congress in foreign policy is not so easy. Deference on the part of opponents of administration policy often reflects an assessment that the balance of power is against them, and that losing in a fruitless effort is worth less than waiting until the balance shifts. In addition, to assess Congress's impact by looking only at cases of changing U.S. foreign policy through binding legislation—particularly on issues of priority to an administration—restricts the discussion to a fairly narrow sample. There are, to be sure, issues on which Congress can exercise influence only through legislation, which dictates one type of political game. Yet there are other cases where legislation is not the only way members of

Congress can bring change, or where they do so by *not* targeting administration policy in the first place.

A more nuanced, and I believe accurate picture is provided by Rebecca Hersman: "Big votes and sweeping legislation tend to grab the headlines and frame the debate about the state of executive-legislative relations, but they only tell part of the story. . . . For the most part, policymakers struggle within porous, fragmented institutions where policy is driven more by like-minded individuals than by disciplined organizations, conflict is as much intrainstitutional as it is interinstitutional, and issue loyalties often outweigh partisan ties or institutional allegiances. In this environment, relations between the branches are characterized as much by collaboration and negotiation as by confrontation and conflict."[26]

Thus the most intense conflict over human rights in Taiwan was within Congress, not between it and the administration. And the congressional power balance was very much in the KMT's favor. It had cultivated broad support in Congress, support that even events like the Kaohsiung Incident did not weaken. The Taiwanese-American community that opposed it was only coming around to pursuing its own congressional strategy in the wake of the Kaohsiung Incident, which in turn would shift the balance somewhat.

Critics like Leach needed that sort of mass support. But they also needed the kind of institutional position that would allow them to exert sufficient leverage in a "porous, fragmented institution" to mount a challenge to the KMT's allies. And they required a strategy to exercise that leverage with effect. In 1980, Leach was not yet a member of the foreign affairs committee, and as a Republican he did not have the sort of agenda-setting capacity that, for example, a subcommittee chairman possesses. (Don Fraser had that position, but he used it on Taiwan only once and then left Congress.) It is no wonder, therefore, that Leach's Kaohsiung resolution did not move through the legislative process. He had to be realistically content with conducting his opposition to the KMT through principled, public statements and quiet cooperation with administration officials, rather than the fruitless pursuit of binding legislation (to suspend arms sales, for example) that would challenge the Executive Branch's authority to conduct foreign policy more than it would attack KMT repression.

The degree of congressional impact on foreign policy, therefore, is a function of the power of those trying to exert influence, their strategy for exerting that influence, and the existence of some outside support. Concerning Taiwan, what was needed was a combination of institutional power, Taiwanese-American activism, and a strategy that provided an appropriate challenge to the KMT and its supporters in Congress. What was needed, in part, was a combination of Don Fraser and Jim Leach—which brings us to Steve Solarz.

The Chairman: Initial Steps

Democrat Steve Solarz was elected to Congress in 1974 at the age of thirty-four from a district in Brooklyn. A member of the Watergate class, he supported the drive to decentralize power in Congress and he benefited from it. A brilliant mind with an insatiable curiosity and a love of policy debate, he did not suffer fools or sloppy thinking gladly, but he was willing to change his mind if given a sound and substantive reason to do so. An antiwar Jewish liberal, he arrived in Washington determined to prevent new Holocausts and to ensure that the United States did not side with right-wing dictatorships and their repression of demands for freedom and social justice. His unyielding approach to the Khmer Rouge was an example of the former impulse, and his opposition to military assistance to the junta in El Salvador was a case of the latter. Although he believed that the United States could protect its interests by cooperating and reaching agreements with "socialist" regimes like China and the Soviet Union, he saw those systems for what they were—Leninist dictatorships that denied human freedom. He was a consistent advocate of democracy everywhere.[27]

Interestingly, he showed only modest interest in Taiwan in the first six years of his congressional career. During the enactment of the Taiwan Relations Act, his attention was focused on security issues. He was aware of the opposition to KMT rule on the island, but apparently played no role in the attempt to get some kind of language on human rights in the legislation. In the mid-1980 hearings at which Leach testified twice on the Kaohsiung Incident, Solarz focused his question on Taiwan views of recent PRC unification overtures.

After he became chairman, almost immediately he began to receive appeals from Taiwanese and others about political prisoners, which he then raised with the Taiwan government (the replies were unresponsive and somewhat patronizing). But at the first hearing of the Asian affairs subcommittee concerning Taiwan after he became chairman, in May 1981, the discussion of human rights got sidetracked into a methodologically complicated comparison of the situation on the island and that in the PRC. Solarz did not minimize the severity of human rights on Taiwan and he demonstrated genuine interest in whether the Taiwan people were ready for a democracy, but he had missed a chance to establish a public position. Jim Leach, who was a member of that subcommittee, was much more effective on that score.[28]

Propelling Solarz in an anti-KMT direction was Cai Tongrong. He approached Solarz in February 1981, right after he became chairman of the Asian affairs subcommittee. Solarz admired Cai because he knew his agenda and was not shy about promoting it. It was from Cai that he learned that there was an active opposition movement in Taiwan and that it had a community of American supporters. And Cai kept Solarz informed about developments on the island. The two had a series of meetings throughout the spring, and then Solarz met with fifty-plus Taiwanese in New York on June 19. That was followed five weeks later by a meeting between Cai and a few others at Solarz's Virginia home. Cai presented the issues on which he thought Solarz could be helpful to Taiwanese so that Solarz could weigh which were feasible and which were not.[29]

It is likely that in these discussions, Solarz sought Cai's views on how Taiwanese-Americans could help him financially. All elected politicians require money to run for office: to hire a campaign staff, to do polling, to print campaign literature, to purchase print, radio, and television advertising, and so on. Having a large war chest is also an effective way for an incumbent member to deter a challenge from an outsider. Solarz was not independently wealthy as Jim Leach was. And in 1981 he had a special problem. In the wake of the 1980 census, the New York State Assembly was to redraw the congressional districts, and because the state was losing population the number of districts would decline. Solarz was afraid that redistricting would require him to compete in the Democratic primary with another sitting congressman, Charles Schumer. That would be an exceptionally expensive race, so Solarz had to raise money as a defensive measure.

Cai knew how the game was played, and this was not the first time that he had approached an American politician to offer a mutually beneficial relationship. Indeed, in 1980 he tried for a political "big score": supporting Ted Kennedy's challenge to a sitting Democratic president. If Kennedy beat Jimmy Carter for the Democratic nomination and then went on to win the presidency, Taiwanese would have extraordinary influence in the U.S. Executive Branch for the first time—or so Cai must have thought. So in April 1980, only two months after first meeting Kennedy, Cai began work on a fundraising party in Los Angeles and he secured commitments for a total of $100,000 in contributions. Among the issues of concern to Taiwanese that Cai brought to Kennedy's attention was the fear that Washington's switch in diplomatic relations from Taipei to Beijing would mean that Taiwan people would have to share a 20,000-person immigration quota with the much larger population of the mainland. The TRA permitted a separate quota but had not required it. At the late May event in Los Angeles, Kennedy called for a fairer approach to the quota issue.[30]

In cultivating Solarz in 1981 Cai was setting his sights lower than he had with Kennedy. But for a community that had only recently decided to pursue its goals through the American political process a House subcommittee chairman was a more appropriate level than a presidential candidate. Solarz also had resources that could enhance his effectiveness. With his chairmanship came the opportunity to hire staff. To cover China and Taiwan issues, Solarz had recruited Edward Friedman, a respected China specialist at the University of Wisconsin who had attended the same high school and university as Solarz. Friedman combined a keen mind and moral passion that served him well in the two-plus years he was on the staff. He also understood the need to balance Taiwan initiatives with commitments made to the PRC at the time of normalization.

One of the issues that Cai brought to Solarz's dinner table on July 16 was the immigration quota. Kennedy had urged the State Department to grant it for Taiwan but the department had so far failed to respond. It happened that Solarz's wife, Nina, an expert on immigration issues, was at the dinner and she recommended amending the Immigration and Naturalization Act to require a separate quota if that should be necessary.[31]

Another issue that Cai may have raised with Solarz was the death on July 3 of Chen Wencheng, a Taiwanese-born professor at Carnegie Mellon University, who was detained by the Taiwan Garrison Command during a trip to the island and then fell to his death from the fifth floor of the library of National Taiwan University. If the ROC government wanted to get off to a bad start with Solarz, it could not have found a better way to do it. He held one hearing on Chen's death at the end of July and another at the beginning of October. Jim Leach played a prominent role and Chen Tangshan, then chairman of the World Taiwanese Association, testified. The hearings developed a strong case that Chen had been the object of surveillance by Taiwan security services *in the United States*, and that his death stemmed from that surveillance. The latter hearing also received information from an American forensic scientist who had gone to Taiwan and concluded from an examination of Chen's body that he had been beaten before the fall and thrown to his death.[32]

Chen's murder outraged Solarz and Leach. As Solarz said, "What happens on Taiwan is the business of the officials of Taiwan. But what happens in America is primarily the business of the Congress of the United States, and we cannot and will not tolerate any act to intimidate or harass Taiwanese or other people living in our country." Leach declared, "It is high time for the United States to make clear to the world that our soil will not become a playing field for international hoodlums." Both warned of dire consequences for U.S.–Taiwan relations if the activity continued.[33]

Solarz did not stop with just a rhetorical warning. He took advantage of House floor action on the foreign aid authorization bill in late 1981 to secure passage of an amendment to the Arms Export Control Act that required that arms sales to a foreign government be terminated if it is found to have engaged in a consistent pattern of intimidation and harassment of individuals in the United States. Solarz had created a linkage between the KMT's effort to enforce its orthodoxy in America and what was most important for its security, the means of self-defense. The ROC's friends in Congress, who normally could be counted on to defend its interests, would not oppose the amendment because they were unwilling to condone surveillance in the United States and the deadly actions that flowed from it. (Chiang Ching-kuo apparently did not get the message that off-the-books political violence was undermining Taiwan's interests. He accepted his subordinates' explanation that this was not a government action, even though U.S. officials knew there was evidence of official involvement.)[34]

Solarz and Kennedy also used the foreign aid bill to address the issue of the immigration quota. Taiwanese leaders had appealed to them in early November, reiterating that it was the most important issue for the community. Late in the month, the State Department informed Kennedy that it would not voluntarily create a separate 20,000-person quota for people born in Taiwan. At Solarz's and Kennedy's parallel initiatives, the House and Senate included in the foreign aid bill a provision that amended the Immigration and Naturalization Act (INA) to provide that the sentence of the INA that established the quota "*shall* [that is, must] be considered to have been granted with respect to Taiwan (China)."[35]

Forming the Formosan Association for Public Affairs

About two months after passage of the two amendments, representatives of the Taiwanese community met to consider the future. Cai wanted to mobilize community funding for a clandestine television station to broadcast in Taiwan (which suggests that he had not completely given up political action directed at his homeland). Others at the meeting argued that there needed to be more focus on what was called "diplomatic work"—in effect a revival of the "external affairs" on which Chen Longzhi had labored fifteen years before. It was therefore decided that a new organization was necessary to both promote freedom and democracy in Taiwan and protect the interests of Taiwanese overseas. This new entity would be named the Formosan Association for Public Affairs (FAPA).[36]

FAPA was not, however, created in response to grassroots appeals. It was in fact a conscious decision on the part of the WUFI wing of the network of Taiwanese Associations in America. It will be recalled that WUFI political activists worked quietly within the organizational structure of the more socially focused TAA chapters. As WUFI activists like Cai talked of forming an organization to engage in political activity in the United States, they had considered creating a political element within the TAA. But there was concern that this would scare off TAA members who wished to avoid politics. Hence it was decided to form FAPA, but as a public—not clandestine—organization. Thus Cai insisted that leaders of the new organization use their "true names" and make their association a matter of public record.[37]

Cai did not want to head the organization, nor did Mark Chen or Peng Mingmin, the others who were recommended. In the end Cai gave in and soon set to work writing bylaws, recruiting leaders and members, and opening a Washington office. This was an opportunity, he thought, to activate Taiwanese who had never been organizationally involved. Because FAPA's principal target was Congress, he sought to create a chapter in every state and at least a small group in each congressional district. During 1982 and 1983, he moved around the country, signing up members and raising money. Raising money was important in a specific way; that was one way to gain congressional support. So was educating Taiwanese on how to play the Capitol Hill game, which took place at training sessions every summer.[38]

The Taiwanese community was thus creating its lobby. In FAPA it had an organization that had an explicit political focus. It served as a conduit for campaign contributions, made appeals in Washington to members of Congress to take action consistent with FAPA's goals, and reinforced those appeals at the state and district levels through the membership's grassroots efforts. (And in the process of forming FAPA, the organizational division of labor within the community between political and other activities had been clarified.) In the *Taiwan Communiqué*, Taiwanese-Americans had a publication that stated their case in clear, simple terms. In Solarz, Leach, Pell, and Kennedy—the "gang of four"—they had a critical mass of congressional activists. Solarz, with his subcommittee chairmanship and his energy, was particularly well positioned and had already achieved some success. All that was needed now was a strategy.

Changing Taiwan

Devising a strategy was easier than it might seem. Securing a 20,000-person quota and deterring the ROC government from intimidating and harassing Taiwanese in the United States were certainly good for the Taiwanese-American community and demonstrated that people like Solarz were going to be more active on their behalf. But in a sense they were the easy steps. The Taiwan government's friends in Congress had seen no reason not to permit the bigger quota, and they could not in good conscience oppose the arms sales provision after the Chen killing. But these steps did nothing to change the situation *in Taiwan*. Solarz and his colleagues had used the legislative process to bar KMT political action in the United States (or so they thought).

But how to use that power to get the KMT to change the political system on the island was not so obvious—even if Taipei's supporters did not exist as an obstacle, which they did.

Complicating matters was Solarz's commitment to the development of relations between the United States and China. He did so for geopolitical and practical reasons. The United States needed China's assistance in containing the Soviet Union and it would be harder to secure that help if Congress took actions that in some way contravened the Carter administration's normalization commitments. Solarz did not abandon his views on the nature of the Chinese system, but he believed that it was changing and that the U.S. relationship could accelerate that process. Thus he needed to strike a balance between promoting political change in Taiwan and preserving relations with Beijing. Ed Friedman and I shared that point of departure and saw part of our jobs as ensuring that he understood the China consequences of specific Taiwan initiatives. (Cai, of course, saw less need to worry about Beijing's sensitivities.) Moreover, the early 1980s was a particularly difficult time to find the right balance point because the PRC was exceptionally touchy then about congressional initiatives that it saw as "interference in China's internal affairs." Solarz's solution was to agree with his Taiwanese supporters on the necessity of democracy and human rights on the island but not on their desire for a Republic of Taiwan. Evidence of that balancing act can be found in the wording of the immigration provision discussed above. Cai and others were no doubt unhappy with the "Taiwan (China)" formulation. In Solarz's mind, however, it was necessary to demonstrate that he was not complicit in an independence project.

Another threshold issue that would affect what Solarz did was an assumption about the nature of KMT intentions domestically, and whether it was actually serious about moving toward a democratic system. Friedman and I believed that there were reformers in the Kuomintang and that positive political change would occur only if they worked successfully within the system. Indeed, I believed that the regime and the opposition were divided into moderate and radical camps and that reform was more likely if the moderate elements found a way to work together and isolate their respective radical camps. The radicals on each side fed off each other and used each other's actions to foster polarization and restrain their more moderate colleagues.[39] The implication of that analysis was that outsiders had a responsibility not to undermine KMT moderates if we could help it. Cai tended to see the KMT as more monolithic and impervious to change from within; hence the need to attack it from without.

A third constraining factor was the limits on congressional power. Congress's main tool for influencing American foreign policy is the power of the purse, controlling in one way or another the way in which appropriated funds are used overseas. But economic assistance for Taiwan ended in 1965 and military aid stopped with normalization, so that tool was unavailable. Using arms sales as leverage was another theoretical possibility, since Congress had given itself the power to block individual transfers by a majority vote of both houses. But getting those majorities with respect to Taiwan was problematic because the island faced a legitimate threat from the PRC. It became more of a problem in June 1983, when the Supreme Court in effect required that Congress needed two-thirds majorities in both houses to block an arms sale. Moreover, on issues like arms sales, Solarz correctly took his cues from the people he was trying to help—in this case, the opposition in Taiwan—and they wanted arms sales to continue. If legislation was not an option for promoting reform on Taiwan, what was?

The next best alternative to binding legislation was a nonbinding statement of congressional views. These neither required the U.S. Executive Branch to do anything nor blocked it from doing anything it planned to do. But these sense-of-Congress resolutions could send a signal to target government and affect its contest with the political opposition (assuming there was a contest and some way for opposition forces to learn of the measure).

Nonbinding statements are enacted in two ways. They can be freestanding measures that focus only on one issue and, once introduced, move through the regular legislative process, considered by the relevant subcommittee(s) and full committee and then by the full House or Senate. Or they can be attached to another bill, usually by amendment, as it moves through Congress. Even nonbinding language that is usually found in a resolution can be included in a bill that is otherwise binding in its effect. From a tactical point of view, it is easier to stick such language in a larger bill than it is to enact it on a freestanding basis. But a freestanding resolution has a stronger symbolic value.

The other mode of influence was holding hearings because they could signal American disapproval of a foreign government's repression. Again, they had a greater impact on countries where there was some flow of information, where the political opposition and the public would know that the regime was subject to outside criticism. And they required a sympathetic committee or subcommittee chairman to convene the hearings.

Taiwan was such a country. Press freedom was limited but there was enough for the island's public to learn of congressional initiatives. So it was in the direction of hearings and resolutions that Cai Tongrong pointed his congressional friends. The issues he sought to emphasize in the early period of FAPA's "diplomatic work" were "the abolition of Taiwan's martial law, the release of Kaohsiung Incident political prisoners, and securing the right of self-determination of Taiwan residents."[40]

In May 1982 Cai got Kennedy, Pell, Solarz, and Leach to hold a press conference on martial law, which Taiwan diplomats tried unsuccessfully to block or delay. On the same day, Solarz used his convening power to hold a hearing on martial law. The hearing was not a complete success, mainly because of the lineup of witnesses. Cai and Hamline University professor Richard Kagan made the case against martial law and called for its abolition. Offering justifications for emergency rule on the island were Berkeley professor James Gregor and Wang Yu-san of the Association of Free Chinese in the United States. Gregor was a more effective advocate for the defense than Cai and Kagan were for the prosecution. He was particularly effective in suggesting that countries usually deemed to be democracies (Britain and Israel) imposed restrictions on human and political rights that were similar to those in effect in Taiwan. Moreover, Representative Henry Hyde (R-IL) raised Cai's role in the 1970 attempted assassination of Chiang Ching-kuo and Cai denied any involvement. Still, this was only the second time that Congress had focused attention on the ROC's authoritarian system.[41]

The martial law hearing demonstrated the difficulty of engaging in this kind of signaling exercise. Although Solarz had opened up a new battlefield, the ROC government was fully prepared to fight back to defend and justify its denial of political freedom. It probably used the right of the members in the minority to request witnesses who shared their point of view and suggested Gregor and Wang (Leach certainly would not have picked them). Solarz tended to accommodate to these requests, partly because he wanted to show balance and partly because he liked the give and take with intellectually challenging opponents. Taiwan diplomats probably also fed information to their friends suggesting that Cai had engaged in violence. Solarz had an advantage because he was chairman of the Asian affairs subcommittee, but it was far from an absolute advantage. Holding hearings and promoting resolutions were a form of political combat.

The contest continued in the 98th Congress, which convened in early 1983. The first front was what Cai called self-determination. Because Taiwan had an authoritarian system, there was a danger that, as in the past, the governments in Taipei and Beijing might reach some understanding on the island's future that did not necessarily reflect the people's views. Taiwanese-Americans were very concerned that the mainlander government that had kept their relatives on the island in thrall for almost four decades would sell out their interests. Cai's principal initiative on this front was a resolution that Jim Leach introduced in the House and Claiborne Pell offered in the Senate. They did so at the time of the symbolic anniversary of the 2-28 Incident. The resolution expressed the sense of each body that "Taiwan's future should be settled peacefully, free of coercion and in a manner acceptable to the people on

Taiwan and consistent with the laws enacted by Congress and the communiqués entered into between the United States and Taiwan." Also on February 28, 1983, Solarz convened a hearing to review U.S.–China relations. Among the witnesses were Peng Mingmin, the leading independence activist, and Qiu Hongda (Chiu Hungdah), a professor at the University of Maryland School of Law and a defender of the KMT regime. Each offered the views one might expect, but the hearing was less adversarial than the martial law hearing. Solarz sought to draw them out on the views of the majority of the Taiwan population and whether those views should be respected in determining the future of Taiwan (both Qiu and Peng agreed on that point).[42]

The Pell-Leach resolution sat idle until November 1983. After a hearing on November 9 that Pell dominated, the Senate Foreign Relations Committee on November 15 reported out the resolution. To the surprise of some in the Senate, FAPA had been able to secure enough votes to secure passage. The reason may have been less FAPA's clout than a decision of the ROC government not to fight the legislation. Indeed, it was the PRC that had the stronger reaction. Its Ministry of Foreign Affairs called in U.S. ambassador to China Arthur Hummel to protest the action and there was some suggestion that the action might affect the visit of Chinese premier Zhao Ziyang, scheduled for January 1984. The Senate action put Solarz in a difficult position. On the one hand, he wished to demonstrate to his Taiwanese supporters that he was committed to their cause. On the other hand, he did not wish unnecessarily to create problems for U.S.–China relations, and the Chinese embassy was urging him to avoid any involvement. There was some talk of weakening the resolution to make it less offensive to the PRC, but its opposition was to the fact of the measure, not its content. Solarz then decided that he would not bring up the resolution for consideration in his subcommittee unless the Senate acted, which was unlikely. By the summer of 1984, Pell was seeking to attach the text of the resolution to another bill, which would have forced Solarz to try to gain support for the provision in the House-Senate conference on the larger bill. In the event, Pell failed in his effort and the measure passed into history.[43]

Solarz himself took the lead in promoting a resolution calling for the end of martial law on Taiwan. There had been no progress on the island since the hearing he had held in May 1982. The Kaohsiung prisoners were still in jail. There was new evidence of surveillance and harassment of Taiwanese in the United States. The March 1983 Washington visit of security czar Wang Sheng had had no apparent impact. But as Solarz plotted strategy in early 1983, he knew that the KMT's congressional supporters would argue that it was unfair to single out Taiwan and not the PRC, where conditions were clearly worse. So he explored the utility of including language on human rights on the mainland. He consulted China specialists, American diplomats, some Taiwanese, and other members of Congress. A number of drafts were considered. At one point it looked as if he was ready to mention both sides of the strait, but finally he chose to focus only on Taiwan. The resolution was introduced on May 23 in both the House and the Senate. But that was just the beginning of the battle.[44]

The ROC government sought to make the most of a series of terrorist actions on Taiwan during 1983. It quickly blamed the attacks on the "Taiwan Independence Movement" (TIM), thereby suggesting that Solarz's supporters were supplementing their congressional lobbying with political violence (unfortunately, WUFI elements did not condemn the bombings). At the press conference at which Solarz, Kennedy, and others announced the resolution, materials on "TIM" terrorism were available. Taipei also sought, to put it bluntly, to buy Solarz off. It first was willing to provide financial assistance to one of his constituents who imported apparel from Taiwan but was losing quota because of counterfeiters. It then sought to use the importer to exert pressure on the martial-law resolution. It was able to delay subcommittee consideration of the measure once, in September 1983, but generally Solarz rejected such linkage. Second, the ROC government approached him on behalf of progovernment residents of New York who had expressed an interest in contributing to his campaign. I suspected that this interest was "directed," and argued strongly against it. I wrote: "Those who respect you for your leadership on the Taiwan issue, Taiwanese-Americans and others, believe that you are motivated by your principles and not by the money. You have entered into a common cause with your Taiwanese friends, which in their eyes gives you a purity uncharacteristic of American politicians. It is the KMT that believes you are in this for the money, and would love to be confirmed right by creating a bidding war that will *appear* to divide your loyalties, even if it does not change your policy views. Even if the KMT has not caused this initiative, your Taiwanese friends will assume that they have." To the best of my knowledge, the offer was declined.[45]

Solarz found a way to take the battle into enemy territory. Cai had urged him to make a trip to Taiwan and give a speech to a *dangwai* audience. Solarz made the trip in August 1983, and drafting the speech was my first major task after joining the subcommittee staff in July. The visit was a whirlwind of activity with lots of media attention. Martial law was the focus of press conferences and official meetings. The Interior Ministry leaked the substance of Solarz's conversation with Minister of the Interior Lin Yanggang (Lin Yang-kang), who may have wanted to show his support for emergency rule.

The speech, which Solarz gave at the Ambassador Hotel on August 16 to more than 100 oppositionists, took a higher road. His main theme was that Taiwan, having achieved an economic miracle, was ready for a political miracle. He went through all the justifications for not moving toward democracy (economic level, religious values, need to preserve stability, national security, and so on) and rejected each of them. He encouraged the authorities to take the risks of political change and exercise restraint. He urged the opposition to pursue moderation and eschew violence. His most telling argument in retrospect was the international impact of democratization: "I am convinced that if the United States and other countries in the world have a favorable impression of Taiwan, it will improve the prospects for a secure and prosperous life for the people of Taiwan. But if world opinion is negative, isolation and insecurity are more likely." He was offering the KMT a bargain: if you democratize, I will support you.[46]

The event had its poignant and humorous moments. Poignant was the absence of all the *dangwai* people still in jail, the casualties of past challenges to KMT rule. Among the honored participants was the wife of Lei Zhen, whose presence I realized too late to have Solarz acknowledge her. Humorous was the way in which the personnel from the state-controlled TV stations turned on their lights and rolled the cameras when he said something about Taiwan's progress but turned everything off during the critical passages. Also amusing was the reaction to a quotation from Sun Yat-sen on how Chinese people were ready for democracy, which we had included in the text to spur the KMT to live up to its own ideals. Solarz did not identify the author of the passage before he read it, but one could see the spreading flash of recognition of people in the audience as they realized he was cleverly turning the KMT's own ideology against them. That awareness occurred twice, first among those who understood English and second among those who had to wait for the translation (which was done by Antonio Jiang Junnan).

The Ambassador Hotel speech was significant not just for its substantive message but also for two other reasons. First, it likely resonated with the views of progressives in the KMT who were themselves arguing for political change. This was evident in the republication of most of the speech the next day in the *Zhongguo shibao* (China Times), whose publisher, Yu Jizhong, was one of those progressives and a rather courageous one at that. Second, the speech gave the opposition an international recognition that it did not have. David Reuther, then the chief political officer at the AIT, recalled that "Solarz's attention [to the opposition] assisted their cause and gave them some cover. . . . His address was not as remarkable as the opportunity for the opposition to meet without being arrested." Kang Ningxiang, whom we entrusted with making arrangements for the event and who suffered politically as a result, later wrote: "Your speech was not only appreciated tremendously by the guests who attended the luncheon, . . . [it also] greatly roused the spirits of your friends in the Opposition who have striven with total concentration to advance the cause of political reform."[47]

Thus a focus on the effort to bring political change on the island was emerging by fits and starts from Cai's proposals and Taiwan events. It was to change the moral and political balance of power within the Taiwan political system. This required discrediting and delegitimizing the ROC government for the worst features of its authoritarian rule, while legitimizing the cause of the *dangwai* and giving it some measure of protection. The KMT had kept its mantle of authority in part by branding those who challenged its power monopoly as criminals, as people who with their relatives were unworthy of social respect. But the KMT was vulnerable to those who were willing to expose the regime's abuses and assert a contrary standard of legitimacy. The opposition sought to do that within the boundaries of permissible action. But as individuals and as a group, the *dangwai* needed a defense against the regime's constant effort to delegitimize it and a way of asserting its moral value. Americans like Leach and Solarz could tip the moral balance by shaming the authorities and "de-shaming" its opponents. They could do so visibly through activities like hearings, resolutions, and speeches. But they also acted in quieter ways. Most important was facilitating the visits of countless *dangwai* leaders to the United States: urging the authorities to grant exit permission in the first place, meeting them and seeking their advice, and posing for group pictures that the visitors could then use as a protective talisman once they returned home. This approach of shifting the moral balance, which was never stated explicitly, did have an assumption: that is, at least some of the Kuomintang's rulers did possess some moral sense and could be shamed into reforming the political system so that it conformed with the party's democratic ideals.[48]

Political Combat

Whether there were in fact progressives within the KMT was one reason it was so hard to pass a martial-law resolution in the 98th Congress. In particular, the possibility that those progressives might convince Chiang Ching-kuo to release some of the Kaohsiung prisoners posed a tactical problem. Would movement on the resolution become pressure to bring about a release or a reason to delay it? When was the best time to move? The other obstacle was the strength of the ROC's friends, which created a different kind of dilemma. Should the text of the resolution be so tough that it provoked overwhelming opposition? Or should the language be toned down in order to get more support?

Solarz decided not to act in late 1983 and early 1984. One Kaohsiung prisoner, Presbyterian elder Lin Wenzhen, was released on medical parole in October 1983 and experts like Tian Hongmao (Tien Hung-mao) and David Dean advised against moving quickly. And there were a series of political events looming that Solarz did not want to disrupt: Legislative Yuan elections in December; presidential and vice-presidential elections in March 1984, and the inauguration in May, which sometimes was an occasion for prisoner releases. But when no major Kaohsiung figures were freed, Solarz decided to go ahead with subcommittee action on the resolution. That happened during a hearing on May 31, at which the witnesses were Tian (a centrist), Martin Lasater (more sympathetic to the KMT), and T.K. Lin of Drake University (aligned with FAPA). With some changes to the resolution's text, the resolution was passed and reported to the full committee. The operative language was "it would be highly desirable if the authorities on Taiwan would continue and accelerate progress toward a fully democratic system, in particular by ending martial law and other emergency provisions and by releasing political prisoners, and so guarantee and protect the rights of all the people of Taiwan." That the resolution had even cleared the subcommittee was a modest victory for FAPA, Solarz, and Leach.[49]

The next step was action by the full committee. The arena had changed but the constraints had not. There were signs through the summer that major releases were in the offing. Because Solarz had been appealing for the release of Gao Junmin, Lin Yixiong, and others, he did not wish to be responsible for their spending more time in prison than they had to. Word finally came on August 15 that Gao, Lin, and Xu Qingfu had been released and that Elder Lin's parole had been converted to release. Solarz then decided to push for consideration of the amended resolution in the foreign affairs committee, but he ran into three obstacles. The first was the refusal of the committee chairman, Dante Fascell (D-FL), to consider any thing that was controversial. The second was the insistence of Representative Gus Yatron (D-PA), chairman of the Subcommittee on Human Rights and International Organizations, to which the resolution had also been referred, that his panel had to pass it as well. The third came from members who were friends of the Taiwan government and who wanted no resolution at all. If they mounted significant opposition in the form of a series of amendments, they could water down the measure. There then ensued an effort to accommodate opponents, in order to reduce the level of controversy. In the end, Yatron was satisfied by some additional clauses but others were still opposed and there was too little time left in the session. At the end of the year, it fell to me to explain to a Taiwanese audience why the legislative process and KMT political clout had combined to defeat this effort.[50]

The first two and a half years of FAPA's existence therefore produced only limited success. Solarz and his like-minded colleagues were willing to do public events to call the KMT to account and establish the legitimacy of the *dangwai*. Two different resolutions had made modest progress through the legislative process. At the same time, the ROC government had demonstrated that it had both the will and the resources to block initiatives like the martial-law resolution. Although it would prefer not to be criticized at all, the ability to thwart these challenges reinforced its position at home. It turned out to be self-destructive acts that would be the undoing of KMT authoritarianism.[51]

The Henry Liu Case

Henry Liu Yiliang, known also by his pen name, Jiang Nan, was a writer of uncertain loyalties living in Daly City, California. At various times in his career he had provided information to the U.S., ROC, and PRC governments. What got him in trouble, however, were biographies of Wu Guozhen and Sun Liren that included criticisms of Chiang Ching-kuo. In the summer of 1984, Admiral Wang Xiling, head of the Intelligence Bureau of the Ministry of National Defense, ordered gangsters of the Bamboo Gang, which the bureau used for such jobs, to kill Liu. (There were later strong suggestions that Chiang's son Alex was the real instigator of the killing.) The murder took place on October 14. Soon thereafter, the plot began to unravel and the plotters tried without success to keep the truth from Chiang and the U.S. government. By mid-January 1985, Taipei had to publicly admit that its intelligence services were involved. Chiang Ching-kuo was pained by the whole episode because it undermined good relations with the Reagan administration. Washington was furious that an ROC agency would commit political violence on American soil.[52]

Right after the murder, Solarz had received an initial briefing from the FBI. When news broke about official involvement, he and I were traveling in Central America. He decided on the spot to hold a hearing and issued a statement that raised the possibility of a cutoff of arms sales, pursuant to the provision he had gotten adopted after the Chen Wencheng case. The hearing occurred on February 7 and featured Mrs. Henry Liu, the congressional representative from her district, Norman Mineta (D-CA), William Brown, deputy assistant secretary of state for East Asia, and Michael Glennon, a specialist on foreign-agent activity in the United States. The subcommittee also passed a resolution that urged Taiwan to deliver to the United States the actual perpetrators of the crime and called on the AIT and its counterpart to conclude an extradition agreement that would regulate future cases of this type. The resolution passed the full committee with modest modifications on April 3, and the House on April 12. (Senator Kennedy introduced a companion measure in the Senate but it was never acted upon.) From the initial revelation to passage of the House resolution only two months had elapsed, a stark contrast to the difficulties faced with the martial-law resolution. But because Henry Liu was a victim of political violence in the United States, neither the ROC government nor its congressional supporters had a defense. There was a temporary ceasefire in the normal political combat over Taiwan.[53]

More important than Solarz's and Leach's victory, however, was the shock presented by the case in Taiwan. The case brought the regime significant shame and had a dual political impact. The right wing and the security services were discredited. Progressive officials like Lee Teng-hui, Frederick Qian Fu, James Soong Chuyu, and older liberals were "aghast." This was not the KMT they thought they had joined. Chiang Ching-kuo, who had failed to heed the warning of previous instances of special action, finally brought the intelligence agencies to heel. He also shook up his staff and ordered his new secretary-general, Ma Shuli, to prepare for a full range of democratic reforms over the next couple of years. One year later, in the spring of 1986, a political reform committee was established to study issues like ending martial law, allowing new political parties, and ending mainlander overrepresentation in the Legislative Yuan and National Assembly. The Henry Liu case therefore was like a bank shot in billiards. A stupid action by the security services that saw themselves as the guardians of authoritarian rule provoked a harsh reaction from the United States (both Congress and the Executive Branch), which in turn gave Chiang and his reformist advisers both the embarrassment and leverage they needed to reduce the conservatives' power and open up the political system.[54]

During the 99th Congress (1985–86), Solarz also pursued a resolution on democratization in Taiwan. Cai and FAPA wanted to revive the martial law resolution but I was certain that an emphasis on emergency rule would provoke a spirited opposition from the KMT. I also believed that we had to take seriously the demand that we be evenhanded and not ignore human rights abuses in China. I therefore argued for a two-track approach: develop a Taiwan resolution that did not target martial law but called for allowing opposition political parties, political freedoms, and full representative government; and hold a hearing on human rights in the PRC and develop a resolution on that subject. Solarz agreed with that strategy and we convinced FAPA that it was the only way to achieve what we wanted. We gained the cooperation of Gus Yatron, chairman of the human rights subcommittee, who had slowed us down before, and secured the grudging support of some conservatives, such as Gerald Solomon (D-NY), for the Taiwan measure. Both resolutions cleared the subcommittee and committee hurdles in the summer of 1986, one step further for the Taiwan resolution than in the previous Congress.[55]

Then the strategy ran into trouble. Although Solarz had secured the support of Taiwan's friends on the committee, there were others who were not part of the arrangement. They were perfectly ready to vote on the floor for the PRC resolution and against the Taiwan measure. Also, procedure on the House floor worked against us. We could ask to consider the resolution on a no-amendment basis (under a device called suspension of the rules) but we would need to secure a two-thirds' majority. If we wanted to go for just a simple majority, we would have to open the measure up to amendments. Solarz judged that we would lose either way and the KMT would secure a victory by defeating our resolution. In September, Solarz convinced Peng Mingmin, now the president of FAPA, that withdrawing to fight another day was better than a defeat.[56]

One reason why the ROC government was intent on blocking the Taiwan resolution—and why Solarz had to avoid losing—was the evolving situation in Taiwan. Elections for the Legislative Yuan were scheduled for December and the opposition was more active than ever. Solarz did not want to hurt the *dangwai*'s chances. Then on September 28, opposition leaders decided to brook the wrath of the regime and form an opposition party—the Democratic Progressive Party (DPP). Solarz and I understood immediately the need to call on the government not to crack down. All day on September 28 Washington time, I coordinated a statement with the offices of Leach, Pell, and Kennedy. It praised the courage and unity of the *dangwai* and called on the regime to permit the DPP to "participate in the political process freely and without constraint. . . . After almost forty years of economic and educational progress [on Taiwan], the emergence of a genuine multiparty system is long overdue." The statement was reported in Taiwan newspapers on September 29. Whether it made a difference is not clear, since Chiang already knew that the "gang of four" favored opposition parties and he quickly rejected proposals from within the regime for a repressive response. But the statement did give confidence to the DPP at its most critical time and let the Taiwan public and KMT conservatives know that a crackdown would entail costs. It was probably a more effective and efficient way of signaling than trying to enact resolutions that were difficult to pass, no matter how watered down they were.[57]

Did the activities of members of Congress and their Taiwanese supporters have an impact on Chiang Ching-kuo's decision to begin the liberalization of the political system in 1986, including his announcement on October 7 that he would propose ending martial law? Certainly, more progressive members of the KMT like John Zhang Xiaoyan (Chang Hsiao-yen) in the early

1980s saw the value of reaching out to congressional liberals like Solarz and Leach, and responding to their concerns. Andrew Nathan and Helen Ho concluded that international pressure was one of the factors that drove Chiang to start dismantling authoritarian rule (along with PRC developments, opposition pressure and election timing, the need to reinvigorate the ruling party, the imperatives of health and succession, and Chiang's political values and sense of mission). Martial law had turned into an embarrassment for the ROC government, and was increasingly difficult to justify. Its extension to the United States had been a disaster. Phillip Newell assessed that international isolation was one critical "environmental factor" that impelled Chiang in the direction of reform. Solarz received more evidence of his impact later on, in January 1988, when he paid a call on Lee Teng-hui, who had just become president after the death of Chiang Ching-kuo. Lee insisted that Shen Changhuan, a conservative elder, attend the meeting in order to expose him to an American liberal. Solarz's and Leach's critique of the KMT regime was not sufficient itself to lead Chiang Ching-kuo to the counterintuitive judgment that the way to preserve the party's dominance was to open up the political system. But it certainly helped, along with the promise that a democratic Taiwan would have a stronger claim on American support.[58]

Sustaining Momentum

With Chiang's announcement of the end of martial law and the convening of the 100th Congress in January 1987, there began a transition in the way Congress approached Taiwan's political system. To be sure, much remained to be done in dismantling the pillars of repression and creating democratic institutions; lifting martial law was only a start. But the issue was less whether Taiwan was going to move toward a free and competitive system than it was how fast this would happen and how far it would go. Solarz and his colleagues had a bias toward faster and farther. Yet their job became somewhat easier because the ROC government did not try to defend a fixed line. Rather it engaged in an orderly retreat. Also the action itself shifted to Taiwan. Lee Teng-hui's succession to Chiang Ching-kuo opened the door to more rapid liberalization. The DPP, or at least its moderate wing, became his ally and in a freer press environment it could make the case for more change just as well as its Americans supporters could. The two sides engaged in a complex dance of both conflict and cooperation. External intervention was important at certain key junctures, but not as often. Furthermore, there were changes in the Taiwanese-American community. Their bond with their congressional friends began to weaken as the goal on which they had made common cause—democratization—was gradually achieved. Members of

Congress had promoted democracy as an end in itself; many Taiwanese wanted political freedom as a means to the end of independence. In addition, members of the community chose to return to Taiwan to participate directly in politics there rather than doing so indirectly in the United States. Some were arrested and became the object of congressional lobbying.[59]

Much of this was in the future. In 1987, it was not so clear that the end of martial law and the decriminalization of political opposition would result in true liberalization. In May, therefore, Solarz and Leach introduced an updated version of the resolution on democratization that they had sought to pass in the previous Congress (Kennedy had already introduced it in the Senate). I was pessimistic about the chances of passing the measure on a freestanding basis even if there were one on the PRC. In a change of tactics, therefore, Solarz decided to offer the language as an amendment to the State Department authorization bill. He waited until the last possible minute to have the text inserted in the *Congressional Record*, which was necessary for the amendment to be in order for consideration on the House floor. I worried that this surprise attack would anger conservatives, so on my own I told David Lonie, the staffer for Gerry Solomon, of our intentions so that he would have time to get the text of a Solomon resolution on PRC human rights into the *Record*. That back-channel gesture and the moderate tone of the Taiwan resolution were sufficient to secure the goodwill of the KMT's congressional friends, and the text was adopted in June without controversy (as was the PRC text). The provision survived the House–Senate conference on the bill unscathed, and Congress had for the first time gone on record supporting a set of specific reforms that would bring full democracy on Taiwan: the guarantee of political freedoms and the establishment of representative government. That these were also Lee Teng-hui's objectives no doubt made the measure more tolerable.[60]

From 1987 on, as Taiwan's reformers sought to take new steps in the direction of a fully democratic system, Solarz was always a few paces ahead. He acknowledged sincerely the progress that they had made but urged them on to address outstanding deficiencies. He did this in a variety of ways. First were hearings, which were held on an annual basis. These were balanced and substantive discussions of major milestones that had either just occurred or were about to happen. There was always a witness on the panel who had been suggested by FAPA, but there were also individuals who represented the center and conservative parts of the spectrum. Taiwan reporters attended the hearings religiously and played the sessions' main points back into the Taiwan political debate.[61]

Second, and more privately, Solarz began a practice of writing to Taiwan's presidents. The first occasion was a letter to Chiang Ching-kuo in May 1987.

Solarz both praised Chiang for his liberalizing initiatives and laid out an agenda of steps to complete the process of democratization, including the release of long-time political prisoners and an end to political restrictions on the return of some overseas Taiwanese. After Lee Teng-hui succeeded Chiang in January 1988, Solarz wrote to him about every six months. In most cases, these letters were written in response to a FAPA request that Solarz raise some specific concern at a high level, but those concerns were always embedded in a broader and more balanced discussion.[62]

The third way that Solarz sought to affect events in Taiwan was through pointed public statements in times of crisis. The first of these came in March 1990, just before the National Assembly vote on whether Lee Teng-hui would continue as president. Conservatives in the KMT had mounted a challenge to Lee and it was touch-and-go for awhile. A trusted Taiwanese friend approached me with concerns that military leaders were trying to exert inappropriate influence over the selection. On March 8, Solarz issued a statement that expressed concern that such an action would "provoke instability and undermine democratization." He continued, "Because the National Assembly is unrepresentative, in that it is composed primarily of individuals who last ran for office over forty years ago, it is all the more important that its ultimate choice for president and vice president not deviate sharply from the will and wishes of the Taiwan people." The State Department issued a similar statement and both ran in Taipei papers on March 9.[63]

The second intervention came in the fall of 1991, at a tense time prior to the election for a new National Assembly. The elderly mainlander incumbents had been retired, and the new members would either be elected from Taiwan districts or be picked on a proportional basis. The most pressing issue was a decision of the DPP to amend its charter to make more explicit its goal of a Republic of Taiwan. This had provoked a harsh reaction from Beijing and raised the possibility of a government crackdown on the DPP, since advocating Taiwan independence was still not permitted. Solarz urged Beijing not to engage in saber rattling and called for restraint on the part of the ROC government: "To crack down on parties that advocate Taiwan independence would be a violation of fundamental principles of human rights. It would also betray a distressing lack of confidence in the political wisdom of the people of Taiwan. The real test of the extent of freedom of speech is whether a government is willing to tolerate what it doesn't wish to hear, and is willing to let the people make the ultimate judgment." In the end, the government did not act against the DPP and the KMT successfully made an electoral issue of the DPP's advocacy of independence.[64]

With a democracy resolution passed in 1987, Cai Tongrong had a series of new proposals for Solarz. Some were public relations gambits, such as an

Olympics-style torch relay that began at the Statue of Liberty in October 1987, made stops in the Washington DC and Los Angeles areas, and then culminated in Taiwan. The theme was the unrepresentative character of Taiwan's central elective bodies. Another was a poll, which Solarz sponsored, of Taiwanese-American views of the situation in their homeland. Given a definite bias in selecting who would receive the questionnaire, the results could have been predicted in advance. Another project was a Solarz-led congressional delegation to monitor the 1989 Legislative Yuan elections. Such a delegation was unneeded to prevent balloting abuses, since balloting was the cleanest part of Taiwan's electoral system. Any unfairness would occur in the weeks before the election because of the KMT's control of the media. And it emerged that Cai's real goal was to have the delegation subtly convey support for DPP candidates. That did not happen, and anyway Solarz was distracted from his monitoring mission by an attempted coup in the Philippines. In the end, he pronounced the election the freest and fairest yet in terms of its process but still not fair in terms of the outcome, because the Legislative Yuan nonetheless had a number of members who represented districts on the mainland. Finally, in September 1991, FAPA tried to play up the fortieth anniversary of the San Francisco Peace Treaty concluding World War II and the view that Taiwan's international legal status had been left undetermined. In responding to these ideas, Solarz tried to strike the right balance between satisfying his friends and avoiding diplomatic problems.[65]

One proposal from Cai would have an enduring impact. In April 1988, he suggested that Congress pass a resolution calling for a plebiscite on Taiwan on the question of whether Taiwan should be a part of the PRC. The focus on a plebiscite reflected his long-standing desire to secure for the people on Taiwan the right of self-determination and a more recent concern about the opening of economic and human contacts between the two sides of the strait. I told Solarz that I thought this was a bad idea, in part because it was not appropriate for the U.S. Congress to tell a democratizing Taiwan how to express the popular will, and in part because Beijing, which had been fairly relaxed about Taiwan, would regard such a plebiscite as foreclosing unification and be compelled to react. A resolution would divide Congress concerning Taiwan at a time that it was starting to come together. The matter was dropped, only to be revived in the spring of 1990. This time, Solarz agreed to introduce a resolution, the operative clause of which was "it is the sense of Congress that in determining the future of Taiwan, the will and wishes of the people on the island should be taken into account through effective democratic mechanisms, such as a plebiscite." Thus we satisfied Cai without explicitly advocating a plebiscite. FAPA tried to push for action on the resolution, which I believed would only provoke opposition from both the Taiwan government (and therefore from its conservative friends) and the PRC.[66]

No action occurred in part because an alternative way to make the same basic point emerged, promoted by someone else besides Cai Tongrong. The alternative was a revival of the resolution that Pell and Leach had introduced in 1983. The agent was David Tsai (Cai Wuxiong), who had been associated with WUFI and FAPA but had set up his own organization, the Taiwan Center of International Relations. In the summer of 1989, after the Tiananmen Incident heightened Taiwanese concerns about PRC intentions, Tsai approached Pell about a congressional statement reaffirming the need for a peaceful process and taking Taiwanese views into account. Pell's office developed a shorter and more moderate version of the original self-determination resolution from 1983, and successfully offered it as an amendment to the Senate version of the State Department authorization bill. Tsai then approached me about getting the House to accept the provision in conference. Unfortunately, Solarz was not on the conference committee and Representative Dante Fascell, who was in charge of the bill for the House side wanted a stripped-down bill with as few controversial provisions as possible. In addition, the Coordination Council on North American Affairs (CCNAA), Taiwan's representative office in Washington, was able to mount a lobbying effort against it. I suggested that Tsai mobilize Taiwanese organizations in support of the text provision, which he did. In the end, it was to no avail.[67]

In 1991, Tsai sought my help again on the same provision, but this time he started on the House side. Drawing on my experience with the democracy provision, I advised Solarz to operate by stealth. We used the foreign aid authorization bill as our vehicle, and were able to have the language included in an en bloc amendment that was adopted on June 12. CCNAA was caught off guard. People in the Taiwanese community and in the DPP in Taiwan were very happy, but through Tsai I urged them to be quiet in order to minimize opposition to the provision. That strategy worked and with Pell's help the Senate adopted the measure on July 24. In the end, the foreign aid bill never got enacted because it could never get through conference (which may explain why CCNAA did not fight hard). But the fact was, both houses of Congress were on record supporting the view that "the future of Taiwan should be settled peacefully, free from coercion, and in a manner acceptable to Taiwan." This approach was less provocative substantively, in that it did not mention how acceptability might be determined (a plebiscite, for example), and also in terms of process, since inserting the text as an amendment to a broader bill often is more successful than trying to move a freestanding resolution.[68]

The other reason that FAPA did not exert more pressure on the plebiscite resolution was that Cai Tongrong had returned to Taiwan. He had tried to go back before the 1989 Legislative Yuan elections, and Solarz appealed to the government to give him a visa, but nothing happened. Then, in June 1990, his father-in-law was killed in Taiwan in an auto accident, and Cai saw an opening. With Solarz's assistance, he asked to return to attend the memorial service and fully intended to stay. Somewhat to my surprise, the government agreed. He took his plebiscite idea with him and within a year got the DPP to make it a part of its 1991 charter statement (the one that risked a government crackdown). He would win a seat in the Legislative Yuan in December 1992. But FAPA would suffer somewhat without his energy.

Cai's return was part of a much broader effort by Taiwanese exile activists to reenter the politics of their homeland. They had sought to promote their goals from a distance, but now that the political system was opening up they wanted a chance to compete for power. (As can be imagined, the exiles' return created tensions with people in the DPP who had been risking their freedom on a fairly constant basis while the exiles had been living in the United States, despite their shared opposition to the KMT.)

The returnees who were most problematic were leaders and members of WUFI, in part because of its goal of Taiwan independence and in part because of the allegations that it had used violent means. All were on the so-called blacklist and could not usually secure visas. They began applying in the late 1980s, and some sought and received letters of support from Solarz. The effort intensified in 1991 as the National Assembly elections loomed. Inevitably, some of the exiles were arrested once they got home, for example, Guo Peihong, Li Yingyuan, and Kang Luwang. Solarz had a multipronged response. He issued statements criticizing the arrests. He wrote Lee Teng-hui and other officials encouraging restraint and clemency. And he introduced a resolution calling on the government to end the blacklist. He chose not to move the resolution because of likely ROC opposition, and soon the government relaxed the policy.[69]

Epilogue and Conclusion

In December 1992, elections were held for a new Legislative Yuan. As with the National Assembly elections a year earlier, the result, in terms of each party's share of seats, reflected more or less the balance of opinion on the island. Gone were the "old thieves," members who had run on the mainland in the late 1940s and held seats for decades. The island now had all the formal institutions of a full democracy. The only remaining issue was whether the president would be elected directly by the people or indirectly by the National Assembly. In 1994 the constitution would be amended to allow for direct elections and in 1996 Lee Teng-hui would become the first chief executive in a Chinese political system to be chosen by popular ballot. With democratization achieved, the former *dangwai* shifted its agenda to gaining power and asserting Taiwan's identity.

Also at the end of 1992, Steve Solarz left Congress. His reputation had been tarnished in a Republican-engineered controversy over an internal House financial agency, and the New York State Assembly, required to reduce the number of congressional districts by three, chose not to ensure his previously safe seat. Another New Yorker, Gary Ackerman, took his place as chairman of the Asian and Pacific affairs subcommittee but he focused on other issues. As Taiwanese-Americans shifted their emphasis toward the goal of independence, members of Congress would be reluctant to support them because it put them at odds with U.S. policy and the fundamentals of American relations with the PRC. Moreover, the leading activists of the community had returned to Taiwan.

By 1995, the game had changed again. President Lee Teng-hui decided that he wanted to visit the United States. His Foreign Ministry, which controlled the various consulting firms that lobbied on Taiwan's behalf, resisted that idea because, in its view, it would alienate the island's only protector. Lee ignored that advice and hired his own lobbying firm, Cassidy and Associates. Cassidy then mounted a very effective public relations campaign, which built strong congressional and media pressure on the Clinton administration. Whatever their party affiliation or ideological tendency, members supported the Lee visit. Democratization on the island had replaced the American liberal-conservative split concerning Taiwan with wall-to-wall support. Increasingly, FAPA activists and Taiwan diplomats would mount parallel efforts even if they did not directly cooperate.

In the literature about American politics, there are few objective and analytic discussions of ethnic lobbies. The effort of the Taiwanese-American community and their friends in Congress revealed here offers a useful case study of what is possible and what is not in influencing the foreign policy of the United States and the politics of the home country of the ethnic lobby. What stand out are the huge obstacles to effective influence.[70]

First, the ethnic group must attain a critical political mass *and* decide to pursue its goals through the American political process. Taiwanese-Americans did not really establish themselves as even a potential political force in the United States until the mid-1970s. By then, the graduate students of the 1950s and 1960s had become professionals with the time and—frankly—the money to press their case with members of Congress and presidential candidates. Their initial efforts at lobbying were aborted after the attack on Chiang

Ching-kuo, and for many years they chose to pursue a strategy of direct, conspiratorial action against the KMT instead. It was only during the letter-writing campaigns after the Kaohsiung Incident that their strategy shifted again.

Second, the task is much more difficult if the target government, in order to protect its interests and regime, has penetrated the U.S. government and the ethnic communities. From the 1940s, the ROC had seen the value of shaping American public opinion and cultivating a base of support in the U.S. Congress as a means of deterring and countering damaging initiatives by the Executive Branch. That influence also came in handy when Taipei saw the need to counter criticism of its political setup, as it regularly did during the 1980s. The KMT also regarded the United States as a legitimate arena for monitoring Taiwan citizens and intimidating them from engaging in opposition activities. This effort was quite successful early and probably undercut those activities. Ironically, it was that very surveillance that led some Taiwanese to strike back. It was the excessive application of that policy that had the most damaging impact on the ROC's position because its American friends refused to defend them.

Third, it is harder to influence either Executive Branch policy or the target government if a U.S. administration both regards the country in question as a strategic asset and does not believe that the human rights problems undermine American interests to such a degree that it is necessary to push the regime to show restraint. Although the Truman administration had periodically urged the ROC to promote political reform to ensure survival and American interests, the Eisenhower administration was sufficiently convinced of the ROC's geopolitical value that it did not continue those efforts (see Chapter 3). But by the late 1970s, with the rise of the human rights issue, congressional lobbying by Taiwanese-Americans, and Taiwan's growing isolation, the State Department began to urge Taipei to improve its image in America by restraining human rights abuses. That quiet diplomacy reinforced the public calls by members like Solarz and Leach, just as their appeals reinforced administration pleadings. But if Solarz and Leach had coupled their calls for democratization with advocacy of Taiwan independence—thus satisfying their more radical Taiwanese supporters but undermining the China policy of the Executive Branch—they would not have been so effective. It was precisely because they were careful to balance their approaches to China and Taiwan that they had the tacit support of the administration.

Fourth, ethnic lobbies do not always agree with their congressional allies because of conflicting interests. The latent disagreement that existed between Solarz and Leach on the one hand and Taiwanese-American activists on the other threatened to undermine their cooperation, and therefore their influence.

Some Taiwanese accepted Solarz's and Leach's focus on democratization for its own sake, their need to pursue their Taiwan initiatives while keeping U.S.–PRC relations in mind, and perhaps their assumption that the KMT had a reformist wing. But the bias of the community was to pursue independence as the fundamental goal with democratization as the means. The KMT, in their view, was incapable of reform. Provocation of both Taipei and Beijing was preferred over balance and moderation. Symbols were preferred over substance. Cai Tongrong pursued this latter agenda fairly relentlessly, and ethnic communities like the Taiwanese probably needed aggressive leaders like that. With Solarz at least, he had the leverage of campaign contributions. It fell to Solarz and his staff to set the limits of what was appropriate and what was not.

Even when an administration is quietly supportive of congressional pressure for political change by a foreign government, and even when the lobby and its congressional supporters are on the same wavelength, an absence of tools can hurt the effort. The KMT's critics lacked important convening power until Solarz became chairman of the Asia and Pacific affairs subcommittee in January 1981. Even so, and even though binding provisions were enacted concerning the immigration quota and intimidation and harassment in the United States, he and Leach had very few options for influencing the situation in Taiwan. There was no economic or security assistance to deny or condition. Blocking arms sales was a political nonstarter and bad policy as well. All that was left was holding hearings and promoting nonbinding resolutions. Even these were problematic, for hearings had to include pro-KMT witnesses and the Taipei government could mobilize its friends to block the resolutions. In the end, Solarz only got one freestanding resolution through the House, and that was in response to the indefensible murder of Henry Liu. He ultimately secured adoption of the text of a couple of resolutions as provisions in larger bills, a procedure that was more likely to succeed but lacked the symbolic value of passing freestanding resolutions. In effect, his power was to shame the KMT into reform, to warn it away from worse repression, and to promise a better relationship with the United States if it moved toward democracy.

In this particular case, conditions happened to be right for successful influence. The KMT's restrictions on the press were not so tight that news of Solarz–Leach initiatives could not get through. The elections that took place demonstrated that the government did not have overwhelming support. There were reformers within the Kuomintang who took seriously its democratic objectives, who believed the party could stay in power even in a more competitive environment, and who saw the value of a better relationship with the United States when formal ties had already been cut.

Chiang Ching-kuo was open to their arguments and had time to start the process before his death. Lee Teng-hui proved to be surprisingly effective in completing Chiang's mission.

Yet without a courageous domestic opposition, the pace and direction of change would not have been so certain. The *dangwai* demonstrated that there was a popular constituency for change on the island, not just among overseas exiles. It was an indigenous force that Solarz and Leach could provide with recognition and protection, which they did, and from which they could secure advice on tactics, which they also did.

In short, members of Congress and their Taiwanese-American supporters made but a tertiary contribution to the democratization of Taiwan, after the *dangwai* opposition and KMT reformers. It was the interaction between the two Taiwan forces that was crucial, but the impact of outsiders on that interaction was far from trivial.

7

Taiwan Policy Making Since Tiananmen

Navigating Through Shifting Waters

Analysts of the evolution of the People's Republic of China (PRC) and of U.S.–PRC–Taiwan relations have observed a tendency for major shifts to occur more or less in ten-year increments. Thus it was in the late 1950s, ten years after the founding of the PRC and the Sino-Soviet alliance, that Beijing moved down the road to radicalism at home and parallel hostility to both Moscow and Washington abroad. Rapprochement between the United States and the PRC, with all that meant for the Nationalist regime on Taiwan, began almost as soon as Richard Nixon took office in 1969 and culminated in formal normalization under Jimmy Carter ten years later.

The most striking example of this apparent pattern of decade-by-decade transitions has been the last decade of the twentieth century. The year 1989 brought the Tiananmen tragedy and with it the sharp decline in the American public's support for a policy of engagement and cooperation with the PRC. The end of the 1980s was also the point at which democratization within Taiwan began to accelerate under Lee Teng-hui's leadership and the long-closed door between the two sides of the strait began to open. As the 1990s proceeded, there were significant gains in Chinese economic and military power, and 1997 saw the reversion of Hong Kong to PRC sovereignty.

In this chapter I examine one dimension of the post-1989 environment: the formation of U.S. policy toward Taiwan during the Bush and Clinton administrations. American policy makers in the 1990s faced unprecedented challenges in preserving U.S. interests as they accommodated the new forces at play. It had been one thing, for example, to interact with a Taiwan government in which a small number of individuals made decisions; now the Taiwan public was playing an increasingly significant role.

In this chapter I follow an approach that is more thematic and analytical than factual. Three recently published books provide detailed accounts of the period: James Mann, *About Face;* Linda Chao and Ramon Myers, *The First Chinese Democracy;* and Ralph Clough, *Cooperation and Conflict in the Taiwan Strait?*[1] The tensions of 1995–96, when the decade's new forces came together, are the focus of discussion.

Context

At the outset, it is important to establish some points of broad context that shaped how the U.S. government addressed the Taiwan issue in the Bush and Clinton administrations. First is the priority that Washington has placed since the end of World War II on preserving peace and stability in East Asia. Specifically, the United States would deny dominance of the region to any hostile power, by deterrence if possible and by warfare if necessary. Alliances, forward deployment of U.S. forces, global economic liberalization, and the encouragement of open societies were all means to that end.

Second has been the long-standing belief that a strong and positive U.S. relationship with mainland China would foster peace and stability in East Asia. This vision was a fantasy at the time of Franklin Roosevelt but was realized by Richard Nixon and Jimmy Carter in the 1970s. The disappearance of the Soviet Union and the absence of a global adversary have not negated the view that cooperation between Washington and Beijing contributes to geopolitical equilibrium, even though the rationale is not as short or simple as it was in the 1970s. (To be sure, there is growing in America an alternative view that the current PRC regime will be the adversary that challenges the United States for dominance in East Asia.)

The third point of context concerns the role of the U.S. Congress. Our separation-of-powers system, the powers that the constitution confers on Congress, the campaign financing "system," the existence of immigrant communities, and a variety of other factors guarantee that the legislative branch will play a role on any major foreign-policy issue and a number of minor ones as well. This is a reality whether or not foreign governments choose to protect and enhance their interests by cultivating the Congress. And there is nothing illegal about foreign representatives in Washington stating their case to members of Congress or hiring American entities to serve as their agents to do so. The Kuomintang (KMT) leadership may have been one of the first to garner support on Capitol Hill but by now it is only one among many. Moreover, members of Congress will often take action concerning a foreign country solely on their own initiative and not because the representatives of that country ask them to do so. Thus any administration, its wishes to the contrary notwithstanding, must accept the reality that Congress or at least some of its members will seek to influence foreign policy, including toward Taiwan.

A fourth point of context for considering the events of the 1990s includes the essential elements of U.S. policy toward the PRC and Taiwan. Viewed from outside the Executive Branch, these are sometimes seen as inconvenient or anachronistic impediments to the proposal of the moment (if they are remembered at all). For those responsible for the daily conduct of American policy, past commitments provide on a cumulative basis the contours that must be taken into account as future action is considered. They are often also the basis on which the PRC makes commitments that are beneficial to the United States.

On its fundamental stance concerning the two sides of the strait, the United States in the 1978 normalization communiqué acknowledged "the Chinese position" that there is but one China and that Taiwan is a part of China. As early as July 1971, and on a number of occasions since, high-level U.S. officials have made policy statements that are corollaries to this "one-China" principle: that Washington does not support two Chinas, one China and one Taiwan, or Taiwan independence. Another corollary was implicit: that the PRC would represent China in international organizations. Finally, having recognized the PRC as the "sole legal government of China," the United States agreed to have unofficial relations with Taiwan.

Concerning Taiwan's security, every administration has insisted that the Taiwan Strait issue be resolved peacefully. In addition, the Taiwan Relations Act (TRA) lays out the following guidelines: that hostile action by the PRC against Taiwan would be regarded as a threat to the peace and security of the Western Pacific and a matter of grave concern to the United States; that the United States should maintain the capacity to resist such hostile action; that the president and Congress would consult and take appropriate action in response to any threat to Taiwan's security and danger to U.S. interests.

On arms sales to Taiwan, the Carter administration made clear to the PRC in the run up to normalization that transfers would continue but also pledged that the weaponry would be defensive in nature.[2] The TRA mandated that the United States should provide defense articles and services necessary for Taiwan to maintain a sufficient ability to defend itself. In the August 1982 communiqué with the PRC, in light of Beijing's assertion of a "fundamental policy to strive for a peaceful solution to the Taiwan question," the United States committed to show restraint in its arms sales. At the same time, Washington informed Taipei that it had neither set a date for the end of arms sales nor would it hold prior consultations with Beijing on arms sales.[3]

On how to resolve the Taiwan Strait issue, the United States has indicated that any arrangement should be worked out by the two sides themselves and that it would accept any solution that they craft, as long as it is done peacefully. In addition, Washington informed Taipei in July 1982 that it would not pressure Taiwan into negotiations with the PRC nor would it seek to mediate the dispute. In addition to these specific commitments on cross-strait relations is an underlying approach that was first expressed publicly by Secretary of State George Shultz (under President Ronald Reagan) in February 1987 and has remained in place until this day. In his statement, Shultz welcomed developments such as cross-strait trade and travel that contributed to a relaxation of tensions. "Our steadfast policy," he said, "seeks to foster an environment within which such developments can continue to take place." This approach of context creation is part of the generally benign stance that the United States has taken toward East Asia. The positive environment that the United States has sought to foster, in part through good relations with the PRC, has contributed to Taiwan's economic and democratic progress and preserved its security, as well as improved the climate across the strait.

The Bush Administration

As the Bush administration came to office, its foreign policy team had legitimate reason to believe that the Taiwan issue was becoming less salient in U.S. policy toward East Asia and that they could manage it easily. Trends that began in the late Reagan years had been positive and continuity would be the order of the day. (Indeed, many of Bush's officials had worked in the second Reagan administration.) In the wake of the August 1982 communiqué, the Reagan team had hit on a mix of sales and technology transfer to meet Taiwan's defense needs. Taiwan's leadership and foreign-policy establishment had adapted to the norms of unofficial relations. The island's first tentative steps of political liberalization and democratization promised to mitigate congressional criticism of the KMT's human rights record. Cross-strait contacts and exchanges had begun. George Shultz's cautious optimism of early 1987 was still justified.

And for much of the Bush administration, the forces that would converge to increase Taiwan tensions in the mid-1990s were only beginning to build. The administration had to spend most of its effort contending with the collapse in public support for U.S.–PRC relations caused by the events at Tiananmen in 1989 and its aftermath. Policy toward Taiwan was marked by basic continuity combined with adjustments to deal with unanticipated problems.

Over the course of the Bush administration, Taiwan's image in Congress and the American public took a significant turn for the better. For decades, a segment of American opinion was critical of the Kuomintang's authoritarian rule and abuse of human rights. The Kaohsiung Incident of December 1979 had exposed the regime's antidemocratic nature, and native Taiwanese in the United States sought congressional support in putting human rights on the agenda of U.S. policy. There resulted during the 1980s a series of skirmishes in Congress between some liberals who supported the native Taiwanese aspiration for democracy and the KMT's old friends, mostly conservatives, who argued that the regime's human rights performance was far better than that of the PRC. With the process of liberalization and democratization on Taiwan that began in the late 1980s and continued into the 1990s, Taiwan's political system was no longer an issue of congressional debate. Between liberals and conservatives, there emerged a broad consensus in support of Taiwan, which was reinforced by the contrast with the simultaneous deterioration of the human rights situation on the mainland and American liberals' reevaluation of the PRC. This new consensus in favor of Taiwan as a fellow democracy would become a significant factor in future policy debates.

With the beginning of democratization, the late 1980s saw a shift in Taiwan's external behavior, in particular the opening of cross-strait relations and the incremental expansion of the island's international role. These trends not only seemed to pose no fundamental problem for U.S. policy; they also strengthened U.S. confidence in the wisdom of its policies. Indeed, it seemed to be an optimal situation, for Washington could continue to balance its interests with both sides of the strait at low costs. To the extent that increased contacts and integration across the Taiwan Strait reduced tensions, they were consistent with Washington's hope for a peaceful solution.

Another early 1990s trend that worked against U.S. interests was growing economic competition among advanced industrial economies for Taiwan's business. European governments began sending economic ministers to Taipei to encourage favorable consideration of bids by their companies, and did so despite Beijing's protests. The United States would remain at a competitive disadvantage as long as the government's guidelines restricted visits to sub-Cabinet officials. That constraint was relaxed at the end of the Bush administration, when Carla Hills, the U.S. trade representative, traveled to Taiwan to speak at a conference of business organizations. The Bush administration was also successful in hewing to an evenhanded approach with respect to international economic organizations. In 1991, it had facilitated the simultaneous entry on an equal basis of the PRC, "Chinese Taipei," and Hong Kong into the forum on Asia Pacific Economic Cooperation (APEC). And it took the position with Beijing that Taiwan's entry into the General Agreement on Tariffs and Trade ([GATT], later the World Trade Organization [WTO]) would not necessarily be delayed until the PRC joined.[4]

Competition was fiercest in the area of weapons. The collapse of the Soviet Union had reduced the demand for arms by the United States and its allies but it had not as quickly reduced the supply of arms, or the desire among Western and Russian defense firms to keep production lines open. This affected Taiwan in two ways. On the one hand, the Russian Republic suddenly gave the PRC access to advanced weapons systems at affordable prices. In March 1992, a contract was signed concerning the transfer of the *Sukhoi*-27 (Su-27) aircraft, which was more capable than any aircraft hitherto faced by Taiwan's Air Force. Second, foreign defense contractors began to press their governments for the opportunity to market systems to Taiwan that had long been off-limits. Thus the French firm Dassault promoted the *Mirage* 2000 and General Dynamics the F-16, each as remedies for Taiwan's aging fighter fleet.

As described by James Mann, the Bush administration's decision to approve the F-16 for Taiwan reflected a mix of security concerns, institutional priorities, commercial interests, and electoral politics. The Su-27 transfer and the age of Taiwan's planes pushed the Pentagon to worry about the shifting air balance in the Taiwan Strait. The State Department placed more emphasis on the U.S. undertakings to the PRC to restrain arms sales to Taiwan (to which was tied the important PRC commitment to strive to resolve the Taiwan issue peacefully). There were reports that Taiwan was about to buy the *Mirage*. And the Bush White House was worried about the president's reelection and the need to hold Texas, home of General Dynamics. Mann concludes that the United States would have ultimately transferred F-16s to Taiwan in order to preserve Taiwan's security, but the timing of the decision was governed by the pressures of the 1992 presidential campaign.[5]

A review of the Bush period would be incomplete without a brief discussion of cross-strait ties. Whereas U.S.–PRC relations were roiled by the aftermath of Tiananmen, and U.S.–Taiwan relations saw modest improvement, relations across the Taiwan Strait made significant progress, releasing a potential that had been pent up for decades. Taipei gradually relaxed its past restrictions on travel, trade, and outward investment. Taiwan residents in large numbers visited their native places and owners of labor-intensive factories began moving their production to the mainland. Even in the political realm, there was a reduction of tensions. On the Taiwan side, President Lee Teng-hui in 1991 announced the end of a policy of hostility toward the mainland and canceled the temporary provisions for the period of mobilization. On each side, organizations were set up to formulate cross-strait policy and to conduct semiofficial contacts (for the latter, Taipei established the Straits Exchange Foundation [SEF] and Beijing set up the Association for Relations Across the Taiwan Strait [ARATS]). Progress was impeded for a while by disagreements over the definition of the "one-China principle," but the two sides addressed that in 1992 by agreeing that there was one China but that each could define it as it wished (*gezi biaoshu*).[6] The engagement that began in 1987 culminated in the first meeting of the heads of the SEF and ARATS— Gu Zhenfu (Koo Chen-fu) and Wang Daohan—in Singapore in April 1993. Throughout this process, the United States maintained a stance of distanced approval, consistent with the principle that cross-strait differences should be resolved by the two sides themselves.

The Clinton Administration: Prelude to Cornell

As with the Bush administration, Taiwan was not high on the agenda of the Clinton team as it came into office. Its attention was focused on how to fulfill the president's campaign pledge to use the annual extension of the PRC's most-favored-nation (MFN) trading status as leverage over its human rights policies. In Congress, however, initiatives regarding Taiwan soon surfaced.

The first pressure came over arms sales. Senator Frank Murkowski (R-AK) attached an amendment to the Senate version of the State Department authorization bill that would have amended the Taiwan Relations Act to say that the TRA's arms-sales provisions superseded the August 1982 communiqué. It had been the position of the State Department that as a matter of law, the relevant sections of the Taiwan Relations Act took precedence over the analogous language of the communiqué's political undertakings; domestic law clearly has priority over statements of policy. Yet the Murkowski amendment would have had the TRA language supersede that of the communiqué, thus abrogating or setting aside the communiqué's political undertakings. The legislation, it seemed, was canceling an American policy commitment to the PRC at the same time that the Clinton administration was trying to get Beijing to make new or better policy undertakings in the areas of human rights, nonproliferation, and trade.

The issue remained unresolved until the spring of 1994, when the House–Senate conference on the State Department bill convened. Through the intervention of Representative Lee Hamilton (D-IN), chairman of the House Foreign Affairs Committee, a compromise was worked out whereby Congress made a nonbinding declaration reaffirming the State Department's traditional view of the legal relationship between the two documents. Hamilton also sought to encourage better communication between defense contractors and the State Department.

Shortly after the Hamilton compromise was reached, a Taiwan delegation, headed by President Lee, had planned a trip to Central America and to South Africa and sought Washington's permission to make a transit stop in Hawaii that would have included an overnight stay and a round of golf. When the administration decided only to permit a refueling stop at Hickham Air Force Base, President Lee took offense and declined to get off the airplane. Taiwan's friends in Congress soon learned of the incident and took the administration to task, seeking during the fall to pass legislation that would require the Executive Branch to grant Lee a visa in the future should he wish to come to the United States for certain purposes.[7]

Administration critics said the decision to deny a transit stop was the wrong call, reflecting a too-tender concern for Beijing's sensitivities. In defense of the administration, however, it is worth noting that the transit request came at a particularly critical time in U.S.–PRC relations. Washington was trying to extract final human-rights concessions from Beijing in the hope that President Clinton would be able to affirm that the PRC had fully met the terms of his MFN executive order. Negotiations concerning intellectual property rights were going down to the wire. And the situation on the Korean peninsula was at the brink, with the United States pushing toward UN Security Council sanctions and Pyongyang vowing to unleash a "sea of fire." On that issue in particular, it was in Washington's fundamental interest that Beijing's position be close to that of the United States, and that nothing be done to sow unnecessary division. The transit request reached Washington at the worst possible time, therefore, and the administration response was probably a function of the higher priority it placed on those issues.[8]

The other Taiwan event of 1994 was the completion of the Taiwan policy review. This effort was one of many assessments that the Clinton White House undertook after it came into office, as is typical of a new administration. But it also was a response to the desire by some in Congress to improve the institutional mechanics of U.S.–Taiwan relations, particularly given the Europeans' continuing tendency to enhance their commercial advantage through ministerial visits (which the Bush administration had already had to face). The review was not completed until September 1994, to ensure that it did not conflict with the handling of the Murkowski amendment and the MFN renewal decision. In the end, the administration took a number of steps that sought, in an incremental fashion, to respond to Taiwan's concerns, including the following:

- The name of Taiwan's offices in the United States were changed from the Coordination Council for North American Affairs to the Taipei Economic and Cultural Representative Office (for the office in Washington, DC) and Taipei Economic and Cultural Office (elsewhere in the United States). As a result, the public would now know that the organization had something to do with Taiwan.
- Taiwan's representatives could now visit U.S. officials in their offices, with the exception of the State Department, the Old Executive Office Building, and the White House.
- Cabinet-level officials in economic and functional agencies were permitted when appropriate to visit Taipei.
- Taiwan's president, vice president, premier, and vice premier would be allowed to make low-profile transit stops in the United States for their convenience, safety, and comfort (the sort of stop that Taiwan had sought for President Lee four months before).

- Although the United States would not support Taiwan's membership in international organizations where statehood was a prerequisite (in effect U.S. policy since 1979), it would support ways for its "voice to be heard" in those institutions and also support its membership in organizations where statehood was not a prerequisite (such as the World Trade Organization).

These steps satisfied no one. Beijing complained that the United States was not sticking to its commitment to have only unofficial relations with the island. Taiwan, although it appreciated the better treatment, would have liked even more. And the members of Congress who had pushed for improved practice were underwhelmed, particularly after the transit decision back in the spring. But sometimes a policy step is successful at least to the extent that it dissatisfies each of the affected parties equally.

Cornell and Its Aftermath

These congressional initiatives were only a prelude to the campaign to convince the president to grant a visa to President Lee so that he could visit the United States and his alma mater, Cornell University. Early evidence of that campaign occurred at a hearing of the House Asia and Pacific Affairs Subcommittee in February 1995, where the assistant secretary of state for East Asia, Winston Lord, was to provide a general overview of U.S. policy toward the region. Two things were surprising—even unprecedented—at the hearing. First, each member of the subcommittee and some nonmembers as well attended. Second, each wanted to speak on only one subject: why the administration should approve a visa for Lee. Such phenomena do not occur on Capitol Hill by chance. There was, it was clear, a concerted effort under way in which all points of leverage would be pushed and no angle of influence would be ignored. It was, in the end, one of the most sophisticated operations to influence foreign policy in recent memory.[9]

The administration was caught in a tremendous bind. On the one hand, the United States had made a commitment to Beijing at the time of normalization that its relations with Taiwan would be unofficial. Although Beijing was well aware that the U.S. ties with Taiwan are robust and substantive, and although the line between official and unofficial is not precise, a public visit to the United States by Taiwan's top official—even in a private capacity—arguably stretched the meaning of "unofficial" to the breaking point. To draw an analogy, suppose that Jefferson Davis had been a graduate of Oxford University, and suppose that he proposed to pay a personal visit to his alma mater in 1862 in the middle of the Civil War at the very time that

Britain was mulling the idea of recognizing the Confederate States of America. How would Abraham Lincoln have reacted?

On the other hand, there was the reality of the congressional pressure. The administration was at a built-in disadvantage in explaining why its one-China policy made Lee's visit inappropriate, particularly when those favoring the trip framed their case in terms of Taiwan's democracy, Lee's affection for Cornell, and the fact that Beijing was the party most opposed. By this point, most members of Congress had not been in office when even the 1982 communiqué was negotiated, much less the other two. Moreover, it was clear that if necessary those who favored Lee's visit would not stop at the nonbinding resolutions that passed both Houses with little or no dissent. They would pass binding legislation to force the president to allow Lee's entry. In April 1995, Secretary of State Warren Christopher reportedly sought to warn PRC foreign minister Qian Qichen that Congress might well overrule the department's view on the matter. In the end, that is basically what happened.[10]

The PRC responded by conducting two rounds of military exercises, one in the summer and fall of 1995 in advance of Taiwan's Legislative Yuan elections, and the other in March 1996 before the presidential elections. This was not the first time that Beijing had used exercises to make a point at the time of Taiwan elections. But these two rounds were larger in scale and closer geographically to Taiwan (especially the March round) than any that had come before. How the U.S. government interpreted these actions was publicly discussed in congressional testimony by Winston Lord in March 1996.[11]

Lord asserted that the PRC actions, which he characterized as "intimidation and psychological warfare," were Beijing's reaction to recent Taiwan actions, as it interpreted them:

> Recent PRC demonstrations of military strength are designed to send a message to the Taiwan authorities to curb what the PRC regards as efforts to establish an independent Taiwan. Recent Taiwan policies, including last June's private visit to the U.S. by President Lee Teng-hui, have been interpreted by the PRC as a step toward independence. The Chinese position, acknowledged by us, is that Taiwan is a part of China, and the PRC interprets these developments in Taiwan as a challenge to the acceptance of a "one China" policy by Taipei. Beijing's leaders are especially sensitive on this issue, which involves questions of sovereignty and national integrity.

Lord informed the subcommittee that the administration had concluded that the PRC exercises did not pose an "imminent threat" to the island that might trigger actions under the TRA. The situation was not without risk, however:

The PRC wishes to influence Taiwan's presidential election, and more fundamentally, to restrain Taiwan's international activities. The PRC does not in our judgment intend to take direct military action against Taiwan. We understand the Taiwan authorities have reached the same conclusion. While the PRC is bent on intimidation and psychological warfare, they know that resorting to force would severely damage their own interests. Nonetheless, their recent actions clearly carry the risk of accidents or miscalculation that could lead to escalation. . . . Although neither Taiwan nor the PRC wants a military confrontation, there is a danger that misunderstandings and strong emotions on both sides could lead to a further increase in tensions and even unanticipated conflict. Democratic development in Taiwan has permitted the free expression by a portion of the Taiwan populace of a desire for a separate Taiwan identity—a desire largely suppressed under the previous political leadership in Taiwan.

The administration, Lord said, did not believe that the PRC had abandoned its fundamental policy of striving for peaceful reunification with Taiwan as stated in the August 1982 communiqué.

Lord described a series of steps that the administration had taken to warn Beijing of the seriousness with which the United States viewed the situation:

During the past several weeks the President and his advisors have expressed our strong concerns in a number of private and public messages. Last week, all our top national security officials met with a senior PRC official and urged his government to exercise restraint and caution. We have made clear that any military attack on Taiwan would have grave consequences. We also have taken a number of prudent, precautionary steps—including certain naval deployments in international waters near Taiwan—to underscore our interests, deter the use of force and prevent any miscalculation. We have been closely consulting with other countries in the region, many of whom have expressed their own concerns directly to Beijing. . . . A resort to force with respect to Taiwan would directly involve American national interests and would carry grave risks. There should be no ambiguity about our posture in Beijing, Taipei or anywhere else.

With respect to Taiwan, Lord made two different points. On the one hand, he suggested that the United States did not agree with the PRC's definition of the situation. He cited statements by Premier and vice-presidential candidate Lien Chan that Lee Teng-hui's administration "is adamant in its pursuit of national reunification and strong opposition to Taiwan independence. . . . The outcome of this election will not alter our government's steadfast pursuit of national reunification." Lee Teng-hui, Lord said, "continues to reiterate his commitment to reunification in his speeches on the campaign trail." On the other hand, Lord indicated that the administration had counseled Taipei to avoid actions that might cause a negative PRC reaction.

> While urging restraint by Beijing, we have also made clear to Taiwan's leaders that restraint is in their interest. We oppose provocation by either side. We strongly urge both sides to resume their high level dialogue. . . . We have also told the Taiwan authorities that we expect them to avoid any actions that put at risk the interests of all parties concerned. In recent days we have reaffirmed these themes to both parties. The United States strongly opposes both aggression and provocation.

More fundamentally, avoiding future tensions would depend on the willingness of Beijing and Taipei to sit down and resolve their differences.

> It is critical to recognize that the U.S. does not unilaterally have the capability to impose a solution which would guarantee peace and stability in the Taiwan Strait. A lasting peace requires Taiwan and the PRC eventually to find a common framework for addressing their relationship. Both sides need to avoid provocative political or military actions that have the potential to destabilize the situation. They must together actively seek ways to address their differences peacefully. This is the only long-term guarantee of Taiwan's security. . . . Only the resumption of positive dialogue directly between Beijing and Taipei can lead to a peaceful and lasting settlement.

So the United States found itself in a situation where the Lee visit, the product of congressional pressure, had led Beijing to employ coercive diplomacy to reverse what it regarded as a fundamentally threatening political trend. The United States deployed both military assets and diplomacy to encourage restraint by all sides and prevent a deeper crisis caused by accident or miscalculation.

Beyond the Strait Tensions

Yet more was occurring in 1995 and 1996 than an increase in cross-strait tensions. The Lee visit was only the foreground of a dark picture that Beijing was drawing concerning American intentions (just as the PRC response increased American concerns about Chinese intentions). For the first time since the 1970s, there was a broad and growing consensus in the PRC that the United States had adopted a fundamentally hostile policy, a return to the containment of the 1950s and 1960s. Washington, it was asserted, was intent on blocking China's rise to political, economic, and military power in modern East Asia. Any U.S. action that PRC observers saw in a vaguely negative light became pieces of this paranoid mosaic. Thus, it was said, Washington crafted its policies on the PRC's entry into the World Trade Organization, on protection of intellectual property, and on technology transfer to retard China's economic growth. The American emphasis on human rights was designed to strengthen dissident elements and so undermine the Leninist regime. And wherever "separatism" reared its ugly head—Taiwan, Hong Kong, Tibet, Xinjiang, and so on—the United States had to be involved.

This perception was not only wrong, it was also detrimental to U.S. interests. As Winston Lord testified when cross-strait tensions were at their highest: "We have an enormous stake in preserving stability in Asia and maintaining a productive relationship with the PRC. We will continue to engage the Chinese Government on issues of mutual interest and encourage the PRC's positive participation in the international community. We seek engagement, not confrontation, but this effort must be reciprocated by the PRC."

And so there began a two-year process of restoring the shaken foundation of U.S.–PRC relations, culminating in Jiang Zemin's visit to Washington in fall 1997 and President Clinton's June 1998 trip to the PRC. Part of that process was reaffirming the basic principles concerning Taiwan that were first stated in Henry Kissinger's July 1971 secret trip to Beijing and further elaborated later in communiqués, high-level communications, and the Taiwan Relations Act. This approach of reconsolidation through restatement was the genesis of the president's statement in Shanghai (the so-called Three Nos), that the United States did not support "two Chinas" or "one China, one Taiwan," "Taiwan independence," and Taiwan's membership in international organizations for which statehood was a prerequisite.

Unfortunately, the significance of the president's statement was exaggerated because its history was so badly misunderstood. The points concerning Taiwan's status go back to the initial U.S.–PRC rapprochement. In Henry Kissinger's first meeting with Zhou in July 1971, he began by stating that the United States did not seek two Chinas, a one-China, one-Taiwan solution, nor an independent Taiwan (Zhou's response: "Good, these talks may now proceed"). Nixon himself told Zhou that there was one China, that Taiwan was a part of it, and that the United States would not support any Taiwan independence movement. Zbigniew Brzezinski repeated those principles in his pivotal visit to Beijing in May 1978. The nonsupport of two Chinas and one China–one Taiwan is included in the August 1982 communiqué. The statement concerning international organizations should not have been a surprise, since it was part of the Taiwan policy review of 1994. And since most international organizations have a seat for "China," and since the United

States recognized at the time of normalization that the PRC was the sole, legal government of "China," it follows that Washington would not support Taiwan's membership. (Note that the verb in all three statements is "does not support"; if the PRC were to accommodate to arrangements more favorable to Taiwan, the United States would certainly support them.) None of these statements should have been a surprise because they had been made by other U.S. officials, most notably Secretary of State Madeleine Albright in Beijing in April 1998. Most telling, perhaps, is Lee Teng-hui's view: "President Clinton's remark [in Shanghai] did not represent a change in U.S. policy." Indeed, all the elements of U.S. policy toward Taiwan stated at the outset of this essay remain in place.[12]

Moreover, I would argue that the president's restatement of the point that the United States does not support Taiwan independence was both necessary and beneficial. It was necessary because there were indications that some in Taiwan had drawn an excessive conclusion from the dispatch of the two carrier battle groups in March 1996 that the United States would defend Taiwan under any circumstances, even a drastic change in the status quo by Taiwan itself. It was beneficial because people on Taiwan are demonstrating greater care as they discuss future choices.

Even as the Clinton administration worked to restore a constructive relationship with Beijing, in part by restating old principles, it did not otherwise sacrifice Taiwan's interests. In the context of the two summits, Washington and Taipei sought to improve their communications, which became somewhat ragged during 1995 and 1996. Washington strongly supported Taiwan's application to enter the WTO on its commercial merits alone and independent of the PRC's application. No changes have been made in our arms-sales policy, and the PRC's growing missile assets capable of hitting Taiwan are a matter of growing concern. And consistent with its pledges concerning cross-strait relations, the U.S. government did not go beyond offering encouragement on a restoration of dialogue.

Dialogue: On Again, Off Again

Beijing had canceled cross-strait dialogue in response to Lee Teng-hui's visit to the United States. For two years thereafter, the two sides fenced over the terms on which a resumption would occur. In early 1998, in the context of improving U.S.–PRC relations and stable U.S.–Taiwan ties, the two sides took incremental positive steps. (Taipei took the initiative to resume the dialogue out of a clear, and I believe correct, understanding of the island's interest, and not because of any U.S. pressure.) The outcome was SEF leader Gu

Zhenfu's visit to Shanghai and Beijing in October and a consensus that the process of reengagement would continue. Reinforcing that process is the deepening economic interdependence: annual two-way trade is now on the order of $25 billion, and Taiwan firms have more than $20 billion in realized investment. Impeding reengagement is the substantial mistrust that each side feels about the intentions of the other.

The Clinton administration welcomed the return to dialogue and took steps to provide some elaboration of its long-standing policy. In my capacity as AIT chairman, I identified five elements of the administration's approach to cross-strait relations:

- The Taiwan Strait issue must be resolved peacefully.
- Constructive and meaningful dialogue is the best way to resolve cross-strait differences.
- Differences should be resolved by the two sides themselves.
- The United States will remain evenhanded in its approach to cross-strait dialogue, and not apply pressure to either side.
- Any arrangements concluded between Beijing and Taipei should be on a mutually acceptable basis.

"Special State-to-State Relations"

The July 9 statement by Taiwan's president, Lee Teng-hui, that cross-strait relations constituted a "special state-to-state relationship" sparked increased tensions between Taiwan and the PRC. There was not only an intense propaganda barrage from Beijing but also increased air activity over the Taiwan Strait by both sides, creating the risk of accident or miscalculation that might in turn lead to escalation. President Clinton quickly enunciated what has become known as the "three pillars": reaffirmation of America's one-China policy; insistence on a peaceful resolution of the Taiwan issue; and encouragement of a resumption of cross-strait dialogue. In addition, after a series of interagency meetings the administration decided to send me to Taiwan and Stanley Roth, assistant secretary of state for Asian and Pacific affairs, and Kenneth Lieberthal, National Security Council senior director for Asia, to Beijing, each carrying a message appropriate to our interlocutors.

My airport departure statement was deliberately crafted to reflect the content of my private conversations and to address the main issues. First, I said that I did get a better understanding of Taipei's views on cross-strait relations. That was not just empty talk. I indeed learned more than we had known before I left, particularly about Taipei's increasingly negative view of the negotiating game that it was playing and the perceived fear that Beijing was backing it into a corner. Faced with the inevitability of political negotiations and Beijing's insistence on the one country, two systems formula, Taipei had to reassert—albeit in new and more explicit terms—its view that the governing authorities on the island possessed sovereignty within the overall context of China.

Second, I said that Taipei had a better understanding of Washington's views, both on President Lee's statement and the process by which it was released. I did not go just to listen.

Third, I reaffirmed that all the elements of the administration's policy toward Taiwan remain in place.

Fourth, I stressed the abiding U.S. interest in the peaceful resolution of the cross-strait issue, and said that the administration had a simple approach to this very complicated issue. That is, steps that promote a reduction of tensions, cross-strait dialogue, and peace and stability in the region are good. Steps that result in increased tensions, a freezing of dialogue, and regional instability and conflict are not good. Obviously, progress must occur on a mutually acceptable basis, but each side must have some measure of confidence in the intentions of the other.

Fifth, I emphasized the "one-China" principle as the cornerstone of U.S. policy. This comment was designed to speak to the impression—or misperception—created that Taiwan had abandoned its commitment to the unification of China. I noted in addition that how specifically to define the "one-China" principle and how concretely to realize it are best left to the two sides of the strait on a mutually acceptable basis.

Critics of administration foreign policy have asserted that President Lee's statement was primarily a response to a shift in U.S. policy concerning Taiwan's status. In particular, they point to the Three Nos and Stanley Roth's March 1999 suggestion that the two sides consider "interim agreements" that were less than a final solution but would lead to a significant reduction of tensions. There are some in Taiwan who hold that view, but it appears that the government does not. In a January 2000 interview with *Zhongguo shibao* (China Times), Lin Bihao, deputy secretary-general of the Office of the President, addressed this question, saying, "Mainly it [the special state-to-state formula] is to ensure Taiwan's status as a sovereign state in the international community and in cross-Strait exchange."[13]

The mini-crisis wound down at the time of the Auckland meeting of the APEC forum in mid-September. President Clinton, during his meeting with Jiang Zemin, acknowledged that Lee's statement had "created trouble." But he also stressed to Jiang that if the PRC were to resort to military force, there would be grave consequences in the United States. Simultaneously, air activity in the strait subsided. It appears that through quick and clear action, the United States had induced restraint by both Beijing and Taipei—at least for the moment.

New Security Issues

During the fall of 1999, some in Congress pushed the administration with the Taiwan Security Enhancement Act (TSEA). This bill, sponsored by Jesse Helms (R-NC) and Robert Torricelli (D-NJ) in the Senate and Tom DeLay (R-TX) in the House, sought to insert Congress more deeply into the decision-making process on arms sales to Taiwan, to increase links between the two security establishments in areas other than procurement, and to call greater attention to the PRC's military buildup. The original version of the bill "authorized" the Executive Branch to provide a number of advanced weapons systems, such as diesel submarines and AAMRAM missiles (actually, the president already had that authority; he just chose not to exercise it as a matter of policy).

The administration opposed the TSEA on the grounds that it interfered with the president's constitutional powers as commander-in-chief and chief foreign-policy officer, and because it would arguably restore a measure of officiality to the U.S.–Taiwan relationship, a breach of the normalization commitment. The administration also feared that it would raise expectations both in the PRC and on Taiwan that the United States was significantly expanding its security commitment to Taiwan, beyond the requirements of the TRA. Either side or both might take unwarranted actions based on those expectations. Beijing virulently opposed the bill while Taipei took basically a neutral stance.

The House passed the TSEA in late January 2000 by a wide margin. At that point, it appeared that opposition in the Senate would prevent it from being brought to the floor. In any event, a presidential veto would probably be sustained.

On February 21, 2000, twenty-six days before Taiwan's presidential election, the Taiwan Affairs Office and Information Office of the PRC's State Council issued a white paper on the Taiwan Strait issue. Embedded in a fairly routine reiteration of Beijing's position was a new condition under which the PRC might use force: "if . . . the Taiwan authorities refuse, sine die, the peaceful settlement of cross-Strait reunification." Previously, the PRC "redlines" had been actions that Beijing opposed (such as, a Taiwan declaration of independence). This new *casus belli* was different: Taiwan's not taking an action that Beijing favored.

The Clinton administration was quick to respond to Beijing's declaration. Spokesmen at both the White House and the State Department stated that the United States "rejected" the use of force or the threat of force. The same week President Clinton said, "We'll also continue to make absolutely clear that the issues between Beijing and Taiwan must be resolved peacefully and with the assent of the people of Taiwan."

Beijing's statement threatened to shift the Taiwan issue to a new and more dangerous plane. Even with flexibility at the margins, the one country, two systems formula has been a formula for reunification that neither Taiwan's leadership nor its public is likely to accept. This new redline was only the latest in a series of actions that alienated the Taiwan public and heightened its sense of insecurity. Its approach to Taiwan—diplomatic, political, and military—may have deterred what it wishes to block, but it is also making less and less likely what it wishes to achieve. Its latest warning only deepened fears and suspicions about its intentions.

This new redline was also counterproductive in the United States. The TSEA was only a symptom of the new situation created by the PRC's military modernization. Its acquisition of short-range ballistic missiles, *Kilo*-class submarines, *Sovremenny* destroyers, and other systems fostered new perceptions of Taiwan's defense needs under the Taiwan Relations Act and debate over the clarity of U.S. commitments to safeguard peace and stability in the Taiwan Strait. The February 21 statement seriously undercut the position of those opposing the TSEA.

Conclusion

There is a subtext that has run through this discussion of commitments questioned and commitments reaffirmed, and of tussles between the Congress and the Executive Branch over foreign policy. That is, how valuable to American interests is the U.S. relationship with the PRC? If one believes, as some Americans do, that PRC behavior is antithetical to U.S. global, regional, and bilateral interests, and to the security of Taiwan, then the commitments concerning Taiwan made by successive administrations might be questioned, along with many other aspects of U.S. policy. Yet such a radical shift from current policy would confirm the views of those in the PRC who fear that U.S. policy is indeed hostile, and the prophecy will fulfill itself. If we treat China as the enemy, it will become the enemy.

If on the other hand one believes—as several administrations have asserted and I personally believe—that for all its difficulties, the U.S.–PRC relationship can and does contribute to a more peaceful world, to an international system that is governed by rule-based regimes, to peace in the Taiwan Strait, and to the well-being of people on the Chinese mainland and on Taiwan, then one would not lightly abandon the series of pledges made to Beijing concerning Taiwan. Those pledges, combined with commitments made to Taipei, do not require the people of Taiwan, through their democratic system, to do anything they do not wish to do—a point reinforced by Clinton's statement that the issues between Beijing and Taiwan must be resolved peace-fully and with the assent of the people of Taiwan.

Yet to anchor the U.S.–PRC relationship on the fundamental commitments made at its inception must be reciprocal. If Beijing believes that its U.S. relationship is important—as it has—then it has an obligation to take into account clear-cut and long-standing American concerns as it shapes its ap-proach to Taiwan.

Such questions were not posed in 1989. After the Bush administration assumed office, a variety of exogenous forces combined to constrain the Executive Branch as it sought to formulate and implement policy, such as the following:

- The Tiananmen Incident and the collapse of the Soviet Union, which reduced public support in the United States for the PRC relationship and willingness to sacrifice Taiwan's interests for the sake of larger strategic imperatives.
- Democratization on Taiwan, which allowed discussion of long-suppressed views on Taiwan's future, and allowed the ruling party to seek a greater international role for the island in order to deprive the opposition of a potent political issue.
- The modernization of the People's Liberation Army, particularly through the acquisition of systems like ballistic missiles that put Taiwan at greater risk than at any time since 1949.
- Growing conflict over Taiwan policy in the United States, as reflected most clearly by congressional efforts to shape administration policy on visits by Taiwan leaders, arms sales, and the broader security relationship.
- The increased complexity of the cross-strait issue as political negotia-tions grew more likely and as the two sides adopted mutually exclusive substantive positions and questioned the intentions of the other.

Even in this environment, there is nothing essentially wrong with the policy approach that George Shultz enunciated in early 1987: to foster an environ-ment in the Taiwan Strait area within which positive developments can con-tinue to take place. Such a policy does not threaten the fundamental interests of either side of the strait. Reasonable people can and will disagree on whether the execution of that policy at any point in time has been skillful or not. They can and will disagree on whether rancorous conflict over policy within the Congress and outside contributes to Taiwan's and America's security. There is, on balance, no compelling reason for the administration to state in ad-vance the details of its response to the use of force against Taiwan. Clearly, a war in the Taiwan Strait would have devastating consequences for all concerned, but spelling out exactly what the United States would do is not a good idea. As Winston Lord put it in March 1996:

> We have stated that grave consequences would flow from a use of force against Taiwan, and we have spelled out our determination to see that the future of Taiwan is worked out in a peaceful manner. We cannot and should not be more precise in advance about hypothetical scenarios. I am confident our message is clear. A resort to force with respect to Taiwan would directly involve American national interests and would carry grave risks. There should be no ambiguity about our posture in Beijing, Taipei or anywhere else.

(Indeed, one might say that U.S. policy is one of strategic clarity and tactical ambiguity.)

Democracy on Taiwan does not in and of itself create instability in the Taiwan Strait and undermine the search for a durable peace. True, the results of cross-strait dialogue must be acceptable to the people on Taiwan and the island's leaders have a responsibility to build public support for an objectively sound outcome. But the Taiwan public is usually sensible enough to support responsible approaches regarding the future, and any outcome of the dialogue that enjoys broad support will be more lasting as a consequence.

What would undermine the Shultz approach is an action by either Taipei or Beijing (or both) that irreversibly rules out the ultimate resolution of the Taiwan Strait issue on a mutually acceptable and peaceful basis—or the creation of an irrefutable perception to that effect. A policy of context creation may not be appropriate to such a situation. Devising and building support for an alternative would be a daunting challenge, for it entails fundamentally what sort of relationship the United States should have with the PRC.

8

Epilogue

When the George W. Bush administration came into office, its foreign policy team had a clear set of views concerning Taiwan policy that were defined in part by what it regarded as the defects of the Clinton approach. It had deep admiration for democratization on Taiwan, as manifested most clearly by the victory of Chen Shui-bian in the March 2000 presidential election, and believed that the Clinton administration's treatment of Taiwan's leaders had been shaped too much by the desire to avoid giving offense to China and too little by the significance of the island's democratic achievement. With respect to cross-strait relations, the Bush team viewed the Clinton administration as too tough on Taiwan, pressuring it into resuming dialogue without proper regard for the impact that it had on the Republic of China's (ROC's) negotiating position, and too soft on China. Clinton had sought to reassure China when it should have been firm (and, conversely, been firm toward Taiwan when it should have sought to reassure). This was particularly apparent in the summer of 1999, when Republicans asserted that, in view of China's belligerent response to Lee Teng-hui's special state-to-state formula, the United States should announce that it would defend Taiwan under any circumstances. Such a declaration, they said, would reduce the chances of Chinese miscalculation. Moreover, they felt that clarity was necessary because China was likely to pose a larger challenge to U.S. interests in East Asia, and that it was over Taiwan that Beijing would likely test America intentions first.[1]

So it came as no surprise that the Bush administration acted on these views once it took office. It accorded Chen Shui-bian better treatment on a transit through the United States in late May and early June of 2001, in order to accord him the dignity that it believed a democratically elected leader deserved. It has offered growing yet still modest support for Taiwan's desire to participate in international organizations. In April 2001, it agreed to provide a "robust" package of weapons systems so that the island's armed forces would be better able to deter People's Republic of China (PRC) military action and to mount a defense if deterrence failed. President Bush, in a series of statements around the same time, stated more clearly than ever that the United States would defend Taiwan under just about any circumstances.

Administration officials avoided rhetorical formulations of policy that reassured Beijing and irritated Taipei. And it was firm in the face of complaints from Beijing about its shift in policy. If the late Clinton approach had been one of dual deterrence, the early Bush policy was more single deterrence, and done very deliberately.

Since the middle of 2001, three things have happened. The first was the attack on the World Trade Center and the Pentagon on September 11 and its aftermath, which forced the Bush administration to reassess China's strategic significance. No longer was China seen simply as a likely rival in East Asia tomorrow, against which the United States had to hedge. That view did not completely disappear, but it was replaced in importance by a perception that Washington needed Beijing's cooperation *today* on a variety of foreign policy issues. These included counterterrorism, the war in Afghanistan, a potential nuclear crisis in South Asia, the war in Iraq, and the nuclear crisis on the Korean peninsula. The Bush administration did not drop its concern about China's military buildup, which had a very Taiwan focus, but subordinated that anxiety to more pressing objectives of American foreign policy. The continuing opportunities that China's economy offered to American companies and their international partners, including firms on Taiwan, only reinforced this shift.

The second development was China's return to a Taiwan policy of economic attraction rather than military intimidation. Until the epidemic of severe acute respiratory syndrome (SARS) broke out in spring 2003, business across the strait was booming. Two-way trade was around $40 billion annually, and the mainland has become Taiwan's largest export market, displacing the United States. Taiwan companies continue to invest in the PRC at record rates, in order to keep their products competitive through cheaper mainland labor. The product mix of Taiwan factories on the mainland is shifting from items like shoes and toys to high-end goods like semiconductors and notebook computers. As machinery moves, so do people, and the number of Taiwan people living most of the time in the PRC is in the hundreds of thousands.

Even more encouraging is the PRC's confidence that it has hit upon a strategy to bring Taiwan peacefully into the China fold. Economic ties, Beijing believes, will ameliorate political frictions and gradually bring a shift in political opinion on the island away from separatism and toward unification on China's terms. Time is on its side, it believes. The PRC will continue gradually to build up its military power, as a hedge against Taiwanese provocations, but it sees less need for regular military threats, which only alienate people on the island anyway.

This policy of economic attraction had a corollary. That was to refuse any contact with the Chen government unless it accepted PRC preconditions that spoke to Taiwan's ultimate relationship with China. Chen was unwilling to meet those conditions because he believed that they would place him in a weak position in any future political negotiations. So Beijing, as part of its united-front strategy and in order to deny Chen any politically beneficial achievements, continued its silent treatment.

The third development was on Taiwan itself, the result of the island's divided, fractious, democratic system. After his inauguration, President Chen Shui-bian faced a Legislative Yuan that was firmly in the control of opposition parties—the Kuomintang (KMT) and the People's First Party (PFP) founded by James Soong. The Democratic Progressive Party (DPP) improved its position in the legislative elections of December 2001, and was further aided by the emergence of the Taiwan Solidarity Union, engineered by Lee Teng-hui. Despite this, the balance of power was even, and the Chen administration had to struggle to advance even the basic items on its agenda.

Furthermore, the imperative of closer economic interdependence with the mainland, particularly in the economic recession that began in the summer of 2000, had a political impact. It created political interests in Taiwan—corporations and the parties that they supported—in favor of a more flexible mainland policy. The KMT and the PFP thus charged that what they saw as Chen's overly rigid approach to cross-strait relations was hurting Taiwan's economic competitiveness. The government found it hard to explain why giving in to Beijing's preconditions would undermine Taiwan's fundamental interests.

Economic cooperation with the mainland plus greater social contact also altered Taiwan threat perceptions. It was harder to make the case that the PRC's military buildup required the dedication of budgetary resources for the purchase of advanced weapons systems in order to improve the island's deterrent. The source of those systems—the U.S. government—became increasingly critical of Taiwan's indecisiveness.

Finally, there was an election looming. Chen would be hard pressed to win a second term because of the economic downturn and the public's perception that his performance had fallen short of the expectations he had created. The only achievement he could point to was the improvement in Taiwan's relations with the United States, and some believed that he had leaned too far in the American direction at the expense of economic and other ties with the PRC.

Part of Chen's task in winning reelection was solidifying his DPP base. And at least some of that base believed that he had done too little as president to further the party's agenda. One response to that complaint came on August 3, 2002, when Chen addressed by video teleconference a large group of overseas supporters. He expressed support for legislation authorizing referenda—long a DPP objective—and proclaimed that there was a *guo* (country, nation, state) on each side of the Taiwan Strait. This cheered the DPP faithful, but the multiple meanings of the Chinese term *guo* created uncertainty. Was Chen simply restating traditional Taiwan policy in a new rhetorical way? Or was he breaking new ground and offending Beijing in the process? It was more the former than the latter, and Beijing's hardball tactics in the international arena had left Chen frustrated as well. But the memory of Lee Teng-hui's special state-to-state formula was still fresh, and Washington moved quickly to contain the episode.

Yet Chen will not have the luxury, as he did in the 2000 election, of a divided opposition. For 2004, the Kuomintang and the People's First Party have united behind a ticket composed of their respective leaders, Lien Chan and James Soong, Chen's opponents in 2000. There is emerging on Taiwan a two-bloc political system. The "Blue" parties (the KMT and PFP) are more accommodating toward China, while the "Green" ones (the DPP and Lee Teng-hui's Taiwan Solidarity Union) are more suspicious. A united opposition will force Chen to move beyond his base to compete for voters in the middle.

Several themes that run through the preceding chapters have a contemporary relevance. The first and main one is the role—or nonrole—of the Taiwan public in shaping the decisions about its destiny. KMT repression after 1945 and U.S. policy in the war and postwar periods denied such a role. It was only with the democratization that began in the mid-1980s that the Taiwan public gained a voice on national policy, including policy toward the mainland.

Second, the definition of the legal status of the territory and of the ROC government has been complex and enduring. Whether Taiwan is a part of China and how the ROC government might be part of the Chinese state have been the key substantive questions at the heart of cross-strait relations and U.S. policy. Successive U.S. administrations have taken different positions on whether Taiwan was returned to China (with the early Truman administration the most explicit), and the relative status of Beijing and Taipei (with the Kennedy and Johnson administrations the most innovative).

Third, the United States has been deeply enmeshed in the Taiwan Strait issue from the beginning. For reasons of national security and domestic politics, Washington has set at least some of the parameters within which the PRC and the ROC operate. Although sometimes taking a hands-off attitude, Washington policy has more often than not been one of dual deterrence, constraining both Beijing and Taipei. The stakes are usually too high and the political pressures too complicated for Washington to disengage. The danger of getting trapped in an unnecessary conflict has been too great. Also,

America's views on the legal status of Taiwan and the ROC and its willingness to help Taiwan defend itself can tilt the negotiating balance between the two sides of the strait.

Thus democracy and identity on Taiwan were at cross-purposes throughout the last six decades of the twentieth century, with the United States often caught in the middle. Democracy, identify, and American policy still interact at the beginning of the twenty-first century, but in new ways. As described above, the Bush administration came into office focused on the shifting balance of military power between the two sides of the strait and committed to redressing that balance somewhat. China's acquisition of more advanced air, naval, and missile capabilities over time will provide it with military options—such as intimidation—that it has never possessed. The fact that there has been no cross-strait dialogue since 1999 to address the political issues that divide the two sides intensifies the concern. At the same time, and somewhat to American surprise, Taiwan's sense of its own vulnerability has declined, either because Beijing's "soft" policy is working or because of an assumption that the U.S. defense commitment renders a robust Taiwan defense establishment unnecessary. For at least some in Washington, neither explanation is particularly comforting. A small minority sees Taiwan as a strategic asset and wants to deny it to Beijing. Others worry that somehow the Taiwan tail may wag the American dog (shades of the Chiang Kai-shek era). Whatever the case, the United States will face new challenges as it seeks to prevent this complicated dispute from spinning out of control.

One reason for the complexity is that the status of Taiwan and the ROC—another of our themes—remains the key substantive issue separating Beijing and Taipei. Taiwan's leaders, across the political spectrum, have asserted that their government is a sovereign entity and that any approach to unification must accommodate that reality. But China has offered a formula—one country, two systems—that would confer home rule on Taiwan but not sovereignty.

This issue of the legal identity of the governing authority on Taiwan keeps popping up in most of the disputes of cross-strait relations. For example, there has been little progress on opening direct transportation links between the two sides due to an argument over how to discuss bringing them about. China says that private associations should hold the discussions. Chen has said that governments should. He sees in the PRC proposal a not-so-subtle ploy to undermine the legitimacy of his government and deny him face. The PRC regards Chen's proposal as an effort to gain the political credibility that it prefers not to confer.

The sovereignty question is not new. Just as it was a major concern in American diplomacy from 1950 to 1972, it has been the sticking point in cross-strait relations since contacts resumed in the late 1980s. There has been some evolution but the fundamentals have not changed. The Taiwan and

China positions are sufficiently at odds that they cannot be papered over. If the stalemate is to be broken peacefully, either Beijing will have to abandon one country, two systems, or Taipei will have to accept it.

This leads us to Taiwan's democratic system, through which any consideration of one country, two systems would have to occur. Although Lee Teng-hui did not initially see democratization as antithetical to unification, he came to regard it as a useful defense against an overly easy accommodation with the mainland. And that has been the result. Successive presidential and legislative elections have moved the island's political center away from unification and confirmed a mainstream preference for the status quo. It was public opinion that drove the government to try to reenter the international community, through leadership travel and campaigns to join international organizations like the United Nations, challenging the PRC's definition of the ROC's legal status in the process.

Democracy on Taiwan has effectively given the Taiwan people a seat at the negotiating table. Any Taiwan government that enters into negotiations with Beijing on the permanent future of the island's 23 million people will be cautious, because 12 million of those people vote. Sentiment concerning one country, two systems has varied over time but it has never gotten close to 50 percent. And if there is to be some kind of ultimate solution, the broad majority of the Taiwan populace will have to be satisfied that it is in their interest, and some 30–40 percent of the public is very afraid of the PRC.

Taiwan's democratic system thus provides a veto over initiatives on mainland policy that do not have broad support. Yet it is fairly recent vintage and arguably has yet to be consolidated. The formal institutions of democracy— elections, civil liberties, and so on—are well established and foster a very lively political life. Yet procedural democracy does not necessarily yield substantive democracy. All democratic systems distort to some degree the popular will and new democracies can do so more than mature ones. Money corrupts politics in Taiwan just as it does in the United States. And, as a result of the elections of 2000 and 2001, Taiwan's political system is now divided between rival blocs. Policy issues tend to be politicized. The political system does not necessarily promote the public interest.

That Taiwan may at some time face fundamental choices about its ultimate future makes it all the more important that the Taiwan political system be consolidated and reformed so that it better—if not perfectly—reflects the popular will. The fundamental issues—sovereignty, security, the U.S. relationship— are complex. The public will accept the decisions that are made in its name only if it has confidence in the institutions that make them. The alternative is serious polarization. Reconciling democracy and identity over the past six decades has never been easy. The biggest challenge, however, is yet to come.

Notes

Notes to Chapter 1

1. The best single treatment of U.S.–Taiwan relations since World War II is Nancy Bernkopf Tucker, *Taiwan, Hong Kong, and the United States, 1945–1992: Uncertain Friendships* (New York: Twayne, 1994).

2. For the wartime record, see Herbert Feis, *The China Tangle: The American Effort in China from Pearl Harbor to the Marshall Mission* (Princeton: Princeton University Press, 1953); John W. Garver, "China's Wartime Diplomacy," in *China's Bitter Victory: The War With Japan, 1937–1945*, ed. James C. Hsiung and Steven I. Levine (Armonk, NY: M.E. Sharpe, 1992); Tang Tsou, *America's Failure in China, 1941–50*, 2 vols. (Chicago: University of Chicago Press, 1963); Barbara Tuchman, *Stilwell and the American Experience in China, 1911–1945* (New York: Macmillan, 1970); and Michael Schaller, *The American Crusade in China, 1938–1945* (New York: Columbia University Press, 1979).

3. On the Marshall Mission and the civil war period, see Tsou, *America's Failure in China*; Forrest C. Pogue, *George C. Marshall: Statesman, 1945–1959* (New York: Viking, 1987); William Stueck, "The Marshall and Wedemeyer Missions: A Quadrilateral Perspective," in *Sino American Relations, 1945–1955: A Joint Reassessment of a Critical Decade*, ed. Harry Harding and Yuan Ming (Wilmington, DE: Scholarly Resource Books, 1989). On the February 28 Incident, see George H. Kerr, *Formosa Betrayed* (London: Eyre and Spottiswoode, 1965); and Lai Tse-han, Ramon H. Myers, and Wei Hou, *A Tragic Beginning: The Taiwan Uprising of February 28, 1947* (Stanford: Stanford University Press, 1991).

4. On Washington decision making at the end of the Chinese civil war, see David M. Finkelstein, *Washington's Taiwan Dilemma, 1949–1950* (Fairfax, VA: George Mason University Press, 1993).

5. On the U.S.–ROC alliance, see John W. Garver, *The Sino-American Alliance: Nationalist China and American Cold War Strategy in Asia* (Armonk, NY: M.E. Sharpe, 1997); and Robert Accinelli, *Crisis and Commitment: United States Policy toward Taiwan, 1950–1955* (Chapel Hill: University of North Carolina Press, 1996).

6. For Taiwan's political evolution, see Denny Roy, *Taiwan: A Political History* (Ithaca: Cornell University Press, 2003). For several contemporaneous perspectives on KMT rule in the early 1960s, see Mark Mancall, ed., *Formosa Today* (New York: Praeger, 1964). For the experience of a Taiwanese opponent of the regime, see Peng Ming-min, *A Taste of Freedom: Memoirs of a Formosan Independence Leader* (New York: Holt, Rinehart and Winston, 1972). For an inside look at Chiang Ching-kuo's role, see Jay Taylor, *The Generalissimo's Son: Chiang Ching-kuo and the Revolutions in China and Taiwan* (Cambridge: Harvard University Press, 2000). On Taiwan's

economic development and the U.S. role, see Thomas B. Gold, *State and Society in the Taiwan Miracle* (Armonk, NY: M.E. Sharpe, 1986).

7. For an excellent study of the reorientation of U.S. relations with China and Taiwan and its strategic context, see Robert S. Ross, *Negotiating Cooperation: The United States and China, 1969–1989* (Stanford: Stanford University Press, 1995).

8. For accounts of political developments in Taiwan in the 1970s and 1980s, see Hung-mao Tien, *The Great Transition: Political and Social Change in the Republic of China* (Stanford, CA: Hoover Institution Press, 1989); Mab Huang, *Intellectual Ferment for Political Reforms in Taiwan, 1971–1973* (Ann Arbor: University of Michigan Center for Chinese Studies, 1976); Edwin Winckler, "Institutionalization and Participation on Taiwan: From Hard to Soft Authoritarianism," *China Quarterly* 99 (September 1984): 491–99; Taylor, *The Generalissimo's Son*; Linda Chao and Ramon H. Myers, *The First Chinese Democracy: Political Life in the Republic of China on Taiwan* (Baltimore: Johns Hopkins University Press, 1988); Steven J. Hood, *The Kuomintang and the Democratization of Taiwan* (Boulder, CO: Westview Press, 1997); and Alan M. Wachman, *Taiwan: National Identity and Democratization* (Armonk, NY: M.E. Sharpe, 1994).

9. On U.S.–China relations after Tiananmen, see Robert L. Suettinger, *Beyond Tiananmen: The Politics of U.S.–China Relations 1989–2000* (Washington, DC: Brookings Institution Press, 2003).

Notes to Chapter 2

1. The Potsdam Declaration of July 1945 formally adopted the "purpose" of the Cairo Declaration concerning Taiwan and other Japanese-held territory, and the Japanese instrument of surrender in September accepted the Potsdam terms. Note: Almost all English sources from this time use the Portuguese term "Formosa" instead of the Chinese name "Taiwan." In this essay, "Taiwan" will be used except in direct quotations, where "Formosa" will be retained.

2. See, for example, Munakata Takayuki (Song Tiongjong), Jay T. Loo, trans., *The True Nature and Solution of the Taiwan Problem* (Taipei: Taiwan International Interchange Foundation, 1998).

3. Taiwanese who hope for a Republic of Taiwan also assert that the intentions of the Allied leaders were never executed, for Japan gave up title to Taiwan at the time of the San Francisco peace conference without transferring title to another party.

4. Frank S.T. Hsiao and Lawrence R. Sullivan, "The Chinese Communist Party and the Status of Taiwan," *Pacific Affairs* 52 (Fall 1979): 446–67. See, for example, Chiang's April 1, 1938, speech to the KMT's provisional National Convention in which he stressed the importance of denying Taiwan to Japan and of "setting free" the people of Taiwan in order to promote East Asian stability, but did not call for the island's return to China; extract cited in Hungdah Chiu, ed., *China and the Question of Taiwan: Documents and Analysis* (New York: Praeger, 1973), 203.

5. For the ROC's declaration of war, see *Foreign Relations of the United States, Diplomatic Papers, 1941*, vol. 5, *The Far East* (Washington, DC: Government Printing Office, 1956), 550–51.

The rest of this paragraph is drawn from J. Bruce Jacobs, "Taiwanese and the Chinese Nationalists, 1937–1945: The Origins of Taiwan's 'Half-Mountain People' (Banshan ren)," *Modern China* 16 (January 1990): 85–86, 88–92, 105. The major source on the Taiwan Revolutionary League is Lu Fang-shang, "Taiwan geming tongmenghui yu Taiwan guangfu yundong" (The Taiwan Revolutionary League and the Movement for the Restoration of Taiwan), in *Zhongguo xiandaishi quanti yanjiu baogao* (Report of Seminar on Contemporary Chinese History), vol. 3 (Taipei: Zhonghua minguo shiliao yanjiu zhongxin, 1973), 255–315. Jacobs also describes the establishment of the Taiwan Volunteers, a military arm of the League, and the KMT's Taiwan Party Headquarters.

6. Embassy Chongqing to Department, March 31, 1942, 894.01A/16, Department of State General Records (hereafter DS), Record Group 59, U.S. National Archives and Records Administration, College Park, MD. On the March meeting, see also Leonard Gordon, "American Planning for Taiwan, 1942–1945," *Pacific Historical Review* 37 (May 1968): 201–28. Sun's remarks were reported in the United States within two weeks; see *New York Times* (*NYT*), April 6, 1942. On the *Yishibao* editorial, see Formosa, Box No. 797, Military Intelligence Service Records, Records of the War Department General and Special Staffs, Military Intelligence Division Regional Files, 1942–44, Record Group 165 (hereafter MISR), U.S. National Archives and Records Administration, College Park, MD.

7. *Foreign Relations of the United States, Diplomatic Papers, 1942: China* (Washington, DC: Government Printing Office, 1956), 732–33 (hereafter *FRUS 1942 China*).

8. "Principal Points of a Report by Owen Lattimore on China and Chinese Opinion on Postwar Problems," T[erritorial Subcommittee]-44, August 21, 1942; Box 60, Notter Files, Records of the State Department Advisory Committee on Post-War Foreign Policy, 1942–1945, Record Group 59, U.S. National Archives and Records Administration, College Park, MD (hereafter Notter Files). Lattimore heard a more definitive view from Chiang Kai-shek on November 16; see below.

9. Zhongguo Guomindang zhongyang weiyuanhui dangshi weiyuanhui, *Zhonghua minguo zhongyao shiliao chubian: Dui Ri kangzhan shiqi*, disanbian *Zhanshi waijiao (yi)*, (Initial Compendium of Important Historical Documents of the Republic of China: Period of the War of Resistance Against Japan, third collection, Wartime Diplomacy; section 1, China–United States Relations) (Taipei, 1981), 777 (hereafter *Zhanshi waijiao*). (During his visit, Wilkie had nothing to do with the American embassy in Chongqing, so there is no diplomatic reporting on his conversations with Chiang; see *FRUS 1942 China*, 161–65.) Taiwan did not come up in Laughlin Currie's conversations with Chiang in August 1942; during those, Chiang focused on the necessity of returning Manchuria; see *Zhanshi waijiao*, 681–82. Soong's statement about Taiwan was reported in the *NYT*, November 4, 1942.

10. Qin Xiaoyi, ed., *Jiang zongtong ji* (Collected Works of President Chiang), vol. 1 (Taipei: Zhonghuan xueshuyuan, 1974), 120. The translation is from Chiang Kai-shek, *China's Destiny and Chinese Economic Theory, with Notes and Commentary by Philip Jaffe* (New York: Roy Publishers, 1947), 36, 38, 34.

11. *War and Peace in the Pacific: A Preliminary Report of the Eighth Conference of the Institute of Pacific Relations on Wartime and Post-war Cooperation of the United Nations in the Pacific and the Far East, Mont Tremblant, Quebec, December 4–14, 1942* (New York: Institute of Pacific Relations, 1943), 155, 159–60.

12. *War and Peace in the Pacific*, 16, 43–44, 37, 85. This scheme for supervising dependent territories was different from FDR's "Four Policemen" idea, which is discussed below.

13. Robert P. Newman, *Owen Lattimore and the "Loss" of China* (Berkeley: University of California Press, 1992), 95; *FRUS 1942 China*, 185; The handwritten notes

of Lattimore's November 16–17, 1942, conversations with Chiang are in Container 27, Owen Lattimore Papers, Library of Congress, Washington, DC. It is not clear whether Roosevelt learned of the ROC desire for the return of Taiwan from Wendell Wilkie, since there are no records in the Roosevelt Library of any report by Wilkie to the president on his trip; communication from Franklin Delano Roosevelt Library. Lattimore also attended part of the Mont Tremblant conference.

14. As one measure of Taiwan's relative unimportance, it came up only briefly in Chiang's conversations with Wendell Wilkie. As another indicator, Christopher Thorne's *Allies of a Kind: The United States, Britain and the War Against Japan, 1941–1945* (London: Hamish Hamilton, 1978), a comprehensive inventory of outstanding issues between the United States and Great Britain during the war, has only nine references to Taiwan. Four concern the prosecution of the war, four concern postwar bases on the island, and none mention its return to China.

15. "Formosa," February 17, 1942, 894.01/2, DS.

16. George Kerr, *Formosa Betrayed* (London: Eyre and Spottiswoode, 1965), 18. Kerr's memorandum was not in the papers concerning Taiwan in the Military Intelligence Service's regional file, but based on his recollection it appears to have been similar in content to his July memorandum.

17. "The occupation and subsequent administration of Formosa," July 31, 1942, MISR. For Kerr's recollection of the policy debate over Taiwan in the U.S. government, see Kerr, *Formosa Betrayed*, 18–19.

18. P[olitical Problems Subcommittee] Minutes [of Meeting] 20, August 1, 1942, summary and detailed versions, Box 55, Political Problems Subcommittee, Notter Files; "Tentative Conclusions of the Security Subcommittee Concerning the Disposition of Japanese Insular Possessions," September 22, 1942, S Document 38, Box 77, Notter Files.

19. William Roger Louis, *Imperialism at Bay: The United States and the Decolonization of the British Empire, 1941–1945* (New York: Oxford University Press, 1978), chapter 8. This discussion presaged the drafting of a draft declaration on dependent peoples, presented to Roosevelt on March 9, 1943. Its focus, however, was on the colonial possessions of the members of the United Nations. The emphasis of the declaration on preparing dependent peoples for self-government and independence might have been applied to Taiwan. For the text, see Harley A. Notter, *Postwar Foreign Policy Preparation, 1939–1945* (Washington, DC: Government Printing Office, 1950), 470–72.

20. Louis, *Imperialism at Bay*, chapter 9, especially 183–86.

21. Louis, *Imperialism at Bay*, 261–62, 263–64.

22. "Tentative Views of the Subcommittee on Political Problems," P 214, March 12, 1943, 14, Box 57, Notter Files; "Tentative Views of the Security Subcommittee," P 214-d, March 12, 1943, 4, Box 57, Notter Files; Minutes of Political Problems Subcommittee Meeting 47, March 13, 1943, Box 55, Notter Files; "Political Subcommittee, Summary of Views, March 1942 to July 1943," P-236, July 2, 1943, 18, Box 57, Notter Files. There was also a Security-Technical Subcommittee that tended to favor transferring Taiwan to China while still ensuring that the island could be used for bases; see Minutes 16, May 7, 1943 (Summary) and Minutes 18, May 19, 1943 (Summary), Box 79, Notter Files.

23. "Formosa," T-325, May 25, 1943, Box 63, Notter Files.

24. T Minutes 51 (Summary), June 25, 1943, Box 59, Notter Files.

25. "Memorandum: Politico-Economic Problems in Formosa," MISR. The version

of the memorandum in the MISR files was prepared either in late 1943 or 1944, but there is a note attached that it was virtually the same "as it was written in September 1943." There is also the wry comment that "Certain questions here raised were answered in the Cairo Declaration"—no doubt a reference to the decision on Taiwan's reversion to China. In *Formosa Betrayed* (page 19), Kerr suggests that three options for Taiwan were considered in 1942 and 1943: independence (impracticable because of certain Chinese objections); return to China (also problematic because the KMT incapacity and preoccupation with the mainland situation); and a "temporary Allied trusteeship, during which the Formosans themselves would prepare for a plebiscite to determine their ultimate political fate." The available documentation suggests that Kerr's definition of the choices at the time was similar but not identical to his later description.

26. Kerr, *Formosa Betrayed*, 18–22.

27. *FRUS 1942 China*, 185.

28. File on Talks with FDR, 1942–44, Box 54, Notter Files. Myron Taylor was an industrialist and member of the advisory committee. Isaiah Bowman, president of Johns Hopkins, chaired the Department's territorial subcommittee. Leo Pasvolsky was special assistant to Secretary Hull and executive director of the advisory committee. This item pushes back by a month the earliest point at which FDR is said to have expressed himself on Taiwan's disposition. Previously, since the publication of Hull's memoir in 1948, the earliest known date was March 27, 1943; see Cordell Hull, *The Memoirs of Cordell Hull*, vol. 2 (New York: Macmillan, 1948), 1595–96. Five years later, Herbert Feis noted FDR's recommendation in his *The China Tangle: The American Effort in China from Pearl Harbor to the Marshall Mission* (Princeton: Princeton University Press, 1953), 106. The fact of the February 22 meeting and a partial list of attendees were publicly reported in the *New York Times* the next day, but without any reference to the Taiwan decision.

29. *Foreign Relations of the United States, Diplomatic Papers, 1943*, Vol. 3: *The British Commonwealth, Eastern Europe, the Far East* (Washington, DC: Government Printing Office, 1963), 37 (hereafter cited as *FRUS 1943 British Commonwealth*).

30. *Foreign Relations of the United States, Diplomatic Papers*, 1943, China (Washington, DC: Government Printing Office, 1957), 845–46 (hereafter *FRUS 1943 China*). It is not clear who else in the U.S. government knew that Welles had briefed Soong on these issues. Cordell Hull would later assert that Welles had a habit of acting beyond his authority in dealing with Roosevelt, foreign diplomats, and U.S. missions, and did not always keep him informed. Ultimately, in August 1943, Roosevelt, who was an old family friend of Welles, asked him to resign for unrelated reasons. See Hull, *Memoirs of Cordell Hull*, 2, 1227–31.

31. *FRUS 1943 China*, 14–15; ST [Security-Technical Subcommittee] Minutes 18, May 19, 1943 (Summary), Box 79, Notter Files (emphasis added). Cordell Hull's papers are held at the Library of Congress. Cordell Hull suggests in his memoirs that Roosevelt did not consult him on the Taiwan decision in November 1943 at Cairo (see Hull, *Memoirs of Cordell Hull*, 2, 1584). That statement appears to be inaccurate, since FDR had raised the matter with Hull the previous February. Also, George Kerr appears to date the beginning of the State Department's opposition to any option other than returning Taiwan to China in 1943 (see *Formosa Betrayed*, 21–22). Although Department officials individually probably tended to favor retrocession even in 1942, their advocacy of that position thereafter may have reflected as much their knowledge that Roosevelt had already made a decision as it did an institutional position.

32. Gaddis Smith, *American Diplomacy During the Second World War, 1941–1945* (New York: Knopf, 1985), 6–7; Louis, *Imperialism at Bay*, 87.

33. *FRUS 1943 British Commonwealth*, 13, 14, 16, 33. See Willard Range, *Franklin D. Roosevelt's World Order* (Athens: University of Georgia Press, 1959), 114–19, for a general discussion of FDR's emphasis on self-determination and his confidence in plebiscites.

34. Notes of Conversation with Chiang Kai-shek, November 16 and 17, 1942, Owen Lattimore Papers.

35. For discussions along these lines, see Feis, *The China Tangle*, 108–9; and John Garver, "China's Wartime Diplomacy," in *China's Bitter Victory: The War with Japan, 1937–1945*, ed. James C. Hsiung and Steven I. Levine (Armonk, NY: M.E. Sharpe, 1992), 22–23.

36. Smith, *American Diplomacy During the Second World War*, 15; Charles F. Romanus and Riley Sunderland, *Stilwell's Mission to China, United States Army in World War II, China-Burma-India Theater* (Washington, DC: Office of the Chief of Military History, Department of the Army, 1953), 279; *FRUS 1943 British Commonwealth*, 35.

37. Romanus and Sunderland, *Stilwell's Mission to China*, 277–79. It is also worth noting that improving Chinese morale was not a factor in the discussions on Taiwan by the State Department's advisory committee; see Notter Files.

38. Romanus and Sunderland, *Stilwell's Mission to China*, 276, 321–27, 329 (quoted passage is on 329). Unlike the advisory committee, State Department officials with day-to-day responsibility for China were quite sensitive to the problem of ROC morale; their solution to that problem was increasing supplies; see *FRUS 1943 China*, 4–9, 9–11.

39. The discussion of the "Four Policemen" is based primarily on Robert A. Divine, *Roosevelt and World War II* (Baltimore: Johns Hopkins University Press, 1969), 57–61. For a more recent treatment, see "'The Family Circle': Roosevelt's Vision of the Postwar World," in Warren F. Kimball, *The Juggler: Franklin Roosevelt as Wartime Statesman* (Princeton: Princeton University Press, 1991), 83–106.

40. *Foreign Relations of the United States: The Conferences at Washington, 1941–1942, and Casablanca, 1943* (Washington, DC: Government Printing Office, 1968), 444–45.

41. *Zhanshi waijiao*, 1, 680, 767–68, 762, 769.

42. *Zhanshi waijiao*, 1, 777–78; communication from the Franklin Delano Roosevelt Library.

43. Notes of November 16–17, 1942, conversation with Chiang Kai-shek, Owen Lattimore Papers.

44. *FRUS 1942 China*, 185–86. In the draft letter, there was a general statement on the disposition of colonial territories in Asia. This discussion tracks well with the points that Chiang had made to Lattimore in mid-November. In some cases in the Lattimore draft, trusteeship as a transition to self-government was deemed preferable to restoration of the colonial power.

45. *FRUS 1942 China*, 185–86; see the footnotes of this document for clarification of which sentences were deleted and added.

46. Louis, *Imperialism at Bay*, 259. It was perhaps this request that led the navy's general board to draw up a list of possible bases in the Pacific; see above.

47. Earl of Avon, *The Memoirs of Anthony Eden: The Reckoning* (Boston: Houghton Mifflin, 1965), 437–38; *FRUS 1943 British Commonwealth*, 26, 35–36, 37, 39.

48. *FRUS 1942 China*, 175.

49. For gossipy accounts of Madame Chiang's demanding nature, see Barbara Tuchman, *Stilwell and the American Experience in China, 1911–1945* (New York: Macmillan, 1970), 351; and Michael Schaller, *The American Crusade in China, 1938–1945* (New York: Columbia University Press, 1979), 119–20.

50. Sumner Welles, *The Time for Decision* (New York: Harper, 1944), 283–84; William D. Leahy, *I Was There: The Personal Story of the Chief of Staff to Presidents Roosevelt and Truman Based on His Notes and Diaries Made at the Time* (New York: McGraw-Hill, 1950), 154–55; Earl of Avon, *The Reckoning*, 437.

51. Hull, *Memoirs of Cordell Hull*, 2, 1587; Hornbeck to Welles, February 17, 1943, 893.44 Chiang Kai-shek/44, DS.

52. Robert E. Sherwood, *Roosevelt and Hopkins: An Intimate History*, rev. ed. (New York: Harper & Brothers, 1950), 706, 976; *Zongtong jianggong dashi changbian chugao* (Preliminary Extensive Chronology of President Chiang) (Taipei: Zhongguo Guomindang zhongyang weiyuanhui dangshi weiyuanhui, 1978), vol. 5, 2126–27; "Zhongguo nuxing shijie zhizui: Song Meiling kangzhan fangmeixing" (World-class Chinese Women; Soong Mei-ling's American Trip During the War of Resistance Against Japan), *Zhongwai zazhi* 63 (1998): 109. The report cited in *Zongtong jianggong dashi changbian chugao* was dated April 15, but since Madame Chiang did not return to Washington until early May, the conversation must have taken place during her February visit.

53. Sherwood, *Roosevelt and Hopkins*, 707, 976.

54. *Zongtong jianggong dashi changbian chugao*, 5, 2170–71; cited in John W. Garver, *Chinese-Soviet Relations, 1937–1945: The Diplomacy of Chinese Nationalism* (New York: Oxford University Press, 1988), 198, 232. Chiang had cabled his wife on June 18 to make clear that the two northeast bases would be used by China and the United States alone (i.e., not by the Soviet Union).

55. Zhongguo Guomindang zhongyang weiyuanhui dangshi weiyuanhui, *Zhonghua minguo zhongyao shiliao chubian: Dui Ri kangzhan shiqi*, disanbian *Zhanshi waijiao (liu)*, (Initial Compendium of Important Historical Documents of the Republic of China: Period of the War of Resistance Against Japan, third collection, Wartime Diplomacy; section 6, Contacts Concerning War-making by the Allied Countries) (Taipei, 1981), 499, 505, 527 (hereafter cited as *Zhanshi waijiao Cairo*). The first of these items, by the staff office of the Military Commission, also mentioned the Liuqiu Islands. A translation of the latter document, a draft paper on postwar cooperation among the Big Four, is reproduced in *FRUS, The Conferences at Cairo and Tehran, 1943* (Washington, DC: Government Printing Office, 1961), 387–89 (hereafter cited as *FRUS Cairo and Tehran*).

56. Louis, *Imperialism at Bay*, 268, 270; *FRUS Cairo and Tehran*, 258–59, 263–65.

57. *FRUS Cairo and Tehran*, 323–25. The fact that Taiwan was not mentioned as a possible site for a base is a function of the weakness of the documentary record of the Cairo conference. When it came time for State Department historians to prepare *FRUS Cairo and Tehran* in 1956, the United States had no record of the Roosevelt-Chiang meeting and had to secure a summary of the conversation from the ROC government. By 1956, even a retrospective mention of base rights on Taiwan would have complicated relations with the United States, so the issue was probably left out. Confirming that hypothesis is the version of the meeting that was published in 1981 in the ROC's Chinese-language version. It does not even mention base rights for Lushun; see *Zhanshi waijiao Cairo*, 527–28. Hopkins discussed the possibility of Taiwan serving as a site

for naval and air bases "in the event that Formosa was returned to China" with Eden and Molotov; see *FRUS Cairo and Tehran*, 570.

58. *Zhanshi waijiao Cairo*, 530–33. The initial American draft of the declaration said that Manchuria, Taiwan, and "the Bonins" were to be returned to China. The Chinese delegation correctly surmised that the reference to "the Bonins," which are almost 1,500 miles from Taiwan, should have been "the Pescadores" and got Harry Hopkins to correct the error; *Zhanshi waijiao Cairo*, 530–31.

59. *Zongtong jianggong dashi changbian chugao*, vol. 5, 2127; *FRUS 1943 British Commonwealth*, 18; Hull, *Memoirs*, 2, 1596; *FRUS Cairo and Tehran*, 324, 887, 888.

60. Leonard Gordon, "American Planning for Taiwan, 1942–1945," *Pacific Historical Review* 37 (May 1968): 209–10, 225.

61. For these two templates as they were discussed in the State Department's advisory committee, see Louis, *Imperialism at Bay*, 79. For Welles's approach to the decolonization template, see his *The Time for Decision*, 300–303.

62. The public versions of the U.S. position were expressed in the 1972 Shanghai Communiqué, where the United States acknowledged "that all Chinese on either side of the Taiwan Strait maintain there is but one China and that Taiwan is a part of China," and stated that it did not challenge that position; and the normalization communiqué of December 1978, where Washington acknowledged "the Chinese position that there is but one China and Taiwan is a part of China." For the private version, see Chapter 5.

Notes to Chapter 3

1 . Nancy Bernkopf Tucker, *Taiwan, Hong Kong, and the United States, 1945–1992: Uncertain Friendships* (New York: Twayne, 1994), 77.

2. George H. Kerr, *Formosa Betrayed* (London: Eyre and Spottiswoode, 1965), 264.

3. Kerr, *Formosa Betrayed*, 146–49, 153, 224. Kerr notes that he provided his superiors with adequate warning that an explosion was coming but was ignored. In a report to the U.S. Embassy in Nanjing and the State Department toward the end of 1946, he said that "tensions within Formosa were near the breaking point, a violent crisis might be upon us at any time." Kerr learned later that someone (probably Blake) had sent forward a follow-up note that advised the embassy not to take his predictions too seriously. Setting aside the latter message, it is not clear what the U.S. government might have done to forestall the crisis. See Kerr, *Formosa Betrayed*, 153, 323fn.

4. Kerr, *Formosa Betrayed*, 91, 148, 206, 223 (cited passages on 206 and 223); *Foreign Relations of the United States 1947, Vol. 7, The Far East: China* (Washington, DC: Government Printing Office, 1972), 423–26 (hereafter cited as *FRUS 1947*).

5. *FRUS 1947*, 427–28; Kerr, *Formosa Betrayed*, 260–61.

6. Embassy Nanjing to Department of State (hereafter cited as Department), March 13, 1947, 894A.00/3-1347, Department of State General Records (hereafter cited as DS), Record Group 59, National Archives and Records Administration, College Park, MD.

7. Embassy Nanjing to Department, March 13, 1947, 894A.00/3-1347, DS.

8. *FRUS 1947*, 429–30, 435–36; Embassy Nanjing to Department, March 3, 1947, 894A.00/3-547, DS. Kerr says that he was unable later to find any record of the delegation's manifesto, but the embassy did report the meeting.

9. *FRUS 1947*, 433. Kerr does not report this recommendation in *Formosa Betrayed*.

10. *FRUS 1947*, 434–35. Kerr does not report the evacuation recommendation in *Formosa Betrayed*.

11. *FRUS 1947*, 437; Embassy Nanjing to Department, March 13, 1947, Taipei Consulate (hereafter cited as Consulate) to Embassy Nanjing, March 7, 1947, 894A.00/3-1347, DS.

12. Kerr, *Formosa Betrayed*, 312–13, including footnote on 313; *FRUS 1947*, 440–41.

13. Consulate to Embassy Nanjing, March 10, 1947, 894A.00/3-1347, DS. Kerr does not mention this memorandum or recommendation in *Formosa Betrayed*. Kerr prepared another memorandum also dated March 10, which reported the thirty-two demands that the Settlement Committee submitted to Chen Yi; Consulate to Embassy Nanjing, March 10, 1947, 894A.00/3-1347, DS.

14. *FRUS 1947*, 71–72, 87; Kerr, *Formosa Betrayed*, 321. It is interesting that embassy officers like Consul Ralph Blake apparently thought that they had to explain Kerr's undiplomatic writing even as they agreed with his views in substance. For another example, see *FRUS 1947*, 445.

15. Kerr, *Formosa Betrayed*, 275, 307–8, 316; *FRUS 1947*, 442.

16. *FRUS 1947*, 72, 90. Embassy officers continued to provide Nationalist officials with its views on what had happened on Taiwan; see *FRUS 1947*, 444.

17. For the full text of Kerr's report, see U.S. Department of State, *United States Relations with China* (Washington, DC: Government Printing Office, 1949) or *The China White Paper: August 1949* (Stanford: Stanford University Press, 1967), vol. 2, 923–38; cited passages on 935–38. In early May a senior embassy officer made similar comments to Wei Daoming, who was named to replace Chen Yi; see *FRUS 1947*, 464–65.

18. Kerr, *Formosa Betrayed*, 325; *FRUS 1947*, 450–51. As noted above, Kerr does not mention his March 10 memorandum in *Formosa Betrayed*.

19. See, for example, the discussion of Taiwan in briefing papers for the Wedemeyer mission in August (in *FRUS 1947*, 745) and Wedemeyer's own conclusions (see Department of State, *United States Relations with China*, vol. 1, 309).

20. *FRUS 1947*, 467–68.

21. "Table of Post-War Taiwan Political Cases," *Renquan zhi dao: Taiwan minzhu renquan huigu* (The Road of Human Rights: A Retrospective on Taiwan's Democracy and Human Rights; English title: The Road to Freedom) (Taipei: Wushu tushu, 2002), 17–24.

22. Jay Taylor, *The Generalissimo's Son: Chiang Ching-kuo and the Revolutions in China and Taiwan* (Cambridge: Harvard University Press, 2000), 191.

23. Taylor, *The Generalissimo's Son*, 191–92.

24. *Foreign Relations of the United States 1949*, Vol. 9, *The Far East: China* (Washington, DC: Government Printing Office, 1974), 283, 378 (hereafter cited as *FRUS 1949*); Taipei Consulate-General (hereafter cited as Consulate-General) to Department, October 26, 1949, 894A.00/10-2649, DS. American newspapers were also limited in their coverage; during 1949, there was only one article in the *New York Times* that made reference to the repression on Taiwan (August 23), while there were several in 1950.

25. *FRUS 1949*, 451–55.

26. *FRUS 1949*, 281–82, 290–92.

27. *FRUS 1949*, 337–41; cited passage on 338.

28. *FRUS 1949*, 346–49.

29. *FRUS 1949*, 365–67, 368.

30. *FRUS 1949*, 401–3, 406–7.

31. *FRUS 1949*, 456. Once the central government moved to Taiwan, there were two administrations ruling basically the same territory, a redundancy that was necessary to preserve the myth that the ROC was the government of all of China. The provincial government, to which Taiwanese were appointed, had very little power.

32. Nancy Bernkopf Tucker, ed., *China Confidential: American Diplomats and Sino-American Relations, 1945–1995* (New York: Columbia University Press, 2001), 76.

33. Consulate-General to Department, February 9, 1950, 794A.00/2-950, DS.

34. Consulate-General to Department, April 8, 1950, 794A.00/4-850, DS.

35. Consulate-General to Department, May 3, 1950, 794A.00/5-350, DS.

36. Consulate-General to Department, May 19, 1950, 794A.00/5-1950, DS.

37. Consulate-General to Department, July 21, 1950, 794A.00/7-2150, DS.

38. Consulate-General to Department, January 2, 1950, 794A.00/1-250, DS; Department to Consulate-General, January 2, 1950, 794A.00/1-250, DS; Consulate-General to Department, August 3, 1950, 794A.00/8-350, DS; "Memorandum of conversation between Phillip Sprouse and Ko Tai-shan," April 5, 1950, 794A.00/4-550, DS.

39. For the TDPA issue see Consulate-General to Department, February 8, 1950, 794A.00/2-850; Consulate-General to Department, February 22, 1950, 794A.00/2-2250; Consulate-General to Department, March 10, 1950, 794A.00/3-1050, DS; Consulate-General to Department March 22, 1950, 794A.00/3-2250, DS; Consulate-General to Department, April 4, 1950, 794A.00/4-450, DS; Department to Consulate-General, April 4, 1950, 794A.00/4-450, DS; Consulate-General to Department, April 8, 1950, 794A.00/4-850, DS. The long quoted passage is from the last item.

40. Consulate-General to Department, "Relations of D.L. Osborn with Formosan League for Reemancipation," July 14, 1950, 794A.00/7-1450, DS; Consulate-General to Department, March 31, 1950, 794A.00/3-3150, DS.

41. Consulate-General to Department, June 2, 1950, 794A.00/6-250, DS; Department to Consulate-General, June 2, 1950, 794A.00/6-250, DS; Consulate-General to Department, June 8, 1950, 794A.00/6-850, DS. In early June, to protect the consulate, Strong had Osborn prepare a memo on his contacts with the FLR; see previous note.

42. For evidence of Taipei's elevation to an embassy, see Department to Embassy Taipei (hereafter cited as Embassy), July 7, 1950, 794A.00/7-750, DS. For the discussions with Wu, see Embassy to Department, July 7, 1950, 794A.00/7-750, DS; Embassy to Department, July 13, 1950, 794A.00/7-1350, DS; Department to Embassy, July 13, 1950, 794A.00/7-1350, DS; Embassy to Department, July 17, 1950, 794A.00/7-1750, DS; Department to Embassy, July 17, 1950, 794A.00/7-1750, DS.

43. Memorandum, Robert Strong to O. Edmund Clubb, September 6, 1950, "Summary of Views on Formosa as of Late August 1950," September 6, 1950, 794A.00/9-650, DS; Embassy to Department, July 20, 1950, 794A.00/7-2050, DS. The latter item provides an inventory of political reforms that Strong felt the ROC government should take to improve relations with the Taiwanese.

44. Sebald to Department, August 3, 1950, 794A.00/8-350, DS.

45. Karl Lott Rankin, *China Assignment* (Seattle: University of Washington Press, 1964), 55; Kerr, *Formosa Betrayed*, 408; Tucker, *Taiwan, Hong Kong, and the United States*, 37; Tucker, *China Confidential*, 121–22.

46. Embassy to Department, August 26, 1950, 794A.00 (W)/8-2650, DS; Embassy

to Department, October 28, 1950, 794A.00 (W)/10-2850, DS; Embassy to Department, November 18, 1950, 794A.00 (W)/11-1850, DS.

47. Embassy to Department, October 28, 1950, 794A.00 (W)/10-2850, DS; Embassy to Department, September 30, 1950, 794A.00 (W)/9-3050, DS; Embassy to Department, November 4, 1950, 794A.00 (W)/11-450, DS; Embassy to Department, December 9, 1950, 794A.00 (W)/12-950, DS; Embassy to Department, January 6, 1951, 794A.00 (W)/1-651, DS; Embassy to Department, January 13, 1951, 794A.00 (W)/1-1351, DS.

48. Embassy to Department, October 10, 1952, 794A.00/10652, DS; Embassy to Department, January 29, 1953, 794A.00/1-2953, DS. In May 1951, the State Department's office of intelligence research prepared a long report on Taiwan, including a frank discussion of the ways in which ROC government policy continued to alienate the Taiwanese populace. The embassy provided its views on the report in August but did not object in any substantial way to the report's analysis. See "The Current Situation on Taiwan," Office of Intelligence Research Report No. 5529, May 4, 1951, 794A.00/5-451, DS; Embassy to Department, August 1, 1951, 794A.00/8-151, DS.

49. Rusk to Wu, August 18, 1950, 794A.00/8-1850, DS. Another instance of Washington's negativism can be found in a commentary that Charles Ogburn wrote at the end of the Truman administration in an article in *The Reporter* on U.S. China policy. Ogburn concluded that the political system in "Free China" was such an embarrassment to the United States that Washington should in effect take over the island and reshape its government in its own image. See Office Memorandum, December 5, 1952, 794A.00/12-552.

50. Rankin, *China Assignment*, 74.

51. Ibid., 142.

52. Ibid., 51.

53. Ibid., 143.

54. Ibid., viii, 137.

55. For examples of senators' concerns about giving Chiang a blank check, see U.S. Congress, Senate Committee on Foreign Relations, *Executive Sessions of the Senate Foreign Relations Committee (Historical Series)*, vol. 7, 84th Cong., 1st sess., 1955, 259.

56. *Executive Sessions*, 752, 242.

57. *Executive Sessions*, 310, 340.

58. *Executive Sessions*, 140, 128, 69.

59. *Executive Sessions*, 317, 327, 331.

60. *Executive Sessions*, 349–50. Morse indirectly raised the criticisms of U.S. policy by Wu Guozhen, who by then had fled to the United States after intense political conflict with Chiang Ching-kuo. Dulles claimed no personal knowledge but did say that some believed Wu "has a sort of persecution complex"; *Executive Sessions*, 350.

61. *Executive Sessions*, 350.

62. Douglas Mendel, *The Politics of Formosan Nationalism* (Berkeley: University of California Press, 1970), 114–16.

63. Embassy to Department, March 2, March 9, April 28, June 8, June 9, July 27, 1960, 793.00/3-260, 793.00/3-960, 793.00/4-2860, 793.00/6-860, 793.00/6960, 793.00/7-2760, DS. The ROC was already concerned about U.S. intentions because of the Conlon Report, which advocated a two-China policy; February 23, 1960, 793.00/2-2360, DS.

64. Embassy to Department, July 27, 1960, 793.00/7-2760, DS; Embassy to Department, February 16, 1960, 793.00/2-1660, DS; Memorandum of Conversation, Edwin Martin and James Dickson, August 26, 1960, 793.00/8-2660, DS.

65. Embassy to Department, June 8, 1960, 793.00/6-860, DS; April 6, 1960, 793.00/4-860, DS.

66. Embassy to Department, 793.00/11-160. It was later learned that the Garrison Command arrested Lei and his confederates in early September because Chiang wanted them out of the way before the imminent arrival in Taiwan of Hu Shi, the most prestigious Chinese liberal; see Embassy to Department, November 15, 1960, 793.00/11-1560, DS.

67. Correspondence between Department and Rep. Charles Porter, September 5, 1960, 993.62/9-560, DS.

68. Correspondence between Department and Rep. Charles Porter, September 5, 1960, 993.62/ 9-560, DS; Department to Embassy, September 10, 1960, 993.62/9-560, DS.

69. Embassy to Department, September 13, 1960, 993.62/9-1360, DS; Department to Embassy, September 14, 1960, 993.62/9-1460, DS; Memorandum of Conversation, September 13, 1960, 993.62/9-1360, DS.

70. For correspondence with cited members of Congress and others during September and October 1960, see 993.62/9-1360, 993.62/9-1460, 993.62/9-1660, 993.62/9-1960, 993.62/9-2260, 993.62/9-2960, 993.62/9-3060, 993.62/10-660, 993.62/20-760, 993.62/10-1360, all DS.

71. *Foreign Relations of the United States 1958–1960*, Vol. 19, *China* (Washington, DC: Government Printing Office, 1996), 724fn (hereafter cited as *FRUS 1958–1960*).

72. Tucker, *China Confidential*, 134; *FRUS 1958–1960*, 724–27.

73. Embassy to Department, September 29, 1960, 793.00/9-2960, DS; Embassy to Department, October 6, 1960, 793.00/10-660, DS.

74. Office Memorandum (Martin to Steeves), October 14, 1960, 993.62/10-1460, DS; Memorandum of Conversation (Steeves and Ye), October 24, 1960, 993.62/10-2460, DS; Department to Embassy, October 25, 1960, 793.00/10-2560, DS.

75. Department to Embassy, October 25, 1960, 793.00/10-2560, DS; Embassy to Department, November 8, 1960, 793.00/11-860, DS.

76. Embassy to Department, November 15, 1960, 793.00/11-1560, DS.

77. Embassy to Department, November 24, 1960, 793.00/11-2460, DS; Memorandum from Parsons to Merchant, November 28, 1960, 993.62/11-2860, DS; Memorandum of Conversation (Merchant and Ye), November 28, 1960, 993.62/11-2860, DS.

78. *FRUS 1958–1960*, 736–38.

79. Embassy to Department, February 10, 1961, 793.00/2-1061, DS; Embassy to Department, February 26, 1961, 793.00/2-2661, DS.

80. Embassy to Department, January 25, 1965, POL 29 CHINAT, DS. Peng recalls these encounters and that the American embassy reportedly had a thick file on him; see Peng Ming-min, *A Taste of Freedom: Memoirs of a Formosan Independence Leader* (New York: Holt, Rinehart and Winston, 1972), 123.

81. For Peng's career up to the point of his proclamation, see Peng, *A Taste of Freedom*; the cited passage is on page 131. For the declaration itself, see Mendel, *Politics of Formosan Nationalism*, 249–60.

82. Embassy to Department, February 15, 1964, POL 23–9 CHINAT, DS; Embassy to Department, March 14, 1964, POL 18–1 CHINAT, DS; Embassy to Department,

July 1, 1964, POL 23 CHINAT, DS; Embassy to Department, July 15, 1964, POL 18 CHINAT, DS; Embassy to Department, July 22, 1964, POL 12 CHINAT, DS; Embassy to Department, July 1, 1964, POL 23 CHINAT, DS. For Taiwan's political climate in the early 1960s, as perceived by several Western China specialists, see Mark Mancall, ed., *Formosa Today* (New York: Praeger, 1964).

83. Embassy to Department, October 3, 1964, POL 29 CHINAT, DS; Embassy to Department, October 9, 1964, POL 29 CHINAT, DS; Embassy to Department, October 24, 1964, POL 29 CHINAT, DS; Embassy to Department, October 30, 1964, POL 29 CHINAT, DS.

84. Embassy to Department, October 24, 1964, POL 29 CHINAT, DS. For the progress of Peng's case from his point of view, see *A Taste of Freedom*, chapters 9 to 12.

85. Department to Taipei, November 10, 1964, POL 29 CHINAT, DS; November 16, 1964, POL 29 CHINAT, DS; Peng, *A Taste of Freedom*, 150; Embassy to Department, November 12, 1964, POL 29 CHINAT, DS.

86. Department to Embassy, November 25, 1964, POL 29 CHINAT, DS; Embassy to Department, November 28, 1964, POL 29 CHINAT, DS.

87. For example, see Department Memorandum of Conversation, November 30, 1964, POL 29 CHINAT, DS.

88. Embassy to Department, December 4, 1964, POL 29 CHINAT, DS.

89. Embassy to Department, December 24, 1964, POL 29 CHINAT, DS.

90. Letter from the Department of State to John King Fairbank, December 9, 1964, POL 29 CHINAT, DS. There are a fair number of reports of the case that have yet to be declassified (perhaps because Peng is still politically active). I am confident, however, that this account is basically accurate.

91. Embassy to Department, January 20, 1965, POL 7 CHINAT, DS; Department to Embassy, January 26, 1965, POL 7 CHINAT, DS; Embassy to Department, January 29, 1965, POL 7 CHINAT, DS; Department to Embassy, February 1, 1965, POL 7 CHINAT, DS; Taylor, *The Generalissimo's Son*, 271; Department Memorandum of Conversation, February 3, 1965, POL 7 CHINAT, DS; Department Memorandum to Office of the Vice President, February 5, 1965, POL 7 CHINAT, DS; Embassy to Department, February 9, 1965, POL 7 CHINAT, DS. It appears that government officials in Washington were at least prepared to say the Peng had in fact been guilty of sedition. See Tucker, *Taiwan, Hong Kong, and the United States*, 115 and 274, n77.

92. Embassy to Department, January 25, 1965, POL 29 CHINAT, DS; Embassy to Department, February 6, 1965, POL 29 CHINAT, DS; Peng, *A Taste of Freedom*, 143. Later in February, a member of the Legislative Yuan hinted that American diplomats were linked to the "Taiwan independence movement"; see Embassy to Department, February 26, 1965, POL 23 CHINAT, DS.

93. Embassy to Department, January 27, 1965, POL 29 CHINAT, DS; Embassy to Department, February 6, 1965, POL 29 CHINAT, DS.

94. Embassy to Department, March 26, 1965, POL 29 CHINAT, DS; Embassy to Department, April 16, 1965, POL 29 CHINAT, DS.

95. Embassy to Department, June 16, 1965, POL 29 CHINAT, DS.

96. Taylor, *The Generalissimo's Son*, 280–81; Tucker, *China Confidential*, 234–35; recollection of Mary Ball Bush, December 22, 2002; Memorandum of Conversation between ROC Ambassador Chow Shu-kai and Marshall Green, April 29, 1970, POL 2 CHINAT, DS; Peng, *A Taste of Freedom*, 230–32.

97. Peng, *A Taste of Freedom*, 151.

98. Embassy to Department, November 9, 1966, POL 2 CHINAT, DS.

99. Embassy to Department, January 22, 1965, POL 2–3 CHINAT, DS. For other reporting that stressed the KMT's political monopoly and the futility of any challenge, see Embassy to Department, July 1, 1964, POL 2–3 CHINAT, DS; Embassy to Department, July 22, 1964, POL 12 CHINAT, DS; Embassy to Department, January 12, 1965, POL 12 CHINAT, DS; Embassy to Department, January 27, 1965, POL 15 CHINAT, DS; Embassy to Department, February 9, 1965, POL 15–1 CHINAT, DS; Embassy to Department, May 21, 1965, POL 11 CHINAT, DS.

100. Embassy to Department, December 4, 1965, POL 29 CHINAT, DS.

101. Mendel, *Politics of Formosan Nationalism*, 179–81.

102. For a detailed and dramatic account of the 1971–1973 movement, see Mab Huang, *Intellectual Ferment for Political Reforms in Taiwan, 1971–1973* (Ann Arbor: University of Michigan Center for Chinese Studies, 1976).

103. "Republic of China: Reformist Pressures," Intelligence Note, INR, February 15, 1972; Embassy to Department, September 8, 1972, POL 2 CHINAT, DS; Embassy to Department, April 12, 1973, POL 2 CHINAT, DS.

104. Interview with Mark Pratt, September 27, 2002.

105. Interviews with David Dean, August 30, 2002, and Mark Pratt, September 27, 2002.

106. Taylor, *The Generalissimo's Son*, 350–54, provides a balanced account of the Kaohsiung Incident, based primarily on John Kaplan, *The Court-Martial of the Kaohsiung Defendants* (Berkeley, CA: Institute of East Asian Studies, University of California, 1981); interview with David Dean, August 30, 2002.

107. Interview with Mark Pratt, September 27, 2002; Taylor, *The Generalissimo's Son*, 351. For confirmation of Chiang's intention to make Taiwan a democracy dating from early 1982, see Tucker, *China Confidential*, 420–21.

108. *New York Times*, February 27, 1980.

109. Interview with Mark Pratt, September 27, 2002; Taylor, *The Generalissimo's Son*, 353.

110. Interview with Mark Pratt, September 27, 2002; interview with David Dean, August 30, 2002.

111. Interview with Mark Pratt, September 27, 2002. On the issue of open and civilian trials, AIT was aided by both Chiang's reformist advisers and a group of prominent Chinese intellectuals led by writer Chen Ruoxi (Chen Jo-hsi). See the *New York Times*, January 24, 1980; Taylor, *The Generalissimo's Son*, 356–57.

112. Interview with David Dean, August 30, 2002; interview with Mark Chen Tangshan (Tan Sun Chen), August 4, 2002.

113. Interview with Mark Pratt, September 27, 2002; interview with David Dean, August 30, 2002.

114. U.S. Congress, House Committee on Foreign Affairs and Senate Committee on Foreign Relations, *Country Reports on Human Rights Practices for 1979*, 96th Cong., 2d sess., February 4, 1980, 526–36.

115. Taylor, *The Generalissimo's Son*, 357–58.

116. Interview with Mark Pratt, September 27, 2002.

117. Taylor, *The Generalissimo's Son*, 359.

118. Charles T. Cross, *Born a Foreigner: A Memoir of the American Presence in Asia* (Lanham, MD: Rowman & Littlefield, 2000), 270; interview with David Dean, August 30, 2002.

Notes to Chapter 4

1. *Department of State Bulletin*, vol. 22, no. 550, January 16, 1950, 79, 80; Document 2, Memorandum of Conversation, Tuesday, February 22, 1972, 2:10 pm to 6:20 pm, Record of Richard Nixon-Zhou Enlai Talks, February 1972, National Security Archive, www.gwi/~nsarchiv/nsa/publications/.

2. Robert Accinelli, *Crisis and Commitment: United States Policy toward Taiwan, 1950–1955* (Chapel Hill: University of North Carolina Press, 1996), 229; Nancy Bernkopf Tucker, "John Foster Dulles and the Taiwan Roots of the 'Two Chinas' Policy," in *John Foster Dulles and the Diplomacy of the Cold War*, ed. Richard H. Immerman (Princeton: Princeton University Press, 1990), 235–62; Wang Jisi, "The Origins of America's 'Two China' Policy," in *Sino American Relations, 1945–1955: A Joint Reassessment of a Critical Decade*, ed. Harry Harding and Yuan Ming (Wilmington, DE: Scholarly Resources Books, 1989), 198–212.

3. These are the themes of David M. Finkelstein, *Washington's Taiwan Dilemma, 1949–1950: From Abandonment to Salvation* (Fairfax, VA: George Mason University Press, 1993) and Nancy Bernkopf Tucker, *Patterns in the Dust: Chinese-American Relations and the Recognition Controversy, 1949–1950* (New York: Columbia University Press, 1983).

4. Wang, "The Origins of America's 'Two China' Policy," 199. The legal rationales behind these proposals were not new. They bear a resemblance to the options discussed in the State Department's postwar planning process discussed in Chapter 2. The key document is "Alternative Political Solutions," an annex to "Formosa," Document 325 of the Territorial Subcommittee of the State Department's Advisory Committee on Post-War Foreign Policy, May 25, 1943, Box 63, Notter Files, Records of the State Department Advisory Committee on Post-War Foreign Policy, 1942–1945, Record Group 59, U.S. National Archives and Records Administration, College Park, MD; see Appendix 2.1.

5. Finkelstein, *Washington's Taiwan Dilemma*, 178–81. Taiwan was not the only late-forties territorial problem for which the foreign policy establishment recommended trusteeship as a solution. In the spring of 1948, State and Defense officials who opposed the emergence of an independent Jewish state urged that Palestine be made a United Nations trusteeship. Among those pushing for such an outcome, which Truman ultimately blocked, was Dean Rusk, who would soon offer a similar proposal regarding Taiwan. See Clark Clifford, *Counsel to the President* (New York: Random House, 1991), 5, 10, 18, 22–23.

6. Wang, "The Origins of America's 'Two China' Policy," 199. In addition, MacArthur in December 1949 proposed setting up Taiwan as a separate country in the context of a peace agreement.

7. *Department of State Bulletin*, vol. 22, no. 550, January 16, 1950, 79, 80.

8. Dulles's memorandum to Rusk is cited in Finkelstein, *Washington's Taiwan Dilemma*, 307–9. Rusk's proposal can be found in *Foreign Relations of the United States, 1950*, Vol. 6, *East Asia and the Pacific* (Washington, DC: Government Printing Office, 1976), 347–50 (hereafter cited as *FRUS 1950*).

9. *Foreign Relations of the United States, 1950*, Vol. 7, *Korea* (Washington, DC: Government Printing Office, 1976), 157–58, 180.

10. Hungdah Chiu, ed., *China and the Question of Taiwan: Documents and Analysis* (New York: Praeger, 1973), 229; Ye-Strong conversation, June 29, 1950, 794A.5/

6–2950, Department of State General Records (hereafter cited as DS), Record Group 59, National Archives and Records Administration, College Park, MD; Gu-Dulles conversation, China File, Files of John Foster Dulles, 1947–1952, Lot Files 54-D-423 (concerning Japanese Peace Treaty), Record Group 59, National Archives and Records Administration, College Park, MD (hereafter cited as Dulles Files).

11. *FRUS 1950*, 438; abbreviations in the original.

12. John Leighton Stuart, *Fifty Years in China: The Memoirs of John Leighton Stuart, Missionary and Ambassador* (New York: Random House, 1954), 285–87; Karl Lott Rankin, *China Assignment* (Seattle: University of Washington Press, 1964), 29. There was a proposal in 1951 to seek Stuart's resignation but it was never carried out. In July 1952 Stuart asked to be sent to Taiwan but Acheson refused. With Eisenhower's election, Stuart finally resigned; see *Foreign Relations of the United States, 1952–1954*, Vol. 14, *China and Japan* (Washington, DC: Government Printing Office, 1985), 81–82, including footnotes (hereafter cited as *FRUS 1952–1954*).

13. *FRUS 1950*, 398; *Department of State Bulletin*, vol. 23, October 2, 1950, 526. The full array of American ideas was laid out in a position paper the State Department prepared August 28, 1950, prior to consultations with the French and the British. The paper presented five hypothetical recommendations that a UN commission might make: (1) incorporation in the PRC; (2) restoration to Japan; (3) independence; (4) a UN trusteeship; and (5) a UN plebiscite to determine which outcome the island's population wanted. Most of the options obviously were intended to give the people on Taiwan a say, as well as to deny the island to Beijing. See "State Department Position Paper on Formosa," August 28, 1950, cited in Accinelli, *Crisis and Commitment*, 48–49. Note the similarity of the set of options to those laid out in "Alternative Political Solutions," cited in note 4.

14. *FRUS 1950*, 534–36. This was not the first time that Dulles had expressed sympathy for the sentiments of "the Formosans." Writing to Senator Arthur Vandenberg in January, he opined that Cairo had been overtaken by events, that it was "scandalous" for the United States to adopt the position that Taiwan was part of China and that therefore "the Formosans must be subjected to the cruel fate of being the final battleground" between the KMT and CCP. "It seems to me that the tragedy of Formosa is the Formosans. . . . I would think that we ought to have had some respect for the six or seven million people in Formosa who, ever since Cairo, have been dealt with from a standpoint of the strategy and prestige of great powers without regard to their own welfare or desires." See John Foster Dulles to Arthur Vandenberg, January 6, 1950, Papers of John Foster Dulles, Box 48, Mudd Library, Princeton University, as cited in Finkelstein, *Washington's Taiwan Dilemma*, 302.

15. *FRUS 1950*, 543–44. Note that Dulles is making implicit reference to the two ways of disposing of territory after an international conflict. The traditional way is pursuant to a decision by the victorious states. The more recent way is through consulting the people of the territory in question.

16. U.S. Mission to the UN to Department of State (hereafter cited as Department), August 30, 1950, 794A.00 /8-3050, DS; Embassy Taipei (hereafter cited as Embassy) to Department, August 30, 1950, 611.94A/8-3150, DS; Embassy to Department, September 4, 1950, 794A.00 /9-450, DS. The Department's reply to that last message expressed irritation at the ROC's emphasis on its legal position: "It is appreciated CHI GOVT will doubtless have recurring worries arising from its concept that it is the only legal CHI GOVT and SHLD receive international treatment as such. This concept not held generally by rest of world. . . . CHI GOVT therefore be

advised to appreciate realties of tenuous position it now occupies." Department to Embassy, September 4, 1950, 794A.00 /9-450, DS.

17. In 1951, the situation in the UN improved but the State Department was ready in case there was pressure to seat the PRC. The underlying premise of much of its planning was that Taiwan was a former colony that should be treated as a separate unit and its people should have some say in their future. See Accinelli, *Crisis and Commitment*, 79–80; *Foreign Relations of the United States, 1951*, Vol. 7, *Korea and China* (Washington, DC: Government Printing Office, 1983), 1859–63.

18. The discussion that follows is based in part on Accinelli, *Crisis and Commitment*, 78–89; Su-ya Chang, "The United States and the Long-term Disposition of Taiwan in the Making of Peace with Japan, 1950–1952," *Asian Profile* 16 (October 1988): 459–70; and Michael M. Yoshitsu, *Japan and the San Francisco Peace Settlement* (New York: Columbia University Press, 1982), 67–83.

19. *Foreign Relations of the United States, 1951*, Vol. 6, *Asia and the Pacific* (Washington, DC: Government Printing Office, 1977), 1044–45, 1050,1107–9 (hereafter cited as *FRUS 1951*).

20. Some of Dulles's arguments were political: that the United States Senate would not ratify the peace treaties if the process tilted too much against the ROC. This reflected, to some extent, the indirect influence that Taipei could exert on the treaty. See *FRUS 1951*, 977 fn, 1045, 1050, 1156–59.

21. Dulles to Acheson, December 12, 1951, Dulles Papers.

22. For the ROC's objections to the treaty draft, see *FRUS 1951*, 1057, 1059–60. The Chinese text of Chiang's statement may be found in Qin Xiaoyi, ed., *Jiang zongtong ji* (Collected Works of President Chiang), vol. 2 (Taipei: Zhonghua xueshuyuan, 1974), 2267–68.

23. Legal Adviser's Office memorandum to Office of Chinese Affairs, June 6, 1951, Dulles Papers (see under August 23, 1951); Acheson to Dulles, December 15, 1951, and Dulles to Acheson, December 17, 1951, Dulles Papers.

24. Gu-Dulles conversations, October 3, 1950, December 9, 1950, December 19, 1950, March 20, 1951, Dulles Papers (the December 9 memo is at the beginning of the 1951 file). Note that on this issue there is no evidence that the ROC's American supporters played any role, as they had on the ROC's participation in the treaty-making process, in shaping the American position; see note 20 above.

25. *FRUS, 1951*, 978.

26. Accinelli, *Crisis and Commitment*, 81; Chang, "The United States and the Long-term Disposition of Taiwan," 461.

27. Ye's statement is cited in U.S. Congress, Senate Committee on Foreign Relations, *Executive Sessions of the Senate Foreign Relations Committee (Historical Series)*, vol. 7, 84th Cong., 1st sess., 1955, 335.

28. For DOD's increasing stake in Taiwan, see the relevant chapters of Accinelli, *Crisis and Commitment*.

29. Accinelli, *Crisis and Commitment*, 112.

30. Rankin, *China Assignment*, 159; *FRUS 1952–1954*, 307.

31. This summary is based on chapters 8–11 of Accinelli, *Crisis and Commitment*. On Dulles's concern that Congress and the public would not support action to defend Jinmen and Mazu in the absence of stronger authorization, see *FRUS 1952–1954*, 611.

32. On ROC resistance to prior approval for offensive action, see *FRUS 1952–1954*,

872–80, 887–92, 895–903, 904–11, 921. On its desire for a public pledge on the off-shore islands, see Accinelli, *Crisis and Commitment*, 195–200.

33. *FRUS 1952–1954*, 760; *Foreign Relations of the United States, 1955–1957*, Vol. 2, *China* (Washington, DC: Government Printing Office, 1986), 115–16, 393, 598, 619–20, 683–84 (hereafter cited as *FRUS 1955–1957*, 2).

34. *Executive Sessions*, 83–84, 98, 315, 324, 330. Dulles was asked in these closed sessions about a UN trusteeship for Taiwan and said that it was undesirable because "the people of Formosa" [the ROC government?] would not accept it and so it would have to be imposed by war; *Executive Sessions*, 345. The statement in the Committee report that the treaty did not change Taiwan's status is at page 791 of *Executive Sessions*. The full citation of the report is U.S. Congress, Senate Committee on Foreign Relations, *Mutual Defense Treaty with the Republic of China: Report*, 84th Cong., 1st sess., February 8, 1955. In July 1955, Robertson mentioned Dulles's squatter's-rights formulation to Gu, saying, "While the juridical status of Taiwan is in limbo, certainly the Chinese Nationalists have the best right to it of anyone." See *FRUS 1955–1957*, 2, 683–84.

35. *FRUS 1952–1954*, 801, 848, 860. Chiang's statement is reproduced in Chiu, *China and the Question of Taiwan*, 259.

36. This paragraph is based on chapters 9–11 of Accinelli, *Crisis and Commitment*.

37. On the renunciation-of-force discussions, see Kenneth Young, *Negotiating with the Chinese Communists: The United States Experience, 1953–1967* (New York: McGraw-Hill, 1968), 91–115, 414–17.

38. *FRUS 1952–1954*, 781; *FRUS 1955–1957*, 2, 146. Taiwan officials worried that a UN resolution might have a different effect: starting a movement to a complete redefinition of Taiwan's status. Chiang Kai-shek, for example, believed that cease-fire and neutralization of the offshore islands was the first step in a careful plan, to be followed by the same steps for Taiwan itself, a UN trusteeship for Taiwan, UN membership for the PRC, then PRC takeover of Taiwan. See *FRUS 1952–1954*, 612, 651, 700, 732, 1034.

39. *FRUS 1955–1957*, 2, 156–57.

40. *Foreign Relations of the United States, 1955–1957*, Vol. 3, *China* (Washington, DC: Government Printing Office, 1986), 110 (hereafter cited as *FRUS 1955–1957*, 3).

41. For documentation of Taipei's objections to negotiations on a renunciation of force, see *FRUS 1955–1957*, 3, 143, 176, 279–82, 295–301, 305–7. Not all in the U.S. government were happy with the course that Dulles charted with respect to the PRC and Taiwan. For objections from within the State Department to a two-China trend, see *FRUS 1955–1957*, 2, 361–62; *FRUS 1955–1957*, 3, 513.

42. During the crisis, friendly governments raised a trusteeship or a plebiscite as ways out but Dulles did not pursue those ideas and Chiang opposed all of them. Dulles did acknowledge at one point that the trends on Taiwan, particularly the Taiwanization of the military, would diminish the impulse to return to the mainland and so encourage a two-China outcome. See *Foreign Relations of the United States, 1958–1960*, Vol. 19, *China* (Washington, DC: Government Printing Office, 1996), 226, 240, 247, 281, 297 (hereafter cited as *FRUS 1958–1960*).

43. *FRUS 1958–1960*, 401, 414–16, 422, 443, 452, 469.

44. For Bowie's effort, see *FRUS 1955–1957*, 3, 470–73, 491–92. On the Dulles-Bowie relationship, see Nancy Bernkopf Tucker, "A House Divided: The United States, the Department of State, and China," in Warren I. Cohen and Akira Iriye, ed., *The*

Great Powers in East Asia, 1953–1960 (New York: Columbia University Press, 1990), 35–62, especially 39–40. For other two-China efforts, see *FRUS 1955–1957*, 3, 491–92, 660–73, 668–69.

45. John Foster Dulles, *War or Peace* (New York: Macmillan, 1950), 190; *FRUS 1955–1957*, 2, 626; *FRUS 1958–1960*, 392, 438. In the late 1950s, there were two proposals from outside the government for a new approach. The first was in a study commissioned by the Senate Foreign Relations Committee on U.S. policy toward China and Taiwan and prepared by Conlon Associates (the "Conlon Report"). It suggested "admission of Communist China to the United Nations; recognition of the Republic of Taiwan; the seating of this Republic in the Assembly." See U.S. Congress, Senate Committee on Foreign Relations, *United State Foreign Policy: Asia*, 84th Cong., 1st sess., November 1, 1959. The second proposal came from Chester Bowles, a foreign-policy adviser to John Kennedy. He rejected dual recognition or dual UN representation but suggested "an independent Sino-Formosan nation." See Chester Bowles, "The 'China Problem' Reconsidered," *Foreign Affairs* 38 (April 1960): 476–86; Chester Bowles, *Promises to Keep: My Years in Public Life, 1941–1969* (New York: Harper and Row, 1971), 391–96. There is no evidence that either proposal had any direct impact on Kennedy administration policy.

46. On the Eisenhower factor, see *Foreign Relations of the United States, 1961–1963*, Vol. 22, *Northeast Asia* (Washington, DC: Government Printing Office, 1996), 33–36 (hereafter cited as *FRUS 1961–1963*). Nancy Tucker does not believe that Eisenhower ever made that threat. What is important, however, is whether Kennedy believed it—as he apparently did—and that he encouraged his staff to believe it, as he most assuredly did.

47. *FRUS 1958–1960*, 749–50; and the five items in Document no. 499 in the microfiche supplement to vol. 19 of *FRUS 1958–1960*.

48. "Chinese Representation in the United Nations," part of Document no. 499, n.d., microfiche supplement, *FRUS 1958–1960*, 2–4.

49. "Some Possible Alternatives for Dealing with the Question of Chinese Representation in the United Nations (Tab B)," part of Document no. 499, microfiche supplement, *FRUS 1958–1960*, 1–2.

50. "Some Possible Alternatives for Dealing with the Question of Chinese Representation in the United Nations (Tab B)," 3.

51. The "important question" idea was also discussed in the December 1960 memoranda; see "Alternative Courses to the Moratorium Procedure," part of Document no. 499, microfiche supplement, *FRUS 1958–1960*, 1–3.

52. *FRUS 1961–1963*, 48–49.

53. *FRUS 1961–1963*, 4–9, 33–36, 37–38, 42–45, 46–48, 50–51, 58–62, 63–65, 66–69.

54. *FRUS 1961–1963*, 76–79, 99–101, 104–10. UN Ambassador Adlai Stevenson remained enamored of the successor-state idea and quietly tried to push it; see *FRUS 1961–1963*, 112–13, 133–34, 135–36, 151–52.

55. *FRUS 1961–1963*, 152–54, 156–57. Ironically, the Kennedy pledge would have been less effective than the way it was portrayed. State Department lawyers later argued that the only circumstance under which the United States would have the right to veto PRC entry would have been if Beijing were entering as a new member of the General Assembly. No veto power was available on a vote to seat the PRC as the representative of *China*, which was already a member. Moreover, in the Security Council, representation would likely be cast as a procedural, not substantive, issue,

on which a veto was not allowed. See Memorandum by Lloyd Meeker, October 31, 1964, UN 6 CHICOM, DS.

56. *Public Papers of the Presidents of the United States: John F. Kennedy, 1963*, 845–46; James C. Thomson Jr., "On the Making of U.S. China Policy, 1961–1969: A Study in Bureaucratic Politics," *China Quarterly* 50 (April–June 1972): 230. This is a good account of the frustrations experienced by advocates of a new China policy in the Kennedy and Johnson administrations. The Kennedy administration continued two other manifestations of a de facto acceptance of the PRC: the ambassadorial talks and constraints on ROC offensive action against the mainland, particularly in the spring of 1962.

57. *Foreign Relations of the United States, 1964–1968*, Vol. 30, *China* (Washington, DC: Government Printing Office, 1998), 92–93 (hereafter cited as *FRUS 1964–1968*). The first Taiwan test for the Johnson administration was France's recognition of the PRC. Washington hoped that Taipei would keep its diplomats in Paris in order to impose a difficult choice on Beijing and it mounted a vigorous effort to convince Taipei. In the end, the ROC could not stand the insult and pulled out. For this episode, see *FRUS 1964–1968*, 1, 5, 8–9, 10–11, 12–13, 14–15, 20, 22–23.

58. *FRUS 1964–1968*, 117–20, 120–23; "Political Perspective," November 1, 1964, UN 6 CHICOM, DS.

59. *FRUS 1964–1968*, 126–28. Eight days later Robert Komer of the NSC staff did prepare a follow-up memo for McGeorge Bundy that accepted Rusk's point about credibility and acknowledged Chiang's stubbornness, but then restated the case for a pragmatic policy adjustment. On the question of the ROC's status, however, he returned to the concept of John Foster Dulles: "What we need to do is to stem the rapid erosion of Taiwan's international position by getting it internationally recognized that China is a divided country (like Germany, Korea, and Vietnam)." See *FRUS 1964–1968*, 130–32.

60. *FRUS 1964–1968*, 223–24.

61. On Johnson's desire for a new look, see *FRUS 1964–1968*, 289, 295. On the Bundy-Sisco proposal, see ibid., 261, 271.

62. *FRUS 1964–1968*, 285.

63. *FRUS 1964–1968*, 289–292. Sisco believed that the main contest was over the General Assembly. Preserving the ROC's seat on the Security Council was a less immediate and more manageable problem.

64. *FRUS 1964–1968*, 292, 294–95; "Memorandum," April 30, 1966, UN 6 CHICOM, DS.

65. *FRUS 1964–1968*, 301–3.

66. *FRUS 1964–1968*, 344 fn., 344–48.

67. *FRUS 1964–1968*, 348–50.

68. *FRUS 1964–1968*, 407, 409–10, including 409 fn., 412–14, 418–19.

69. *FRUS 1964–1968*, 427 fn., 437–40, 443–45, quoted passage on 444, 445–52, quoted passage on 450, 458–59, 462–66, 467–69.

70. *FRUS 1964–1968*, 468.

71. *FRUS 1964–1968*, 638–41, 645–46, 649 (emphasis added), 672–74.

72. Document 2, Memorandum of Conversation, Tuesday, February 22, 1972, 2:10 pm to 6:20 pm, Record of Richard Nixon-Zhou Enlai Talks, February 1972, the National Security Archive, www.gwi/~nsarchiv/nsa/publications/.

73. Henry Kissinger, *White House Years* (Boston: Little, Brown, 1979), 770–71, 719–20.

74. "Talking Points for NSC Meeting on Chinese Representation in the UN," March 23, 1971, UN 6 CHICOM, DS.

75. "Talking Points for NSC Meeting on Chinese Representation in the UN"; "Chirep Scenario and Draft Resolution, July 28, 1971, UN 6 CHICOM. The principle of universality raised the question of a UN presence for the two Germanys, Koreas, Vietnams. Because Germany was particularly sensitive, the universality principle received little emphasis.

76. "Talking Points for NSC Meeting on Chinese Representation in the UN"; Kissinger, *White House Years*, 772. On April 28, Charles Bray, the department's spokesman, reiterated the two-decade American view that "sovereignty over Taiwan and the Pescadores is an unsettled question subject to future international resolution." He acknowledged the intention of the Cairo and Potsdam declarations but that objective was not carried out, particularly in the Japan peace treaty. He indicated that the United States regarded the ROC as "exercising legitimate authority over Taiwan and the Pescadores," but only because Japanese forces on Taiwan had been ordered to surrender to ROC forces at the end of World War II. He acknowledged that Beijing and Taipei disagreed with the U.S. position on Taiwan's sovereignty and that Washington could not resolve the dispute between the two. "Whatever the ultimate resolution of the dispute between the Republic of China on Taiwan and the PRC on the mainland, it should be accomplished by peaceful means," and noted that the dispute could be resolved either "internationally or directly by the two governments" (see Chiu, *China and the Question of Taiwan*, 340–41, for an extract of Bray's statement). But this episode did not represent a shift in U.S. policy. It was, rather, a more routine answer to a reporter's question that drew on very standard formulations. The response that it provoked in both Taipei and Beijing (see, for example, Embassy to Department, May 1, 1971, UN 6 CHICOM, DS) was unexpected by the department. Personal communication from Charles Bray to the author, October 4, 2001.

77. For the record of the Washington-Taipei discussions on UN strategy, see the many items in UN 6 CHICOM, DS.

78. On the spokesman incident, see note 76. Kissinger, *White House* Years, 708, 719–21, 770–74; "Memcon, Kissinger and Zhou, 10 July 1971, Afternoon," in "The Beijing-Washington Back-Channel and Henry Kissinger's Secret Trip to China," National Security Archive Electronic Briefing Book, no. 66, www.gwu.edu/~nsarchiv/NSAEBB/NSAEBB66/ch-35.pdf, 15–16. The cross-purposes characterizing American diplomacy during this period are demonstrated with particularly ironic clarity by a memorandum prepared by the legal adviser's office that presented in detail the case that Taiwan's legal status was undetermined. The memo is dated July 13, 1971, at which point Kissinger was jetting his way home from the PRC; see "Legal Status of Taiwan," July 13, 1971, POL 19 TAIWAN, DS.

79. "ViceMin Yang's Efforts toward GRC Flexibility on Chirep and Chirec," July 20, 1971, UN 6 CHICOM, DS.

80. U.S. Congress, Senate Subcommittee on Separation of Powers, *Taiwan Communiqué and Separation of Powers*, 97th Cong., 2d sess., September 17 and 27, 1982, 140.

Notes to Chapter 5

1. Most of the documents considered in this chapter can be found in Stephen P. Gibert and William M. Carpenter, *America and Island China* (Lanham, MD: University Press of America, 1989), as follows: Shanghai communiqué, 111–14; normalization communiqué, 201–3, U.S. normalization statement, 203; Carter oral statement,

204–5; PRC normalization statement, 206; Taiwan Relations Act, 222–29; 1982 communiqué, 312–14; Reagan oral statement, 305–6; PRC statement, 306–7. For Hua Guofeng's press conference at the time of normalization, see *Peking Review,* December 22, 1978, 9–11. For the statement of the Standing Committee of the PRC National People's Congress, see *Beijing Review,* January 5, 1979, 16–17, 104–7. For the Chinese versions of the three communiqués, see Xie Xide and Ni Shixiong, *Quzhe di licheng: Zhongmei jianjiao 20 nian* (Circuitous Course: The Twenty Years Since the Establishment of China–U.S. Relations) (Shanghai: Fudan daxue chubanshe, 1999), 228–34. For an ambitious study of the broader context surrounding the three communiqués, one that links bilateral U.S.–PRC negotiations and their strategic context, see Robert S. Ross, *Negotiating Cooperation: The United States and China, 1969–1989* (Stanford: Stanford University Press, 1995).

2. John H. Holdridge, *Crossing the Divide: An Insider's Account of Normalization of U.S.-China Relations* (Lanham, MD: Rowman and Littlefield, 1997), 68; Henry Kissinger, *White House Years* (Boston: Little, Brown, 1979), 781–82.

3. Kissinger, *White House Years,* 782–83, 747.

4. Ibid., 783, 1075; "Memcon, Kissinger and Zhou, 'President's Visit, Taiwan and Japan,' 21 October 1971, 10:30 A.M.–1:45 P.M.," Negotiating U.S.-Chinese Rapprochement, New American and Chinese Documentation Leading Up to Nixon's 1972 Trip, National Security Archive Electronic Briefing Book, no. 70, www.gwu.edu/~nsarchiv/NSAEBB/NSAEBB70/doc11.pdf, 26.

5. Kissinger, *White House Years,* 1072, 1080, 1075.

6. Ibid., 1077–79. Kissinger stressed to Zhou that if the PRC refused the American desire to make some statement about peaceful resolution, it would have to state its conditions unilaterally.

7. Ibid., 1082–84; Holdridge, *Crossing the Divide,* 92–93.

8. Kissinger, *White House Years,* 1080. There is disagreement on another point. John Holdridge's account says that Green objected to use of the term "all people" on both sides of the Taiwan Strait, because some residents of Taiwan would not necessarily ascribe to that view. Kissinger's account says the term was "all Chinese," which Green wanted to change to "the Chinese." The fact that the phrase in the October drafts of the communiqué is "all Chinese" indicates that Kissinger's recollections were correct.

9. Ibid., 783, 1075. On the latter page, Kissinger indicates that the added phrase was a product of the October discussions. Recall that Kissinger borrowed the initial "The United States acknowledges . . ." formulation from a State Department planning document from the 1950s. At that time, it would have been unthinkable to include in such a formulation a statement that Taiwan was a part of China, since the U.S. position was that the island's legal status had yet to be determined.

10. Ibid., 1079.

11. See, for example, "Memcon, Kissinger and Zhou, 10 July 1971, Afternoon, 'The Beijing-Washington Back-Channel and Henry Kissinger's Secret Trip to China,'" National Security Archive Electronic Briefing Book, no. 66, www.gwu.edu/~nsarchiv/NSAEBB/NSAEBB66/ch-35.pdf, 4; "Memcon, Kissinger and Zhou, 'President's Visit, Taiwan and Japan,' 21 October 1971, 10:30 A.M.–1:45 P.M."

12. Kissinger, *White House Years,* 1084–85. Kissinger also says that the American side did not check the Chinese translation. But Charles Freeman, a member of the State Department team in the Nixon delegation, stated that he indeed had checked it; see Charles W. Freeman Jr., "The Process of Rapprochement: Achievements and

Problems," in Gene T. Hsiao and Mike Witunski, ed., *Sino-American Normalization and Its Policy Implications* (New York: Praeger, 1983), 9.

13. Holdridge, *Crossing the Divide*, 90; Document 2, Memorandum of Conversation, Tuesday, February 22, 1972, 2:10 p.m.–6:20 p.m., Record of Richard Nixon-Zhou Enlai Talks, February 1972, the National Security Archive, see www.gwu.edu/~nsarchiv/nsa/publications/DOC_readers/kissinger/nixzhou/, 5. The other principles were that the United States would discourage Japan from taking its place in Taiwan; that it would support any peaceful resolution regarding Taiwan; and that it would work to achieve normalization.

14. For example, Kissinger said to Zhou in October 1971, "Let me separate what we can say and what our policy is"; see "Memcon, Kissinger, and Zhou, 'President's Visit, Taiwan and Japan,' 21 October 1971, 10:30 A.M.–1:45 P.M.," 26.

15. Holdridge, *Crossing the Divide*, 92. That the U.S. statement was intended as a substantive response to the Chinese statement is indicated by the order of paragraphs in the English and Chinese texts. In the sections where the two sides detailed their disagreement on *international* issues, the U.S. statement came first in the English version and the PRC statement came first in the Chinese version. Yet in the discussion of the *Taiwan* issue, the PRC statement came first in both versions. That would be appropriate only if the U.S. statement was in some way a response to the PRC statement. This inference is strengthened by the note in Kissinger's memoirs that State Department officials had suggested at the last minute that the communiqué follow diplomatic practice and place the American position first in the English version (see Kissinger, *White House Years*, 1083). Kissinger agreed with that general point, but still the American position on Taiwan came second. So there was a deliberate decision to do so. Moreover, Nixon's explicit and implicit rejection of various formulae inconsistent with the idea of one China in his conversation with Zhou Enlai (see above) validates the Holdridge claim that there was a deliberate link between the end of the Chinese statement on Taiwan and the beginning of the American one.

16. Su Ge, *Meiguo duihua zhengce yu Taiwan wenti* (The China Policy of the United States and the Taiwan Question) (Beijing: Shijie zhishi chubanshe, 1998), 382–86.

17. William Burr, ed., *The Kissinger Transcripts: The Top-Secret Talks with Beijing and Moscow* (New York: New Press, 1999), 66–68. For a discussion of prior U.S. efforts to secure renunciations of the use of force from both Taipei and Beijing, see Leonard H.D. Gordon, "United States Opposition to Use of Force in the Taiwan Strait, 1954–1962," *Journal of American History* 72 (December 1985): 637–60. In November 1973, Mao told Kissinger that he did not believe in a peaceful solution; see Burr, *The Kissinger Transcripts*, 186–87.

18. This was not the first time that Beijing had pushed the five principles on the United States. In April 1964 during the Warsaw talks, for example, the PRC representative proposed that the two conclude an agreement that they would coexist peacefully on the basis of the five principles, and that accordingly the United States would withdraw militarily from Taiwan and the Taiwan Strait. See *Foreign Relations of the United States, 1964–1968*, Vol. 30, *China* (Washington, DC: Government Printing Office, 1998), 37–38.

19. *Department of State Bulletin* 66, March 20, 1972, 435; Memorandum of Conversation, Tuesday, February 22, 1972, 6–7; Burr, *The Kissinger Transcripts*, 294–98.

20. Kissinger, *White House Years*, 1080.

21. Patrick Tyler, *A Great Wall: Six Presidents and China: An Investigative History* (New York: Public Affairs, 1999), 266; Freeman, "The Process of Rapprochement," 13.

22. Ross, *Negotiating Cooperation*, 86; conversation with Michel Oksenberg.

23. Michel Oksenberg, "A Decade of Sino-American Relations," *Foreign Affairs* 61 (Fall 1982): 181–82.

24. Ibid., 182. As late as July 1975, Kissinger's advisers had held out the hope that a unilateral PRC statement might be an element in a normalization package; see Burr, *The Kissinger Transcripts*, 376–77. This proposal also acknowledged the arms sales issue. Note that Carter's approach on peaceful resolution was similar to how Kissinger had handled the security treaty in 1972: reaffirm the commitment and ask Beijing not to contest the statement.

25. Cyrus Vance, *Hard Choices: Critical Years in America's Foreign Policy* (New York: Simon and Schuster, 1983), 79, 81–82; Oksenberg, "A Decade of Sino-American Relations," 182. There are variations among the accounts of the normalization negotiations as to when the Carter administration reached its bottom line on the future U.S. presence on Taiwan and on how to address the use-of-force issue. Accounts from Carter's officials (such as Vance and Oksenberg) indicate that they actually recognized early on that both were nonstarters. Outsider accounts suggest that the hopes for getting a liaison office in Taipei and a unilateral PRC statement of peaceful intent lasted longer. In any event, the solutions on both were locked in by the time of the Brzezinski trip.

26. Zbigniew Brzezinski, *Power and Principle: Memoirs of a National Security Adviser* (New York: Farrar, Straus and Giroux, 1983), 224–25; Oksenberg, "A Decade of Sino-American Relations," 185–86.

27. Oksenberg, "A Decade of Sino-American Relations," 186–87; Brzezinski, *Power and Principle*, 229; Tyler, *A Great Wall*, 257–58. In Tyler's telling of the story, Woodcock suggested that Washington basically ignored Huang's response. By inference, if Beijing was prepared to negotiate a communiqué in spite of Carter's statement to Chai, that constituted tacit acceptance of continued arms sales. But Tyler does not really document his point that the Carter administration assumed that PRC silence meant consent, and it may well be his own interpretation. Might the reverse apply, that the PRC believed that the Carter statement was merely for the record and that Washington's movement on a communiqué that did not include the arms sales issue constituted tacit acceptance by the United States that arms sales would *not* continue? It might be argued that Deng Xiaoping's request for a one-year moratorium on arms sales during the period when the U.S.–Taiwan defense treaty would be terminated constituted recognition that arms sales would continue. But that is only implicit. When he visited Washington in early 1979, he told Carter that he was opposed to arms sales but hoped that Washington would be extremely prudent; another hint, but not conclusive. There was certainly no formal agreement reached, and Deng reserved the right to revisit the issue. Context thus became important and Ronald Reagan changed the context. See Tyler, *A Great Wall*, 268, 277.

28. Jimmy Carter, *Keeping Faith: Memoirs of a President* (New York: Bantam Books, 1982), 197–98.

29. Conversation with an American official who was directly involved in negotiating the communiqué and ancillary documents.

30. Oksenberg, "A Decade of Sino-American Relations," 187–88.

31. Ibid., 188; Brzezinski, *Power and Principle*, 231; Tyler, *A Great Wall*, 266–69.

32. I reach that conclusion because the arms sales deadlock occurred at the very end of the negotiations when time was pressing. It seems a bit unlikely that the two sides would take the time—or even remember—to make the change in the text.

Moreover, Oksenberg, who was the chief China specialist on the National Security Council staff at the time of normalization and who played a critical role in drafting the communiqué, confirmed for me the significance of the omission. The normalization communiqué did not repeat from the Shanghai communiqué the somewhat redundant warning against collusive behavior by any major country and against division of the world into spheres of influence, nor the now unnecessary pledge to keep in touch.

33. Brzezinski, *Power and Principle*, 214.

34. Lester L. Wolff and David L. Simon, *Legislative History of the Taiwan Relations Act* (New York: American Association for Chinese Studies, 1982), 310–11.

35. Su, *Meiguo duihua zhengce yu Taiwan wenti*, 423–27.

36. See Burr, *Kissinger Transcripts*, 295–98.

37. For the first time, the term "reunifying" was used to describe the process of reintegrating Taiwan and the mainland.

38. The United States responded to the first of these points in the communiqué. As was the case in the Shanghai communiqué, it chose not to address the second.

39. Note, however, that the normalization statement used the term "reunifying," which was less politically charged than "liberation," which was in the Shanghai communiqué.

40. Why the contradiction between the PRC statement that said that the Taiwan issue had been resolved and Hua's indication that normalization had preceded without agreement on arms sales? The most likely explanation is the confused conclusion of the negotiations. The written statement had likely been prepared before the last-minute agreement to disagree on arms sales and no one thought to take out the categorical statement that the Taiwan issue had been resolved.

41. Burr, *Kissinger Transcripts*, 295–98; Vance, *Hard Choices*, 82–83; Brzezinski, *Power and Principle*, 213–14, 218; Hungdah Chiu, ed., *China and the Taiwan Issue* (New York: Praeger, 1979), 184.

42. Tyler, *A Great Wall*, 262–63.

43. That this was actually the outcome on the arms sales issue is confirmed in the second paragraph of the arms sales communiqué; see below.

44. Harvey J. Feldman, "The Taiwan Relations Act—Past, and Perhaps Future" (paper presented at University of Maryland, March 4, 1999), 2–3.

45. Feldman, "The Taiwan Relations Act," 4–5. For the text of the administration bill, see Gibert and Carpenter, *America and Island China*, 211–13.

46. David Tawei Lee, *The Making of the Taiwan Relations Act: Twenty Years in Retrospect* (New York: Oxford University Press, 2000), 47–48, 64–70, 76–79.

47. It is also unnecessary, in light of the publication of Lee, *Making of the Taiwan Relations Act*, which provides an excellent chronological account.

48. Lee, *Making of the Taiwan Relations Act*, 122–24, provides a summary of the differences as the bills came out of committee.

49. As will become clear in the discussion below, these provisions are not phrased in a way that constitutes a binding order on the Executive Branch.

50. On the corrosive effect of mistrust, see U.S. Congress, House Committee on Foreign Affairs, *Executive-Legislative Consultations on China Policy, 1978–1979*, Congress and Foreign Policy Series, no. 1.

51. The remainder of this section draws on a section of my essay, "Helping the Republic of China to Defend Itself," in *A Unique Relationship: The United States and the Republic of China Under the Taiwan Relations Act*, ed. Ramon H. Myers (Stanford: Hoover Institution Press, 1989), 83–86.

52. The reference to "peace and security" was a deliberate effort to echo the United Nations Charter, and so internationalize the Taiwan Strait issue.

53. It should be noted that the Taiwan Relations Act defined the word "Taiwan" to include only the island of Taiwan itself and the Pescadores. Excluded from the definition were Jinmen, Mazu, and other Nationalist-controlled offshore islands.

54. Interview with a member of the staff of the House Office of Legislative Counsel who was deeply involved in the drafting of the Taiwan Relations Act.

55. Richard M. Pious, "The Taiwan Relations Act: The Constitutional and Legal Context," in *Congress, the Presidency, and the Taiwan Relations Act*, ed. Louis W. Keonig, James C. Hsiung, and King-yuh Chang (New York: Praeger, 1985), 161.

56. Jacob K. Javits, "Congress and Foreign Relations: The Taiwan Relations Act," *Foreign Affairs* 60 (Fall 1981): 60.

57. Interview with a member of the staff of the House Office of Legislative Counsel.

58. U.S. Congress, House Committee on Foreign Affairs, *Implementation of the Taiwan Relations Act*, 96th Cong., 1st sess., October 23 and November 8, 1979, 51.

59. Interview with a staff member of the House Office of Legislative Counsel who was deeply involved in the drafting of the Taiwan Relations Act.

60. U.S. General Accounting Office report. The passage quoted is from an unclassified section of a document whose overall classification is "secret."

61. Indeed, when President Carter reluctantly signed the Taiwan Relations Act, he interpreted the new law to emphasize what Congress had not done, and so buttressed the power of the Executive Branch. He stated: "In a number of sections of this legislation, the Congress has wisely granted discretion in a manner consistent with our interest in the well-being of the people on Taiwan, and with the understanding we reached on the normalization with the People's Republic of China." See U.S. President, *Public Papers of the Presidents of the United States. Jimmy Carter, 1979,* Book 1 (Washington, DC: Government Printing Office, 1980), 640–41. A Carter administration official told me that the president claimed that the Taiwan Relations Act empowered him to do what he felt was appropriate vis-à-vis Taiwan and bound him in no significant way

62. Tyler, *A Great Wall*, 269, based on interviews; Ross, *Negotiating Cooperation*, 181; Zhang Zuqian, "National Defense Modernization and the Taiwan Problem," *Zhanlue yu guanli*, December 30, 1999, trans. in Foreign Broadcast Information Service, CPP 20000215000116, February 15, 2000.

63. Ross, *Negotiating Cooperation*, 182; Alexander M. Haig Jr., *Caveat: Realism, Reagan, and Foreign Policy* (New York: Macmillan, 1984), 209–11; Holdridge, *Crossing the Divide*, 213. In light of the linkage in the PRC mind between U.S. arms sales and Taiwan's willingness to negotiate, note the fact that the new overture to Taiwan (Ye Jianying's nine points) was made at the same time as a push on arms sales. For the text of the nine points, see Gibert and Carpenter, *America and Island China*, 288–90.

64. Haig, *Caveat*, 212; Holdridge, *Crossing the Divide*, 216–18, 230–31, 222; Ross, *Negotiating Cooperation*, 189.

65. Haig, *Caveat*, 212; Holdridge, *Crossing the Divide*, 222–23; Ross, *Negotiating Cooperation*, 194. For the text of Reagan's letter to Zhao, see Gibert and Carpenter, *America and Island China*, 297–98.

66. Haig, *Caveat*, 213–14; Holdridge, *Crossing the Divide*, 222–23; Ross, *Negotiating Cooperation*, 195–96. Haig includes in his account of his last proposal to Reagan his opposition to doing anything in secret, which suggests that someone may have been making such a recommendation; see Haig, *Caveat*, 214.

67. Holdridge, *Crossing the Divide*, 235–38; Ross, *Negotiating Cooperation*, 195–98.

68. Holdridge. *Crossing the Divide*, 235–36.

69. See, for example, Oksenberg, "A Decade of Sino-American Relations," 188; Tyler, *A Great Wall*, 177.

70. Tyler, *A Great Wall*, 277.

71. See most importantly John Holdridge's testimony before the two foreign policy committees of the Congress, in U.S. Senate, Committee on Foreign Relations, *U.S. Policy toward China and Taiwan*, 97th Cong., 2d sess., August 17, 1982, and U.S. House, Committee on Foreign Affairs, *China-Taiwan: United States Policy*, 97th Cong., 2d sess., August 18, 1982.

72. Consulted were R.H. Mathews, ed., *Mathews' Chinese-English Dictionary* (Cambridge : Harvard University Press, 1966); *Cihai* (Taibei: Taiwan zhonghua shuju, 1974); *The Chinese-English Dictionary* (Hong Kong: Commercial Press, 1979); *Far East Chinese-English Dictionary* (Taibei: Yuandong tushu gongsi, 1992); Dennis J. Doolin and Charles P. Ridley, eds., *A Chinese-English Dictionary of Communist Chinese Terminology* (Stanford, CA: Hoover Institution Press, 1973); and *Hanying cidian* (Beijing: Foreign Language Teaching and Research Press, 1995). It is only in the latter dictionary that the term *dazheng fangzhen* appears. The term *dazheng* does not appear on its own.

73. In his meetings with Haig in the fall of 1981 Huang Hua asserted that the United States was pursuing a "two China" policy; Holdridge, *Crossing the Divide*, 213.

74. Finally, the two sides vowed to strengthen their ties across the board. They also reaffirmed the principles of the other two communiqués, partly in order to oppose aggression and expansion (a reference, at least for the United States, to the Soviet Union).

75. Holdridge, *Crossing the Divide*, 232. Holdridge's account misstates one of the assurances.

76. For the hearings, see U.S. Congress, Senate Subcommittee on Separation of Powers, *Taiwan Communiqué and Separation of Powers*, 97th Cong., 2d sess., September 17 and 27, 1982 and 98th Cong., 1st sess., March 2, 1983; and *Report on the Taiwan Relations Act and the Joint Communiqué Signed by the United States and China*, 98th Cong., 1st sess., June 1983. The statement concerning Taiwan's sovereignty appears on page 140 of the hearing report for the September 17 and 27, 1982, sessions.

Notes to Chapter 6

1. U.S. Congress, House Subcommittee on International Organizations and Movements, *Human Rights in the World Community: A Call for U.S. Leadership*, 93d Cong., 2d sess., March 27, 1974, 1, 9.

2. Laurie S. Wiseberg and Harry M. Scoble, "Monitoring Human Rights Violations: The Role of Nongovernmental Organizations," in *Human Rights and American Foreign Policy*, ed. Donald P. Kommers and Gilburt D. Loescher (Notre Dame: University of Notre Dame Press, 1978), 179–210; William Korey, *NGOs and the Universal Declaration of Human Rights: "A Curious Grapevine"* (New York: St. Martin's Press, 1998), 139–58, 181–202; Jerome J. Shestack and Roberta Cohen, "International Human Rights: A Role for the United States," *Virginia Journal of International*

Law 14 (Summer 1974): 673–701. There was no major NGO specifically focused on Taiwan. There were small groups organized by Taiwanese in a few cities around the country, and, by 1977, the International Committee for the Defense of Human Rights in Taiwan, headed by Lynn Miles.

3. Roberta Cohen, "Human Rights Decision-Making in the Executive Branch: Some Proposals for a Coordinated Strategy," in Kommers and Loescher, *Human Rights and American Foreign Policy*, 217.

4. U.S. Congress, Senate Committee on Foreign Relations, *Human Rights Reports Prepared by the Department of State in accordance with Section 502(b) of the Foreign Assistance Act, as amended*, 95th Cong., 1st sess., March 1977, 5–6.

5. Interview with Roberta Cohen, July 26, 2002.

6. Marc J. Cohen, *Taiwan at the Crossroads: Human Rights, Political Development and Social Change on the Beautiful Island* (Washington, DC: Asia Resource Center, 1988), 289–90; Douglas Mendel, *The Politics of Formosan Nationalism* (Berkeley: University of California Press, 1970), 163–65.

7. Cohen, *Taiwan at the Crossroads*, 290; Cai Tongrong, *Wo yao huiqu* (I Want to Return) (Kaohsiung, Taiwan: Tun-li, 1990), 11.

8. Lung-chu Chen and Harold D. Lasswell, *Formosa, China, and the United Nation: Formosa in the World Community* (New York: St. Martin's Press, 1967).

9. Interview with Chen Longzhi (Chen Lung-chu), April 2, 2003.

10. Interview with David Tsai, September 13, 2002; interview with Hong Jilong (Keelung Hong), November 12, 2002; interview with Chen Longzhi, April 2, 2003.

11. Interview with Chen Longzhi, April 2, 2003.

12. Mendel, *Politics of Formosan Nationalism*, 165–69; David E. Kaplan, *Fires of the Dragon, Politics, Murder, and the Kuomintang* (New York: Atheneum, 1992), 148–54, 160–61, 176–78; Winston T. Dang, comp. and ed., *Taiwangate: Blacklist Policy and Human Rights* (Washington, DC: Center for Taiwan International Relations, 1991); U.S. Congress, House Subcommittee on Asian and Pacific Affairs and Subcommittee on Human Rights and International Organizations, *Taiwan Agents in America and the Death of Prof. Wen-chen Chen*, 97th Cong., 1st sess., July 30 and October 6, 1981.

13. Interview with Mark Tan Sun Chen, August 4, 2002; interview with John Salzberg, August 9, 2002; U.S. Congress, House Subcommittee on International Organizations, *Human Rights in Taiwan*, 95th Cong., 1st sess., June 14, 1977, 111–19. Cranston's office had received complaints about human rights in Taiwan from a Taiwanese-American scholar at Berkeley, Hong Jilong (Keelung Hong); interview with Keelung Hong, November 12, 2002. Fraser already possessed some understanding of the Taiwan situation. At an October 1970 hearing of the House Subcommittee on Asian and Pacific Affairs, he had asked State Department witness Marshall Green about the past record of U.S. government representations to the ROC government urging the enlargement of political rights for the entire Taiwan population; see Marshall Green to Rep. Donald Fraser, January 12, 1971, POL 1 CHINAT 1970–73, Department of State General Records, Record Group 59, National Archives and Records Administration, College Park, MD.

14. Interview with Cynthia Sprunger Fogelman, November 11, 2002; communication from Fulton Armstrong, December 18, 2002.

15. *Congressional Record*, March 8, 1979, H-4488–4489; interview with Mark Tan Sun Chen, August 4, 2002; communication with Mark Tan Sun Chen, August 12, 2002.

16. U.S. Congress, Senate Committee on Foreign Relations, *Senate Report to Accompany S. 245*, March 1, 1979, 45, 26; *Congressional Record*, March 13, 1979, S-4850.

17. U.S. Congress, House Subcommittee on Asian and Pacific Affairs, *Implementation of Taiwan Relations Act: Issues and Concerns*, 96th Cong, 1st sess., February 14 and 15, 1979, 65–72; David Tawei Lee, *The Making of the Taiwan Relations Act* (New York: Oxford University Press, 2000), 140, 135; Issue 25, "Taiwan Conference Issue Papers," House Foreign Affairs Committee Document, n.d., Richard Bush Papers, TRA File; *Congressional Record*, March 8, 1979, H-4488–4489 and March 13, 1979, H-4777; interview with Cynthia Sprunger Fogelman, November 11, 2002. Derwinski described his motivation for offering the motion to recommit with instructions in an interview he gave to David Lee in 1986; see *Making of the Taiwan Relations Act*, 135. N.B. The title of the first work cited in this note suggests that the hearing was held after the enactment of the TRA; in fact, it was held in February 1979.

18. Issue 25, "Taiwan Conference Issue Papers"; Communication from Mark Tan Sun Chen, August 12, 2002; interview with Cynthia Sprunger Fogelman, November 11, 2002.

19. U.S. Congress, House Subcommittee on Asian and Pacific Affairs and Subcommittee on International Organizations, *Human Rights in Asia: Non-Communist Countries*, 96th Cong., 2d sess., February 4, 6, 7, 1980, 106–40, 146–48. During the hearing (see pages 147–48), Kagan cited the *New York Times* article that said that AIT took the position that it could not interfere in human rights cases because of the absence of diplomatic relations. Representative Wolff publicly agreed that AIT was restrained in what it could do. He was either misled by AIT's deception or was a party to it.

20. *Human Rights in Asia: Non-Communist Countries*, 160–63.

21. U.S. Congress, House Subcommittee on Asian and Pacific Affairs, *Implementation of the Taiwan Relations Act*, 96th Cong., 2d sess., June 11, 17, and July 30, 1980, 4–5, 20, 26, 30, 53, 60–73, 98–103, 107. Representative Pete Stark also introduced a resolution that sought to limit U.S. arms sales in light of Taiwan's human rights situation; see U.S. Congress, Senate Subcommittee on East Asian and Pacific Affairs, *Oversight of the Taiwan Relations Act*, 96th Cong., 2d session, May 14, 1980, 35–36. Neither resolution was acted on, even at the subcommittee level.

22. Cai, *Wo yao huiqu*, 69–70; *New York Times*, March 18, 1980; *Oversight of the Taiwan Relations Act*, 12.

23. Communication from Gerrit van der Wees, August 31, 2002.

24. House Resolution 708 called on Taiwan to "relax restrictions on the *constitutional* rights of freedom of expression"; to "*return* to recent policies allowing for the development of participatory democracy"; and urged a "spirit of reconciliation" concerning the Kaohsiung Incident. See *Implementation of the Taiwan Relations Act*, 107.

25. Stephen R. Weissman, *A Culture of Deference: Congress's Failure of Leadership in Foreign Policy* (New York: Basic Books, 1995), 3; Barbara Hinckley, *Less Than Meets the Eye* (Chicago: University of Chicago Press, 1994), 5.

26. Rebecca K.C. Hersman, *Friends and Foes: How Congress and the President Really Make Foreign Policy* (Washington, DC: Brookings Institution Press, 2000), 3, 4.

27. In the interest of full disclosure, I was Steven Solarz's staffer for China and Taiwan issues on the House Subcommittee on Asian and Pacific Affairs from July 1983 to December 1992. The discussion that follows probably exaggerates Solarz's

role and impact relative to other members of Congress and other factors, simply because it is drawn from my own files and I did not always know what other actors were doing. I have tried, however, to present as objective an assessment as possible.

28. Communication from Stanley Roth, November 19, 2002; U.S. Congress, House Committee on Foreign Affairs, *Taiwan Legislation*, 96th Cong., 1st sess., February 7 and 8, 1979, 16–17, 44–46, 62–63; Lester L. Wolff and David L. Simon, ed., *Legislative History of the Taiwan Relations Act: An Analytic Compilation with Documents on Subsequent Developments* (Jamaica, NY: American Association for Chinese Studies, 1982), 89, 158; U.S. Congress, House Subcommittee on Asian and Pacific Affairs, *The New Era in East Asia*, 97th Cong., 1st sess., May 19, 1981, 2–5, 36–37, 56–66; included in the hearing report was a two-page statement on religious freedom submitted by Cai Tongrong. For correspondence on human-rights cases, see Stanley Fu to Solarz, February 14, 1981; Solarz to Wang Ching-hsi [Jingxi] (Taiwan Garrison Command), March 24, 1981; Wang Ching-hsi to Solarz, April 24, 1981; Solarz to Wang Ching-hsi, September 10, 1981, all in Richard Bush Papers, 97th Congress Items File.

29. Cai, *Wo yao huiqu*, 75–76; interview with Steve Solarz, December 31, 2002.

30. Cai, *Wo yao huiqu*, 70–71.

31. Ibid., 72–76.

32. See *Taiwan Agents in America*. Strangely, Cai's memoir does not mention the Chen case and the congressional reaction.

33. Ibid., 2, 7.

34. Jay Taylor, *The Generalissimo's Son: Chiang Ching-kuo and the Revolutions in China and Taiwan* (Cambridge: Harvard University Press, 2000), 374.

35. Cai, *Wo yao huiqu*, 74, 76–77; Simon and Wolff, *Legislative History*, 195.

36. Cai, *Wo yao huiqu*, 81–82. Cai later wrote that FAPA was an appealing English acronym because it sounded like the Taiwanese for "shout and hit"; see his *Wo yao huiqu*, 83. The term "diplomatic work" suggests that some in FAPA saw themselves as a government-in-exile.

37. Interview with David Tsai, September 13, 2002; Cai, *Wo yao huiqu*, 82, 85. Years later, some associated with FAPA remained afraid that WUFI had not given up its clandestine effort to manipulate more public organizations.

38. Cai, *Wo yao huiqu*, 83–87.

39. For a good statement of this view, see Tien Hung-mao, "Uncertain Future: Politics in Taiwan," in *China Briefing, 1980*, ed. Robert B. Oxnam and Richard C. Bush (Boulder, CO: Westview Press, 1980), 87–99. Friedman and I were basically correct in our assumption that Chiang Ching-kuo wanted to move toward a democracy. Early in 1982 he sent a message to James Lilley, who was about to become director of the Taipei office of the American Institute in Taiwan, that "(a) I'm going to democratize, (b) its going to become a Taiwan process, (c) I'm going to maintain prosperity because I have to, and (d) I'm going to open up to China." See Nancy Bernkopf Tucker, ed., *China Confidential: American Diplomats and Sino-American Relations, 1945–1995* (New York: Columbia University Press, 2001), 420–21.

40. Cai, *Wo yao huiqu*, 87.

41. U.S. Congress, House Subcommittee on Asian and Pacific Affairs, *Martial Law on Taiwan and United States Foreign Policy Interests*, 97th Cong., 2d sess., May 20, 1982. The accusations about Cai and his rebuttal can be found on pages 124 and 125.

42. U.S. Congress, House Subcommittee on Asian and Pacific Affairs, *United*

States-China Relations 11 Years After the Shanghai Communique, 98th Cong., 1st sess., February 28, 1983.

43. Cai and FAPA were not happy with the revisions that Pell had made in the initial draft in order to accommodate senators who were concerned about Taipei's and Beijing's reactions; see Cai, *Wo yao huiqu*, 91–94. For other materials on the resolution, including documents and notes from the November 9 hearing, translations of the PRC reaction, and follow-up memos and notes, see Richard Bush Papers, Future of Taiwan Resolution File and 98th Congress Items File.

44. For materials on the resolution, see Richard Bush Papers, Martial Law 83–84 (Resn) File and 98th Congress Items File. Solarz had introduced a resolution on martial law in September 1982, but that was too late in the session for any action.

45. Richard Bush Papers, Martial Law 83–84 (Resn) File and 98th Congress Items File.

46. For a text of the speech, see Stephen J. Solarz, "Democracy and the Future of Taiwan," *Freedom at Issue* 77 (March–April 1984): 18–21.

47. Tucker, *China Confidential*, 421; Kang to Solarz, October 1983, Richard Bush Papers, SJS August 83 Speech File.

48. Interview with Mark Pratt, September 17, 2002.

49. Richard Bush Papers, Martial Law 83–84 (Resn) File and 98th Congress Items File; U.S. Congress, House Subcommittee on Asian and Pacific Affairs, *Political Developments in Taiwan*, 98th Cong., 2d sess., May 31, 1984.

50. Richard Bush Papers, Martial Law 83–84 (Resn) File.

51. In late 1983, at Solarz's encouragement, FAPA decided to support Walter Mondale for president. They came with a variety of requests of the candidate, many of which were impracticable. The Mondale campaign was wary of any commitments that would upset U.S.–China relations. See Richard Bush Papers, Mondale Campaign File. At the end of 1983, there was a leadership change at FAPA. Mark Chen became president but Cai became executive director and still retained influence.

52. Taylor, *Generalissimo's Son*, 327–28, 385–94, provides a good summary of the Henry Liu affair. Kaplan, *Fires of the Dragon*, is a more florid account and sympathetic to Liu.

53. Richard Bush Papers, Henry Liu Case File; U.S. Congress, House Subcommittee on Asian and Pacific Affairs, "The Murder of Henry Liu," 99th Cong., 1st sess., February 7, March 21, April 3, 1985.

54. Taylor, *Generalissimo's Son*, 393–96. Demonstrating that the security services were slow to learn their lesson, the Taiwan Garrison Command in September 1985 arrested Lee [Li] Yaping, the editor of the Los Angeles–based, Chinese-language *International Daily News* on the basis of articles published in the United States. Solarz and Leach issued harsh statements, raised the possibility of an arms-sales cutoff, and prepared a resolution. Before action could be taken, Lee was released. See Richard Bush Papers, Lee Ya Ping Case File.

55. Richard Bush Papers, H. Con. Res. 233 (85–86) File; U.S. Congress, House Subcommittee on Human Rights and International Organizations and Subcommittee on Asian and Pacific Affairs, *Implementation of the Taiwan Relations Act*, 99th Cong., 2d sess., May 7, June 25, August 1, 1986.

56. Richard Bush Papers, H. Con. Res. 233 (85–86) File.

57. Richard Bush Papers, 99th Congress Items File; Taylor, *Generalissimo's Son*, 405–7. The September 28th statement was made in the name of the Committee for Democracy in Taiwan, which Cai asked Solarz, Leach, Pell, and Kennedy to form in

the spring of 1986, for reasons that are still a mystery to me. There were two other developments in late 1986. First, Cai asked Solarz to support Xu Xinliang's return to Taiwan. I opposed that because Xu had been too closely associated with political violence when he was in the United States and he was also competing organizationally with the DPP. Solarz agreed with me (see Richard Bush Papers, Hsu Hsin-liang File). Second, I led an election-observation team to Taiwan to witness the December elections. See U.S. Congress, House Committee on Foreign Affairs, *Elections in Taiwan: Report of a Staff Study Mission to Taiwan*, 100th Cong., 1st sess., August 1988.

58. "Zhang Xiaoyan tan duimei waijiao" (Chang Hsiao-yen Talks About Diplomacy Toward the United States), *Shibao zazhi* 176, April 17, 1983; Andrew J. Nathan and Helena V.S. Ho, "Chiang Ching-kuo's Decision for Political Reform," in *Chiang Ching-kuo's Leadership in the Development of the Republic of China on Taiwan*, ed. Shao-chuan Leng (Lanham, MD: University Press of America, 1993), 31–61, especially 35–36; Phillip Newell, "President Chiang Ching-kuo and Taiwan's Transition to Democracy," *Harvard Studies on Taiwan: Papers of the Taiwan Studies Workshop* 1 (1995): 79–80; Richard Bush Papers, 1988 Trip File.

59. There were also a series of splits in FAPA; see Richard Bush Papers, 100th Congress Items File and 101st Congress Items File.

60. Richard Bush Papers, 1987 State Bill Taiwan Democracy Amendment File.

61. U.S. Congress, House Subcommittee on Asian and Pacific Affairs, *Political Trends in Taiwan Since the Death of Chiang Ching-kuo*, 100th Cong., 2d sess., May 26, 1988; U.S. Congress, House Subcommittee on Asian and Pacific Affairs, *The Upcoming Elections in Taiwan*, 100th Cong., 2d sess., November 15, 1989; U.S. Congress, House Subcommittee on Asian and Pacific Affairs, *Taiwan: The National Affairs Council and Implications for Democracy*, 101st Cong., 2d sess., October 11, 1990; U.S. Congress, House Subcommittee on Asian and Pacific Affairs, *Taiwan: The Upcoming National Assembly Elections*, 101st Cong., 1st sess., September 24, 1991.

62. For the letters, see Richard Bush Papers, 100th Congress Items File, 101st Congress Items File, and 102d Congress Items File. Solarz visited Taiwan just a few days after Chiang Ching-kuo died on January 13, 1988. He met with a variety of people inside and outside the government. There were the expected differences of opinion on the issues of the day. But Lee Teng-hui, only five days in office, signaled that the DPP would be able to register even though it advocated independence, and that "representativeness" would be the principle governing reform of the National Assembly and Legislative Yuan. See Richard Bush Papers, 1988 Trip File.

63. Richard Bush Papers, 101st Congress Items File.

64. Richard Bush Papers, 102d Congress Items File.

65. Richard Bush Papers, 101st Congress Items File and 1989 Election Delegation File.

66. Richard Bush Papers, Taiwan Plebiscite Res 1990/1991 Res File. As AIT chairman, I helped introduce the idea of "acceptable to the people of Taiwan" into the lexicon of U.S. Executive Branch policy.

67. Richard Bush Papers, 1989/1991 State Bill Future Resolution File, *Ziyou shibao meitongbao*, September 15, 1997; communications with David Tsai, December 3 and 5, 2002. I am grateful to David Tsai for providing a copy of the *Ziyou shibao* article.

68. Richard Bush Papers, 1989/1991 State Bill Future Resolution File, *Ziyou shibao*, September 15, 1997; communications with David Tsai, December 3 and 5, 2002.

69. Richard Bush Papers, 101st Congress Items File and 102d Congress Items File. For a compilation of documents on the blacklist, see Dang, *Taiwangate*.

70. James M. Lindsay and Randall B. Ripley, "Foreign and Defense Policy and Congress: A Research Agenda for the 1990s," *Legislative Studies Quarterly* 17, no. 3 (August 1992): 425.

Notes to Chapter 7

1. James Mann, *About Face: A History of America's Curious Relationship with China, from Nixon to Clinton* (New York: Knopf, 1999); Linda Chao and Ramon H. Myers, *The First Chinese Democracy: Political Life in the Republic of China on Taiwan* (Baltimore, MD: Johns Hopkins University Press, 1988); Ralph N. Clough, *Cooperation and Conflict in the Taiwan Strait?* (Lanham, MD: Rowman and Littlefield, 1999). For a comprehensive account of U.S.–China relations after 1989, see Robert L. Suettinger, *Beyond Tiananmen: The Politics of United States–China Relations 1989–2000* (Washington, DC: Brookings Institution Press, 2003).

2. Zbigniew Brzezinski, *Power and Principle: Memoirs of a National Security Adviser* (New York: Farrar, Straus and Giroux, 1983), 229.

3. The PRC, particularly in the 1990s, has held that the United States has not observed the 1982 communiqué. The United States holds that it is abiding by its commitment.

4. James A. Baker, III, *The Politics of Diplomacy: Revolution, War & Peace, 1989–1992* (New York: G.P. Putnam's Sons, 1995), 591. The Bush administration's position on Taiwan and GATT was linked to a series of objectives that it had pledged to moderate senators that it would pursue in return for their support on continuing the PRC's MFN status. Incidentally, Taiwan was quietly supportive of maintaining normal trade status for the PRC, since its companies were in the process of relocating their production to the mainland.

5. The main points of Mann's account (see *About Face*, 264–68) have been confirmed by a participant in the decision process.

6. The PRC now denies that such a consensus ever existed, or claims that it applied only to the interaction between the SEF and ARATS.

7. For Mann's account of the Hawaii transit, see *About Face*, 315–17.

8. It is worth noting that after September 1997, in the context of improving U.S.–PRC relations, the United States permitted several transits by President Lee, Vice President Lien Chan, and Premier Vincent Siew, including golf and overnight stays.

9. For more details on Taiwan's legislative and public relations activities in the United States, see James Mann, "Congress and Taiwan: Understanding the Bond," in *Making China Policy: Lessons from the Bush and Clinton Administrations*, ed. Ramon H. Myers, Michel C. Oksenberg, and David Shambaugh (Lanham, MD: Rowman and Littlefield, 2001), 201–22.

10. *Los Angeles Times*, July 31, 1995. In Mann's account, the working levels of the State Department opposed the Lee trip almost to the bitter end; high-level foreign policy officials believed that the costs of denying the trip were greater than those of allowing it; and President Clinton was basically sympathetic to Lee's coming and resented Beijing's hard-line opposition. See Mann, *About Face*, 320–26.

11. See "The United States and the Security of Taiwan," Winston Lord, Assistant Secretary of State for East Asian and Pacific Affairs, Testimony before the House International Relations Committee, Subcommittee on East Asia and the Pacific, March 14, 1996, accessible at the State Department's Web site, www.state.gov.

12. Holdridge, *Crossing the Divide,* 90; Document 2, Memorandum of Conversation, Tuesday, February 22, 1972, 2:10 p.m. to 6:20 p.m., Record of Richard Nixon-Zhou Enlai Talks, February 1972, the National Security Archive, www.gwi/~nsarchiv/nsa/publications.pdf; Brzezinski, *Power and Principle*, 214; Lee Teng-hui, *The Road to Democracy: Taiwan's Pursuit of Identity* (Tokyo: PHP Institute, 1999), 130.

13. "Taiwan Officials on U.S. Straits Policy," *Zhongguo shibao* (China Times), January 29, 2000, in Foreign Broadcast Information Service, CPP20000205000021. For a Taiwanese interpretation of Lee's statement that places much of the blame on the United States, see Hung-mao Tien, "Taiwan's Perspective on Cross-Strait Relations and U.S. Policy," *American Foreign Policy Interests* 21, no. 6 (December 1999): 13–19.

Note to Chapter 8

1. See Project for the New American Century, "Statement on the Defense of Taiwan," August 20, 1999, www.newamericacentury.org/Taiwandefensestatement.htm.

Index

A

Accinelli, Robert, 85
Acheson, Dean, 87, 90
Advisory Committee on Post-War
	Foreign Policy, 15–16
Ainsworth, Thomas, 52
Albright, Madeleine, 232
American Institute in Taiwan (AIT),
	78–79, 80, 151–153, 187
See also Bush, Richard
Arms Export Control Act, 158, 159
Arms Sales Communiqué
	creation of, 160–163
	interpretation and language of,
		overview, 163–164, 166–168
	overview of, 160, 166–167, 168
	text of, 169–173
Arms sales to Taiwan. *See* Arms
	Sales Communiqué; Taiwan,
	arms sales to, from U.S.; Taiwan
	Relations Act

B

Benninghoff, H. Merrell, 24
Blake, Robert, 41, 43–44
Borton, Hugh, 24
Bowie, Robert, 103
Brzezinski, Zbigniew
	Chinese leaders meet with, 142, 143,
		145, 231
	on Taiwan issues facing U.S., 148–149
Bundy, William, 110–111

Bush, George H. W., and administration
		of
	China policies, overview of, 117,
		161–162, 222
	*See also names of individuals in
		administration*
Bush, George W., and administration of
	China policies, overview of, 239, 243
	*See also names of individuals in
		administration*
Bush, Richard
	advisor on Taiwan initiatives, 198, 202,
		207, 213, 233–234
	AIT official, 3

C

Cai Tongrong
	activism of, 194–195, 199, 200,
		211–213, 214
	political organizations led by, 182, 190,
		197
Cairo Conference, 3, 34–36
Cairo Declaration, 9, 10, 90
Carter, Jimmy, and administration of
	China-Taiwan policies, overview of, 5,
		137, 141, 151
	Chinese leaders, meetings with,
		142–143, 160–161
	Taiwan relations terminated by,
		141–142
	Taiwan security issues and, 147–148,
		164
	*See also names of individuals in
		administration*

Catto, Robert, 41–42
Chai Zemin, 142–143
Chao, Linda, 219
Chen, James, 53
Chen Cheng, 51, 61
Chen Longzhi, 183, 184, 196
Chen Shui-bian, 239, 241–242, 243
Chen Wencheng, 195
Chen Yi
    February 28 Incident, reaction to, 43,
        45, 46
    governor-general of Taiwan, 41, 47
Chennault, Claire, 26, 34
Chiang Ching-kuo
    assassination attempt on, 183, 184
    Kaohsiung Incident and, 77, 78, 80,
        82
    liberalization efforts of, 40, 75, 76, 78,
        208–209
    political repression cases and, 71, 206,
        207
    U.S. influence on regime of, 83, 84,
        210–211
    White Terror and, 50
Chiang Kai-shek
    authoritarian style of, 76, 83
    China's Destiny drafted by, 12
    Lei Zhen condemned by, 62, 64, 65
    East Asian issues addressed by, 25
    February 28 Incident, response to, 46,
        47
    ideology and principles of, 87, 113,
        120, 178
    joint bases sought by, 29, 31, 38
    ROC government moved to Taiwan by,
        4, 50
    Taiwan government, views on, 59–60,
        93, 105
    Taiwan's status, views on, 22, 99
    on U.S. "two-China" approach, 112,
        113, 119–120, 123
    and United Nations membership,
        116–117
    on U.S. defense issues and policies, 95,
        98, 100, 102–103

Chiang Kai-shek *(continued)*
    U.S. presidents, dealings with, 3,
        25–26, 27, 35–36, 108
    U.S. support of, during wars, 4, 27
Chiang Kai-shek, Madam (Soong
        Meiling), 31–34
China
    civil war in, 3–4, 49–50
    economic interaction with Taiwan,
        6, 223
    Japanese issues, 10–11, 16
    normalization with U.S., overview
        of, 121, 147, 219
    offshore islands, status of, 97, 123
    "Sacred Texts" in U.S. relations,
        overview of, 124–125,
        175–176
    Taiwan issues, overview, 9, 12–13,
        21, 34
    United Nations membership,
        103–104, 106–109, 115–117
China Democratic Party, 61, 62
    See also Lei Zhen
Christopher, Warren, 228
Church, Frank, 69–70
Churchill, Winston, 9, 13, 30, 36
Cleveland, Harlan, 110
Clinton, Bill, and administration of
China policies, overview of, 122, 225,
        226, 232
    *See also names of individuals in
        administration*
Clough, Ralph, 71, 219
Colville, Cabot, 20
Communism, U.S. containment of, 4,
        6–7, 40, 50–51, 100
Congress, U.S.
    foreign policy, influence on, 191–192,
        198–199, 209, 220
    Kaohsiung Incident, reaction to,
        188–190
    KMT repression addressed by, 186,
        188–190, 197–198, 213
    political imprisonment addressed by,
        205
Cross, Charles, 78, 79

D

Dangwai. See names of individual opposition groups
Dean, David, 78, 79
DeLay, Tom, 235
Democratic Progressive Party (DPP), 208, 211, 241
Deng Xiaoping
  on arms sales from U.S., 162, 165
  national reunification efforts, 149, 150, 160
  U.S. relations with, 143–144, 162, 174–175
Derwinski, Edward, 187, 188
Diaoyutai Islands, 75–76
Divine, Robert, 27
Douglas, Lewis, 90
Drumright, Everett, 64, 65, 66, 67, 84
Dulles, John Foster
  legal status of Taiwan, views on, 92, 93–95, 99
  peace treaty, duties regarding, 93
  security of Taiwan, views on, 59, 60, 91–92, 97
  and "two-China" and "divided country" policies, 101–102, 104–105, 117–118

E

East, John, 174
Eden, Anthony, 23, 24, 30, 34
Eisenhower, Dwight, and administration of
China-Taiwan policies, overview, 58, 59, 96–97, 99–100
See also names of individuals in administration

F

Fascell, Dante, 213
February 28 Incident
  description of, 42–43

February 28 Incident *(continued)*
  overview of, 41, 49
  See also Kerr, George
Feldman, Harvey, 151
Ford, Gerald R., and administration of
China-Taiwan policies, overview of, 147
Formosa. *See* Taiwan
Formosa League for Re-emancipation (FLR), 54
Formosa (magazine), 77
Formosan Association for Public Affairs (FAPA), 196–197, 213–214, 215
Formosans for Free Formosa (FFF), 182
Forum for the Improvement of Local Elections (File), 61, 62
Four Policemen (United States, Great Britain, Soviet Union, China), 28–29, 31
Fraser, Donald, 179, 180, 184
Free China Fortnightly, 60–61, 62, 65
Friedman, Edward, 195, 198
Friends of Taiwan, 159
Fu Zuoyi, 166

G

Gao Yushu, 63, 67, 69
Goldberg, Arthur, 111–112
Goldwater, Barry, 185
Great Britain
  empire of, 36
  Taiwan and China, policies on, 35–36, 92–93, 99, 108
Green, Marshall, 127
Gregor, James, 200
Gu Weijun, Wellington, 89
Gu Zhenfu, 232–233
Guomindang. *See* Kuomintang (KMT)

H

Haig, Alexander, 160–161, 162
Hamilton, Lee, 225
Hamilton, Maxwell, 16, 23

Harriman, Averell, 36
Helms, Jesse, 235
Henry Liu Yiliang case, 206–209
Hersman, Rebecca, 192
Hills, Carla, 223
Hinckley, Barbara, 191
Holbrook, Richard, 137, 151
Holdridge, John, 125, 133, 161, 163
Hopkins, Harry, 33, 34, 35
Hornbeck, Stanley, 17
Hsiao, Frank, 10
Hu Shi, 66, 67
Hua Guofeng, 148
Huang, Peter, 54, 55
Huang Hua, 142, 143, 160–161
Hull, Cordell, 17, 23, 32
Human rights and repression in
    Taiwan. *See* February 28 Incident;
    Kaohsiung Incident; Kuomintang,
    repression of Taiwanese, overview
    of; Lei Zhen case; Peng Mingmin
    case; White Terror
Hummel, Arthur, 162, 201
Hyde, Henry, 200

I

Institute of Pacific Relations (IPR)
    conference, 12

J

Jacobs, Bruce, 81
Japan
    Chinese relations with, 10–11
    peace treaties, overview, 92
    Taiwan a colony of, 3, 10
Javits, Jacob, 183, 187
Jiang Tingfu, 91, 92, 101
Johnson, Lyndon, and administration of
    China-Taiwan policies, overview of,
    110–111, 114, 119
    *See also names of individuals in
    administration*

K

Kagan, Richard, 188, 189, 200
Kang Ningxiang, 203–204
Kaohsiung Incident
    overview of, 76, 82, 222
    trials for defendants in, 81–82
Kennan, George, 87
Kennedy, John F., and administration of
    China's entry into UN opposed by, 109
    China-Taiwan policies, overview,
        105–106, 119
    with Great Britain on China policy, 108
    *See also names of individuals in
    administration*
Kennedy, Ted, 194, 195
Kerr, George
    February 28 Incident described by, 41,
        43, 45, 46–47
    Formosa Betrayed written by, 41
    on Taiwan's security and administration,
        14–15, 21, 48–49
Kissinger, Henry
    China visited by, 117, 125, 126,
        231–232
    on human rights in China, 181
    security issue addressed by, 148
    and Shanghai Communiqué, 125–126,
        127, 131, 133, 135–136
KMT. *See* Kuomintang
Korea, 23, 35, 64, 88, 90
Kuomintang (KMT)
    in Chinese civil war, 49–50
    opposition to, among Taiwanese, 61, 77,
        204, 217, 241
    repression of Taiwanese, overview of,
        4–5, 40–41, 82–84, 242
    retreat to Taiwan, 4, 50
    and Taiwan's relation to China, 38
    See also Chiang Kai-shek

L

Lagomarsino, Robert, 158
Lasswell, Harold, 183

Lattimore, Owen
  FDR's advisor to Chiang Kai-shek, 12,
    13, 22, 25, 29–30
  Madam Chiang Kai-shek meets with, 32
Leach, Jim, 186, 187, 188–190, 191, 192
Lee Teng-hui
  liberalization accelerated by, 6, 7, 219,
    244
  presidency of, 209, 215, 218
  on reunification of China, 123, 233, 234
  trip to U.S., controversy surrounding,
    225, 227–228, 230
Lei Wang, Emily Dequan, 62–63
Lei Zhen, 61, 62–64, 65–67
Lei Zhen case, overview of, 60–61, 67
Levin, Burton, 185
Li Wanju, 63
Lian Zhan, 242
Lien Chan, 229
Lin Biahao, 234
Lin Yixiong, 80–81
Liu, Henry, 206–209
Lord, Winston, 227, 228–230, 231, 238

M

MacArthur, Douglas, 56, 87
Mann, James, 219, 224
Mao Zedong, 125, 126
Marks, Lee, 151
Marshall, George, 3–4, 44, 46, 49
Martin, Edwin, 62
McCarthy, Joseph, 56
McConaughy, Walter, 73, 112, 113, 114
Mendel, Douglas, 74
Merchant, Livingston, 51, 66
Military, U.S.
  leaders' post–WWII priorities, 14,
    36–37
  U.S. Navy deployments, 4, 35, 36, 232
Military aid to Taiwan. See Arms Sales
    Communiqué; Taiwan, arms sales to,
    from U.S.; Taiwan Relations Act
Morse, Wayne, 179
Murkowski, Frank, 225, 226

Myers, Ramon, 219

N

National People's Congress (NPC),
    149–150
Nationalists. See Kuomintang (KMT)
Navy, U.S., 4, 35, 36, 232
Nixon, Richard, and administration of
  China visited by, 117, 125, 126,
    231–232
  China-Taiwan policies, overview of, 5,
    85, 114–117, 118, 181
  See also names of individuals in
    administration
Normalization. See Carter, Jimmy, and
    administration of; Nixon, Richard,
    and administration of; Normalization
    Communiqué; United States, foreign
    policy, normalization with China,
    overview of
Normalization Communiqué
  interpretation and language of,
    144–147
  overview of, 136–137, 146–147, 221
  text of, 138–141
Notter, Harley, 22–23

P

Parsons, Graham, 63
Pease, Donald, 186–187
Pell, Claiborne, 186–188, 201
Peng Mingmin
  activism and career, 68–69, 208
  arrest and trial for sabotage, 69–70,
    71–72
Peng Mingmin case, overview of, 67–68,
    74
People's First Party (PFP), 241, 242
People's Liberation Army (PLA), 50
People's Republic of China (PRC). See
    China
Peter Huang Wenxiong, 183
Porter, Charles, 62–63

Q

Qiao Guanhua, 127

R

Radford, Admiral, 59
Rankin, Karl
  ambassador to ROC, 52, 96
  and containment of communism,
    56, 57–58
  and Taiwan relations, 56, 84, 90,
    96
Reagan, Ronald, and administration
  of China and Taiwan policies,
  overview, 5, 161–163, 167,
  174–175
  *See also names of individuals in
    administration*
Republic of China (ROC). *See*
  Taiwan, government and
  administration of
Reuther, David, 203
Rhee, Syngman, 64
Rogers, William, 115
Roosevelt, Franklin D., and
  administration of
  Chiang Kai-shek, dealings with, 3,
    25–26, 27, 35–36
  China-Taiwan policies, overview of,
    22, 23, 27–28, 37–38
  territorial issues addressed by, 17,
    24–25, 36
  *See also names of individuals in
    administration*
Rostow, Walt, 112
Roth, Stanley, 233, 234
Rusk, Dean
  on Taiwan's UN prospects, 106–109
  on "two-China" approach, 106, 109,
    111, 112–113, 114
  to Wu Guozhen, on representative
    government, 55

S

"Sacred Texts," overview of, 124–125,
    176–177
  See also Arms Sales Communiqué;
    Normalization Communiqué;
    Shanghai Communiqué; Taiwan
    Relations Act
Salzberg, John, 184
San Francisco Peace Conference, 92, 212
Service, John Stewart, 11
Seymour, James, 185
Shanghai Communiqué
  China's stances on, 128–129,
    133
  interpretation and language of,
    overview, 127–129, 134,
    136
  overview of, 125–127, 136
  text of, 128
  U.S. statement in, 129–130
Shi Mingde, 78, 81
Shimonoseki, Treaty of, 10–11
Shoesmith, Thomas, 114
Shultz, George, 221–222, 237
Sisco, Joseph, 111
Solarz, Steve
  Cai Tongrong, works with, 193–194,
    195, 202, 211–212
  Chinese relations addressed by,
    198
  on human rights cases and freedoms,
    195–196, 200–201, 205,
    206–207
  immigration quotas addressed by,
    196
  personal background, 193
  support of, by Taiwanese activists,
    194, 202
  Taiwan democratic reforms sought
    by, 207–209, 210–211, 217
  trip to Taiwan, meetings with
    officials, 202–203
Solomon, Richard, 132

Soong Meiling, 31–34
Soong, James, 241, 242
Soong, T.V., 12, 23, 34, 48
Soviet Union, 109–110
Sprunger, Cynthia, 186
Stalin, Joseph, 9
Stevenson, Adlai, 110, 111
Stilwell, Robert, 26
Strong, Robert, 52–56, 89
Stuart, John Leighton, 47, 49, 82, 90
Su Ge, 133, 146
Sullivan, Lawrence, 10
Sun Fo, 11

T

Taiwan
 government and administration of
  arms sales to, from U.S., 121, 137,
    155–159, 219, 223–224 (see
    also Arms Sales Communiqué;
    Taiwan Relations Act)
  communiqués and U.S. relations
    with, 126, 144–145 (see also
    names of individual
    communiqués)
  defense treaty with U.S., 59–60, 96
  economy and industry, 223,
    240–241
  ideology of ROC, 59–60 (see also
    Chiang Kai-shek, ideology and
    principles of)
  international isolation of, 5
  liberalization and democratization in,
    5–6, 214–215, 219, 223, 244
    (see also Chen Shui-bian;
    Chiang Ching-kuo; Lee Teng-
    hui)
  United Nations membership, 106–109,
    114–116, 184
  in U.S. post–WWII plans, 13–14,
    17, 20, 31
  World Trade Organization
    membership, 223, 232

Taiwan (continued)
 people of
  civil liberties of (see Kuomintang,
    repression of Taiwanese,
    overview of)
  self-determination of, 9, 38–39, 200,
    242, 244
  Taiwanese-American activists,
    overview, 182, 215–217, 222
Taiwan Communiqué (periodical), 190
Taiwan Relations Act, 121
 interpretation and language of,
   152–155, 156–160
 overview of, 150–151, 152–154, 177, 221
 text of, 155
 U.S. Congress and, 152–153,
   156–157, 158–160
Taiwan Revolutionary League, 11
Taiwan Security Enhancement Act
  (TSEA), 235, 236
Taiwan Solidarity Union, 241, 242
Taiwanese Association of America
  (TAA), 190
Taiwanese Democratic People's
  Association (TDPA), 53
Thompson, William P., 189–190
Thomson, James, 110
Tiananmen Incident, 6, 224, 237
Torricelli, Robert, 235
Treaties
 mutual defense, 59–60, 96–97
 peace with Japan, 92, 93
 Shimonoseki, 10–11
Treaty of Shimonoseki, 10–11
Truman, Harry S., and administration of
  China-Taiwan policies, overview of,
  4, 85, 88–90, 95–97, 118
Tsai, David, 213
Tucker, Nancy Bernkopf, 40, 85

U

United Formosans for Independence,
  182

United Formosans in America for
    Independence (UFAI), 182
United Nations Security Council, 31
United States
    Arms Sales Communiqué, response to,
        168, 173–174
    February 28 Incident, response to,
        41–42, 45–46, 49–50
    foreign policy
        containment of communism, 4, 6–7,
            50–51, 100
        "divided country," 101–102
        dual deterrence and use of force, 7,
            235, 239–240
        human rights in China, overview of,
            79–80, 82–83, 226, 231
        normalization with China, overview
            of, 121, 147, 219
        "one-China," overview of, 114, 219,
            221, 234
        "successor state," 106, 107–108,
            122–123
        trusteeship system, 8, 16–17, 23, 25,
            87
        "two-China," overview of, 85–88,
            101, 103, 117–118, 121–122
    Kaohsiung case, response to, 78, 222
    Lei Zhen case, response to, 64, 70
    mutual defense treaty with Taiwan,
        59–60, 96–97
    Normalization Communiqué, overview
        of, 136–137, 146–147
    Peng Mingmin case, response to, 72, 73,
        74, 83–84
    "Sacred Texts" of Chinese relations,
        overview of, 124–125, 176–177
    Shanghai Communiqué, overview of,
        125, 136
    Taiwan elections, response to, 61–62
    Taiwan Relations Act, overview of,
        150–151, 152–154
    Tiananmen Square incident, effect on
        Chinese relations, 224
    White Terror, response to, 83
U.S. Congress. See Congress, U.S.

V

Vance, Cyrus, 142, 143, 148

W

Wang Xiling, 206
Wang Yu-san, 200
Wees, Gerrit van der, 190
Wees, Mei-chin van der, 190
Wei Daoming, 48, 68, 69, 72, 113
Weissman, Stephen, 191
Welles, Sumner, 16, 23, 30, 32
White Terror, overview of, 49–50
Willkie, Wendell, 12, 28–29
Woodcock, Leonard, 142, 143–144, 164
World Trade Organization (WTO), 223,
    231, 232
World United Formosans for
    Independence (WUFI), 182, 183
Wu Guozhen
    governor of Taiwan Province, 51, 57
    and repression of political activism, 53,
        54, 55

X

Xie Zongmin, 68, 69, 72

Y

Yager, Joseph, 109–110
Yang Xikun, 120
Yang Yunzhu, 11–12
Yatron, Gus, 205, 207
Ye Gongzhao
    on Lei Zhen case, 65
    on Taiwan's legal status, 89, 92, 99,
        101–102

Z

Zhao Ziyang, 160–161, 201
Zhou Enlai
    Nixon administration, dealings with,
        117, 125, 131–132, 134, 231
    and Shanghai Communiqué, 131–132,
        136
    Taiwan security issues and, 100

About the Author

Richard C. Bush is a senior fellow at the Brookings Institution in Washington, DC, and director of its Center for Northeast Asian Policy Studies. A graduate of Lawrence University, he received his doctorate in political science from Columbia University in 1978. He began his professional career with the China Council of the Asia Society in 1977. From 1983 to 1995 he served on the staff of the House International Relations Committee, first with the Subcommittee on Asian and Pacific Affairs and on the full committee after 1992. In July 1995 he became National Intelligence Officer for East Asia and a member of the National Intelligence Council. In September 1997 he assumed the positions of chairman and managing director of the American Institute in Taiwan, which he held until July 2002.